Water for Texas

NUMBER SIX:
Texas A&M University Agriculture Series
C. Allan Jones, General Editor

Water for Texas

Edited by

Jim Norwine

John R. Giardino

and Sushma Krishnamurthy

FOREWORD BY LEO SAYAVEDRA

Texas A&M University Press

College Station

The paper used in this book meets the minimum requirements
of the American National Standard for Permanence
of Paper for Printed Library Materials, Z39.48-1984.
Binding materials have been chosen for durability.

Library of Congress Cataloging-in-Publication Data

Water for Texas / edited by Jim Norwine, John R. Giardino and
Sushma Krishnamurthy ; foreword by Leo Sayavedra. — 1st ed.
p. cm.
Includes bibliographical references.
ISBN 1-58544-326-3 (cloth : alk. paper)
1. Water resources development — Texas. 2. Water supply — Texas.
3. Climatic changes — Texas. 4. Water quality — Texas. I. Norwine, Jim.
II. Giardino, John R. III. Krishnamurthy, Sushma.
TC424.T4W3823 2004
333.91'009764—dc22
2004004789

CONTENTS

Foreword, by Leo Sayavedra, *vii*

Acknowledgments, *ix*

Introduction, by Jim Norwine, John R. Giardino, and Sushma Krishnamurthy, *xi*

Part I. Texas Water in the Past, Present, and Future, 3

1. A Half Century of Water Resource Planning and Policy, 1950–2000, by Joe G. Moore, Jr., *5*
2. Texas Water at the Century's Turn: Perspectives, Reflections, and a Comfort Bag, by George H. Ward, Jr., *17*
3. Administration and Modeling of the Water Rights System, by Ralph A. Wurbs, *44*
4. Water Use Patterns and Trends: The Future in Texas, by Rima Petrossian, *52*

Part II. Regional Assessment, 63

5. Water Resources of the Panhandle and Upper Colorado Regions of Texas, by Lloyd V. Urban and A. Wayne Wyatt, *65*
6. Major Water Issues Facing South-Central Texas, by Richard A. Earl and Todd H. Votteler, *75*
7. The Present and Future Status of Water in the Coastal Bend Area, by C. Alan Berkebile, Karen K. Dodson, Rick Hay, and James A. Dodson, *89*
8. Houston Water Issues, by Philip B. Bedient, Hanadi S. Rifai, Monica P. Suarez, Rik M. Hovinga, and Burke Nixon, *107*
9. Status and Trends of North-Central Texas Water Resources: The Integrity of the Trinity River, by Glenn C. Clingenpeel, *122*

Part III. Climate and Water Quantity, 135

10. Will We Have Enough Water? An Overview, by Jurgen Schmandt, *137*
11. Water and Climate Change in the Twenty-first Century, by Gerald R. North, *144*
12. Climate and Water: Precipitation, Evapotranspiration, and Hydroclimatological Aspects, by David R. Legates, *149*
13. The El Niño/Southern Oscillation and Impacts on Climate Anomalies in Texas, by Kent M. McGregor, *153*
14. Influence of Climatic Variability on Texas Reservoirs, by Alan W. Groeger, Bruce G. Kelley, and Joe Martin, *159*
15. Landscape Water Conservation through Xeriscape, by Douglas F. Welsh, *164*
16. Changes in Flow Regime following Dam Construction, Yegua Creek, South-Central Texas, by Anne Chin and Jean Ann Bowman, *166*

Part IV. Water Quality, 179

17.   Using a Geographic Information System to Identify Impacts from 4,200 Closed Municipal Solid Waste Landfills, by Robert D. Larsen and Ronald J. Stephenson, *181*

18.   Nonpoint-Source Pollution from Silviculture in Texas, by Michael G. Messina and R. Scott Beasley, *185*

19.   Long-Term Trends in the Water Quality of Barton Springs, Austin, Texas, by Martha A. Turner and David A. Johns, *200*

20.   Educating the Public about Water Resources Research at Texas Universities, by Ric Jensen, *210*

21.   Reuse as a Viable Option in Water Resource Development: A Discussion of the Legal Framework Governing Reuse Projects, by Edmond R. McCarthy, Jr., and Michael A. Gershon, *218*

Part V. International Issues in the Rio Grande Valley, 227

22.   Water Resources of Far West Texas: El Paso–Ciudad Juarez, by Robert H. Schmidt, *229*

23.   Geographical Hydrology of the El Paso–Ciudad Juarez Border Region, by Richard A. Marston and William J. Lloyd, *242*

24.   Instream Salinity Modeling of Mid–Rio Grande and Wichita Basins, by R. S. Muttiah, S. Miyamoto, M. Borah, and C. H. Walker, *249*

25.   Water in the Lower Rio Grande Border Region: A Binational Perspective, by Mitchell L. Mathis, *273*

FOREWORD

Leo Sayavedra

Vice Chancellor for Academic and Student Affairs

Texas A&M University System

It is my great fortune to know Rick Giardino, professor of geology, geophysics, and geography at Texas A&M University, and Jim Norwine, professor of geosciences at Texas A&M University–Kingsville. Both these distinguished scholars are at the forefront of research and education on the earth's resources and processes.

About five years ago, they approached me with an idea for a conference on water resource issues in Texas. While it is obvious that abundant and available water is crucial to Texas in the twenty-first century, nobody had yet gathered together the best experts to assess the subject. But it is imperative that this problem of the present and future status of water in the state be addressed. I am pleased that the Texas A&M University System, with its educational and research initiatives toward real-world issues such as water, could take the lead in this endeavor.

Rick and Jim first commissioned leading authorities to write white paper summaries on key topics. The project then brought them together for a two-day scholarly conference, culminating with the publication of a book by Texas A&M University Press. (And of course, good professors that they are, it was not merely my wise imprimatur they came seeking.)

It is with pleasure that we offer the resulting work to the thinkers, decision makers, and above all the citizens of Texas, who are avidly concerned about water resource planning. Citizens encouraged experts to gather the scientific data that are the foundation of statewide water planning efforts. The research compiled in this book will make a significant contribution toward those efforts and for the future of our great and beloved State of Texas. I am proud to have been a part of *Water for Texas*.

ACKNOWLEDGMENTS

We would like to thank the Texas A&M University System, Texas A&M University, Texas A&M University–Kingsville, and the Center for Earth and Environmental Studies at Texas A&M International University for their support. And we would like to thank Carla Lee Suson for the help she provided in preparing this manuscript.

INTRODUCTION

Jim Norwine

Regents Professor, Department of Physics/Geosciences

Texas A&M University–Kingsville

John R. Giardino

Dean of Graduate Studies

Texas A&M University

Sushma Krishnamurthy

Associate Professor of Biology, Department of Biology and Chemistry

Texas A&M International University

While it is already a commonplace idea that water will be the world's most crucial natural resource in the new century, the disturbing implications of serious—even disastrous—water shortages are less obvious. They will probably be limited to a handful of locations, led by the Middle East, where the first "water wars" are likely to occur. These locations share most or all of the following characteristics:

- limited water supplies (often these are tropical or subtropical, arid, semiarid, or subhumid climatic regimes);
- expanding populations, increasing expectations, and growing water demand;
- glaring imbalance between water-rich and water-poor sections;
- transnational water disputes; and
- potential for drier futures due to global "greenhouse" warming.

The American Southwest generally, and Texas specifically, share all of these attributes and thus constitute the North American region with the greatest and most worrying water challenge. Water is *the* defining issue that this region faces. Economy, immigration, and environment are important issues all, but they pale in comparison with water. Water is fundamental and non-negotiable. In the decades ahead, water may become the most daunting challenge Texas has faced since European settlement. This is not something we can finesse, spin, or rationalize away: the future of Texas depends on how we respond to this test of our collective character and ingenuity.

Water for Texas is a general, state-of-knowledge survey of and report on the status of water in Texas. Our goal is to enhance understanding of current and prospective water quantity and quality. As the work is aimed equally at public education and scholarly exchange, a premium has been placed on readable overviews synthesizing key themes pertaining to Texas water, including assessments of each of the major regions of the state.

The project grew out of a knowledge-oriented (as opposed to policy-oriented) conference held at Texas A&M University in College Station in the autumn of 2000. Scholars at work on water-related topics in the sciences, engineering, agriculture, business, government, and the social sciences were invited to participate. This legacy of that gathering of leading Texas water scholars at century's turn is intended to serve as a benchmark and resource for researchers, policy makers, and most of all for present and future Texans.

We hope the book honors the Texas that was, but its real subject is the Texas that will be. We will be pleased if it suggests answers or at least directions for planning and policies, but it is chiefly designed to focus on knowledge and questions—above all, the question: Where are we heading? We have aimed to present in a useful and transparent manner the current state of knowledge among the very best authorities. *Water for Texas* is dedicated to the citizens, leaders, and scholars of our state: they will determine the Texas that will be.

Water for Texas

PART I

Texas Water in the Past, Present, and Future

The disastrous drought of the 1950s and recent bout of water shortages in 1996 left little doubt that water is a valuable and increasingly limited natural resource. With the Texas population continuing to rise, the problem of dwindling water supplies will only worsen. Plans are now being developed to attempt to meet needs for the next fifty years, not only for periods of normal weather but particularly for those times of recurring drought that are an inevitable part of the Texas climate.

However, before we begin to study, control, or legislate about the state's existing water systems, we must understand the role of water in a historical, geographical, and meteorological context. We need to examine past attempts at supply control to see how successful they were at lessening flooding and droughts; we need to gather data on water movement and recharging through the ground and on the surface; and we need to understand what

rights, claims, and legal issues affect proper water rationing and conservation.

This first section is an overview that offers a perspective on the current status of Texas water and on legislation now being developed. Joe G. Moore, Jr., notes that historically, legal plans were motivated only by a response to catastrophic events such as floods or droughts or by the "threat" of federalization of state lands. Once the panic passed, progress on meeting future needs slowed to a near standstill. By the time of the 1950s drought, state officials finally had to take a serious, long-term view of statewide water plans. However, any plans had to balance carefully the concerns of regional ownership of water rights, conservation of natural resources, nonregional needs for water, and growth of municipal centers.

George H. Ward, Jr., discusses water problems over the last century from a climatological and developmental view. He notes that one fundamental problem with Texas water is that the "flashiness" of runoff and recharge creates an unstable situation that perpetuates a cycle of floods and droughts. He suggests that water supply development may be reaching its feasible limit due to several issues involving irrigation, municipalities, business, and power usage that will continue to grow during the twenty-first century.

Ralph A. Wurbs takes a look at the two types of water rights used in the state: riparian and prior appropriation. These two systems were melded together with some difficulty into one law that covered the different categories of water. He describes in detail the water rights permit system established pursuant to the Water Rights Adjudica-tion Act of 1967. He also discusses the water availability modeling system, which uses historical data on water usage to help decide future permits involving surface waters located in streams, rivers, and lakes.

Rima Petrossian reviews the current plan coming out of Senate Bill 1 and compares it to plans made in 1961, after the worst drought on record. Through Senate Bill 1, sixteen new regional water planning programs were created around the state. Each program included representatives from all categories of city, agricultural, business, conservation, and energy plant concerns. She examines some of the sixteen individual plans under development and their recommendations for the next fifty years.

CHAPTER 1

A Half Century of Water Resource Planning and Policy, 1950–2000

Joe G. Moore, Jr.

Distinguished Professor, Department of Geography

Texas State University–San Marcos

Abstract

Water supply crises such as floods and droughts or fears about control of water sources generate governmental attention to water resources policy in Texas. The last half century of water planning has been dominated by the drought of the 1950s (now the worst "drought of record") and the floods that ended it. Subsequent years have seen less extensive water shortages or excesses. In the mid-twentieth century there was also concern that federal agencies, namely the U.S. Army Corps of Engineers and the Bureau of Reclamation, would preempt the state's ability to choose its own water supply solutions. Legislation has been adopted over the years producing a series of fifty-year water plans—1968, 1984, 1990, 1992, and 1997—with a new one (using a different approach) effective in 2002. Residents in river basins, now estimated to have water in excess of their fifty-year future needs, fear that this excess will be diverted to the nearest metropolitan centers in other basins. During the decades since 1950, Texas groundwater law has moved away from the "rule of capture."

Historically, citizen and legislative attention to Texas water supply issues has been precipitated by catastrophic physical events—droughts and floods—and by institutional threats from government, such as federal water agency planning and implementation by Congress. Real or imagined crises generate a flurry of activity, but this is followed by periods of little or moderate progress toward meeting future water needs until a new crisis emerges. Decision makers often react to events rather than anticipating them and rarely devote attention to resolution of water problems without the stress of a crisis.

Constitutional Status of Water Resources in the State

In 1904, article 3, section 52 was added to the Texas Constitution authorizing any defined district to levy and collect taxes in order to support bonded indebtedness within specified limitations, for the purposes of "(1) the improvement of rivers, creeks, and streams to prevent overflows, and to permit the navigation thereof, or irrigation thereof, or to aid in such purposes; [and] (2) the construction on maintenance of pools, lakes, reservoirs, dams, canals and waterways for the purpose of irrigation, drainage or navigation, or in the aid thereof."[1] This amendment was adopted because "the populace had awakened to the fact that water conservation and the utilization of water resources was one of the most important problems facing the state." Nearly a century later there is a renewed awakening.

Article 16, section 59(a), added to the Texas Constitution in 1917, provides:

Table 1. Evolution of Texas surface water rights regimes

Sovereign	Date	Water Rights Regime
Spain	1600–1821	Spanish civil law
Mexico	1821–1835	Mexican civil law
Republic of Texas	1836–1840	Presumably riparian
	1840–1845	Riparian law*
State of Texas	1845–1888	Riparian law
	1889–1912	Limited prior appropriation and riparian law
	1913–1966	Mixed prior appropriation and riparian law
	1967–present	Unified to prior appropriation

Source: Ronald A. Kaiser, "Evolving Paradigms in Texas Surface Water Law," Texas Water Law Institute Seminar, Austin, October 23–24, 1997, 5.

*Riparian law holds that ownership of land adjoining a lake or stream includes the right to use such waters (Haas v. Choussardl 17 Tex 558, 1856).

The conservation and development of all of the natural resources of this State, including the control, storing, preservation and distribution of its storm and flood waters, the waters of its rivers and streams, for irrigation, power and all other useful purposes, the reclamation and irrigation of its arid, semi-arid and other lands needing irrigation, the reclamation and drainage of its overflowed lands, and other lands needing drainage, the conservation and development of its forests, water and hydro-electric power, the navigation of its inland and coastal waters, and the preservation and conservation of all such natural resources of the State are each and all hereby declared public rights and duties; and the Legislature shall pass all such laws as may be appropriate thereto.

Section 59(b) authorizes creation of conservation and reclamation districts. These constitutional provisions were "inspired by terrific floods in Texas during 1913 and 1914."[2] Article 3, section 49-d contains the declaration that "public waters of the state . . . are held in trust for the use and benefit of the public" and "the policy of the State" is "to encourage the optimum regional development of systems built for the filtration, treatment, and transmission of water."

Rights to Use Texas Surface and Groundwater

In Texas, surface and groundwater are governed by two different legal concepts. While all users of surface water must secure a permit from a state agency (now the Texas Natural Resource Conservation Commission, TNRCC), any landowner can drill a well and pump unlimited groundwater for beneficial use even though such pumping may withdraw water from under a neighbor's land or cause a neighbor's well to go dry.

Rights to Surface Water

Surface water law is derived from property law. Thus, Texas has experienced several regulatory regimes, as reflected in table 1.

The prior appropriation surface water rights doctrine has two significant components: (1) "first in time is first in right"; and (2) "use it or lose it." In the event of shortage in the source, rights to quantities are supplied in chronological order, the oldest being met first. While Texas law also provides for any part of the permitted amount not used during a ten-year period to be subject to a reduction in the permit, such rights are rarely if ever involuntarily canceled for non-use. Stock tanks with a capacity of less than two hundred acre-feet of water on an owner's land are exempt from state regulation, as is sufficient water from adjoining streams and rivers for domestic and livestock use.

Several controversies arising from Texas' historical water rights regimes have clarified state water law or generated legislative action. The source of original land grants, either from Spain or Mexico, impacted surface water rights for irrigation. In *State v. Valmont Plantation*, the Texas Supreme Court enunciated the rule that any grant of water for irrigation had to be explicitly stated; it cannot be implied from the laws of either of these countries at the time of the grant.[3] During the 1950s drought, when the flow in the lower Rio Grande was inadequate to meet all claims based on civil law, riparian law, and the prior appropriation system, Texas filed suit to have these competing claims resolved. In *State v. Hidalgo County WCID No. 18* some three thousand parties generated $10 million in court costs and attorneys' fees during the thirteen years of litigation.[4] This litigation led to the enactment of the Water Rights Adjudication Act of 1967.[5] All riparian and civil law surface water rights were to be converted to appropriative rights by court judgments to be entered for each river basin. Constitutionality of this act was affirmed by the Texas Supreme Court in 1982 and 1988.[6] All subsequent surface water rights in Texas are now determined by the Texas Natural Resource Conservation Commission.

Rights to Groundwater

While the prior appropriation regime for rights to surface water is based on statutes enacted by the legislature, groundwater rights in Texas are based on a 1904 Texas Supreme Court ruling. In *Houston and Texas Central Railway Co. v. East,* the justices adopted language from an 1861 Ohio case stating that "the movement and course of such waters and the causes which govern and direct their movements, are so secret, occult and concealed that an attempt to administer any set of legal rules in respect to them would be involved in hopeless uncertainty and would be, therefore, practically impossible."[7]

Thus most groundwater underlying Texas is governed by the "rule of capture," which states that the owner of the overlying land may "capture" and beneficially use not only the groundwater underlying his or her own land but also that from under the land of adjoining neighbors. Only if the withdrawal causes land subsidence is there liability for damages.[8] This rule originated in English common law concerning disputes over wild animals. An 1804 New York case applies the rule to the claims of two neighbors over a dead fox.[9] Initially applied to minerals underground, the rule was extended to oil and gas in Texas when these resources were discovered. Eventually, this application of the rule was replaced to prevent waste of these resources. However, as late as May, 1999, the Texas Supreme Court reaffirmed the rule's application to groundwater in *Sipriano et al. v. Great Spring Water of America, Inc. Ozarka.*[10]

While most groundwater districts created pursuant to article 16, section 59(a), exercise limited control on the spacing of wells and on water conservation to present waste, only eight counties in Texas are subject to real limits in groundwater pumping. In three counties—Harris, Montgomery, and Galveston—pumping is restricted by districts created to prevent land subsidence; and in Hays, Comal, Bexar, Medina, and Uvalde counties, and in parts of Atascosa and Guadalupe counties, pumping is limited to assure minimum flows from Comal Springs in New Braunfels and San Marcos Springs in San Marcos. These springs also provide a constant minimum flow downstream to the Guadalupe River. Statutes modifying the rule of capture in both these areas have been upheld as constitutional by the Texas Supreme Court.[11]

Drought Motivates Water Planning

Average annual precipitation in Texas varies from some fifty-six inches in the Beaumont–Port Arthur area to eight inches in the vicinity of El Paso.[12] Ambient surface temperature also affects water availability through evaporation and evapotranspiration. "Mean annual net evaporation rates vary from zero inches in East Texas near the Sabine River to approximately 100 inches in the Trans-Pecos, near El Paso."[13]

Between 1891 and 1960 Texas experienced eleven significant drought periods of varying severity and areal extent. They are ranked in the *Texas Water Plan.*

Most severe	1954–56
Second	1916–18
Third	1909–12
Fourth	1901
Fifth	1953
Sixth	1933–34
Seventh	1950–52
Eighth	1924–25
Ninth	1891–93
Tenth	1937–39
Eleventh	1986–89

Accompanying commentary indicates how bad things were in the early 1950s: "As the 1954–1956 drought was the most severe, and since it was immediately preceded by the fifth and seventh ranked droughts comprising a continuous series of years of rainfall deficiencies, this series—1950 through 1956—comprises the most intense 7-year drought period that the State as a whole has experienced within the 70-year period of rainfall records. Dendrochronological studies [analysis of annual tree growth rings to determine dates and order of past events] in the southwestern part of the United States suggest that the 1950–1956 drought period ranks among the most severe droughts of the past 400 years."[14] The drought ended in 1957 with a statewide flood.

Thus for statewide water planning purposes, the period 1950–56 is generally characterized as the drought of record. Projects to meet future water requirements must be planned to assure water supply for any repeat of this drought term.

Texas Water Planning in the 1950s and 1960s

State Planning Efforts

The Texas Board of Water Engineers (TBWE) was created by the Irrigation Act of 1913 to administer a system of surface water rights that came to be known as "certified filings." Acute concern about adequacy of the state's water supply surfaced during the drought of record. As a result of recommendations made by the Thomas Commission, named by Governor Price Daniel, the Texas Water Development Board was created by legislative act in 1957. In a constitutional amendment adopted the same year, the board was named to administer the $200 million Texas Water Development Fund, which supplied loans to "political subdivisions and bodies politic and corporate" for water resource development projects.[15]

In 1961, at the governor's request and in response to the drought of record and federal water planning, the board delivered to Governor Daniel and the legislature *A Plan for Meeting the 1980 Water Requirements of Texas*. The document begins: "Nature within the past decade has inscribed upon the wide-spreading landscape grim warnings of greater disasters to come if development of the State's water resources [is] neglected. . . . It was the drought beginning in 1950 and extending through 1956 that awoke Texans to the real seriousness of the problem."[16]

The Texas Water Resources Planning Division was created within the board by the 1957 Planning Act, and a progress report entitled "Texas Water Resources Planning at the End of the Year 1958" was submitted to the 56th Legislature in 1959. Governor Daniel met with the board several times during development of the plan. Two significant factors were cited as constraints to the plan. The first was the Wagstaff Act, which established priority preferences for domestic and municipal ("classed as superior and coequal") and industrial uses ahead of water for irrigation, mining, hydroelectric power, navigation, and recreation; the act was repealed in 1997.[17] The second was that "ground-water has not been subjected to state control."[18] When the report was being prepared, "14 major reservoirs" (those with five thousand acre-feet of storage or more) were under construction; "the yield of 7 of these reservoirs [was] to be utilized completely before 1980," and only "small amounts" would remain available from the other seven. The plan proposed forty-five new major reservoirs and the enlargement of two existing ones and claimed: "This study demonstrates that Texas has water resources to meet the State's municipal and industrial needs of 1980."[19]

Federal Planning Efforts

Three cabinet departments have been involved in planning and constructing water supply projects in Texas. The U.S. Army Corps of Engineers in the Defense Department is responsible for navigation and flood control, as well as municipal and industrial water supply, primarily in the eastern part of the state. The Bureau of Reclamation of the Department of the Interior operates in the twelve contiguous western states where there is extensive federal ownership of public lands. Texas did not initially fit within the bureau's jurisdiction, as there are no federal public lands in Texas except for those purchased by the federal government because of the compromise forced on the state at the time of its annexation. The state had to repay its then existing national debt in exchange for retaining all public lands. In 1905 and 1906, the bureau's jurisdiction was extended to Texas, with most of its activity occurring west of the 100th meridian. The Soil Conservation Service (now the National Resources Conservation Service) of the Department of Agriculture has historically constructed small flood retardation and sediment control structures on private lands, with cooperation of landowners or soil and water conservation districts, in order to collect sediment and slow floodwaters. These projects can be authorized to include as much as five thousand acre-feet of storage for water supply. An acre-foot is enough water to cover an acre to a depth of one foot, or 325,851 gallons. Tension and competition among these federal agencies was of sufficient concern to Senator Lyndon Johnson for him to secure a memorandum of understanding executed by the secretaries of Defense, Interior, and Agriculture clearly delineating their respective federal roles in Texas water planning and development.

Three significant federal efforts have affected Texas state water resource planning. A 1953 Bureau of Reclamation proposal, developed at the request of Senator Johnson, discussed large interbasin transfers of water across Texas rivers, except for the Sabine, Rio Grande, Red, and their tributaries.[20] Designated the Gulf Basins Project, the bureau's proposal included a canal from Beaumont to Corpus Christi and ending in the Rio Grande Valley, collecting river flows to meet coastal needs and expanded irrigation in the Valley and Coastal Bend areas. This canal came to be known as "Burleigh's Ditch" in honor of Harry Burleigh of the Austin Bureau of Reclamation office.

In 1958, a second document detailing water plans for Texas rivers was published.[21] Covering all Texas rivers except the Red and Rio Grande and their tributaries, this product was a joint effort of the TBWE, Corps of Engineers, Soil Conservation Service, and Bureau of Reclamation.

In 1959, through the leadership of Senator Johnson, Congress created the U.S. Study Commission–Texas.[22] Chaired by long-time Johnson friend and financial supporter George Brown of the Brown and Root construction firm, the commission developed a fifty-year plan for the same river basins as in the 1958 document. The plan was issued in March of 1962, elaborating the Texas Basins Project with cost estimates of $1.1 billion by 1975 plus an additional $3 billion by 2010.

The 1968 Texas Water Plan

John Connally became governor in 1963 after defeating Governor Price Daniel in the Democratic primary election and Ralph Yarborough in the primary runoff. Alarmed at the prospect that federal water planning and construction agencies would preempt state preferences, the Texas Water Commission (successor to the TBWE and now part of the Texas Natural Resource Conservation Commission) requested a study of state water planning needs from the Texas Research League, a business-financed, nonprofit research agency organized to minimize the costs of state government. In its report, the league concluded: "Only the State has broad enough jurisdiction to plan the most effective coordination of water project development, and up until now the State has dispatched its responsibility for such coordination very poorly."[23]

With release of the bureau's Texas Basins Project report and while the league's study was under way, the Texas Water Commission Chair Joe Carter and Chief Engineer John Vandertulip met with Governor Connally in August, 1964, to request an emergency allocation of funds to un-

dertake a comprehensive water plan covering the entire state. The governor's response, in a letter dated August 12, 1964, is quoted in the 1968 *Texas Water Plan:*

The Bureau of Reclamation and Corps of Engineers have proposed broad water development projects for Texas far beyond the plans of the Texas Water Commission report, "A Plan for Meeting the 1980 Water Requirements of Texas." In my opinion, these plans fall short of satisfying the water needs for all of Texas.

Furthermore, the Congress is presently considering a Federal water pollution control bill, which will supplant state authority in this field. I have long been concerned that the State exercises its responsibility in all areas of water conservation and development. The recently enacted Water Resources Act of 1964 does provide an opportunity for state participation in federal water research programs. . . .

I cannot properly evaluate some proposed federal projects without a longer-range State Water Plan for Texas. Therefore, . . . I hereby request the Texas Water Commission . . . to begin at once to develop a comprehensive State Water Plan. In the public interest and to aid the economic growth and general welfare of the State, I urge that you explore all reasonable alternatives for development and distribution of all our water resources to benefit the entire State, including proposals contained in preliminary reports to the federal agencies.[24]

In the 1965 legislative session, Governor Connally proposed a detailed water planning statute; a constitutional amendment to enlarge the purposes for which proceeds from bond sales in the Texas Water Development Fund might be spent; and a Water Rights Adjudication Act to clarify all surface water rights in the state and compel conversion of any riparian rights to state permits. In the planning statute, water resource planning was transferred from the Texas Water Commission to the Texas Water Development Board. Senator George Parkhouse of Dallas sponsored these proposals.

During the evolution of the planning legislation, legislators from East Texas became alarmed at the prospect that surface water from rivers or reservoirs in their area might be transported to meet metropolitan or irrigation water demands in other river basins. Senator Jack Strong of Longview spoke for East Texas interests; he was also sponsor of Governor Connally's education legislation relating to public school teachers' pay. Governor Connally directed his staff to accommodate Senator Strong's views on interbasin transfers of surface water. Compromise language in 1965 provided that the Water Development Board "shall not prepare or formulate a plan that contemplates or results in the removal of surface water from the river basin of origin if the water supply involved will be required for reasonably foreseeable water supply requirements within the river basin of origin during the next ensuing 50-year period, except on a temporary, interim basis."[25] Since a water plan had to be reviewed and if necessary revised every five years, East Texas legislators deemed this language adequate protection for their future needs.

Also being considered was the constitutional amendment authorizing Texas Water Development Fund bond proceeds to be spent "for the additional purposes of acquiring and developing storage facilities, and any system or works necessary for the filtration, treatment and transportation of water."[26] Senator Strong insisted on the addition of language in the amendment so that neither the Texas Water Development Fund nor "any other state fund" could be used to finance any project that would have the same results as those prohibited in the planning statute. In a Senate Constitutional Amendment Committee hearing, Senator Parkhouse mistakenly advised his colleagues that the proposed amendment doubled the Water Development Fund by adding $200 million to the authorized total of bonds that could be issued; at his insistence, the necessary change was made to increase the fund from $200 to $400 million to "keep him honest." The people of Texas approved the amendment on November 6, 1966. No further increase in total bond proceeds for water supply development projects was approved until November 5, 1985. The Water Rights Adjudication Act proved too complex and too controversial for adoption in the 1965 session. It was passed in 1967.

Two major issues dominating water resource planning in the 1960s were irrigation and inflows to the bays. Irrigation farmers on the Texas High Plains overlying the Ogallala aquifer, and their supporters, insisted that their need for water to replace groundwater being mined from the aquifer must be met. Annual recharge to the aquifer is roughly one-tenth of the amount withdrawn. Meeting this need would require water importation from out of state. The final 1968 plan contemplated two significant parts: (1) The Trans-Texas Division, distributing 7.5 million acre-feet to West Texas for irrigation, 1 million acre-feet for municipal and industrial use, and 1.5 million acre-

feet to New Mexico, for a total of 10 million acre-feet; and (2) the Coastal Division, distributing 1.8 million acre-feet for irrigation, 0.5 million acre-feet for municipal and industrial use, and 2.5 million acre-feet for fish, wildlife, and freshwater inflows to Texas bays and estuaries, for a total of 4.8 million acre-feet.[27] Of the 14.8 million acre-feet to be transported in the two divisions, 12–13 million acre-feet were required from the Mississippi River, with only 1.8–2.8 million acre-feet coming from interbasin transfers within Texas. In addition to the two major canal systems, the plan proposed some sixty-two new major reservoirs and two salt water barriers. As of 2000, only six of these had been constructed.

The total cost of the intrastate facilities in the plan was $9 billion in 1967 dollars for its implementation to the year 2020.[28] The Texas Legislature proposed a constitutional amendment to authorize an additional $3.5 billion in Texas Water Development Fund bonds, and it was on the election ballot on August 5, 1969. It failed in a vote of 315,793 against and 309,516 for, a margin of 6,277 votes; a major factor in defeat of the proposal was organized vocal opposition by the Sierra Club.[29] Meeting irrigation water shortages on the Texas High Plains because of overdrafting the Ogallala aquifer frustrated Texas water planners for the ensuing sixteen years.

The other major issue was allocation for freshwater inflows to the bays and estuaries. Noncoastal water users felt such an allocation was a waste. At a conference on "Texas Water Problems and Possible Solutions" held at Southwest Texas State Teachers College (now Texas State University–San Marcos) on July 20, 1954, during the drought of record, Guy C. Jackson, president of the Texas Water Conservation Association, listed one of several problems as "increased water escaping into the sea" with the "mean annual unused run-off at 54 million acre-feet" compared with then "consumptive uses at 8 million acre-feet."[30]

Water Planning Efforts in the 1970s

Despite the defeat of the bond issue that would have financed the start of implementation of the 1968 water plan, residents and political leaders on the Texas High Plains continued to advocate delivery of water to replace depletion of the Ogallala. The Public Works Appropriation Act of 1967 authorized the Bureau of Reclamation, Corps of Engineers, and Mississippi River Commission to analyze a project to divert Mississippi River water to West Texas and eastern New Mexico.[31] The final 1973 report, *West Texas and Eastern New Mexico Import Project*, concluded that the $16.6 billion cost, with a cost-benefit ratio of 0.27, "could not be justified economically or financially using present procedures." Still West Texas persisted in its support of an import scheme.[32]

The Texas Water Development Board contracted with an engineering firm in Little Rock, Arkansas, which in December, 1976, produced "An Assessment of Surface Water Supplies of Arkansas with Computations of Surplus Supplies and a Conceptual Plan for Import to Texas." The report concluded: "Mutual benefits can be derived by both Arkansas and Texas if surplus water is exported from Arkansas to the water short areas of Texas. Should New Mexico, Oklahoma and Louisiana join with Texas and Arkansas in a water transfer plan, the water supply and delivery system could probably be enlarged and a more cost effective system designed and constructed. The leadership to explore this concept could be provided by the Arkansas-White-Red Basins Inter-Agency Committee (AWRBIAC)." The latter agency was the vehicle for negotiating the Red River Compact.[33]

An attempt in 1976 to double the Water Development Fund to $800 million failed, despite twenty "forums" sponsored by the Water Development Board around the state. The vote was 1,234,451 against and 937,921 in favor.[34]

In May of 1977, a draft report titled *Continuing Water Resources Planning and Development for Texas, Phase I* was issued by the Texas Department of Water Resources, into which the TWDB had been incorporated by the legislature. No final phase I report was ever issued, and a draft for phase II was not produced.

Congressman George Mahon of Lubbock was chair of the U.S. House Committee on Appropriations during these years. In 1976, Congress appropriated funds to the U.S. Department of Commerce "to examine the feasibility of various alternatives to provide adequate water supplies" for the six-state High Plains region and "to assure the continued growth and vitality of the region."[35] Because the Ogallala underlies the parts of six states, the governors of those states formed a High Plains Study Council. No significant actions were initiated following the report of High Plains Associates in March, 1982, addressed to the commerce secretary, the Honorable Malcolm Baldridge.[36] The advent of the Carter and Reagan administrations and the elimination of substantial federal funding for water supply projects ended hope for substantial water importation.

In the 1990 TWDB plan, the agency stated: "Under present circumstances and during the 50-year planning horizon used in this update, major interstate importation of water, distinguished from local efforts to import ground water and interstate division of surface water within a shared river basin through existing or interstate compact agreements, is not necessary to meet projected demands."[37]

The surface waters of all interstate rivers and their tributaries—the Canadian, Red, Sabine, Pecos, and Rio Grande—are allocated according to compacts with the states in those basins, administered by compact commissions. In addition, allocation of the waters of the Rio Grande from El Paso to Brownsville is governed by treaties with Mexico administered through the International Boundary and Water Commission, a unit of the U.S. State Department, headquartered in El Paso, Texas.

In the same 1990 report, the TWDB notes that "the 69th Texas Legislature created the Multi-State Water Resources Planning Commission to study the water importation question and actions to work with other states in an attempt to identify available water supplies and cost-effective import supply alternatives. However, the Multi-State Commission was never provided funding by the Legislature to begin a program of work."[38]

Various measures to provide additional state water resources funding were attempted by several governors and Texas legislatures. None were successful, largely because of opposition from the Sierra Club.[39] While Texas environmental groups had mustered sufficient strength to prevent adoption of policies adverse to their interests, they were not yet sufficiently strong to compel adoption of their ideas.

Accommodation in the 1980s

Accommodation between water developers and some environmental groups was finally achieved in the 1980s. When a new constitutional amendment for water project funding failed in 1981, many leaders recognized that additional money could be provided only if the Sierra Club and its allies were satisfied.

The first significant formal revision of the 1968 water plan was produced by the TWDB in November, 1984. Coincidentally, the state was experiencing one of its periodic droughts. The plan contemplated the construction of forty-four major reservoirs between 1984 and 2020.[40] For the first time, estimates of substantial freshwater inflows to bays and estuaries were included as water requirements, and water conservation and direct reuse were discussed as means to reduce demand.[41]

In the 1985 legislative session, a compromise approach

to assuring freshwater inflows was at last achieved. Simultaneously, the legislature proposed constitutional amendments including (1) an additional $400 million for the Water Development Fund for water supply storage, transportation, and treatment projects; (2) $200 million for flood control; (3) $250 million for an insurance program to guarantee repayment of bonds issued by local political subdivisions for water supply and wastewater projects; and (4) provisions for a $200 million program administered by TWDB that would lend money to irrigators for installation of efficient irrigation equipment.[42] The environmental community was split in the election at which these amendments were considered. "The Sierra Club, the Sportsmen's Clubs of Texas (the state's National Wildlife Federation affiliate), the League of Women Voters, and others remained neutral or supported adoption of the amendments. Only the Audubon Society and the Texas Committee on Natural Resources (TCONR), led by Dallas attorney Edward Fritz, publicly opposed the package. [It] was approved by a vote of 705,678 to 251,031 in November 1985."[43]

Further Planning in the 1990s

The TWDB issued three water plans in the 1990s. The first extended the planning horizon to 2040. A number of recommendations were made and explained.[44] Among them was the proposal that the legislature should "remove the requirement that only surface water in excess of the 50-year water supply requirements of an originating basin may be considered for interbasin water transfers."[45] In 1991 the legislature eliminated this provision from the planning statute. The TWDB subsequently contracted with HDR Engineering, Inc., to develop what became known as the Trans-Texas Water Program. The program included only those areas of the state in which future water shortage would most likely be affected by interbasin transfers, such as the Beaumont–Port Arthur–Orange, Houston, Austin, San Antonio, and Corpus Christi metropolitan areas, and the available water resources in these regions.[46] The fears of residents in basins of origin for water transfers were rekindled, and this effort was overtaken by the planning process mandated by Senate Bill 1, passed in 1997.

In 1992, the TWDB issued an update of its 1990 plan.[47] It contains about one hundred pages of recommendations and "Area/Project Assessments." Many of the recommendations in the 1990 and 1992 plans are still valid and worthy of consideration by the legislature.

Texas was again plagued with a severe drought in 1996. Before the 1997 legislative session, Lieutenant Governor Bob Bullock requested recommendations for water legislation from the Texas Natural Resource Conservation Commission, the Texas Parks and Wildlife Department, and the Texas Water Development Board in order to enable the state to mitigate repeated water shortages and drought. These agencies responded with a twenty-five-page document addressed to Governor George Bush, Lieutenant Governor Bullock, and House Speaker Pete Laney.[48] With these recommendations as a basis, Bullock developed a legislative proposal that became Senate Bill 1 in the 1997 Texas legislative session, sponsored by Senator "Buster" Brown, chair of the Natural Resources Committee. It was enacted after extended hearings and considerable debate in both houses.

Significant provisions restructured the state water resources planning process. Instead of the traditional "top-down" approach from the TWDB at the state level, Senate Bill 1 ordered a "bottom-up" approach from planning groups operating within regions designated by the TWDB prepared regional plans. The board delineated sixteen regions after publication of proposed boundaries, a comment period, and revisions. By law, each regional water planning group (RWPG) must have members representing counties, municipalities, industries, agriculture, environmental groups, small businesses, electric generating utilities, river authorities, water districts, water utilities, the public, and any other interest groups appropriate to the region. The TWDB named the initial members in its rule establishing the RWPGs. The regional planning period is fifty years, and regional plans are submitted to the TWDB upon completion. Each region is required to coordinate its plan with all adjoining regions. Any unresolved conflicts between plans were to be resolved by the TWDB and consolidated into a statewide plan by September 1, 2001 (extended to January 1, 2002). Any water resource project requiring a state permit during the five years following the completion of the initial and subsequent plans must be included in the final plans before a permit will be granted. The process must be repeated every five years to update initial plans. Executive Administrator Craig D. Pedersen reported that as of September, 2000, the process had been successful with remarkable consistency among the plans.[49]

The most critical statutory changes in Senate Bill 1 that affect future water resource planning and supply are those restricting interbasin transfers of surface water. First, the legislature provided that any such proposed transfer will be "junior" in priority to any water right in the receiving basin.[50] Since all Texas river basins are over-appropriated (i.e., there are verified rights to more water than is normally available in the basin), any right to transferred water becomes very uncertain during periods of low surface water flow. In addition, the law requires the applicant to provide a long list of specific information about the proposed transfer to any person without cost.[51] These provisions severely inhibit future interbasin transfers.

Provisions of Senate Bill 1 requiring water conservation plans for any utility seeking a permit should provide a basis for reducing future demand. Similar requirements for drought management plans should enable the state eventually to develop a statewide plan. Also, groundwater districts were required to file management plans detailing how they would conserve water.

The TWDB was in the process of updating its 1992 plan as Senate Bill 1 was being formulated. That process ended with publication of *Water for Texas, A Consensus-Based Update of the State Water Plan* in August, 1997.[52] This publication is particularly significant since it constitutes the baseline against which the current "bottom-up" planning effort will be measured.

In Texas, the twentieth century ended with incipient drought. The year 2000 ended with widespread heavy rainfall that produced scattered local flooding. Thus there is added motivation to prepare to meet the water demands of Texas' multiplying population in the new century. Proposals by Ozarka to pump more East Texas groundwater in areas where there are springs and a proposal by T. Boone Pickens, an oil and gas entrepreneur and Panhandle rancher, to pump some 100,000–200,000 acre-feet of Ogallala groundwater from Parker County to Dallas–Fort Worth or San Antonio at prices competitive with surface water guarantee further attention to the rule of capture. At the request of Senator Brown of the Senate Natural Resources Committee, the TWDB funded "a study to work with stake-holders to build consensus recommendations for improving groundwater management in Texas." Five proposed statutory changes resulted: (1) support the TWDB's groundwater availability modeling; (2) continue and expand the TWDB's grants for groundwater conservation equipment purchases; (3) make the current voluntary groundwater use survey mandatory; (4) expand the state's real-time groundwater and well level monitoring network; and (5) appropriate additional funds to the TWDB to provide pay for flexibility to enable TWDB to hire and retain qualified modeling and data collection personnel.[53]

Some of the Senate Bill 1 RWPG plans in the eastern half of the state propose meeting water requirements with new surface water reservoirs. Meeting San Antonio's projected needs includes further interbasin transfers and desalination of Gulf seawater. Both the Senate and House Natural Resources Committees held hearings throughout the state during the interim between the 1999 and 2001 legislative sessions, and their members generated additional proposals for legislation. Senate Bill 2, sponsored by Senator Brown in the 2001 legislative session, was adopted after substantial controversy and amendment. It strengthens the role of groundwater districts in regulating withdrawals to accommodate a reliable "firm annual yield" and to limit exports. The most pressing issues remain: (1) achieving adequate levels of water conservation; (2) integrating planning and use of groundwater and surface water; (3) regional or local modification of the rule of capture for groundwater; (4) assuring reasonable environmental protection and instream and estuarine water requirements; and (5) simplifying interbasin transfers of surface water by removing the many obstacles added in 1997, while protecting the "reasonably foreseeable water supply requirements within the river basin of origin during the next ensuing fifty year period."[54]

Observations after Fifty Years of Water Resource Planning in Texas Drought

Periodic drought is inevitable in Texas. Water use for all purposes has reached levels such that at least one region of the state is likely to experience water shortage every three to five years, and widespread drought may occur in ten- to fifteen-year cycles. Advance preparation to minimize hardship is essential. The TWDB and the TNRCC should be given authority to prescribe standards for determining when a region, or the state, is experiencing drought. They should also develop regional and statewide triggers for various stages of water use reductions during droughts. The duty to declare a regional or more extensive drought, and the definition of the affected geographical area, should be assigned to the TWDB; the TNRCC should be charged with enforcement of water use restrictions during drought in each region or the entire state.

Water Conservation and Reuse
The people of Texas cannot conserve enough water from current uses to meet projected fifty-year water requirements. St. Augustine lawn grass and tropical shrubbery should be outlawed except where it can survive with

normal rainfall. Every municipal and existing water utility should establish ten-year goals for gallons per capita per day (gpcd) of water use, and the TNRCC should monitor progress toward achieving these goals. The TNRCC should develop guidelines for all major industrial and commercial water users against which their uses can be evaluated to assure maximum conservation. All major irrigation water users should be required to adopt timetables, with state assistance if necessary, for installing the most efficient irrigation equipment consistent with economic efficiency. Properties with water-based landscaping and recreational facilities such as swimming pools and fountains should be penalized with higher water rates. Reuse of treated municipal and industrial wastewater should be practiced whenever possible, consistent with the protection of public health and downstream surface water rights.

Water for the Environment
A reasonable level of instream water requirements and freshwater inflow to bays and estuaries is as legitimate a water use as are needs for municipal, industrial, commercial, and irrigation activities. Refinement of the quantities required and timing of deliveries should continue as these flows are essential to the preservation of these ecosystems.

Weather Modification
While precipitation enhancement is popular in the public imagination, it will not deliver the quantities of water where they will be needed by Texans in the next fifty years. Rainfall occurring in one place precludes it occurring in another place. The potential range of legal liabilities, as well as evidence of benefits being limited, restricts this alternative within the fifty-year planning time frame.

Desalination
Promoting desalting of Gulf of Mexico salt water provides solace and comfort for those unable or unwilling to consider more practical solutions that should be initiated now to avoid inevitable shortage. Costs—especially for transporting the desalted water to points of use—and environmental consequences are speculative for the short term. Investment in improving the technology, however, should continue.

River Basin Reservoir and Groundwater Management
Where this is not already practiced, all major surface reservoirs in a river basin should be operated jointly so as to optimize distribution of the available surface water.

Efforts should begin now to determine for each major aquifer underlying part of any river basin an annual maximum groundwater withdrawal amount that can be sustained for the drought of record—that is, a "firm annual yield" similar to that for surface water reservoirs. The state legislature should formulate new laws that will allow joint planning, management, and use of all surface water in a river basin and the supplies of groundwater from any major aquifers or parts of aquifers underlying that basin. Where major aquifers underlie more than one surface water basin, methods should be devised for allocating the groundwater between them.

Bottom-Up Planning
The initial results of the Senate Bill 1 planning process are impressive, but the devil may lie in the details. It pays to be skeptical of a product with "consensus" in its title. Almost any solution to a significant fifty-year water supply shortage in any part of Texas is controversial. Large or expensive projects that are initially acceptable are often derailed as the plans and costs become more definitive. Even if all stakeholders are pleased at first, there are risks that the solutions were ill-defined or not well understood and that the consequences (in cost or perceived environmental or other damage or loss) have not been documented or fully explored. Water development and distribution in Texas will remain volatile issues as the potential shortages are fully revealed.

Use of Models to Assist Decision Making
All computer models are extensions of human imagination; they are not a substitution for the human brain—they cannot decide. Models have limitations, and their output should be carefully evaluated, as would the product of any other tool available to assist in the making of choices. Too often, model results are presented as the absolute truth; they are only way stations.

Data
The most glaring shortcoming of all current water resource planning efforts in Texas is the fact that the state today is collecting less water data from fewer locations than it was thirty-five years ago. Discontinuance of monitoring data not only shortchanges the future; it also invalidates the past. A terminated data chain makes the data already collected useless. Often, data collection and analysis fall victim to real or imagined state or local budget crises; at those times, the numbers have no defenders. All agencies involved in water resource planning should de-

velop a statewide essential data needs inventory that will survive scrutiny by the legislature, and they should initiate a program to obtain public support for its implementation.

New Surface Reservoirs

Prospects for new surface water reservoirs are dim. It takes twenty-five years from initiating a plan for a reservoir before water is impounded. There are major environmental considerations—endangered species, loss of habitat, alteration of ecosystems, archeological considerations, etc. Unless all water now used for irrigation is to be converted to municipal, commercial, and industrial use, and groundwater dangerously depleted, additional surface water reservoirs are an absolute necessity at some future date. Efforts must continue to assure their timely completion to meet expected needs after all other alternatives are exhausted.

Aquifer Storage and Recovery

Storing surface or groundwater excess to current needs in empty existing aquifers avoids substantial evaporation and seepage losses that occur in surface reservoirs. Prospects are favorable for this solution in appropriate areas of the state.

The Rule of Capture for Groundwater

Continued modification of the rule of capture is inevitable. Proposals for pumping and transport of substantial quantities of groundwater generate attention. Although this rule was once thought to be protective of the surface landowner's right to water under the land, plans for extensive well fields and long-distance transport of groundwater demonstrate the fragility of the presumed right to groundwater. Outright termination of the rule is unlikely; the number of groundwater districts and their areal extent militate against a radical change. Modifications to meet local concerns are probable.

Interbasin Transfers of Surface Water

Texans have demonstrated their unwillingness to reside "where the water is." They expect the water to be moved to where they want to live. Further interbasin transfer of surface water is inevitable. When there is unused water available in other river basins, people will not accept severe restrictions on their water use, especially during drought. Despite public perception, water in Texas does not "belong" to residents within a basin; all surface water is held in trust for all the people of the state. Redistribution to population concentrations is a people problem, a political issue; it will be resolved politically. When a majority of Texans conclude that restrictions on interbasin transfers are a serious threat to their livelihoods and quality of life, they will repeal or modify such limits to suit the majority of Texans.

Notes

1. *Vernon's Annotated Constitution of the State of Texas,* vol. 1A (West Publishing Co.), 402.

2. Ibid.

3. *State v. Valmont Plantation,* 355 SW 2d 502 (1962).

4. *State v. Hidalgo County WCID No. 18,* 433 SW 2d 728, Texas Civ. App.–Corpus Christi (1969), writ ref'd, n.r.e.; Ronald A. Kaiser, "Evolving Paradigms in Texas Surface Water Law," Texas Water Law Institute Seminar, Austin, October 23–24, 1997, 7, footnote 30, citing Caroom and Elliot, "Water Rights Adjudication—Texas Style," *Texas Bar Journal* 1183 (November, 1981).

5. Water Rights Adjudication Act of 1967, Texas Water Code 3311, 301–41.

6. *In re Adjudication of Water Rights of the Upper Guadalupe Segment,* 642 SW 2d 438, Tex. (1982) and *In re Adjudication of Water Rights of Brazos III Segment,* 746 SW 2d 207, Tex. (1988).

7. *Houston and Texas Central Railway Co. v. East* 98 Tex. 146, 81 SW 279 (1904); *Frazier v. Brown,* 12 Ohio St. 294, 311 (1861).

8. *Friendswood Development Co. v. Smith–Southwest Industries, Inc.* 576 SW 2d 21, Tex. (1978).

9. *Pierson v. Post,* 3 Cai R 175, N.Y. Sup. Ct. (1804).

10. *Sipriano et al. v. Great Spring Water of America, Inc. Ozarka* SW 2d 1-29-98, Tex. (1999).

11. *Beckendorf v. Harris-Galveston Coastal Subsidence District* 558 SW 2d 75, Tex. (1978), affirmed; *Barshop, et al. v. Medina County Underground Water Conservation District, et al.* no. 95-881, slip op. 20, Tex. (June 28, 1996).

12. *Water for Texas: A Comprehensive Plan for the Future,* 2 vols., Texas Water Development Board, Document GP-4-1 (November, 1984), fig. 5, 1:16.

13. Ibid., 2:3.

14. *The Texas Water Plan,* Texas Water Development Board, Austin (November, 1968), II-2, II-3.

15. Article 3, sec. 40-c.

16. *A Plan for Meeting the 1980 Water Requirements of Texas,* Texas Board Water Engineers (May, 1961), 5.

17. S.B. 93, Chapter 128, *General Laws of Texas* (1931), 42nd Legislative, Regular Session.

18. *Plan for Meeting the 1980 Water Requirements,* 7.

19. Ibid., 3.

20. *Water Supply and the Texas Economy: An Appraisal of the Texas Water Problem,* U.S. Senate Document 57, 83rd Congress (1953).

21. *Water Development and Potentialities of the State of Texas,* Senate Document III, 85th Congress (1958).

22. U.S. Congress PL 85-843 (1959).

23. Texas Research League, "A Pattern of Intergovernmental Relations for Water Resource Management in Texas," Austin (February, 1966), 10.

24. *Texas Water Plan* (November, 1968), vii–viii.

25. *Vernon's Texas Codes Annotated, Water,* vol. 1, sec. 16.052.

26. Article 3, sec. 49-d.

27. *Texas Water Plan* (November, 1968), 12, 14.

28. Ibid., table 1-4, I-25–I-28.

29. "The Texas Water Plan: Biggest Boondoggle in History," *Texas Observer,* August 1, 1969, entire issue.

30. *Bulletin of Southwest Texas State Teachers College* 20, no. 4 (December, 1954): 32.

31. The Public Works Appropriation Act of 1967, PL 89-689.

32. See Gregory Curtis, "Lubbock, World's Largest City with *No* Water," *Texas Monthly,* December, 1974, 76.

33. "An Assessment of Surface Water Supplies of Arkansas with Computations of Surplus Supplies and a Conceptual Plan for Import to Texas." Report to Texas Water Development Board, December, 1976.

34. Ibid., TWDB, 111.

35. PL 94-587, sec. 193, 90 Stat. 2943.

36. *Six State High Plains Ogallala Aquifer Regional Study,* High Plains Associates (March, 1982).

37. *Water for Texas, Today and Tomorrow,* Texas Water Development Board, Document no. GP-5-1 (December, 1990), 4-11.

38. Ibid.

39. TWDB, December, 1976, 104–14.

40. *Water for Texas: A Comprehensive Plan for the Future* (November, 1984), vol. 1, fig. 15, 39.

41. Ibid., table 3, 36, and 29–33.

42. *Texas Constitution,* Article 3, secs. 49-d.2, 49-d.3, 49-d.4, 50-d.

43. TWDB, December 1985, 143–44.

44. *Water for Texas Today and Tomorrow,* Texas Water Development Board Document no. GP-5-1 (December, 1990), 4-1 through 4-46.

45. Ibid., 4-8.

46. For example, see *Trans-Texas Water Program,* West Central Study Area, Phase II, Summary Report of Water Supply Alternatives, HDR Engineering, Inc. (March, 1998).

47. *Water for Texas, Today and Tomorrow,* Recommendations for the 1992 update of the Texas Water Plan, Texas Water Development Board, Document no. GP-6-1 (December, 1992).

48. *Water for Texas, Today and Tomorrow,* "Legislative Summary of the 1996 Consensus-based Update of the State Water Plan," prepared by the Texas Water Development Board in conjunction with the Texas Natural Resources Conservation Commission [and the] Texas Parks and Wildlife Department (January, 1997), with transmittal letter dated January 20, 1997.

49. "Senate Bill 1 Planning: Status, Challenges and Implementation," *Texas Water Law 2000,* Texas Water Law Institute, September 15, 2000, Austin, Texas.

50. *Texas Water Code,* sec. 11.085(a).

51. Ibid., secs. 11.085(b) and (c). The TNRCC must consider a similar laundry list of factors before granting a permit for the transfer, as specified in sec. 11.085(k).

52. *Water for Texas, A Consensus-Based Update of the State Water Plan,* vol. 2, "Technical Planning Appendix," Document no. GP-6-12. Austin: Texas Water Development Board, 1997.

53. "Future of Groundwater Management in Texas, A Consensus Building Effort," Texas Water Development Board (May 2, 2000–August 31, 2000), 2.

54. Ibid.

CHAPTER 2

Texas Water at the Century's Turn

Perspectives, Reflections, and a Comfort Bag

George H. Ward, Jr.

Center for Research in Water Resources

University of Texas at Austin

Abstract

The purpose is to assess the similarities maintained and the changes wrought in water problems and their management over the intervening century. The state exhibits a wide range of hydroclimatology, the greatest of any of the contiguous states. Runoff derives mainly from deep convection, largely associated with equinoctial midlatitude storms and landfalling tropical depressions; the resulting streamflow is flashy. There is a near balance between rainfall and evapotranspiration, making their difference—the water source for both runoff and recharge—susceptible to slight variations in either. The instability of and flashiness in runoff and recharge together comprise the fundamental problem of Texas water supply.

The close of both the nineteenth and twentieth centuries found Texans reeling from droughts and floods. Population growth in the state over the last decade of both centuries was about 30 percent. In the twentieth century, Texas population has multiplied by an order of magnitude and has shifted from rural to urban. Then, as now, the predominant consumption of water was for irrigation, but the volume of this consumption grew substantially during the twentieth century. A ubiquitous pattern in Texas water use was a shift in supply from groundwater to surface water,

and the twentieth century has seen the development of practically the entire Texas reservoir system. During the first decade of the century, rice irrigation came to constitue the predominant demand for surface water. Although in decline over the last decade, it remains the predominant demand. There has been an almost total shift from hydroelectric power to steam generation, but the latter also has a substantial water requirement that is often overlooked in water planning.

The greatest difference between 2000 and 1900 is the sense that Texas water supply development may be approaching its feasible limit. Groundwater supplies have declined due to increasing drafts and decreasing recharge: hundreds of artesian springs across Texas no longer flow; the great Ogallala aquifer has been substantially depleted; and municipal and agricultural pumping can now draw down the entire spring recharge of the Edwards aquifer. The ability of reservoirs to be maintained by a "critical mass" of feeding watershed area, together with the political opposition to such projects, limits present reservoir development. Around 1970, a pronounced reversal in the trend of reservoir storage per capita occurred, coinciding with the defeat of the Texas Water Plan. Looking ahead, interbasin transfer from the eastern water-surplus region of the state will increase, as will reuse strat-egies and conversion of irrigation rights to municipal/industrial uses, resulting in further decline of irrigated agriculture.

Cosmic import aside, the passage of a round number of centuries affords a convenient benchmark for appraisal of water resources and their utilization and management in Texas. Consider the state of Texas at the turn of the twentieth century: after weathering major recessions in the 1880s, Texas entered an economic boom as its population increased by a staggering 35 percent in the closing decade of the century. The preceding several years had been unusually warm, with many record high temperatures, and large regions of the state had suffered from drought. On the national scale, after a harrowing century, the United States emerged in a new position of world leadership and enjoyed relative peace and prosperity. Our last war of the century with an Old World power had been swift and decisive, and while popular at the time, its motivations were subsequently called into question. Politically, the country was in one of its periodic slides to the right, with both houses of Congress controlled by Republicans and the leadership of the House practically reactionary. The business climate was healthy despite consolidation of huge corporations motivating widespread concern about trusts and monopolies. American society was undergoing a revolution driven by the explosion of technology, especially in telecommunications, which created the capacity for exchange of information on an unprecedented scale. Texas especially benefited from technological advancement, notably in the urban areas, where electricity had largely replaced gas lighting and the telephone now permitted instantaneous communication within and between cities.

There are tantalizing parallels between Texas in 1900 and Texas in 2000. One of the most basic parallels is the effect of climate. The backdrop to the growth of population and development of commerce in both 1900 and 2000 includes the vagaries of climate, which plagued Texans throughout the nineteenth and twentieth centuries. Numbing blizzards, searing heat, deadly floods, and fearful windstorms were endemic. However, these were episodes widely scattered in time and space. The climate component that remorselessly stressed the state was water supply. As T. R. Fehrenbach noted in *Seven Keys to Texas,* "the dominant feature of Texas is water, or rather, its scarcity."

Texas Hydroclimate

On the broadest scale, the climates of the North American continent are determined predominantly by the interplay among four factors: the belt of westerlies and their synoptic-scale perturbations; the influx of water vapor from the Gulf of Mexico carried by the easterly limb of the Bermuda High circulation; the physiography of the continent, notably the barrier of the Rocky Mountain cordillera to the west and the relief-free plain in their lee; and the receipt of solar radiation at the surface.

The westerlies impinge on the mountains and are forced up and over the cordillera, releasing their moisture in the process. They then descend to the lee plain as warmed and dried air, establishing a semiarid climate downwind from the mountains—the familiar rain-shadow effect. Onshore flow from the tropical Gulf carries water vapor northward into the lee plain to be entrained back into the air stream. The rate of entrainment is governed by the synoptic-scale disturbances in the westerlies. Surface heating and cooling are controlled by insolation, which reinforces synoptic disturbances by inducing or suppressing convection. If one steps back and squints at the North American continent, its general morphology is seen to be that of an inverted triangle, with the Rocky Mountain cordillera in the west and the moisture source of the Gulf of Mexico from the east converging at its apex (figure 1). At that same apex lies the state of Texas. This geographical fact accounts for one of the dramatic features of the Texas climate, namely its pronounced geo-

Figure 1. Principal determinants of North American climate. Note the position of Texas at the apex of the indicated triangle.

graphical variation, giving rise to the first of five maxims of Texas water.

1. Precipitation and river flow decline markedly from east to west across the state.

There is a six- to sevenfold variation in annual precipitation across Texas, the largest range of variation of the contiguous states (tying with California). The humid eastern sections of Texas are heavily forested, the westward extension of the great eastern forest, while the western sections of the state are desert, the northward extension of Mexico's *tierra caliente*. Between these extremes, much of

Texas is semiarid. Benedict and Lomax (1916) made the tongue-in-cheek observation: "Irrespective of the prohibition issue, Texas is permanently divided into wet and dry." This is exemplified by the patterns of annual precipitation shown in figure 2.[1] The isohyets generally lie along meridians of longitude. Isotherms, in contrast, align mainly along parallels of latitude (fig. 3), evidencing the role of southward-increasing insolation as well as the diminishing effect of synoptic disturbances in the westerlies (the two being interrelated).

Another defining characteristic and the second maxim of Texas water is the source of precipitation.

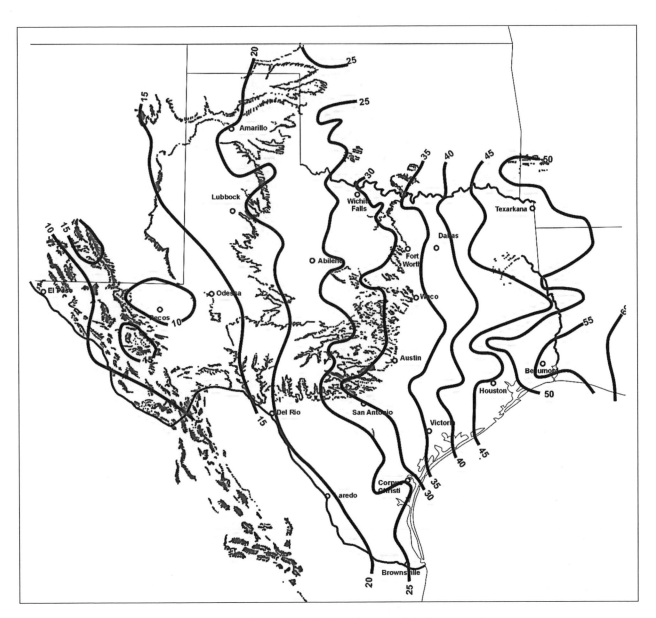

Figure 2. Annual precipitation in Texas (contours in inches per year).

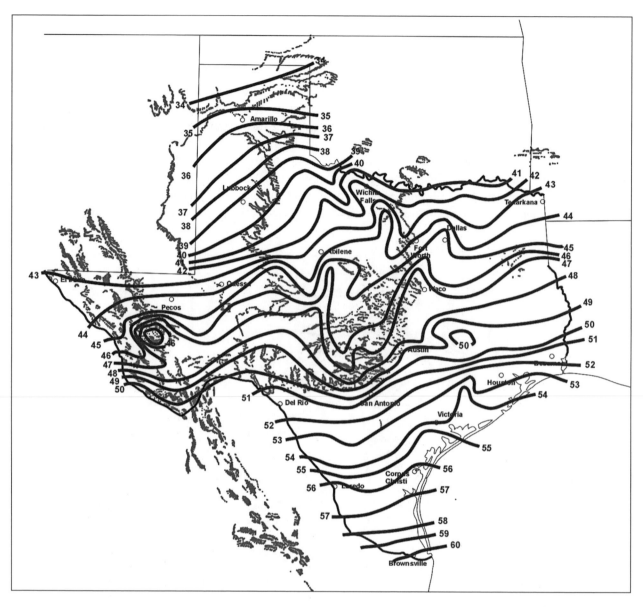

Figure 3. Average January temperatures (degrees F).

2. Precipitation is almost entirely rainfall derived from deep convection.

The implications are that runoff is closely keyed to the occurrence of storms, and the resulting streamflow is flashy. In contrast to other regions of the country, Texas is not routinely visited by large-scale stratiform systems that deliver widespread rainfall at a slow rate over extended periods, and nor is there storage of precipitation in its solid form to melt slowly with the onset of spring.[2]

Maxim 2 also implies that the seasonal pattern of rainfall is governed by synoptic processes that trigger thunderstorms (fig. 4). The geographical occurrences of seasonal maxima in monthly rainfall are shown in figure 4. The spring maximum results from the interplay between midlatitude systems in the westerlies and the increasing influx of moist, unstable air from the Gulf of Mexico, an interplay that is maximized in the late spring months. A fall maximum results from a similar interaction as the summer trades weaken in the early fall and low-pressure systems with their associated surface fronts penetrate more readily to these latitudes. The fall maximum also reflects the occurrence of tropical disturbances entering Texas

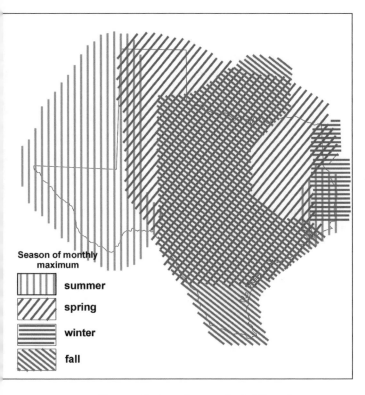

Figure 4. Regions of seasonal rainfall maxima.

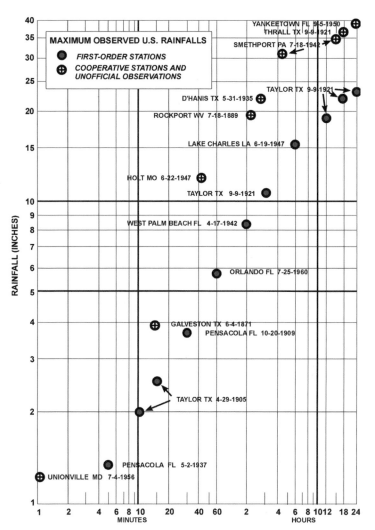

Figure 5. Greatest rainfall volumes for specified duration in contiguous United States, data of U.S. Weather Bureau (Jennings 1942, rev. 1963).

mainly from the Atlantic and Gulf. A large segment of Central Texas has a bimodal rainfall distribution with maxima in both fall and spring. Airmass thunderstorms and disturbances developing along the dryline are the primary source of rainfall in West Texas, the maximum for which occurs in summer.

Monthly rainfall values are in one respect misleading, because the rainfall is actually delivered as isolated storm events of short duration—in effect spikes, or impulses, of rainfall. Figure 5 is a rather famous compilation of magnitude-duration data, originally presented by the U.S. Weather Bureau (Jennings 1942, rev. 1963) and appearing in several standard textbooks on engineering hydrology (e.g., Linsley and Franzini 1964). This figure shows the largest storm event in the entire United States for each duration value, based upon measurements through 1961. It is worth noting that of the twenty data points plotted, 45 percent are from Texas.[3]

Data on Texas hydroclimate and water supply has been analyzed by dividing the state into four broad hydroclimatic zones, as shown in figure 6 (Ward 1993). Surface water budgets for these four component regions and for the state as a whole are presented in table 1. Inspection of these data discloses the next maxim.

3. On both a statewide and a regional basis, apart from the extreme humid eastern section of the state, there is a near balance between precipitation at the land surface and evapotranspiration.

The distribution of the ratio of runoff to rainfall across the state is depicted in figure 7. Even in the humid eastern portions of the state, only a fraction of the rainfall, about 20 percent on average, appears in the drainageways as streamflow. Farther west, this fraction dwindles to only a few percent.

Therefore the two sources for water supply, namely runoff and recharge, are the difference between two large, nearly equal parameters—precipitation (P) and evapotranspiration (E). This is a prescription for instability: a

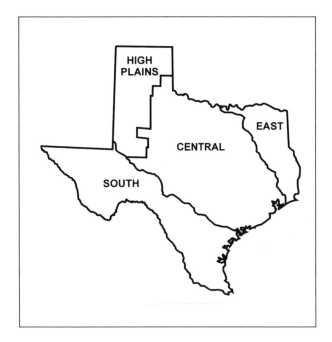

Figure 6. Texas regions used in hydrological data compilation (Ward 1993).

slight change in either is capable of producing a great change in their difference, e.g. in runoff.[4] This consequence of maxim 3 is so important to Texas water supply that it warrants separate identification, as follows.

4. Rainfall and runoff are subject to long-period vacillations. As noted earlier, much of Texas is semiarid. This term, in the present context, does not mean intermediate between arid and humid but rather that some years are humid and some years are arid. Alternation between extended periods of high and low rainfall is in many respects the *central* feature of Texas water, because it determines the limits of natural water supply for human use.

Floods and Droughts

When he visited San Antonio in 1854, Frederick Law Olmsted (1857) noted the existence of irrigation ditches and aqueducts that had been indispensable ten years before but were now unused and in disrepair. This was due to a steady increase in moisture during that period. Apparently unaware of maxim 4, he opined: "By common Mexican report the commencement of this change is coincident with American occupation. It is certainly, if well

Table 1. Regional and statewide water budgets for Texas, normal conditions ca. 1980, rounded to three significant digits, 10^3 acre-feet per year, after Ward (1993)

	Region				
	East	Central	South	High Plains	Texas
Surface water budget					
Inflow from upstream	4,070	912		10	1,530
From: Central	(2,550)	High Plains		N.M.	N.M. & La.
Louisiana	(1,520)				
Precipitation	68,300	193,000	79,400	38,400	379,000
Evapotranspiration	49,800	167,000	75,400	36,900	329,000
Runoff	17500	24,800	3,720	1,180	47,200
Recharge	1,090	2,600	1,090	343	5,130
Downstream flow to:					
other regions/states	8,380	2,550		912	9,330
Texas coast	12,600	21,100	973		34,700
Human activities					
Groundwater withdrawal	246	2,100	1,100	7,190	10,600
Surface water diversion	6,250	17,000	3,380	150	26,800
Surface water return	5,740	15,900	1,500	89	23,200
Consumption	752	3,190	2,990	7,250	14,200
Spills/uncaptured	21,000	23,200	973	1,010	42,700

Note: See Figure 6 for regions.

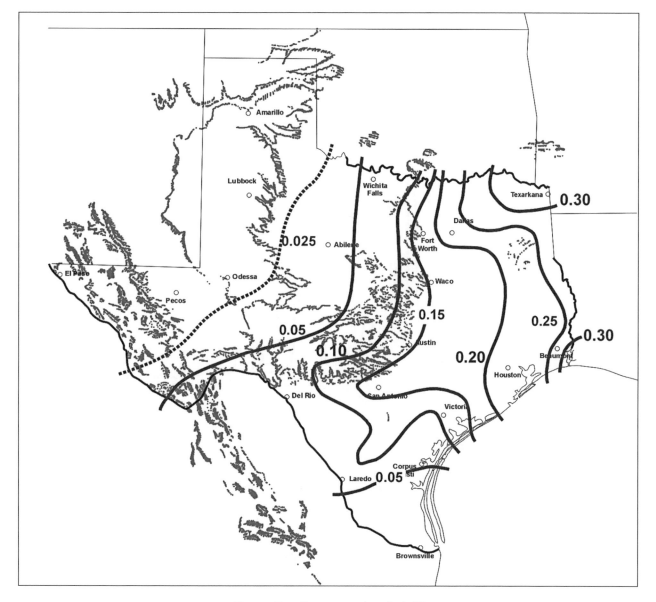

Figure 7. Runoff as a proportion of rainfall.

attested, a remarkable scientific phenomenon. In the settled districts of Western Texas, the evidence seems to have been so palpable as to have become a matter of common allusion." Later in the century, a similar vacillation in the Great Plains climate would lead to the incorrect precept that "rain follows the plow."

Since the nineteenth century, the wide range of flows exhibited by any given Texas river has been noted by travelers and settlers. The same stream can range from "insignificant," as Olmsted (1857) described the Neches when he crossed it in 1854, finding it barely "three rods in width," to a bluff-to-bluff flow, a roaring, roiling froth of brown water. These freshets are, of course, produced by

intense rainfall events, and the time base of the storm is often so short compared to the response of the watershed that the rainfall event appears like an impulse function. The time variation of the resulting streamflow hydrograph is typically a classical impulse-response function (which can be nicely modeled by a two-parameter gamma distribution; Dooge 1979). The spring freshet on the major rivers in the east of the state is a merger of such responses, both in time and with distance down the river channel. With distance to the south or to the west, into the more arid sections of the state, the seasonal freshet becomes resolved into a series of such impulse-responses, such as the freshet on the Trinity shown in figure 8.

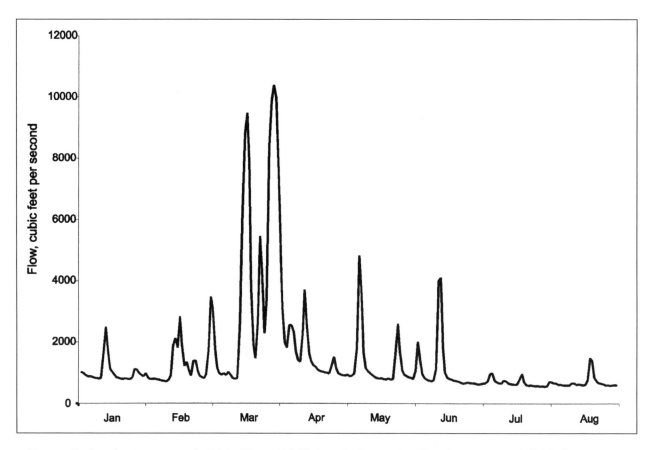

Figure 8. Freshet of spring, 1984, on the Trinity River at Trinidad, resolved as a series of impulse responses to individual storm events.

Particularly intense rainfall events produce hydrographs that exceed the capacity of the channel, resulting in floods that have plagued Texans since the first settlements along rivers.

In 1900 stream gauging was in its infancy, and the only records of nineteenth-century floods were the recollections of amateur observers, usually in the form of high-water marks. Floods were noted on the Colorado in 1843, 1852, and 1870 (Baker 1875), but the greatest of the nineteenth century occurred in 1869. By interviewing old-timers and sifting through newspaper records and similar reports, Taylor (1930) reconstructed the high-water profile and determined that the flood reached a stage of 43 feet, at least seven feet higher than the other floods, relative to the United States Geological Survey (USGS) gauge datum at Austin. At Dallas, the Trinity flooded in 1844, 1866, 1871, 1899, and 1908, all reaching stages around 50 feet (Kimball 1927); the 1866 flood may have been the largest, as one estimate puts the high water at 56.5 feet

The operation of stream gauges and archiving of data are indispensable in the engineering and management of state water resources. Not only do these data provide

objective, consistent quantification of such events, but they also allow rigorous statistical evaluation. It is ironic, therefore, that in the closing years of the twentieth century there was a move afoot in the USGS to reduce the number of operating stream gauges in order to save money (USGS 1998). Table 2 summarizes the record floods on the major rivers of Texas within the gauged record for the twentieth century.[5] Of these record floods, we observe that 50 percent occurred within the last fifteen years of the century. The southeast Texas flood of October, 1994, is especially noteworthy. The meteorology of this event is not well understood but included the ingredients of an open Gulf, a long trade-wind fetch with dew points in the eighties, an approaching surface front, and a Pacific hurricane that jumped the continental divide into northeastern Mexico. The system produced phenomenal rainfall from the Guadalupe to the Calcasieu basins. The precipitation was exceptional in its combination of intensity and duration: in terms of average rainfall on the San Jacinto basin, the maximum daily rainfall during the October, 1994, storm was a one-in-200-year event, but the maximum five-day rainfall had a return period of

Table 2. Record floods on principal Texas rivers. Data of U.S. Geological Survey and International Boundary and Water Commission

River/gauge	Agency number	Reliable gauge record begins	Stage (ft)	Date	Estimated max before period of record
USGS:					
Wichita/Wichita Falls	07312500	1938	24.0	Oct 1941	Jun 1915*
Red/Terral, Okla.	07315500	1938	33.6	Oct 1983	27.2 May 1935**
Red/Index, Ark.	07337000	1936	32.3	May 1990	
Sabine/Beckville	08022040	1938	38.9	Mar 1989	33.8 Apr 1945
Sabine/Bon Wier	08028500	1923	37.9	Jul 1989	43.5 Apr 1913
Neches/Evadale	08041000	1921	20.8	Jul 1989	26.2 May 1884
Trinity/Dallas	08057000	1931	47.1	May 1990	52.6 May 1908
Trinity/Romayor	08066500	1924	45.8	May 1942†	
San Jacinto/Sheldon	08072050	1970	27.1	Oct 1994††	
Brazos/Glen Rose	08091000	1923	35.8	Apr 1990	29.5 May 1922
Brazos/Richmond	08114000	1922	50.3	Oct 1994	61.2 Dec 1913
Colorado/San Saba	08147000	1915	62.2	Jul 1938	
Colorado/Columbus	08161000	1916	48.5	Jun 1935	51.6 Dec 1913
Lavaca/Edna	08164000	1938	35.5	Oct 1994	33.8 May 1936
San Antonio/Falls City	08183500	1925	33.8	Sep 1946‡	
San Antonio/Goliad	08188500	1924	53.7	Sep 1967	1869‡‡
Guadalupe/Victoria	08176500	1934	34.0	Oct 1998	
Nueces/Three Rivers	08210000	1915	37.3	Jun 1987¶	46.0 Sep 1919
Nueces/Mathis	08211000	1939	48.7	Sep 1967	
IBWC					
Pecos/Langtry	08-4474.10	1898	>100	Jun 1954	
Conchos/Ojinaga	08-3730.00	1896	n/a	Sep 1904¶¶	
Rio Grande/Brownsville	08-4749.00	1934	31.5	Oct 1945	

* *1941 peak flow 17,800 cfs; 1915 peak est 50,000 cfs.*

‡ *Max daily 63,600 cfs and instantaneous 70,000 cfs Oct 1998.*

** *Max daily flow Jun 95.*

† *Max daily 117,000 cfs & instantaneous flow 122,000 cfs Oct 94.*

‡‡ *Exceeded 1967 stage by "several feet."*

¶ *Max for 1949, pre and post regulation.*

†† *356,000 cfs Oct 94 measured near flood peak.*

¶¶ *Max flow of 162,000 cfs.*

1,300 years. The peak flow of the San Jacinto at the Sheldon gauge (table 2) had a return period of 2,100 years, and the five-day cumulative flow was off the scale at more than 10,000 years.

However, we are presently concerned with the opposite end of the flow spectrum. Heraclitus said that the same river cannot be stepped in twice. But Heraclitus was not a Texan who would have become accustomed to the often stagnant or even bone-dry streambeds of the state. In his *Seven Keys to Texas*, Fehrenbach (1983) observes, "Although the annual rains across most of central Texas equal those of London in total measure, the moisture tends to fall at scattered periods, long dry spells broken by heavy rains, rainy seasons interspersed by months of extreme aridity." This is the obverse face of convection-derived precipitation. Everywhere in the state there is a low-flow season, which often amounts to a no-flow season. Baker (1875) refers to this in Central Texas as the "usual summer drought." This regular annual drought is inconvenient enough, but when it stretches for months or years, the results are catastrophic.

In the nineteenth century, *the* drought was that of the 1880s, which reached its absolute nadir in South Texas in 1886 but intensified and lingered in Central and West Texas through the early 1890s. The Panhandle and Rolling Plains regions were subjected to repeated occurrences of the infamous Texas "dusters." Farming was devastated statewide, and farmers defaulted in record numbers.[6] To attempt farming west of the Brazos, one reporter wrote, "is folly of the very worst sort" (King 1965). In the cattle industry this was known as the Great Die-off. Many ranchers cashed in. The beef packeries at Fulton and Rockport turned to canning sea turtles. The Red Cross was called to Texas in 1887 and its president Clara Barton made a visit. Through her offices clothes and food were shipped to the state, and the Red Cross became active in motivating additional aid from private sources and from the federal government.

Several devastating droughts occurred during the twentieth century. The drought of the 1930s is the famous Dust Bowl, which at the time seemed to consist of the worst possible drought conditions that could be inflicted upon the state. For most parts of Texas, however, the drought of record is that of the 1950s. This was a six- to nine-year drought, depending upon the region, and it created havoc statewide. President Eisenhower visited San Angelo, where the Bureau of Reclamation made a presentation showing the problems with the groundwater supply and the need for surface storage (Bureau of Reclamation 1957). While the 1950s are the drought of record for most basins, for the Nueces basin an even more intense drought occurred in the 1961–64 period, which is its drought of record (Ward and Proesmans 1996).

Compared to droughts, floods are easy to analyze. They are sharp, well-defined events. They can be unequivocally linked to specific rainfall events. Their occurrence in time is precisely defined in terms of maximum stage or peak flow. Droughts are insidious, unfocused, and shadowy, like silent vampires flitting in the darkness to suck the lifeblood from the state. Their beginnings and ends are indistinct (Karl 1983), and their very existence

may be controversial (see, e.g., Riggio et al. 1987).[7] The contrast between a flood and a drought, from the standpoint of hydrological analysis, is analogous to that between a gunshot wound and consumption. Riggio, Bomard, and Larkin (1987) examined shorter-term droughts in Texas and concluded from an extensive and careful analysis of meteorological data that "the occurrence of 6-month and year-long drought has a greater probability of occurring than either a near-normal or wet-weather spell for the same time frames."

Dendrochronology has provided one means of reconstructing much longer records of drought by employing proxy measures of tree-ring growth. One of the more rigorous such studies is reported by Stahle and Cleaveland (1988), who used post oak to reconstruct the Palmer index for June of the past 283 years. They found the driest decades to be 1772–81, 1855–64, and 1950–59, noting that the proxy Palmer index underestimated the actual intensity of the 1950s drought. They also discovered that of the most severe June droughts since 1917, five out of six had occurred in northern Texas and five out of seven in southern Texas. A long-term positive trend in Palmer index (i.e., increasing drought severity) was disclosed. For present purposes, the most important conclusion relating to Texas water is that there is no evidence that the great drought of the 1950s was in any way unique to the twentieth century or is unlikely to be repeated (or exceeded) in the future.

Water Supply

The population of Texas in 1900 stood at 3,050,000, a spectacular increase from its 1890 value of 2,240,000, and people continued to pour into the state. Droughts only temporarily staunched the influx of population. Benedict and Lomax (1916) commented: "The population flows westward after good seasons and ebbs eastward after bad, each ebb tide leaving increased numbers." In 1900, about 66 percent of the population was rural and 33 percent urban (Benedict and Lomax 1916). By 1940 these proportions had reversed (Steen 1942), with 33 percent of the state population now rural, and, after another thirty years, in 1970 only 20 percent was rural (Rodriguez 1978). These same proportions obtained in the 1990 data (Sharp 1992), and with the boom in high-tech jobs in the 1990s, the shift to urban predominance has no doubt continued.

The major source of domestic water supply in the early part of the twentieth century was groundwater. For a dispersed, largely isolated rural populace with low-volume needs, this made perfect sense: groundwater was widely available and could be had by digging straight down, the water thereby being supplied largely where it was needed without the requirement of infrastructure. The advent of the windmill provided an accessible source of energy. It is a device, along with the Colt revolver and barbed wire, to which Webb (1931) credits the habitation of the Great Plains. Even the majority of the cities relied on groundwater: a photograph of Plainview taken from the dome of the courthouse after 1900 shows a small city bristling with windmills. However, windmills are capable of producing only several hundred gallons of water a day under optimum conditions, and soon after the turn of the century, they began to be replaced by gasoline or electric pumps.

There is, moreover, a short-term limit to the flow that can be economically produced from groundwater. An even more basic long-term limitation is the rate of recharge of the aquifer. Once withdrawal exceeds the rate of recharge, the volume in storage in the aquifer will begin to be depleted. As the water table drops, further withdrawal becomes more difficult until it is either technologically or economically infeasible. This became a familiar pattern of water usage in Texas: what was at first a reliable groundwater supply is subjected to increasing withdrawal until the aquifer can no longer meet the demand. At this point, the second aspect of the water usage pattern occurs—adoption of a surface supply. In many respects, the defining feature of Texas water in the past century has been this consistent usage pattern, which brings us to the fifth maxim.

5. The water supply paradigm is an increasing overdraft of a groundwater source followed by a shift to surface water.
This pattern was repeated across the state, differing only in the volume of withdrawals and the time that passed before the demand exceeded the yield of the aquifer, motivating the change to a surface supply. In Dallas in the nineteenth century, "many springs" furnished the water supply and "water could be found almost everywhere by the mere digging of a well" (Brown 1930). The first artesian well in Dallas was drilled in 1876, and by 1900, Dallas and Fort Worth had artesian wells distributed in and around each city (Brown 1930; Taylor 1930). Following the loss of artesian pressure, the cost of pumping became so great that by then both cities were already shifting to a surface supply. Dallas completed White Rock Lake around 1910 and Fort Worth completed a dam on the West Fork in 1915. By 1877, due to a combination of increasing population and a severe drought, Austin considered construction of a dam on the Colorado and completed Lake McDonald in 1893 (Taylor 1900, 1910). The Austin dam was "one of the largest hydraulic works of the country" (Hutson 1898). Taylor (1901) noted its "immense importance . . . as an engineering structure—it being the largest in the world across a flowing stream." It did not last into the twentieth century; it was carried away by high flows in April of 1900. Lakes were built to supply Abilene, Sweetwater, Stamford, and Wichita Falls (Dowell and Breeding 1967). Houston's artesian wells were frequently unreliable, and after 1879, Buffalo Bayou water was stored in a small reservoir and was used as a backup supply (Burke 1879).

The most spectacular groundwater source for municipal supply in the state is the Edwards aquifer, a complex of water-bearing limestone strata that lies beneath the Balcones escarpment and is recharged on the Edwards Plateau. The limestone formations are porous, being fractured and fissured, so groundwater moves readily into and through the aquifer. The aquifer is also leaky, with numerous springs along the Balcones fault zone, the most important of which are Comal and San Marcos. Together these springs produced on the order of 350,000 acre-feet/ year, discharging to the Guadalupe River, until about 1930. The artesian zone of this aquifer has been tapped for municipal, industrial, and agricultural uses since the nineteenth century (fig. 10). Through the twentieth century, it has served as the sole water supply for the city of San Antonio. The monthly elevation of the water table at the Bexar index well J-17 is plotted in figures 9 and 10. The effect of the 1950s drought, in combination with pumpage from the aquifer, is clear in the depression of the water table. During this drought, Comal Springs ceased flowing for about five months in 1956. The pumpage was about 321,000 acre-feet during that year. In the last two decades, it has nearly doubled the 1956 value, mainly due to increasing usage by San Antonio. The greater excursions in water level during the 1960–90 period evidence the effects of the higher pumpage rates. It is now possible for the withdrawals to approach the annual recharge.

For farming and ranching, enterprises that entailed greater spatial extents than cities, water supply was far more aleatory. A strategy was needed for moving water "from where it is to where it ain't," which involves the practice of irrigation, i.e. the use of canals, laterals, and ditches for the transport of water. Irrigation will be discussed separately.

The temporal variability in water supply, especially a surface water supply, is dealt with by the construction of storage facilities, viz. reservoirs. Reservoirs also serve as

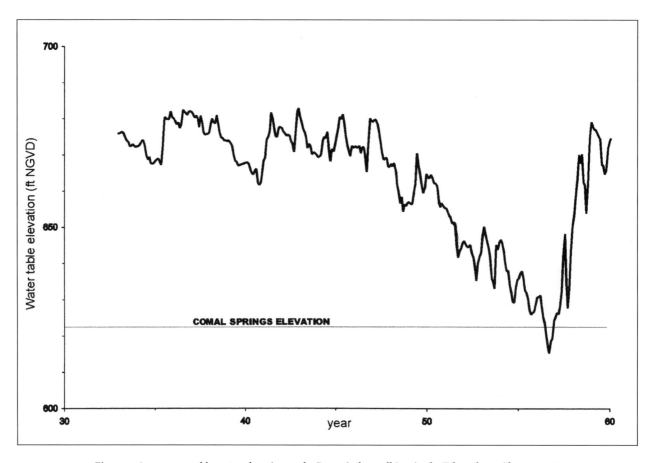

Figure 9. Average monthly water elevation at the Bexar index well J-17 in the Edwards aquifer, 1930–60.

flood control facilities and in power generation. At the beginning of the twentieth century, dam construction was limited mainly to small structures (see Dowell and Breeding 1967). As already noted, several cities constructed reservoirs to ameliorate water supply difficulties, one of which was the ill-fated Austin dam. The first major reservoir constructed in the twentieth century was Lake Medina, capacity 254,000 acre-feet, completed in 1913 on the Medina River about forty miles northwest of San Antonio (Taylor 1930).[8] This was a privately funded reservoir intended for irrigation supply.

Around 1910, a Board of Water Engineers and a Reclamation Department were created at the state level. In August, 1922, Gov. Pat Neff convened the "largest body of engineers ever congregated in Texas," who then adopted resolutions for appropriations from the state and federal governments to gather data needed to design works for dams, reservoirs, and levees (Hughes 1937). Motivated by the State Reclamation Engineer, major reservoirs were later proposed for construction on the Colorado and the

Brazos. The 43rd Legislature in 1933–34 wrestled with the need to create a public agency in order to obtain federal funds—and the presence of the Bureau of Reclamation in the state—to build Hamilton Dam (Lake Buchanan) on the Colorado. In the fourth called session, they created the Lower Colorado River Authority (Adams 1990).

The construction of reservoirs during the twentieth century is depicted in figure 11, composed from data of the Texas Water Development Board. Buchanan inaugurated the heyday of dam construction in Texas, which extended roughly over the period 1940–70. As shown in figure 11, about half of the state reservoir capacity is allocated to flood control, and this has been rather consistent over time, although the proportion on a given river varies substantially depending upon exposure to flooding. By the close of the twentieth century, the state had about 84.3 million acre-feet of combined reservoir capacity, of which 38.8 million acre-feet are allocated to flood control. There are also some 1,500 Soil Conservation Service sediment control reservoirs and perhaps 300,000 stock tanks, farm

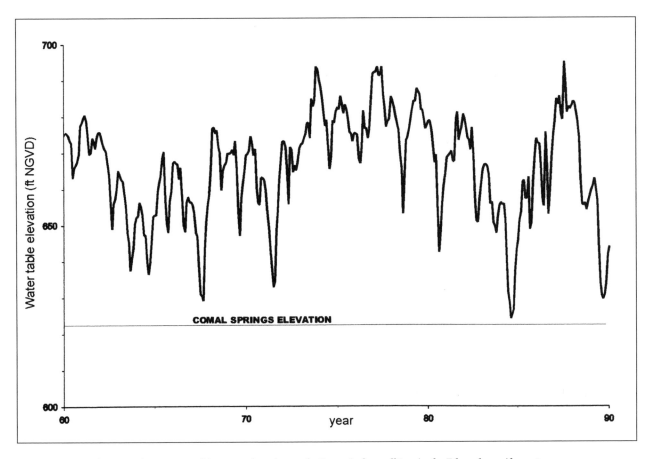

Figure 10. Average monthly water elevation at the Bexar index well J-17 in the Edwards aquifer, 1960–90.

ponds, and recreational reservoirs impounding about 3 million acre-feet (see, e.g., Lowry 1958; Texas Society of Professional Engineers 1974).

This brief survey cannot overlook pluviculture. The drought of the 1880s motivated the first wide-scale attempts at rainmaking in Texas. These were based upon a theory current at the time that loud continuous noise could stimulate rain. This theory was forwarded by an engineer, Edward Powers, who wrote an 1871 book demonstrating a relation of rainfall to battles (Powers 1871). In 1891, under the auspices of the Department of Agriculture, an array of cannons was fired on the prairie near Midland and later El Paso. The results were at best equivocal.[9] Desperate ranchers in the Coastal Bend area tried similar cannonades near Corpus Christi and later San Diego, again with equivocal results.

But the most elaborate such exercises began in 1911, conducted by C. W. Post near Post City, now Post (the first planned community in Texas). Post drove in mule trains of dynamite from DuPont and staged full-scale "rain battles" (Eaves and Hutchinson 1952). Sometimes lit dynamite sticks were carried aloft by kites, but usually Post's men lined up for a mile or more along the rim of the Caprock and set off hundreds of rounds of explosions. At first, these experiments seemed successful, but this was apparently due to a few fluke thunderstorms. As time wore on and the experiments continued, it became apparent that these efforts would not solve the water supply problem of Post.

After World War II, the more soundly derived strategy of cloud seeding became the basis for extensive experimentation in West Texas, and such projects have been under way for the past half century. The experimental region has ranged from the Edwards Plateau to the High Plains, the objectives have ranged from rainfall stimulation to hail suppression, and the financial support has ranged from local through state to federal (notably from the Bureau of Reclamation). At the close of the twentieth century, some form of cloud seeding experiment was under way in more than seventy-five counties in Texas, extend-

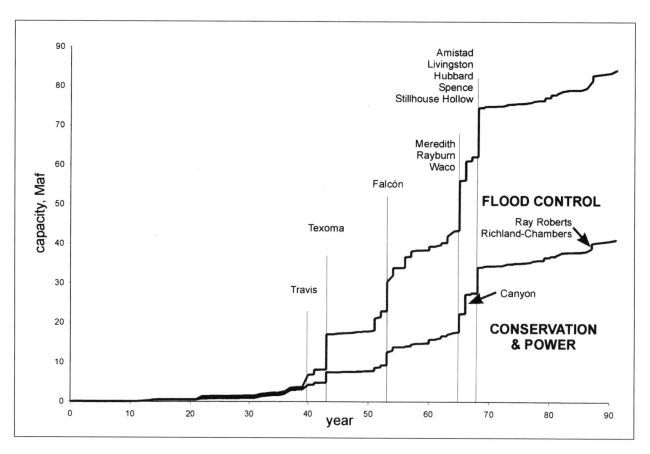

Figure 11. Cumulative reservoir capacity (acre-feet) in Texas.

ing from the northern Panhandle to the Rio Grande. While there is potential scientific value to these experiments in the spin-off information about Texas meteorological processes, it is difficult to document any substantive impact on the Texas surface water budget beyond the contribution of a variety of acronyms to the water resources lexicon.

Irrigation

The beginning of modern irrigation in Texas, meaning large-scale farming with permanent aqueducts, is sometimes marked as 1869 at Del Rio (e.g., Taylor 1901, 1902a; Benedict and Lomax 1916), where San Felipe springs served as a water source and an extensive system of canals was constructed. Other copious springs in the state later served as irrigation supplies for similar canal systems, including Comanche Springs near Fort Stockton (Hutson 1898; Taylor 1901) and those of the Pecos Valley, where springs were described by the 1912 *Texas Almanac* as "inexhaustible" (Galveston-Dallas News 1912). However, such natural artesian sources were rare.

In the closing decade of the nineteenth century, the prospects for large-scale irrigation in the western states grew upon the success of the Spanish and the Mormons (Baker and Conkling 1930) and culminated in the passage of the Newlands Act in 1902, inaugurating the national "reclamation" program of the federal government. Texas did not immediately benefit from the federal initiative for the simple reason that there were no federal lands in Texas as the state retained ownership of its public lands when admitted to statehood. But the attitude engendered by the federal reclamation program proved an intangible benefit to the Texas philosophy that water supply could be engineered by large-scale reservoir construction. The federal government became directly involved in Texas after the first third of the century.

On a parallel track were other developments that were to have profound effects on Texas irrigation: the centrifugal pump, drilling technology, and the low-compression internal combustion engine. All of these came together in East Texas at the start of the twentieth century. By 1900, the 150-year-old centrifugal pump had undergone improvements to become at last efficient and reliable. Rotary drilling technology was stimulated by the Beaumont oil boom, and coincidentally such drillers were in the East Texas area when the Dingley protective tariff was passed (by the Republicans, who had returned to power in the 1896 election), and when the Latin American markets opened after the Spanish-American war. Both events created a demand for rice and an opportunity for Texas production. At first, Texas rice irrigation used groundwater. The exigencies of maintaining a pump pit in East Texas gumbo soil, and clambering in and out of the pit to operate the pump, led to the 1902 creation of a "pitless" pump that could be placed in a drilled well casing. The first such pump was installed at El Campo, and a company was created for its manufacture: the Layne and Bowler Company of Houston. Finally, the low-compression oil-burning engine—the "hot-ball" diesel—began to be widely manufactured in the United States by 1895, providing an economical, autonomous power plant for pumping.

Rice was first planted in Beaumont in 1862–63 for domestic consumption (Benedict and Lomax 1916; Scanlon 1954). For many years before, Cajuns had planted rice in freshwater "pockets" (Phillips 1951). Commercial production began when the first rice mill was constructed in Beaumont in 1892 and irrigation per se, pumping water to rice (a method "peculiar to Texas and Louisiana" according to Benedict and Lomax (1916)), began in 1893. Both subsurface and surface water were used, but the latter became predominant as the industry grew. The first pumping plants were built on Taylor and Hillebrandt bayous (Scanlon 1954). At the beginning of the century, Taylor (1902a, 1902b) described the coastal plain from Sabine Pass to the Rio Grande as the "rice belt" of the state. He noted that there were two well-developed zones: the Beaumont section, including Liberty, Orange, Jasper, and Chambers counties, and the Colorado valley extending from Columbus to the coast, which together accounted for 75 percent of the Texas crop (fig. 12). Figure 12 shows the history of the Texas rice industry. Between 1900 and 1906, the rice industry exploded from 9,000 to 200,000 acres. As of 1910, there were about 250,000 acres planted, primarily on the Sabine near Orange, on the Neches near Beaumont, and on the Colorado from Eagle Lake down

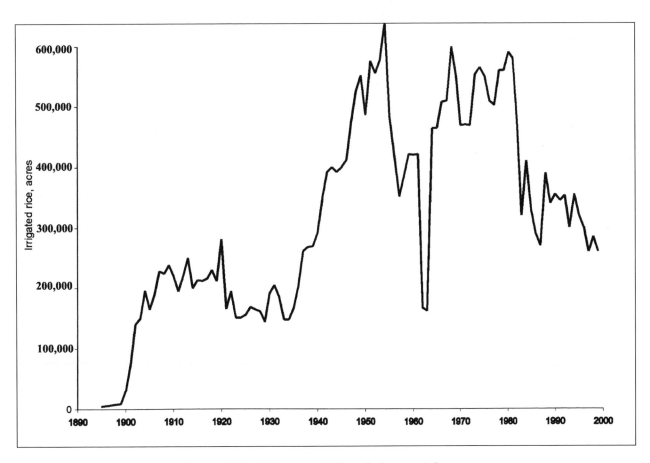

Figure 12. Irrigated rice acreage in Texas during twentieth century.

to Bay City. By midcentury, rice irrigation water was pumped from the Colorado, Brazos, San Jacinto, Trinity, Neches, Sabine, and Guadalupe rivers (Scanlon 1954). The rice industry peaked in the 1970s. In the mid-1980s, about 60 percent of the Texas rice irrigation water came from surface sources and about 40 percent from groundwater (Webb 1990).

The Sabine and Neches were capable of providing a reliable water supply for rice irrigation due to the high runoff in this part of the state. The low flow of the Colorado, in contrast, could not supply the requirements for its rice industry. That a rice industry could be built here in the early part of the century was due to a fluke of nature: a huge log raft that extended from just upstream of Matagorda to Bay City (Clay 1949; Wadsworth 1966). The earliest detailed survey of the log raft was made in 1894, at which time it covered a distance of fifteen to twenty miles. The main raft was described as three hundred feet wide, twenty-five to fifty feet thick, and practically solid, though permitting percolation of water. Trees of two-foot diameter were noted to be growing on its surface. The raft functioned as a natural dam for the lower Colorado (Taylor 1902b), providing storage and a pumping head, until it was eliminated in the 1930s by a combination of snagging and dynamiting.

The importance of the rice industry in a consideration of Texas water is that it is the single greatest use of surface water for irrigation. Timing of the growth of the industry is important. In the nineteenth century after 1840, the use of water was governed according to the riparian doctrine, devolving to the landowner or grantee adjacent to the watercourse, a doctrine that had been imported from the water-rich eastern seaboard, and thence from English common law. As the semiarid regions of the state were settled, the inadequacy of the riparian doctrine in a water-stressed climate became evident, and the state began evolving the notion of ownership of surface water as a separate right. A major step was taken in 1895 when the 24th Legislature enacted a law establishing the prior appropriative system (Hutson 1898), founded upon the concept of seniority in time: "first in time is first in right." In 1913, the Board of Water Engineers established a formal permitting system. Between the years of 1895 and 1913, by sheer coincidence, the rice industry grew from nonexistence to a major industry and in the process established senior water rights from the Colorado to the Sabine.

At the opposite corner of the state, on the Texas High Plains, these same developments in pump technology were used to tap the groundwater resource of that region—the vast Ogallala. By 1900, the existence of substantial groundwater in the High Plains was established through surveys and reports of the U.S. Geological Survey (Green 1973). *The Earth*, a magazine published by the Santa Fe Railroad, stated in 1904 that this water was "inexhaustible" (Green 1973). The problem was lifting the water to the surface. The first successful wells were completed by McDonald near Hereford in 1910 and Green on the Slaton farm at Plainview in 1911. Irrigation was mainly promoted by land speculators, one of whom dubbed the region the "land of the underground rain." From 1913 to 1917, visitors to the Santa Fe depot in Plainview were astonished to see a thirty-acre lake lying across the railroad tracks to the north: Lake Plainview, created by the operation of a single well by the Texas Land and Development Company. The lake provided boating and fishing in the summer and ice-skating in winter (Brunson 1970). A combination of climate and economics, however, prevented widespread growth of irrigation on the High Plains until the drought of the 1930s. Improved technology, reduced capital costs, New Deal financing, and especially a market for cotton and wheat produced an acceleration in irrigation. The number of operating wells increased by an order of magnitude between 1930 and 1940, at which time a quarter of a million acres on the High Plains were "under ditch." This would further increase by another order of magnitude over the next two decades.

At the southern tip of Texas around 1900, there was an initial impetus in irrigation from the Rio Grande, primarily in the Lower Rio Grande Valley. At first truck crops were raised, but by 1910 most of these had converted to field crops. In this area were built some of the largest irrigation plants in the world at the time, with enormous pump stations on the river and hundreds of miles of canals and laterals (Benedict and Lomax 1916). Two canals measured two hundred feet wide by eighteen to twenty feet deep. "Under present regulations and with proper conservation, the water supply is practically assured," said the *Texas Almanac* (Galveston-Dallas News 1912). This proved to be overly optimistic. Irrigators turned to groundwater to supplement the unreliable Rio Grande flow, but the groundwater supply suffered from the same limitation on economics of pumping and rate of recharge as in other regions of the state.[10] The complete potential for agriculture was not realized in the Lower Rio Grande Valley until surface water became available from the international reservoirs Falcón (1953) and Amistad (1968). Less than 1 percent of the irrigation water now comes from groundwater sources (Texas Department of Water Resources 1981; hereafter TDWR).

The two reservoirs are operated in tandem, releases being made from the lower one, Falcón, to meet demands in the Lower Valley. Diversions are made to both the United States and Mexico to supply the municipal and industrial requirements of the cities below Falcón and to meet the heavy irrigation requirements of the extensive agricultural areas in both countries. The strategy of diversion is different for the two countries. Mexico diverts its share of the water mainly at a single point, the Anzalduas canal, which then routes the water to various agricultural areas, principally District 26, and to several cities. In contrast, the U.S. water is diverted at numerous pump stations distributed along the river channel from Falcón to Brownsville. The Valley is extensively plumbed with canals and siphons to effect the transport of this water over a four-county agricultural area. During the 1972–90 period, total U.S. diversions averaged 171,000 acre-feet/month (Ward 1999).[11]

Water and Power

There is an intimate relation between water and electric power generation. Fundamentally, the generation of electric power requires the availability of an enormous amount of water.

Water has been a source of power in Texas since the nineteenth century. At the beginning of the twentieth century, Taylor (1901, 1904) surveyed the use of water power on the principal Texas rivers and determined that these facilities were largely concentrated in the Guadalupe, Brazos, and Colorado basins. The facilities fell into categories of mechanical power (mills and sawmills) and electrical power (including turbine-driven sawmills) and with rare exceptions entailed the construction of a small dam to provide power head. Taylor inventoried nearly seventy dams, with fourteen on the Brazos, seventeen on the Colorado (including ten on the Concho alone), and twenty-eight on the Guadalupe. The Guadalupe was favored because of its stable, spring-driven flow. The dam at Del Rio on San Felipe Creek included one power plant, which ran an electric light plant and an ice plant. San Antonio had separated the San Antonio River into two canals, with a powerhouse built on each, and operated two more dams on the upper river. The river became so low in 1896 that waterpower was abandoned. The largest single power plant was that on the doomed Austin dam.

Many of the large dams in Texas include provisions for hydroelectric generation, beginning with Buchanan in 1937. However, hydroelectric generation represents less than 5 percent of the present electric generation capability in Texas. The combination of stable river flow, suitable dam site, and adequate bed slope is rare in Texas. Benedict and Lomax (1916) summed it up nicely: "Water-power in Texas is scanty, because where there is plenty of water the country is too flat to make a fall, and where there is plenty of fall there is no water." Electrical power in Texas depends, instead, upon steam-electric generation (fig. 13). High-pressure steam, produced from pure water in a boiler, spins a turbine that turns a generator, thus producing electricity. The steam cycle is completed by recondensing the spent steam and feeding the resulting water back into the boiler. Power plants differ in their fuels (natural gas, coal, lignite, fuel oil, nuclear reactions) and in the stack emissions, but they are equivalent insofar as the steam-generation cycle is concerned. The key is the condenser stage, which requires passing great volumes of ambient water in thermal contact with the spent steam, thereby cooling the steam so that it recondenses. In the process, the cooling water is heated and is then rejected

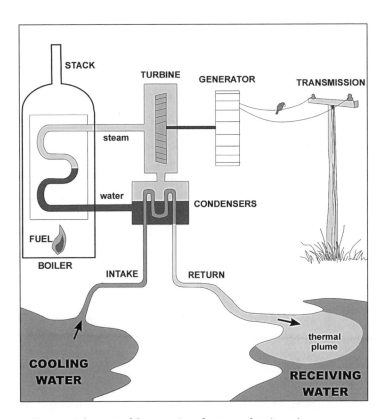

Figure 13. Schematic of the operation of a steam-electric station using once-through cooling (Ward and Huston 1984).

to the external environment. Figure 13 shows a once-through cooling circuit in which the heated water is returned to a receiving water body into which it is mixed. Most steam-electric plants in Texas employ once-through cooling.

From the opening of the twentieth century, steam-electric generation has been a major source of the state's power, increasing in proportion to the growth of population. At present, steam-electric generation represents about 95 percent of the state's generating capacity. Of 177 major reservoirs in the state (i.e., greater than 5,000 acre-feet capacity), 44 have power plants situated on them, and these collectively represent 65 percent of the state's steam-electric capacity.[12] These reservoirs serve both as the source of cooling water and as the receiving water for the thermal effluent. The trick is to site the plant so that the discharge canal is sufficiently far from the intake that the excess heat is dissipated to the atmosphere before the water circulates back to the power-plant intake. More than half of these plants are located on cooling reservoirs, which are small lakes constructed for the express purpose of serving as a cooling water source for the power plant (though most also provide recreational amenities as well). These cooling reservoirs are generally located on minor tributaries off the main stem of rivers and have insufficient watershed to ensure maintenance of water level. So, they have to be made up from some nearby water source.

Surveying the Century

Texas was already undergoing change when the twentieth century opened. The buffalo were gone and their bones had been stacked on the plains, whitening in the summer sun. But even the bones were being gathered in 1900 and shipped off to sugar refineries (Philips 1942). In a few years there was nothing at all left of the great southern herd. Much of the native forest had been cleared, and the effects on turbidity of Texas rivers were evident (Benedict and Lomax 1916). Tarpon—"the greatest in the world"—and sea turtles were still plentiful on the coast; they would be nearly eliminated during the twentieth century. Mesquite was now well established over much of Texas, covering the central prairies and even pushing onto the High Plains, having spread into the state during the latter half of the nineteenth century. Olmsted encountered dense growth west of San Antonio in 1854 (see Olmsted 1857). The boll weevil, armadillo, and Inca dove were extending their range into Texas. However, these were benign; fire ants and killer bees still lay in the future.

The population of Texas in 1900 was about 3 million. In 1990, its population was 17 million and in 2000, 21 million. This represents an order of magnitude increase in population over the span of the twentieth century, and a population growth of 25 percent during the 1990s, nearly the same rate of growth experienced by Texas in the closing decade of the nineteenth century.

The twentieth century encompassed the development (some might say exploitation) of the state's water resources. The century opened with a drought, particularly severe in South Texas, where extensive irrigation was already in operation, both from the Rio Grande and from groundwater sources in the Valley. The main water supply statewide was groundwater at this time, but at some point, the demand exceeded the aquifer yield, as expressed by maxim 5, and surface supplies were sought. For many of the major cities in Texas, this point occurred early in the century. For a few, reliance on groundwater was able to serve well into the century. Groundwater was an important part of the municipal source for Houston until past midcentury.[13] For San Antonio, the Edwards remained the water supply for the city as of 2000, but the limits of that supply had become apparent and the city was seeking surface supplies.

A prominent example of the continued reliance upon groundwater is the High Plains, for which the Ogallala supplied the extensive irrigated agriculture that developed after the 1930s. The growth of this industry is evident in the increasing magnitudes of irrigated acreage (Stockton and Arbingast 1952; TDWR 1981): from 80,000 acres in 1935, to 250,000 acres by 1940, to 2.0 million acres in 1950, and to 5.6 million acres by 1980.

The withdrawals for this aquifer far exceed its recharge, making the term *water mining* appropriate. By 1960, the water table in the region, identified as the "shallow water belt" at the beginning of the century (Green 1973), had declined markedly, about sixty feet on average but with pockets of 100–120 feet of decline (Cronin 1969). By 1979, the decline continued, these areas logging an additional twenty feet or more of depletion since 1960. There is no alternative surface source capable of yielding the volumes of usage by High Plains agriculture.[14] When the groundwater is depleted in a region or becomes uneconomical to lift, the region reverts to dryland farming. By the end of the twentieth century this had occurred in many regions of the High Plains.

Although the detail is beyond the scope of this brief review, we note in passing that groundwater in Texas is governed by the old riparian right of "capture." Throughout the twentieth century, groundwater authorities called for an appropriative doctrine (Hutson 1898; Benedict and Lomax 1916; Texas Society of Professional Engineers 1956, 1974; Hughes and Harman 1969), but the riparian mentality seems ingrained, perhaps because of the central role of petroleum in the state's economy. Hughes and Harman (1969) suggested that the lack of regulation leads to a "use it or lose it" mentality: "The landowner has little choice with respect to the time of use. If he elects to defer use for more propitious times, a large part of his water supply is likely to be drained off and used by his more current-income conscious neighbors. The pressure for income and the lack of area-wide water use restrictions combined with the fixed nature of assets invested in irrigation facilities virtually dictate that a farm operator extract all the water he can gainfully use each year." What they describe is known in ecology as the "tragedy of the commons" (Hardin 1968). No clearer example could be cited than the Ogallala.

In 1960, the pumpage from the Ogallala was estimated at 5 million acre-feet per year (maf/yr; Hughes and Harman 1969). In 1979, a rare wet year, the reported pumpage was 5.7 maf/yr, but the following year it was 7.1 maf/yr (TDWR 1981). The next decade was unusually wet, reducing the irrigation demand and increasing recharge, so that in 1989 the pumpage was reduced to 4.7 maf (Peckham and Ashworth 1993). At the close of the century, improvements in efficiency of water use had been achieved over several decades by various methods of conservation, but there had been corresponding increases in irrigated acreage due to large-scale mechanized farming; irrigated water usage was reported as 5.4 maf/yr (Texas Water Development Board 1997; hereafter TWDB).

The statewide effect of groundwater pumpage on the subsurface resource becomes evident upon reviewing the current condition of Texas springs. Throughout the state, hundreds of springs that were flowing under artesian pressure at the beginning of the century were dry at its end.[15] A sampling of the historical springs that have ceased flowing, or flow at best intermittently, includes Big Spring (Howard County), Carrizo Springs on El Camino Real (Dimmit County), Cherokee Spring and Tyler Springs (Smith County), Comanche Springs (Pecos County), Fort Elliott Springs (Wheeler County), Leon Springs on the Chisolm Trail (Bell County), Mill Spring and Kickapoo Spring (Tom Green County), Nacogdoches and Shawnee Springs on El Camino Real (Nacogdoches County), San Pedro Springs and San Antonio Springs in San Antonio (Bexar County), Santo Rosa Spring (Pecos County), Smith Springs (Galveston County), Sulphur Springs and Mustang Spring on the Comanche Indian trail (Martin County), Walnut Springs in Seguin (Guadalupe County), Willow Springs (Winkler County), and XIT Springs at the XIT Ranch headquarters (Hartley County). Extensive inventories of Texas springs are presented by Brune (1975, 1981).

The twentieth century also encompassed the growth of the USGS stream-gauging network, an enterprise of inestimable value to the hydrologist, water manager, and planner and to the public at large. The Texas network began to be implemented in earnest around 1915 through a cooperative program between the State Board of Water Engineers and the USGS. At midcentury, the Texas Society of Professional Engineers (1954) pleaded for more gauges, noting that only 266 stations existed and "no less than 160" additional stations would be needed. It is sobering to realize that this network reached its zenith around 1970 and continues to decline. A recent report to Congress (USGS 1998; Lanfear and Hirsch 1999) indicates that "more than 100" stations with over thirty years of data are discontinued nationwide *each year* due to lack of funding. An inspection of the data in the report reveals that the situation is worse than that: in the data analyzed through 1996, the rate of discontinuation has increased exponentially to 170 discontinuations in 1996.[16] Specific statistics could not be found for Texas, but of the Hydroclimatic Data Network stations in Texas (Slack and Landwehr 1983), 68 percent had been discontinued as of 1992.

The need for reservoirs became apparent early in the century. As noted earlier, only minor dams existed in 1900, and these were used mainly for waterpower (Taylor 1904). Several municipalities constructed water supply dams in the first couple of decades of the century, including Dallas and Fort Worth. Major droughts occurred in 1915–18 and 1925–32, the latter once again requiring the services of the Red Cross. The Dust Bowl years of the mid-1930s seemed as bad as it could get, but in fact drought conditions were mainly concentrated in the northern regions of the state. The drought of the 1950s demonstrated how bad water shortages can be in Texas.

Large-scale dam building coincided with Bureau of Reclamation involvement in the late 1930s. The majority of dams in the state were completed in the period 1940–70. The better, more economical, higher yielding dam sites were built first; thus, with the passage of time, availability of suitable sites has diminished. The increasing aridity with distance westward (and southward) in Texas conspires against successful reservoir construction. Surface storage is constrained on both sides of the surface water budget—decreasing runoff (fig. 7) and increasing lake-surface evaporation. The more constrained this water budget becomes, the greater the watershed area needed to achieve a desired yield. Or conversely, for a fixed watershed area, the more constrained the water budget, the smaller the yield. But as one proceeds westward in Texas, the watershed areas decrease. It follows that there is a westward limit for an operational reservoir in any particular basin. Some suggestion of how severe this may be is indicated by figure 14, which shows the watershed area necessary to maintain the surface water balance of a given area, assuming an average yield of three times the evaporative loss.[17] The 100:1 line serves as a general boundary of practicality.[18] (We hasten to observe that establishing feasibility of a reservoir is a site-specific matter, and yield may not be an issue; for example, in flood control or power cooling reservoirs. Also, the relation of reservoir surface area to volume, not considered in figure 14, is an important determinant in the actual operation of the project.[19])

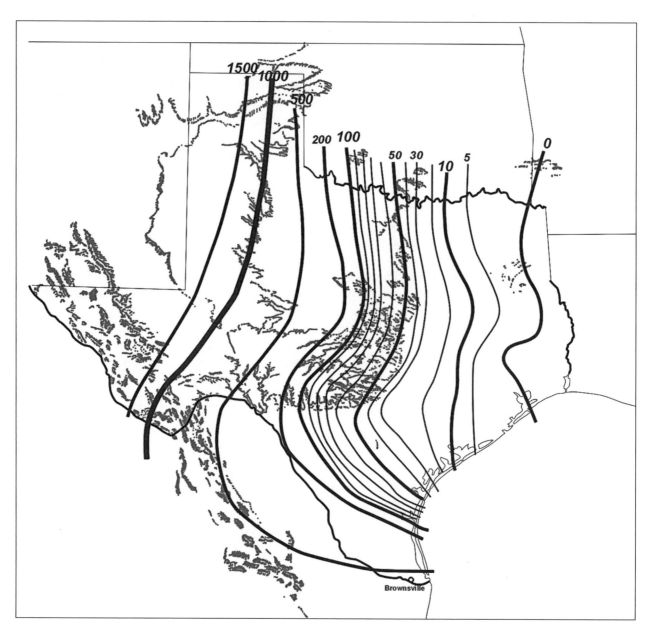

Figure 14. Variation of the ratio of watershed area to reservoir surface area, necessary to maintain average volume against evaporation and yield assumed equal to three times evaporation.

The general distribution of water use among various human activities representative of the close of the twentieth century is summarized in table 3. Groundwater withdrawal is dominated by the High Plains pumpage from the Ogallala, the agricultural pumpage from the Carrizo and Edwards Aquifers in both the central and southern regions (fig. 6), and the municipal usage by the City of San Antonio from the Edwards (central region). If these three activities are deleted from table 3, it can be seen that by the close of the century, water use in Texas had become predominantly surface water. Rice irrigation dominates the surface water diversion for agriculture in the eastern and central regions, and irrigation in the Lower Rio Grande Valley (and to a much lesser extent the Maverick Canal area) dominates the surface diversion for agriculture in southern Texas.

The establishment of the Texas rice industry coincided almost exactly with the beginning of the twentieth century; the industry reached its apex after midcentury and is now in decline (fig. 12). Though economic forces are at work, water has also been a part of this because the senior water rights held by rice irrigators are becoming more valuable to upstream users, especially for municipal supplies, than the economic yield these water rights represent

in a rice crop. The $75 million price paid by the Lower Colorado River Authority in its 1998 acquisition of 133,000 acre-feet per year from the Garwood Irrigation Company would have been unthinkable only a few years ago.[20]

Conversion of irrigation supply to municipal supplies is also under way in the Lower Rio Grande Valley (LRGV). This is partly due to the ability of municipalities to pay top dollar for the water but also reflects intensifying water supply shortages in the Valley. It is difficult to perform an accurate accounting of water uses in the LRGV because the diversions from the various pump stations serve multiple uses. In a recently completed binational study, Schmandt et al. (2000) disaggregated the municipal and industrial usage from the total diversions on both sides of the river to infer the irrigation components. At present, the Valley is practically fully developed for agriculture, in that all available land is in production. Based upon the highest five values in the 1980–93 data record, when uncurtailed deliveries were made to agricultural interests, an annual combined U.S. and Mexico usage of 3.0 billion cubic meters per year (2.4 maf/yr) was judged to represent the potential feasible irrigation usage for the Lower Rio Grande (Schmandt et al. 2000). Under drought condi-

Table 3. Present regional and statewide water uses for Texas, after Ward (1993), rounded to 3 significant digits,
10^3 **acre-feet per year**

	Region				
	East	Central	South	High Plains	Texas
Surface water diversion	1,070	3,380	2,080	132	6,650
M&I	615	1,800	274	110	2,790
Agr	452	1,580	1,810	22	3,860
Groundwater withdrawal	246	2,100	1,100	7190	10,600
M&I	215	995	178	154	1,540
Agr	24	1,080	905	7030	9,040
Electric	7	27	14	8	56
Return flows	624	2,390	210	89	3,310
M&I	468	1,780	154	89	2,490
Agr	156	606	56	0	818
Consumption					
M&I	362	1,020	298	175	1,840
Agr	320	2,050	2,660	7050	12,080
Steam-electric, surface water					
Diversion	5,181	13,601	1,300	15	20,088
Return	5,120	13,500	1,290	0	19,900
Consumption	61	101	10	15	188

Note: M&I = municipal and industrial uses.

tions, when this demand cannot be met, there will of course be a corresponding shortfall. The Schmandt (2000) study was based upon hydrometeorological and socioeconomic data through about 1993, up to which time no serious curtailment of water deliveries from the international reservoirs had ever occurred. The study investigated various stressed-supply scenarios, one of which was the recurrence of a drought similar to that of the 1950s (before construction of the two tandem reservoirs). The analysis and conclusions regarding this scenario proved to be portentive, because since 1993 the LRGV has been experiencing the most intensive drought in many years, with catastrophic impacts on the agriculture of both countries, as anticipated in the analyses of Schmandt et al. (2000).

Another scenario investigated by the Schmandt team may be of particular significance as the new century unfolds. The twentieth century conveniently coincides with the development of riparian diplomacy between the United States and Mexico. The Convention of 1906 established the distribution of river waters above Fort Quitman between Mexico and the United States (Jetton and Kirby 1970). International management of the waters in the Rio Grande from Fort Quitman to the Gulf of Mexico was formalized by the Treaty of 1944 (U.S. Department of State 1946). Among other actions, this treaty authorized construction of international reservoirs for water supply, flood control, and power generation and established a quantitative division of the waters of the river between the two countries. Development of the treaty rules was consummated by a roomful of minutes and memoranda, to which the end-of-century drought contributed yet more.

External to this process, an engineering company has recently accused Mexico of failing to meet its obligated delivery to the Rio Grande system, as mandated by the 1944 treaty (R. J. Brandes Company 2000). The furor raised among Texas water users, who would apparently like to fix blame for the drought conditions somewhere other than upon nature, has (inadvertently) raised an important issue that had already been addressed in the Schmandt study. The obligated delivery by Mexico under the conditions of the Treaty of 1944 is 350,000 acre-feet per year. Since 1924, and also since the tandem operation of the two reservoirs began in 1972, the average inflow from the Mexican tributaries is nearly five times the treaty-mandated minimum flow. Put another way, on average, 80 percent of the past inflow from Mexico is not ob-

ligated under the terms of the treaty. Most of the Mexican inflow to the Rio Grande comes from the Rio Conchos. The Schmandt team (2000) evaluated a scenario in which reservoir construction diverted most of this flow, while meeting the treaty-mandated volume. The net result would be a reduction in yield from the international reservoirs of more than 25 percent (which implicitly assumes optimum management of the available water—a feat that can occur only with perfect predictive ability over the duration of a drought).

From table 3, the greatest single statewide diversion of surface water is for steam-electric generation. However, as a *consumer* of water, power generation is minor, even less than municipal consumption. The reason, of course, is that the diverted water is returned to the water resource, albeit heated somewhat (which accounts for the consumption, because the elevated temperature increases the evaporation slightly over what would naturally have occurred).

In the early twentieth century, the notion was prevalent in Texas that water allowed to escape to the Gulf of Mexico—that is, "uncaptured" water—represented a waste (Benedict and Lomax 1916; Texas Society of Professional Engineers 1956). It is now recognized that the resources downstream from dams have a minimum flow requirement that should be met. Most important is the inflow needed for the Texas bays. These are estuarine systems that serve as spawning or nursery areas for a variety of marine species, including most of the major *Gulf* fisheries. Freshwater inflow into these systems provides nutrients and sediments and maintains a salinity gradient across the bays, all of which are necessary for the estuaries to maintain their ecological function. At the close of the century, the concept of "beneficial inflows" had been incorporated into the Texas Water Code (by the 69th Legislature in 1985), and environmental water needs had become part of project planning (TWDB 1997). A comprehensive methodology for establishing the necessary level of inflows to the Texas estuaries is under development by the Texas Water Development Board and Texas Parks and Wildlife Department (Longley 1994). This methodology is diagrammed in figure 15 and involves application of several sophisticated models and the use of extensive hydrological, hydrographic, chemical, and biological data. An example of the results of this methodology is the pattern of beneficial inflows recommended for Galveston Bay (fig. 16). Apart from the complexity of the methodology, questions remain on how it can be imple-

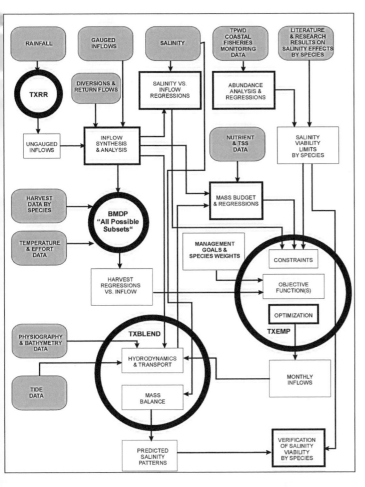

Figure 15. Schematic of state methodology for establishing beneficial inflows to estuary (Longley 1994). Bold circles represent models, shaded oblongs represent external data analysis.

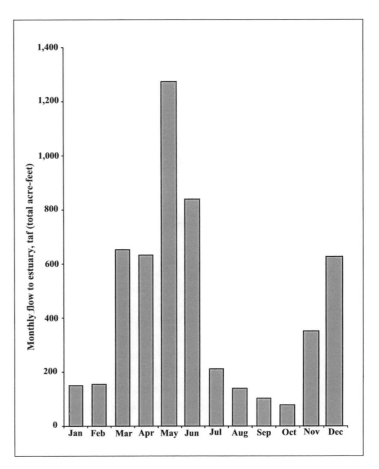

Figure 16. Monthly beneficial inflows recommended for Galveston Bay developed from state methodology (Texas Parks and Wildlife Department 1998).

mented operationally and how it will affect existing water uses in a basin.

Summary

In summary, the hydrometeorological features of Texas that vexed the state at the beginning of the twentieth century, as expressed in maxims 1 through 4, are still with us and dictate the natural water supply. The instability of runoff and recharge, implied by maxim 3, results in the recurrence of drought (among other results, maxim 4). The major feature of water supply in Texas in the twentieth century was an inexorable shift from groundwater to surface water, as expressed in maxim 5. Apart from that, the uses of water in 2000 were very much like those in 1900. They have changed quantitatively, however. Many of the features of Texas water have described a parabolic trajectory over the past century, rising from practically zero at the outset to a maximum and then falling by the close of the century.[21] These include groundwater use, reservoir development, and large-scale irrigation, though the point in time at which the high point of the trajectory was attained is variable. The glaring exception is population, which continues to grow exponentially and at a rate greater than that of the country as a whole. The ratio of reservoir capacity to population underwent a sharp reversal in trend after 1970 (fig. 17). The difficulty of new reservoir construction—both hydrological and political—ensures that this trend will continue. No better symbol of this is the fact that at the close of the century, the Bureau of Reclamation had only a single water supply–related project active in Texas. Moreover, this project was not a reservoir but instead involved the diversion of the

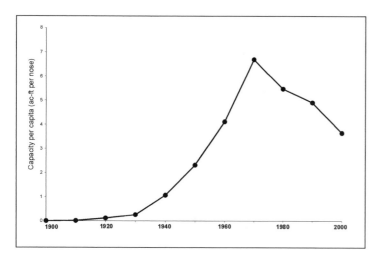

Figure 17. Variation of reservoir capacity per capita during the twentieth century.

Nueces River into its tidal marsh, the frequency of natural overbank flows having been substantially reduced due to construction of reservoirs on the Nueces River.

The most prolific sites for reservoirs in the state, as noted in maxim 1, are in the east (fig. 14), and indeed there is unused water in many of the reservoirs in this region. It is a good bet that this water will be transported westward, primarily to supply municipal/industrial requirements. The Texas Water Plan of 1968 (TWDB 1968) included major conveyances to bring this water westward through Dallas–Fort Worth into the South Plains and southward along the Texas coast. Though voters defeated the water plan on its grand scale (at just about the point in figure 20 that the trend in per capita ratio turned negative), the westward interbasin transfer is taking place, albeit via isolated, uncoordinated, ad hoc conveyances (e.g., the Mary Rhodes Memorial Pipeline from Lake Texana to Corpus Christi).

The relatively modest requirements of cities and industries (compared to those of irrigated agriculture) also allow other alternatives that, though expensive, can be important additional sources. Prominent among these are desalination and water reuse. With respect to the latter, in this brief survey I have completely avoided the issue of water quality, which also circumscribes the use of a watercourse as supply. Suffice it to note that improvements in treatment technology now allow recovery and reuse of effluent water as a viable process.

One aspect of Texas water seems clear: irrigated agriculture will become increasingly difficult to sustain, both in terms of supply and in terms of economic competition for water. As noted earlier, the conversion of irrigation

surface rights to municipal supply is under way on the coast and in the Lower Rio Grande Valley and will no doubt continue. On the Edwards aquifer, San Antonio has competed effectively with irrigation for the groundwater by its pumping capacity, in lieu of a structure of water rights law. On the High Plains, the Ogallala resource is limited and continues to be depleted, advances in conservation and efficiency notwithstanding.

With the decline in reservoir construction there seems to be an associated decline in monitoring and research enterprises, which are the foundation of water management. Stream gauging also followed a parabolic trajectory during the twentieth century and is now declining. Maxim 3 expresses the fact that the ultimate source of water supply is the difference between two large, nearly equal fluxes—precipitation and evapotranspiration. Of all of the elements of the Texas water balance, it is this difference—recharge and runoff—about which we know the least. We have been able to get by because direct measurements of streamflow can be used as a surrogate in reservoir engineering.

Although droughts occurred in the latter half of the twentieth century, thus far there has been no repetition of the great 1950s drought. But this is merely a matter of time. It is noteworthy that of the major reservoirs in Texas, two-thirds were built after the drought of the 1950s. Though water planning in Texas is drought planning, the system has not been truly tested in a major drought. There have been critical droughts in certain areas—North Texas in the 1980s, Corpus Christi in the 1990s, and the Lower Rio Grande Valley at century's end—but nothing of the spatial scale of the droughts of the 1930s and 1950s.

Moreover, almost all of the steam-electric cooling lakes were built after the 1950s drought. The dependency of Texas electric generation on the maintenance of water level in the state's reservoirs does not seem to be given adequate consideration in water planning. Though power generation is a minor consumer of water, a minimum water elevation is necessary, both to allow pumping of the cooling water and to prevent heating of the reservoir and reduced efficiency of generation. In the last two decades, several power plants have been forced offline because of either low water levels or high intake temperatures, but these difficulties have been spasmodic and easily accommodated with the redundancy of the grid. A large-scale drought with widespread reduction in reservoir levels would endanger the state's generating capacity.

There is one other aspect of Texas water that has not changed since 1900. This is the promotion mentality, which expands on the many attributes of the state but disregards the water supply problem. The term in 1900 was *booster*; by 2000 it was *developer*. Benedict and Lomax (1916) observed that "boosters frequently say two things: 'rainfall is increasing' and 'this drought is unusual.'" After a century, the availability of water is still widely ignored in municipal planning and land development. The effectiveness of the state's water districts and river authorities in planning and brokering its water supply is no small factor in this: they make a difficult task look easy. However, there are hydrological limits, and the attitude that somehow the water will be there is no longer tenable. To use an expression current in the year 2000, after a century, it is time to get real.

Notes

1. All climatological data presented in this chapter are derived from the 1941–70 normals. This normal time period coincides most closely with the time periods for which the statistics on streamflow and water demand were computed.

2. One noteworthy exception to this statement is the Rio Grande, which in 1900 derived a substantial amount of its flow from the snowpack in the Rockies. With the completion of Elephant Butte Dam, and the diversion of the entirety of the normal flow above El Paso for water supply and irrigation, the statement in the text is true of the Texas reach of the river.

3. It is also worth noting that of the nine data points from Texas, eight are from stations lying along the Balcones Escarpment. This abrupt rise in topography is frequently a favored region for the development of thunderstorms, particularly associated with the strong inland flow of moist, convectively unstable air from the Gulf of Mexico.

4. The statewide average rainfall for the period of the 1950s drought, 1950–56, was only 20 percent below normal; see, for example, Lowry (1958).

5. Table 2 was compiled in 2000. While there have been several significant floods since then, none has supplanted the gauge data of table 2. Tropical Storm Allison in 2001, in particular, caused extensive flooding in the Houston area. The peak flows at the gauges of table 2 were modest, however.

6. King's 1965 summary of the effects on Texas farmers of this drought is sardonically titled *Wagons East*.

7. For example, at this writing in June of 2000, the cumulative rainfall in Austin is exactly at its long-term average value for this point in the calendar, but Lake Travis on the Colorado is over thirty feet below conservation pool—its lowest such level in twenty years.

8. The 1912 state almanac lists one major reservoir in the state as of 1910, unnamed but with a stated capacity of 91,000 acre-feet (*Galveston-Dallas News*, 1912). This is erroneous.

9. The officer in charge, one General Dyrenforth from Fort Bliss, was dubbed "General Dryhenceforth."

10. In recent years, salination due to leaching in the arid environment of the Valley has emerged as another problem with the groundwater supply.

11. Tandem operation is considered to begin when both reservoirs reach conservation pool, which occurred in 1972.

12. Of the remaining 35 percent of steam-electric capacity, 15 percent is situated on bays or estuaries and 20 percent employs cooling towers.

13. In Houston a separate problem limited continued groundwater withdrawal, namely the resulting subsidence of the land and the consequent encroachment of the sea.

14. There are no alternative surface sources in the High Plains area. The Texas Water Plan of the 1960s (TWDB 1968) included a proposal to move surface waters from East Texas and from the Mississippi.

15. On a personal note, this writer grew up about a hundred yards from a desiccated gully with the paradoxical name of Running Water Draw. On no less authority than that of his seventh-grade history teacher, Mrs. A. B. Cox, this in fact was a perennial flowing stream fed by many springs from the shallow water belt of the Ogallala from prehistoric times until the 1930s, when the springs and the draw went dry.

16. Approximately as $\exp\{0.05\,T\}$ where T is the elapsed time in years since 1921.

17. The Soil Conservation Service (1971) presented data on the variation of "drainage area per unit volume of storage" as a means of estimating reservoir feasibility. This measure, which does not consider yield, appears to be more than it is, because it is in fact simply the reciprocal of runoff.

18. As an example, the surface area of the Lake Corpus Christi–Choke Canyon system is 45,000 acres. From figure 17, about fifty times this area is required for a viable project, or 3,500 square miles. The actual watershed is 17,000 square miles.

19. The Texas Water Rights Commission in 1972 attempted to determine empirically a relation between reservoir capacity and yield based upon permitted withdrawals. It proved noisy, ranging from 0.5 to 10, but this relation reflects a variety of water uses, and moreover, the permitted withdrawal may bear no relation to the reservoir yield. Ward and Proesmans (1996) surveyed reclamation reservoirs to determine such a relation, but actual yield numbers proved to be largely nonexistent.

20. The purchase price was not only for the water rights but also for the physical assets of the Garwood Company, including a low-water dam, two pump stations, and 170 miles of canal. But the purpose of the acquisition was to obtain the water rights; thus the total price paid is a measure of their value.

21. The intended metaphor is a ballistic.

References

Adams, J. A. *Damming the Colorado.* College Station: Texas A&M University Press, 1990.

Baker, D. M., and H. Conkling. *Water Supply and Utilization.* New York: John Wiley and Sons, 1930.

Baker, D. W. C. *A Texas Scrap-Book Made Up of the History, Biography, and Miscellany of Texas and Its People.* New York: A. S. Barnes and Company, 1875.

Benedict, H. Y., and J. A. Lomax. *The Book of Texas.* Garden City, N.Y.: Doubleday, Page and Company, 1916.

Brandes, R. J., Company. "Preliminary Analysis of Mexico's Rio Grande Water Deficit under the 1944 Treaty." Draft Report, R. J. Brandes Company, Austin, 2000.

Brown, E. H. *Trinity River Canalization.* Dallas: Trinity River Canal Association, 1930.

Brune, Gunnar. *Major and Historical Springs of Texas.* Report 189. Austin: Texas Water Development Board, 1975. Reprint, College Station: Texas A&M University Press, 2002.

———. *Springs of Texas.* Vol. 1. Fort Worth: Branch-Smith, 1981.

Brunson, B. R. *The Texas Land and Development Company: A Panhandle Promotion, 1912–1956.* Austin: University of Texas Press, 1970.

Bureau of Reclamation. *Elements of the Texas Water Problem.* Department of the Interior, Bureau of Reclamation (limited distribution), 1957.

Burke, James. *Burke's Texas Almanac 1879.* Facsimile, Austin: Steck Company, 1969.

Clay, C. "The Colorado River Raft." *Southwestern Historical Quarterly* 52 (1949): 410–26.

Cronin, J. G. "Ground Water in the Ogallala Formation in the Southern High Plains of Texas and New Mexico." *Hydrol. Invest.* Atlas HA-330. Washington, D.C.: U.S. Geological Survey, 1969.

Dooge, J. C. I. "Deterministic Input-Output Models." 1–37 in *The Mathematics of Hydrology and Water Resources,* ed. E. Lloyd, T. O'Donnell, and J. Wilkinson. London: Academic Press, 1979.

Dowell, C., and S. Breeding. *Dams and Reservoirs in Texas.* Report 48. Austin: Texas Water Development Board, 1967.

Eaves, C. D., and C. A. Hutchinson. *Post City, Texas: C. W. Post's Colonizing Activities in West Texas.* Austin: Texas State Historical Association, 1952.

Fehrenbach, T. R. *Seven Keys to Texas.* El Paso: Texas Western Press, 1983.

Galveston-Dallas News, *The Texas Almanac and State Industrial Guide, 1912.* New York: A. H. Belo and Company, 1912.

Green, D. E. *Land of the Underground Rain: Irrigation on the Texas High Plains, 1910–1970.* Austin: University of Texas Press, 1973.

Hardin, Garrett. "The Tragedy of the Commons." *Science* 162 (1968): 1243–48.

Hill, R. T., and T. W. Vaughan. "Geology of the Edwards Plateau and Rio Grande Plain Adjacent to Austin and San Antonio, Texas, with Reference to the Occurrence of Underground Waters." 193–322 in *18th Annual Report, U.S. Geological Survey, Part II,* 1897. (55 Congress 2d, HOR Doc. no. 3.)

Hughes, W. F., and W. L. Harman. *Projected Economic Life of Water Resources, Subdivision Number 1, High Plains Underground Water Reservoir.* Tech. Mono. 6, Texas Ag. Exp. Sta., Texas A&M University, College Station, 1969.

Hughs, F. M. *Legends of Texas Rivers and Sagas of the Lone Star State.* Dallas: Mathis, Van Nort and Company, 1937.

Hutson, William F. *Irrigation Systems in Texas.* Water Supply & Irrigation Paper no. 13, U.S. Geological Survey. Washington, D.C.: Government Printing Office, 1898.

Jennings, A. H. "Maximum Recorded United States Point Rainfall for 5 Minutes to 24 Hours at 296 First-order Stations." Tech. Paper no. 2, Weather Bureau, U.S. Dept. of Commerce, Washington, D.C., 1942 (rev. 1963).

Jetton, E., and J. Kirby. "A Study of Precipitation, Streamflow, and Water Usage on the Upper Rio Grande." Report no. 25, Atmospheric Science Group, College of Engineering, University of Texas at Austin, 1970.

Kane, J. W. *Monthly Reservoir Evaporation Rates for Texas, 1940 through 1965.* Report 64. Austin: Texas Water Development Board, 1967.

Karl, T. R. "Some Spatial Characteristics of Drought Duration in the United States." *J. Clim. Appl. Met.* 22 (1983): 1356–66.

Kimball, J. F. *Our City—Dallas.* Dallas: Kessler Plan Association, 1927.

King, C. Richard. *Wagons East: The Great Drought of 1886—an Episode in Natural Disaster, Human Relations, and Press Leadership.* Austin: School of Journalism Development Program, University of Texas, 1965.

Lanfear, K., and R. Hirsch. "USGS Study Reveals a Decline in Long-record Streamgages." *Eos* 80, no. 50 (1999): 605–607.

Linsley, R. K., and J. B. Franzini. *Water-Resources Engineering.* New York: McGraw-Hill Book Company, 1964.

Longley, W. (ed.). *Freshwater Inflows to Texas Bays and Estuaries.* Austin: Texas Water Development Board, 1994.

Lowry, R. L. "Surface Water Resources of Texas." Report to Texas Electric Service Company. Austin: R. L. Lowry, 1958.

Olmsted, F. L. *A Journey Through Texas.* New York: Dix, Edward, 1857. Reprints, Austin: Von Boeckmann-Jones Press, 1962; Austin: University of Texas Press, 1978.

Peckham, D. S., and J. B. Ashworth. *The High Plains Aquifer System of Texas, 1980 to 1990: Overview and Projections.* Report 341. Austin: Texas Water Development Board, 1993.

Philips, Shine. *Big Spring: The Casual Biography of a Prairie Town.* New York: Prentice-Hall, 1942.

Phillips, E. H. "The Gulf Coast Rice Industry." *Agricultural History* 25, no. 1 (1951): 91–95.

Powers, E. D. *War and the Weather, or the Artificial Production of Rain.* Chicago: S. C. Griggs, 1871. Rev. ed., Delavan, Wis.: E. Powers, 1890.

Riggio, R., G. Bomar, and T. Larkin. "Texas Drought: Its Recent History (1931–1985)." Report LP 87-04, Texas Water Commission, Austin, 1987.

Rodriguez, L. J. (ed.). *Dynamics of Growth: an Economic Profile of Texas*. Austin: Madrona Press, 1978.

Scanlon, Sister Francis Assisi. "The Rice Industry of Texas." M.A. thesis, University of Texas at Austin, 1954.

Schmandt, J., I. Águilar-Barajas, M. Mathis, N. Armstrong, L. Chapa-Alemán, S. Contreras-Balderas, R. Edwards, J. Hazleton, J. Navar-Chaidez, E. Vogel, and G. Ward. *Water and Sustainable Development in the Binational Lower Rio Grande/Río Bravo Basin*. Final Report (EPA/NSF Water and Watersheds Grant no. R 824799-01-0). The Woodlands, Tex.: Center for Global Studies, Houston Advanced Research Center, 2000.

Sharp, John. *The Changing Face of Texas*. Special Report, Comptroller of Public Accounts, Austin, 1992.

Slack, J. R., and J. M. Landwehr. "Hydro-Climatic Data Network (HCDN): A U.S. Geological Survey Streamflow Data Set for the United States for the Study of Climate Variations 1874–1988." Open File Report 92-129, USGS, Washington, D.C., 1992.

Soil Conservation Service. *Ponds for Water Supply and Recreation*. SCS Handbook no. 387. Washington, D.C.: Department of Agriculture, 1971.

Stahle, D. W., and M. K. Cleaveland. "Texas Drought History Reconstructed and Analyzed from 1698 to 1980." *J. Clim.* 1, no. 1 (1988): 59–74.

Steen, Ralph W. *Twentieth-Century Texas*. Austin: Steck Company, 1942.

Stockton, J., and S. Arbingast. *Water Requirements Survey, Texas High Plains*. Austin: Bureau of Business Research, University of Texas, 1952.

Taylor, T. U. *The Austin Dam*. U.S. Geological Survey. Washington, D.C.: Government Printing Office, 1900.

———. "The Water Power of Texas." *Trans. Texas Acad. Sci.* 4, part 2 (4). 1901.

———. *Irrigation Systems of Texas*. Water Supply & Irrigation Paper no. 71, U.S. Geological Survey. Washington, D.C.: Government Printing Office, 1902a.

———. "Rice Irrigation in Texas." *Bulletin no. 16 of the University of Texas*, Austin, 1902b.

———. *The Water Powers of Texas*. Water Supply & Irrigation Paper no. 105, U.S. Geological Survey. Washington, D.C.: Government Printing Office, 1904.

———. "The Austin Dam." Scientific Series no. 16, *Bulletin of the University of Texas,* no. 164. 1910.

———. "Silting of Reservoirs." *Bulletin No. 3025,* University of Texas, Austin, 1930.

Texas Department of Water Resources. "Inventories of Irrigation in Texas 1958, 1964, 1969, 1974 and 1979." Report 263. TDWR, Austin, 1981.

Texas Society of Professional Engineers. *Water! A Plain Statement of Some of the Problems Involved in the Development of Texas Water Resources, with Some Recommendations for Their Solution*. Austin: Water Education Committee, TSPE, 1956.

Texas Society of Professional Engineers and Texas Section of the American Society of Civil Engineers. *The Effects of Ponds and Small Reservoirs on the Water Resources of Texas*. Technical report. Austin: TSPE, 1974.

Texas Parks and Wildlife Department. "Freshwater Inflow Recommendation for the Trinity–San Jacinto Estuary." Coastal Studies Program, Resource Protection Division, TPWD, Austin, Texas, May, 1998. Posted at http://www.tpwd.state.tx.us/conserve/sb1/enviro/galvestonbay-trinitysanjac/inlandflow.html, 1998.

Texas Water Development Board. *The Texas Water Plan*. Austin: TWDB, 1968.

———. *Water for Texas*, vol. 2: Technical Planning Appendix. Document GP-6-2. Austin: TWDB, 1997.

U.S. Department of State. *Utilization of Waters of the Colorado and Tijuana Rivers and of the Rio Grande*. Treaty Series 994, Treaty between the United States of America and Mexico. Washington, D.C.: Government Printing Office, 1946.

U.S. Geological Survey, *A New Evaluation of the USGS Streamgaging Network*. Report to Congress, USGS, Washington, D.C. Posted at http://water.usgs.gov/streamgaging/report.pdf, 1998.

Wadsworth, A. "Historical Deltation of the Colorado River, Texas." In *Deltas and Their Geological Framework,* ed. M. Shirley, 99–105. Houston: Houston Geological Society, 1966.

Ward, George H. "A Water Budget for the State of Texas with Climatological Forcing." *Texas Journal of Science* 45, no. 3 (1993): 249–64.

———. "Water Demands and Flows in the Lower Rio Grande/Rio Bravo." Working paper, EPA/NSF Task Force, Houston Advanced Research Center and Instituto Tecnológico y de Estudios Superiores de Monterrey, 1999. (Published as appendix in Schmandt et al., 2000.)

Ward, G. H., and R. J. Huston. *Water and Energy: An Unprecedented Challenge in Resource Management*. Washington, D.C.: Edison Electric Institute, 1984.

Ward, G., and Proesmans. *Hydrological Predictands for Climate-Change Modeling*. Denver: Great Plains Region, Bureau of Reclamation, 1996.

Webb, Walter P. *The Great Plains*. New York: Grosset and Dunlap, 1931.

Webb, William Randall. "An Analysis of the Texas Rice Farming Industry." Prof. Report for Masters in Public Affairs, University of Texas, Austin, 1990.

CHAPTER 3

Administration and Modeling of the Water Rights System

Ralph A. Wurbs

Professor of Civil Engineering

Texas A&M University

Abstract

Allocation of limited water resources among numerous users is a governing concern in water management in Texas. A water rights permit system was developed for the lower Rio Grande during the 1960s in conjunction with a massive lawsuit. A surface water permit system was implemented for the remainder of the state during the 1970s–1980s pursuant to the Water Rights Adjudication Act of 1967. The Texas Natural Resource Conservation Commission administers about seven thousand permits statewide. A water availability modeling system was developed pursuant to the 1997 Senate Bill 1 to support the water rights regulatory program as well as other water resources planning and management activities.

Water right systems provide a basis to (1) allocate water resources among users, (2) protect existing users from having their supplies diminished by new users, and (3) manage limited water resources during droughts, when supplies are inadequate to meet all needs. Legal rights to use streamflow are generally based on two alternative doctrines: riparian and prior appropriation. The basic premise of the riparian doctrine is that water rights are incidental to ownership of land adjacent to a stream. The prior appropriation doctrine is based on the concept of protecting senior water users from having their sup-

plies diminished by newcomers developing water supplies later. In a prior appropriation system, water rights are not inherent in land ownership, and priorities are established based on dates when water is appropriated. Water law in twenty-nine eastern states is based primarily on the riparian doctrine. Nine western states adopted the prior appropriation doctrine from the beginning. Ten other states, including Texas, originally had riparian systems but later converted to appropriation systems while preserving existing riparian rights (Rice and White 1991; Getches 1997).

Water law recognizes four distinct categories of water: (1) diffuse surface runoff; (2) flow in streams and rivers and surface water stored in lakes; (3) percolating groundwater; and (4) underground streams. This chapter is focused specifically on the second category, surface water in streams, rivers, and lakes.

Effective management of the highly variable water resources of a river basin requires an understanding of the reliability with which water use requirements for various types of use can be met, under specified conditions, within institutional constraints. Implementation of a water rights permit system in Texas, during the 1970s–1980s pursuant to the 1967 Water Rights Adjudication Act, has motivated efforts to expand capabilities for assessing water availability at any location on any stream considering the impacts of water management throughout the river basin. Senate Bill 1, enacted by the Texas Legislature in 1997, authorized development of a statewide Water Availability Modeling (WAM) system. The Texas Natural Resource Conservation Commission (TNRCC), its partner agencies, and contractors are developing the WAM system during the period 1997–2001. The modeling effort is built upon the water rights permit system but is designed to support planning as well as regulatory functions. This chapter describes the water rights permit system established pursuant to the Water Rights Adjudication Act of 1967 and the water availability modeling system developed pursuant to Senate Bill 1 enacted in 1997.

Historical Development of Water Rights in Texas

Rights to use streamflow in Texas have been granted over several centuries under Spanish, Mexican, Republic of Texas, and State of Texas laws. Early water rights were based on various versions of the riparian doctrine. The prior appropriation doctrine was adopted in the 1890s while still maintaining existing riparian rights. An essentially unmanageable system evolved as various types of water rights existed simultaneously, and many rights went unrecorded. The drought of the 1950s motivated a twenty-plus-year effort to merge the varied rights into a unified permit system. The 1995–96 drought provided an impetus for further refinements. Two somewhat similar yet distinctly different water rights systems have been developed, one in the Lower Rio Grande Valley below Fort Quitman and another for the remainder of the state.

The Rio Grande is unique relative to the other river basins of Texas, shown in figure 1, from several perspectives. It is an international river shared by two nations; about 50 percent of the contributing watershed lies in the United States, and about 26 percent is in Texas. The intensive agricultural production of the region depends almost exclusively on the Rio Grande, with little use of groundwater. The water rights system for the lower Rio Grande was developed separately and has distinct differences from that of the rest of the state, particularly in regard to the priority system and water-master operations.

The Texas share of the waters of the Rio Grande below Fort Quitman were allocated among numerous water rights holders in conjunction with a massive lawsuit, State of Texas v. Hidalgo County Water Control and Improvement District No. 18, commonly called the Lower Rio Grande Valley water case. The litigants included forty-two water districts and twenty-five hundred individuals. Although the lawsuit was filed in 1956, the trial was not held until 1964–66. The final judgment was filed in 1969,

Figure 1. River basins of Texas.

and regulations implementing the court decision were adopted in 1971. The assorted versions of riparian and appropriative rights were combined into a permit system. The expense and effort involved demonstrated the impracticality of a purely judicial determination of water rights for the entire state and led to enactment of the Water Rights Adjudication Act passed by the Texas Legislature in 1967 (Templer 1981).

The stated purpose of this legislation was to require a recording of all claims for water rights that were not already recorded, to limit the exercise of those claims to actual use, and to provide for the adjudication and administration of water rights. The adjudication process required to merge all existing rights into a permit system was initiated in 1968 and completed in the late 1980s. All unrecorded claims had to be filed with the Texas Water Rights Commission. Minor exceptions were made for those using only small quantities of water for domestic and livestock purposes. Claims were recognized only if valid under existing law and only to the extent of the maximum actual beneficial use of water without waste during any year from 1963 through 1967.

Statewide 11,600 unrecorded claims were filed. Most were for riparian rights, since most appropriative rights were already recorded. More than half the claims were rejected because they showed no water use during the base period. The Texas Water Rights Commission conducted a series of administrative adjudications of water rights by river segment and permits, called certificates of adjudication. The adjudication process was essentially completed in the late 1980s. With the permit system now in place, applications for additional water rights are submitted and processed following prescribed procedures.

Some centralized agency has administered some type of water rights system statewide since 1913. However, the agencies and water rights system have changed over time. The Texas Natural Resource Conservation Commission (TNRCC) was created in 1993 by merging programs of predecessor agencies. The TNRCC is one of the largest and most comprehensive state environmental agencies in the nation. It consists of three full-time commissioners, appointed by the governor, and a professional and administrative staff of more than three thousand employees. Water rights represent just one of many statewide regulatory responsibilities of the TNRCC.

State Water Allocation System

Water rights are granted by a state license, or permit, which allows the holder to divert a specified amount of water annually at a specific location, for a specific purpose, and to store water in reservoirs of specified capacity. The TNRCC currently administers about seven thousand active water rights permits for use of surface water. Numerous other claims and permits have been canceled due to lack of water use or for other reasons. The water rights are held by river authorities, cities, municipal water districts, irrigation districts, individual farmers, companies, and private citizens. The water allocation system described next is applicable to the entire state, except that several significant differences for the Rio Grande below Fort Quitman are noted.

Anyone may submit an application to the TNRCC for a new water right or to change an existing water right at any time. The TNRCC will approve the application if unappropriated water is available, a beneficial use of the water is contemplated, water conservation will be practiced, existing water rights are not impaired, and the water use is not detrimental to the public welfare. After approval of an application, the TNRCC issues a permit giving the applicant the right to use a stated amount of water in a prescribed manner. Once the right to the use of water has been perfected by the issuance of a permit by the TNRCC, the water authorized to be appropriated under the terms of the particular permit is not subject to further appropriation until the permit is canceled. A permit may be canceled if water is not used during a ten-year period.

Special term permits may also be issued, allowing water use for specified periods of time. The Rio Grande has been over-appropriated for many years, with no new rights for additional water use being granted. However, rights are commonly transferred between users in the Rio Grande Basin.

A permit holder has no actual title to the water but only a right to use it. However, a water right can be sold, leased, or transferred to another person. The Lower Rio Grande Valley has been the only region of Texas with an active water market in the past. In 1993, the Texas Legislature established a statewide water bank to be administered by the Texas Water Development Board. Although transfers can be accomplished independent from the water bank, the program was created to encourage and facilitate water marketing, transfer, and reallocation.

The legal right to use or sell the water from a reservoir is usually granted to the owner prior to construction of the project. Many reservoirs are owned and operated by cities to provide water to their citizens for domestic, public, and industrial use. The city holds the permit or water right and sells the water to its citizen customers. Another common case is a reservoir or system of several reservoirs owned and operated by a river authority, which sells the water to a number of cities, water districts, industries, businesses, and/or irrigators. The river authority holds the water right permit. Entities that purchase water from the river authority are not required to hold a water right. The river authority operates the reservoirs to meet its contractual obligations to its customers. Nonfederal project sponsors that contract for the conservation storage in federal reservoirs are responsible for obtaining the appropriate water rights permits through the TNRCC.

Individual farmers, industries, and cities also hold water rights permits not associated with reservoirs. In most major river basins, a number of reservoir operators, all holding appropriate water rights permits, operate reservoirs in the same basin. Reservoir operators are required to make releases, typically not exceeding inflows, to allow senior downstream users not associated with the reservoir access to the water to which they are legally entitled.

The Texas Water Code requires that the TNRCC consider environmental instream flow needs in the water rights permitting process. Such needs include maintenance of aquatic habitat and species, water quality, public recreation, wetlands, and freshwater inflows to bays and estuaries. Instream flow uses have become a major consideration in issuing permits since 1985. However, most water rights in the state were granted earlier, without specifying instream flow requirements. Developing methodologies for establishing instream flow criteria and incorporating them into the water rights system continues to be an important issue.

Although water-master operations are common in other western states, the Rio Grande and South Texas water-master offices, which are components of the TNRCC, are the only such programs in Texas. A water-master office has administered water rights and accounted for water use in the Rio Grande basin since the 1960s. The South Texas water-master was established in the late 1980s to administer water rights allocations in the Guadalupe, Nueces, and San Antonio river basins. Plans during the 1980s to establish water-master programs throughout the state have been abandoned due to political considerations. The TNRCC responds to reports of illegal water use anywhere in the state. However, with the exception of the Lower Rio Grande Valley, water withdrawals are not routinely monitored.

The Texas Water Code is based on the prior appropriation doctrine. For permits issued during the adjudication of existing rights, pursuant to the Water Rights Adjudication Act of 1967, priority dates were established based on historical legal rights and actual water use. Since completion of the adjudication process, priorities for additional new rights are based upon the dates that the permit applications are filed. In general, senior water users are legally protected from more junior appropriators taking their water. However, water marketing is encouraged; rights may be bought and sold. In emergency drought situations, nonmunicipal water users may be forced to sell rights to municipalities.

For the lower Rio Grande, priorities were set in conjunction with the lawsuit previously discussed. Water rights are divided into three categories. Municipal rights have the highest priority. Irrigation rights are divided into Class A and Class B rights, with Class A rights receiving more storage in the Falcón and Amistad international reservoirs' storage accounts during the allocation procedure. Although this weighted priority system for irrigation rights has little significance during years of plentiful water, its effect in water-short years is to distribute the shortage among all users, with the greater shortages occurring on lands with Class B water rights.

Water Availability Modeling

River or reservoir system reliability estimates are fundamental to effective water management. Streamflow, evaporation, and other pertinent variables are characterized by randomness, uncertainty, and great variability, including the extremes of droughts and floods. Water availability is affected by institutional considerations and interactions between multiple water uses, users, and storage facilities. Models for assessing the amount of water that can be supplied by a river basin include features for representing basin hydrology, water use, reservoir storage capacities and operating rules, effects of basinwide water management on streamflows at particular locations of concern, and measures of water supply reliabilities and instream flow frequencies. Administration of the water allocation permit system provides a major motivation for expanding water supply reliability analysis capabilities. However, water availability models provide integrated decision support for planning studies, project development, operations, and other water management activities as well as water rights permitting functions.

Water availability models for eight of the major river basins (Brazos, Colorado, Guadalupe, Lavaca, Nueces, San Antonio, San Jacinto, Trinity) were developed during the 1970s and 1980s in conjunction with the water rights adjudication process. These basin-specific models consisted of Fortran computer programs and data files for analyzing allocation of the surface waters of each river basin under the water rights system. The primary purpose of the models was to determine unappropriated streamflows. Data from past runs of the models have continued to be used along with other information to evaluate permit applications. However, the Fortran programs have not been operative since the early 1990s. The Water Rights Analysis Package (WRAP) model, described later, was applied to the Brazos, San Jacinto, and Lavaca river basins, prior to the 1997 Senate Bill 1, using some input data from the earlier models along with other updated information. The Senate Bill 1 WAM project represents a major new effort to apply a consistent modeling approach to all the basins.

Water Availability Modeling Pursuant to Senate Bill 1

Senate Bill 1, the Brown-Lewis Water Management Plan enacted by the Texas Legislature in 1997, is having a major impact on water resources planning and management in the state. This is a comprehensive water management package that addresses a wide range of issues. Two related programs created by Senate Bill 1 are particularly important: (1) regional planning studies; and (2) water availability modeling.

Committees of local water interests have been established to prepare plans for the orderly development, management, and conservation of the water resources of each of sixteen regions. Consulting firms are providing technical support. Senate Bill 1, as amended in 1999, mandates that the sixteen regional studies be completed by January 2001. The Texas Water Development Board (TWDB) is coordinating the planning studies. The TWDB must incorporate the regional plans into a statewide plan by January 2002. The modeling capabilities developed by the water availability modeling project, described next, are being used whenever feasible in the regional studies.

Another provision of the 1997 Senate Bill 1 directs the TNRCC to develop water availability models for the twenty-two river basins of the state, excluding the Rio Grande. Six river basins are to be completed by December 1999 and the other sixteen by December 2001. The Rio Grande basin will be addressed later under separate legislation. The purpose of the Water Availability Modeling (WAM) project is to develop a WAM system consisting of software and databases to be used by water management entities and their consultants both in planning studies and in preparing permit applications and to be used by the TNRCC in evaluating permit applications. The WRAP simulation model that the regulatory agency (TNRCC) uses in evaluating permit applications, with hydrology and water rights input files for each river basin, is publicly available for use in planning studies and preparation of permit applications.

Modeling Strategy

The river basin water management simulation model adopted for the Water Availability Modeling (WAM) system is called the Water Rights Analysis Package (WRAP). Earlier versions of the WRAP model developed during 1986–96 have been greatly improved and expanded under the Senate Bill 1 WAM project (Wurbs 2000). WRAP is generalized for application to any river/reservoir/use system anywhere, with input files being developed for the particular river basin of concern. The generalized model simulates management of the water resources of a river basin, or multiple-basin region, under a priority-based water allocation system. WRAP facilitates assessment of hydrologic and institutional water availability and reliability for existing and proposed water rights. Basinwide impacts of water resources development projects and management strategies may be evaluated. The public domain software and documentation are distributed by the

Texas Water Resources Institute (http://twri.tamu.edu). Executable programs for desktop computers and Fortran source code are readily available.

The overall WAM system includes water rights and other databases, database management software, a geographic information system (GIS), graphics programs, user interfaces, and WRAP input files and simulation results for individual river basins as well as the generalized WRAP simulation model. WRAP may be applied either independently or in combination with other components of the WAM system.

A typical WRAP simulation study involves assessing capabilities for meeting specified water management and use requirements during a hypothetical repetition of historical hydrology. For example, for a particular application, the analysts may choose to analyze reliabilities of existing or proposed reservoirs and other facilities to supply year 2000 water needs with basin hydrology represented by sequences of monthly naturalized streamflows and reservoir net evaporation-precipitation rates at all pertinent locations for each of the 720 months of a 1940–99 hydrologic period-of-analysis. The model allocates water to meet the year 2000 use requirements during each sequential month of the 720-month simulation.

The overall water availability modeling process for a river basin is outlined as follows.

1. Sequences of monthly naturalized streamflows are developed.
   - Complete sequences of naturalized flows covering the specified period-of-analysis at selected gaging stations are developed by adjusting gaged flows to remove effects of human development.
   - Flows are distributed from gaged to all pertinent ungaged locations based on parameters characterizing the watersheds.
2. Allocation of water to each right in priority order for each month of the hydrologic period-of-analysis is simulated.
3. The simulation results are organized, and reliability and frequency indices are computed.

WRAP uses a monthly time step with no limit on the number of years in the hydrologic period-of-analysis. Water use targets vary seasonally over the twelve months of the year and may also vary as a function of reservoir storage. Water rights requirements include reservoir storage, water supply diversions, return flows, environmental instream flow needs, and hydroelectric power generation. In each sequential month of the hydrologic period-of-analysis, volume accounting computations are performed for each water right in priority order. The simulation results include sequences of monthly and annual values for all pertinent variables, storage and flow frequency statistics, and reliability indices for meeting water use requirements.

A fundamental concept of the model is that available streamflow is allocated to each water right in ranked priority order. The priority-based simulation approach in WRAP is essential for the Texas WAM system. For each month of the simulation, priority numbers are input for each water right, which in turn determine the order in which the rights are considered in the water allocation computational loop. Diversion, instream flow, hydropower, and storage refilling targets for each right are met to the extent allowed by available streamflow and storage prior to considering the requirements of more junior rights. In the Texas prior appropriation water rights system, priority numbers typically represent dates specified in the permits. However, with a little ingenuity, the model user can devise various other schemes for using the priority numbers to model relative priorities for allocating water. A priority scaling option allows rights associated with specified water use types to be conveniently adjusted. For example, all municipal rights could be given priority over all agricultural rights in a particular simulation run. Another option allows water demands to be met in upstream-to-downstream order without regard to priorities.

The spatial configuration of a river/reservoir/use system is represented in WRAP as a set of control points. All system features are assigned control points denoting their locations. Essentially any configuration of stream tributaries and man-made conveyance facilities may be modeled. In the Texas WAM project, the number of control points representing individual river basins has ranged from just a few to well over a thousand for the larger basins. The larger basins have over a thousand diversions and several hundred reservoirs.

Alternative water use scenarios and management strategies are analyzed by alternative simulation runs. Simulation results may be organized in various formats, including the entire time series of monthly or annual values of various variables, water budgets, frequency statistics, and reliability indices. The results of a WRAP simulation are typically viewed from the perspectives of frequency, probability, percent-of-time or reliability of meeting (or risk of failing to meet) water supply,

instream flow, hydropower, and/or reservoir storage requirements.

Volume and period reliabilities may be computed for either water supply diversion or hydroelectric energy generation targets for individual water rights, or for the aggregation of selected groups of rights. Volume reliability (R_v) is the ratio of the water volume supplied or energy generated (v) to the amount demanded (V), expressed as a percentage:

$$R_V = (v / V)(100\%)$$

or, equivalently, the ratio of the mean actual rate supplied to mean target rate. Period reliability (R_P) is the percentage of months in the simulation for which a specified demand target is fully met without shortage:

$$R_P = (n / N)(100\%)$$

where n denotes the number of months during the simulation for which the demand is fully supplied, and N is the total number of months in the simulation. Thus, R_P is an expression of the percentage of time that the demand can be met or, equivalently, the likelihood of the demand being met in any randomly selected month. Tabulations are also developed of both the percentage of months and the percentage of years within the simulation during which the amounts supplied equal or exceed specified magnitudes expressed as a percentage of the target demand.

Exceedance frequency tables may be developed for naturalized flow, regulated flow, unappropriated flow, instream flow shortages, and reservoir storage. Exceedance frequency is defined as:

$$Frequency = (n / N)(100\%)$$

where n is the number of months during the simulation that a particular flow or storage amount is equaled or exceeded, and N is the total number of months in the simulation. Frequency tables also include the mean, standard deviation, minimum, and maximum.

Model Development and Application

The TNRCC is the lead agency for the WAM project. Other key participants include the Texas Water Development Board, Texas Parks and Wildlife Department (TPWD), consulting engineering firms, and two universities (TNRCC 1998; Sokulsky et al. 1998). An administrative management team is composed of staff from the TNRCC, TWDB, and TPWD. Parsons Engineering Science, Inc., serves as the technical manager for the overall project. A Workgroup of Water Use Interests advises on policy issues that arise during development of the modeling system.

During 1997–98, the TNRCC, TWDB, TPWD, and a team of consulting firms evaluated available river/reservoir system simulation models to select a generalized model for the WAM project (TNRCC 1998). Leading models investigated included MODSIM, developed at Colorado State University; STATEMOD, developed by the state of Colorado; MIKE BASIN developed by the Danish Hydraulic Institute, and others. This study resulted in adoption of WRAP, developed at Texas A&M University, and recommendations for expanding and improving WRAP.

The original WRAP has been greatly expanded under a 1998–2001 contract between the TNRCC and the Texas Water Resources Institute (TWRI) of the Texas A&M University System (Wurbs 2000). The WRAP modifications work involves developing modeling methodologies and computer code. Many improvements have been incorporated into WRAP based on suggestions made by the team of agencies and consulting firms involved in both the model evaluation study and application of the generalized model to the various river basins. Numerous meetings, workshops, and informal communications have facilitated interactive feedback between individuals involved in applying WRAP to specific river basins and those responsible for modifying the model.

Methods for distributing naturalized monthly streamflows from gaged to ungaged sites were investigated under a 1997–99 TNRCC/TWRI contract (Wurbs and Sisson 1999). Selected streamflow transfer methodologies incorporated into WRAP require the following watershed parameters for each gaging station and water right location: drainage area, curve number (representing soil type and land use), and mean precipitation. The Center for Research in Water Resources (CRWR) at the University of Texas developed an ArcView-based geographic information system (GIS) for delineating the spatial connectivity of pertinent sites and compiling values for these watershed parameters (Hudgens and Maidment 1998).

Managing voluminous data, including water right, water use, mapping, and hydrologic data, is a major concern. The TNRCC initiated efforts early in the project to expand and refine inhouse database management capabilities (Sokulsky et al. 1998).

Consulting engineering firms working under contracts with the TNRCC are developing WRAP input data sets and applying the model to each of the twenty-two river basins. Six consulting firms working under three TNRCC contracts modeled the initial six river basins in 1998–99. These were the Sulphur, Neches, Nueces, San Antonio, Guadalupe, and San Jacinto river basins. Modeling studies for the other sixteen basins are being conducted during the period 1999–2001. This work consists of developing the WRAP hydrology and water rights input files and executing the model for specified water management scenarios.

The studies for each river basin include simulations for the several alternative scenarios that incorporate assumptions regarding water use, reuse of return flows, and reservoir sedimentation. Alternative water use scenarios include assumptions that (1) all permit holders use their full permitted amounts, (2) all rights not actually used during the last ten years are canceled, and (3) water demands are based on the maximum annual use during the past several years. Term permits are included only in certain simulation scenarios. A portion of the water diverted for beneficial use is returned to the stream as wastewater effluent or other forms of return flow. Alternative assumptions regarding reuse of wastewater effluent are modeled. Reservoir sedimentation alters the storage capacities and the storage volume versus surface area relationships incorporated in the model. Alternative sedimentation conditions include (1) the original topography when the reservoir project was constructed and permits issued and (2) storage volume and surface area versus elevation relationships updated to a specified year based on estimates of sediment accumulation.

The consulting firms document each basin modeling study with a detailed report. The TNRCC furnishes the reports to the regional planning committees, Workgroup of Water Use Interests, and other interested parties. Senate Bill 1 requires that individual permit holders be informed of the reliabilities associated with their water rights. Thus, upon completion of each river basin study, the TNRCC provides pertinent information to all public agencies, private businesses, and individual citizens holding water right permits regarding the reliabilities associated with their specific rights. The WRAP data sets are publicly available from the TNRCC web site (http://www.tceq.state.tx.us). The basic input data sets will continue to be used in the future by the TNRCC and other entities interested in investigating various water management strategies in conjunction with planning studies, permit applications, or other activities.

Conclusion

With growing demands on limited water resources, water rights have become increasingly important in Texas. Implementation and administration of a water allocation system has been a major thrust of water management in Texas since the milestone Water Rights Adjudication Act of 1967. The 1997 Senate Bill 1 is another milestone legislative package greatly affecting statewide water management. Expanding water availability modeling capabilities to support administration of the water rights system is currently a major emphasis. Planning and regulatory functions have become closely integrated. The same computer simulation model and data sets used in planning studies are applied both in preparing and in evaluating permit applications.

References

Getches, D. H. *Water Law,* 3rd ed. St. Paul, Minn.: West Publishing Company, 1997.

Hudgens, B. T., and D. R. Maidment. "Determination of Watershed Parameters Using Geospatial Data." In *Proceedings of 25th Water for Texas Conference, "Water Planning Strategies for Senate Bill 1," Texas Water Resources Institute,* Austin, December 1–2, 1998.

Rice, L., and M. D. White. *Engineering Aspects of Water Law.* Malabar, Fla.: Krieger Publishing Company, 1991.

Sokulsky, K., T. Dacus, L. Bookout, and J. Patek. "Water Availability Modeling Project Concept Plan: Overview of the New Modeling System and Its Role in Regional Planning." In *Proceedings of 25th Water for Texas Conference, "Water Planning Strategies for Senate Bill 1," Texas Water Resources Institute,* Austin, December 1–2, 1998.

Templer, O. T. "The Evolution of Texas Water Law and the Impact of Adjudication." *Water Resources Bulletin* (American Water Resources Association) 17, no. 5 (1981): 789–98.

Texas Natural Resource Conservation Commission. *Water Availability Modeling: An Overview.* GI-245. 1998.

Wurbs, R. A. *Reference and Users Manual for the Water Rights Analysis Package (WRAP).* Texas Water Resources Institute, Technical Report 180. 2000.

Wurbs, R. A., and E. D. Sisson. *Evaluation of Methods for Distributing Naturalized Streamflows from Gaged Watersheds to Ungaged Subwatersheds.* Texas Water Resources Institute, Technical Report 179. 1999.

CHAPTER 4

Water Use Patterns and Trends

The Future in Texas

Rima Petrossian

Manager, Groundwater Technical Assistance Section

Texas Water Development Board

Abstract

The recorded history of water planning in Texas had its initial stirrings in 1904. By 1961 the State of Texas had started compiling and analyzing water data, resulting in statewide water management plans. The first plan referred to drought conditions, and the 2002 plan similarly uses the historical worst-case scenario of drought-of-record conditions. In 1996, during the most recent severe drought, approximately 352 smaller communities, some without any water planning strategies, struggled with water supply shortages. The passage of Senate Bill 1 is the establishment of "bottom up" planning, with the resulting formation of sixteen regional water planning groups (RWPGs). According to the 1997 State Water Plan, groundwater use has stabilized, while surface water use increases each year. Total water use is projected to decrease from 15.912 million acre-feet in 2000 to 14.911 million acre-feet in 2050. The RWPGs are considering several different approaches: the Panhandle Region (A) is maintaining a groundwater availability of 50 percent of the current water in storage in 2050; the Lower Colorado Region (K) is considering using all available groundwater, depending upon the aquifer, for use up to the recharge limits. The final set of strategies adopted by the groups will be presented in the 2002 plan.

Water use and water supplies in Texas have changed dramatically over the past hundred years. The steadily growing population and a resilient economy figure predominantly in the changes. For example, the growth in municipal surface water use has outpaced groundwater use significantly over the past twenty years as smaller cities and rural areas convert from relying on local water supply wells to buying supplies from regional surface water systems. The 1996 drought threatened many of these smaller cities and rural areas that were not prepared for diminished surface water supplies. In response, the 75th Texas Legislature formulated and passed Senate Bill 1 in 1997. Senate Bill 1 implements changes in water supply planning by developing a regional approach to state planning for the first time in Texas history.

History of Texas Water Planning

Water planning proposals have been around since 1904, when voters first authorized the public development of water. The Texas Water Development Board (TWDB, formerly known as the Board of Water Engineers) planned and circulated the first statewide plan in 1961. A total of six plans have been developed and approved over the past thirty-nine years (TWDB 1997).

The 1961 plan was developed in response to legislation, House Joint Resolution 3 and the 1957 Planning Act, following the hallmark drought of the 1950s. The plan consisted of an initial description of the state's water resources, quantified future water supply and demand, and proposed water supply projects. The first page of the plan reads like an article about contemporary water planning issues. Lack of public awareness, inaction, and short-sighted projects solving only local water needs were all mentioned as problems (TWDB 1961).

A striking parallel from the 1961 plan to the anticipated 2002 plan is the consideration of planning for drought conditions. Another parallel is that drought was the driving factor in the late 1950s and mid-1990s initiatives (Texas Board of Water Engineers 1961). The 2002 plan will incorporate planning focused on drought-of-record conditions using data from the historical worst-case scenario.

The 1961 plan focused primarily on surface water. The rationale at the time was that groundwater was not subject to state control, and therefore there was no need to plan for groundwater resources. In vast areas the groundwater resources were not considered well delineated or understood. The plan reported that 79 percent of the communities in the state used groundwater resources. At the time, fourteen major reservoirs were under construction, and the plan proposed forty-five new ones (Texas Board of Water Engineers 1961). In comparison, eight new reservoirs were proposed in the 1997 plan (TWDB 1997). The projections for 1980 in the 1961 plan indicated municipal and industrial needs at 6.547 million acre-feet per year, consisting of 1.300 million acre-feet per year of groundwater and 5.247 million acre-feet per year of surface water (Texas Board of Water Engineers 1961). For comparison purposes, the actual 1980 use for municipal and industrial demands was 4,876,809 acre-feet, consisting of 1,770,567 acre-feet of groundwater and 3,106,242 of surface water (TWDB 1980). The earlier prognosticators concluded that in the 1980s, "new reservoirs and increased use of groundwater [could] provide for the projected needs" (Texas Board of Water Engineers 1961).

Plans developed in 1968 and 1984 continued the trend of recommending additional surface water supply development to meet increasing needs. The 1968 plan indicated that "importation of water from out-of-state sources would be essential," and it referenced the Mississippi River. The plan indicated that the Texas water resources were "grossly inadequate" to meet the future needs (TWDB 1968).

The 1990, 1992, and 1997 plans began to emphasize water demand management (conservation, etc.) as well as planning for the new water supplies. Environmental considerations, including the effect on natural systems from new water supply construction projects and natural flow maintenance, were also being included in the planning process. Both the 1997 and 2002 plans provide specific criteria for instream flows and environmental considerations.

The 1997 Water Plan, a consensus plan between several state agencies and stakeholder groups, discusses both surface water and groundwater supplies. The 1997 plan indicates that 67 percent of communities used groundwater for a total of 8.539 million acre-feet. The 1997 plan projected a total water supply demand for Texas in 2050 of approximately 20.95 million acre-feet. Prognosticators in this plan indicated that "a reasonable plan for water development has been identified in this State Water Plan that can assure an adequate supply of water to meet all anticipated economic needs of the State for the next 50 years." The tools to meet the needs identified in the 1997 plan include water conservation, expanded use of existing local supplies, wastewater reuse, water marketing, reservoir storage reallocation, water quality protection, interbasin transfers, and new water supply development (TWDB 1997).

In 1996, during the most recent severe drought, larger cities suffered less because of their previous water planning and implementation efforts. However, approximately 352 smaller communities, some without any water planning strategies, struggled with water supply shortages (Texas Natural Resource Conservation Commission 2000). The legislature recognized the need to involve smaller communities and other interests in planning for their water needs and responded by formulating and passing Senate Bill 1. Senate Bill 1 is designed to increase local involvement and, consequently, local support for long-term water supply planning.

Senate Bill 1 Planning

The state's goals expressed through the passage of Senate Bill 1 are to develop fifty-year regional plans and a comprehensive state plan to provide for the orderly development, management, and conservation of water resources. Addressing these goals in the plan is intended to ensure that sufficient water will be available during drought conditions at a reasonable cost to provide for public health, safety, and welfare. These goals will further ensure that water will be available for increased economic development and to protect the agricultural and natural resources of the entire state (Texas Water Code, Chapter 16, Section 16.053).

In addition to specifying the particulars of water planning, other topics were addressed by Senate Bill 1. Its passage not only changed the planning process but also addressed:

- groundwater conservation district management plans;
- the priority groundwater management area process;
- funding digital data set compilation for statewide map creation and updating;
- TWDB funding authorizations;
- data collection and dissemination for water resources planning; and
- interbasin transfers of surface water.

Since the passage of Senate Bill 1, a major difference in water resources management has been the change in water rights priority dates for interbasin transfers of surface water. During an interbasin transfer, existing senior water rights become junior rights when the water is transferred from one basin to another, meaning that the new rights have the newest priority date. During a drought, there may not be water available to satisfy the junior right. This change in priority of surface water rights may have accelerated the trend to acquire and transfer groundwater, which is governed in Texas by the rule of capture except where modified by the rules of a groundwater conservation district.

Regional Planning

The TWDB divided Texas into sixteen regions (fig. 1) based on hierarchical criteria and public comment. Initially, proposed planning areas were developed beginning with ten climatic regions described by the National Weather Service. The areas were adjusted based on data characterizing the statutory considerations provided. They include additional changes based on public comment.

Public comment and negotiations were heavily relied upon during the final phase of boundary delineation. Among the additional factors for consideration, mandated by statute, were river basin watersheds, aquifers, water utilities' service areas, demographics, existing water planning areas, political subdivision boundaries, and public comment.

A strong effort was made not to divide major cities between regions. Counties were not divided except at their request. However, there are many instances where a water

Figure 1. TWDB designated regional water planning groups (RWPGs), June, 1998.

source is located in one region and supplies water to other regions. One of the common questions that was asked after the regions were delineated is why the regions were not divided based on the water supplies, either by aquifer or river basin. The answer is because of the data.

The plan administration and management by a regional political subdivision plays a critical part in creating the regional plans. Most of the natural aquifer and basin boundaries do not conform to any political or authority boundaries. The aquifer and basin boundaries do not directly correspond either. The way water is distributed and water use is recorded is based on the responsible political subdivision or supplier accounting systems. A complex web of cooperation between private and public entities reporting water use, and statistical manipulation, would have been necessary to incorporate the many stakeholders if the natural boundaries had been used.

Part of the intricacy in planning involves tracking the supplies in a consistent way between two or more regions. However, once the regions were established, they were allowed to formulate their plans fairly autonomously. This could result in differences ranging from varying methods of calculating supplies to varying ways of allocating shared supplies.

TWDB Rules and Guidelines

The TWDB drafted rules to help guide the planning process. These rules provide guidance on the general format of the plan, funding limitations, document production criteria, coordination with other entities, documentation requirements, definitions of the mandated interests, and other considerations. Draft rules were revised several times to address public comment; twenty-six public meetings were held throughout the state to elicit comments. Out of 431 comments received, 325 resulted in changes to the rules and planning area delineation. All comments and changes are reported in the TWDB document listing the adopted rules. The rules were adopted early in 1998, six months ahead of the statutory deadline. This gave the newly created regions six additional months to develop their plans (TWDB 1998).

Regional Water Planning Groups

As with most new program initiations, the new regional water planning program has some advantages over the old methods. Reasons cited for greater participation in regional water planning include:

- regional cooperation toward a common goal;
- regional acceptance of the resulting plan;
- establishing regional projects and benefiting from shared cost savings;
- eligibility for TWDB funding for water supply projects;
- consideration for Texas Natural Resource Conservation Commission water rights permits or amendments;
- linking planning to the Texas Natural Resource Conservation Commission permitting; and
- establishing a closer relationship between planning and implementation.

To encourage planning participation, representation of specified interest groups for each region was mandated through Senate Bill 1 to ensure adequate representation during water planning. The TWDB made an effort to ensure that each specific area's local interests were adequately represented. Each of the regions has at least one

person representing each of the following interests, if the interest is present in the region: municipal, agriculture, environmental, county, industry, public, small business, electric generating utility, river authority, water district, and water utilities. Nonvoting members include one TWDB staff member per region, a Texas Parks and Wildlife Department representative, a Texas Department of Agriculture representative, adjacent regions' regional water planning group (RWPG) liaisons, and surface water rights holders (representing those holding a thousand acre-feet or more a year) in an adjacent region. Additional members, including other state or federal agencies or representing state, federal, or binational entities sharing water resources with the RWPG, may be added at the discretion of the RWPG. In some regions the nonvoting members actively participate except for voting.

A total of 5,069 nominations were made for membership in the RWPGs. Initial coordinating bodies for each region were formed from these nominees to begin the regional planning process. TWDB representatives identified 1,748 candidates for the initial coordinating bodies. The candidates were asked about their level of personal interest and were considered for their technical understanding of water resources, current role in water planning, interest representation, geographic representation across the planning area, community influence, and leadership.

A total of 270 candidates were selected and agreed to serve on the initial coordinating bodies in the sixteen regions. After adding at least one additional member, as required by statute, and certifying that all interests in the region were adequately represented, the initial coordinating bodies became RWPGs. Nonvoting members ensure that the views of other interested parties are represented, without having the voting control.

Each RWPG is a voluntary group. Group members are not remunerated for their time or expenses unless they are being paid by the organization they represent. Each RWPG member is expected to represent and advocate for his or her constituency's viewpoint, report the group planning results to that constituency, and participate in the planning process. The group ultimately identifies area needs; formulates, reviews, and recommends water management strategies to be used to meet those needs; and adopts the plan.

TWDB Funding

Senate Bill 1 stipulates that future funding from TWDB for projects and future Texas Natural Resource Conservation Commission surface water permits for municipalities will be contingent upon consistency with regional and state water plans. If an entity is applying for TWDB funding for a project, in order to be considered for funding, the plan must list that project as a water management strategy. Currently, some items eligible for the TWDB loan program include brush control, precipitation enhancement, water conservation and reuse, aquifer storage facilities, pipelines, reservoir construction, water well construction, water marketing, monitoring, and drought preparedness and management plans. Senate Bill 1 provided much of the funding, through the TWDB, for the preparation and planning for the 2002 regional plans.

Water Demand Projections

In addition to funding, the TWDB provided each RWPG with the 1997 Water Plan population and water demand projections for each water user group. New regional information based upon more current data resulted from some RWPGs reviewing and updating the 1997 projections. The revised projections served as a base to formulate the entire 2002 plan.

The plan will include projections of population and water demands, assessments of existing supplies, and a determination of a surplus or needs for additional water. The plan is required to meet the needs for the following water user groups: municipal, manufacturing, irrigation, steam electric power generation, mining, and livestock.

The RWPGs developed water management strategies, scenarios, and appropriate strategies to meet the water users' needs identified through the comparison and analysis of the demand projections and the available supplies. In some regions, new studies were performed to determine groundwater availability. The RWPGs considered all the interests of the people they represent in their respective regions, reached a consensus within the group, and considered what their neighboring groups were planning for mutual water resources.

Plan Development

Each RWPG developed a scope of work for their regional water plan. The RWPG designated a political subdivision to apply to the TWDB for a grant to implement the scope of work by August 1, 1998. The political subdivision chosen by each group is a "city, county, district, or authority created under the Texas Constitution . . . any other political subdivision of the state . . . any interstate compact commission to which the state is a party . . . and any non-profit water supply corporation" (TWDB 1998).

Contracts with the TWDB to produce the regional plans are administered by a political subdivision. The political subdivision is responsible to the TWDB for accounting and reporting the monies spent by consultants. The consultants were hired by the political subdivision, as voted on by the RWPG, to research, develop, write, and present a plan to the RWPG for adoption and ultimately for presentation to the TWDB.

The RWPGs have met regularly starting in March–April 1998. All planning meetings are public meetings held in accordance with the Open Meetings Act. The number of meetings held thus far exceeds five hundred. In contrast, twenty-seven public hearings and three public meetings were held regarding the 1968 water plan (TWDB 1968). Public attendance at RWPG meetings is variable, but there is consistently public representation at each meeting. At least one public hearing was held in each region before October 1, 2000, in order to present the plan initially prepared and discuss it with the public prior to adoption by the RWPG.

At the conclusion of the first major planning cycle, January 5, 2001, the TWDB must work with the regions to resolve any conflicts between adopted regional plans. Then the TWDB incorporates the sixteen regional plans into a statewide plan by January 5, 2002, after resolving any remaining conflicts. The state will update the plans every five years through each RWPG's efforts, but the plans may be amended at any time.

Groundwater and Surface Water
Projected Use and Demands

Groundwater and surface water demands, availability, and allocations are being formulated for the 2002 plan and are not available at this time. However, according to the 1997 State Water Plan data presented here, groundwater use has stabilized, while surface water use increases each year. Total water use is projected to decrease from 15.912 million acre-feet in 2000 to 14.911 million acre-feet in 2050 (fig. 2). Municipal groundwater use is lessening statewide, by percent of total supply, while surface water use is increasing (TWDB 1997).

In 1994, groundwater use was 9.352 million acre-feet total. Groundwater use, projected to be 31 percent of the water supply in 2050, is projected to be 4.616 million acre-feet, indicating an overall drop in use. Projections indi-

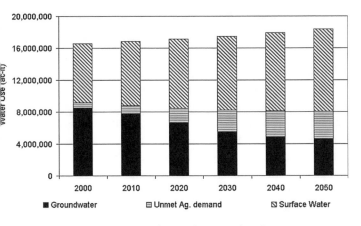

Figure 2. *Projected groundwater and surface water use (TWDB 1997).*

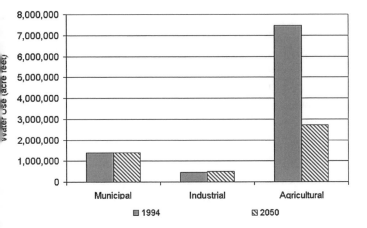

Figure 3. *Composition of current and projected groundwater use for 1994 and 2050 (TWDB 1997).*

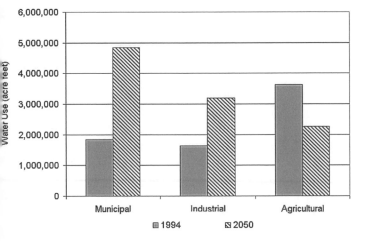

Figure 4. *Composition of current and projected surface water use for 1994 and 2050 (TWDB 1997).*

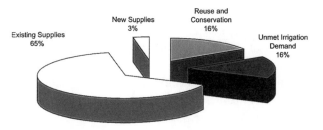

Figure 5. *Water management strategies to meet demands in 2050.*

cate decreased use and unmet needs by agriculture-based entities, the biggest users of groundwater; in addition, agricultural conservation programs are expected to reduce demand. Municipal and industrial use are both projected to double in percent, and agricultural use may drop by about 20 percent (fig. 3; TWDB 1997).

In 1994, surface water use was 7.116 million acre-feet total (fig. 4; TWDB 1997). Surface water use, projected to be 69 percent of the water supply in 2050, is estimated to be 10.295 million acre-feet. Municipal use is projected to almost double; industrial use will increase slightly, while agricultural use will drop to less than half the 1994 use in percent (fig. 4; TWDB 1997). Proposed water management strategies from the 1997 plan to meet demands in 2050 are shown in figure 5. The strategy pie may be sliced significantly differently in the 2002 plan.

Potential Strategies Considered for 2002 and Beyond

Some RWPGs are considering a plethora of surface water and groundwater water management strategies for satisfying water demands and needs. Several of the more innovative approaches are presented here, but the final adopted set of strategies chosen by the groups will be presented in the 2002 plan.

Groundwater

Groundwater extraction beyond the limit of aquifer recharge is considered acceptable in some regions while it is not being considered in other regions as a management strategy. For example, the Coastal Bend Region (N) set drawdown limits in their Gulf Coast aquifer groundwater model based on the current aquifer thickness. The model limits imposed were at 250 feet below predevelopment levels in the confined portion of the aquifer and 125 feet for unconfined portions, with a minimum saturated thickness of 150 feet. An acceptable maximum limit of 250 feet of drawdown is input in the model through 2050.

Another limit being considered in the Panhandle Region (A) is maintaining a groundwater availability of 50 percent of the current water in storage in 2050. Also in this area, a pipeline system carrying groundwater and surface water around the region is being considered to cover smaller entities with needs. In addition, private interests are marketing groundwater.

Several regions are defining groundwater availability as the average annual recharge or projected fifty-year demands. Some regions have developed aquifer availability quantities independent of TWDB research.

The Lower Colorado Region (K) is considering using all available groundwater, depending upon the aquifer, for use up to the recharge limits. In some cases, primarily for irrigation, pumping in excess of annual recharge may be used during drought conditions. Region K is considering off-channel reservoirs—combining surface water and groundwater as appropriate—as another potential solution to meeting needs.

Surface Water

Eight RWPGs recommend a total of seventeen surface water reservoir water management strategies and thirty-nine unique reservoir site designations. Two water management strategies include off-channel reservoirs. The RWPGs recommending surface water sources identified thirty-nine unique sites for reservoir construction as per chapter 357 of the TWDB Regional Planning Guidelines. Specifically, section 357.9 addresses recommending sites of unique value for reservoir construction, including hydrologic, geologic, topographic, water availability, environmental, cultural, and current development characteristics or other pertinent development factors. The reservoirs, listed in table 1, include both new surface water reservoirs and some previously proposed.

Another surface water strategy, considered by the Rio Grande Region (M), is the conversion of water rights by sale of irrigation rights to municipalities. In the Lower Colorado Region (K), off-channel reservoirs are being considered to offset upper-basin municipal shortages, lower-basin irrigation shortages, and municipal and industrial shortages in Region L. This strategy could yield in excess of 300,000 acre-feet per year. The Lavaca Region

(P) is considering seawater desalination in conjunction with surface water resources to supply municipal and industrial needs inland in Region L. This strategy could yield up to 200,000 acre-feet per year.

Region H is considering cost-efficient treatment and reuse of treated effluent at industrial facilities for a gain of 90,000 acre-feet per year. Contractual agreements, if parties are willing, could amount to another 150,000 acre-feet. Also under discussion are interbasin transfers, desalination, irrigation conservation, advanced municipal water conservation, and new reservoirs. Over half of the projected needs would be addressed by contract extensions and drilling additional wells. One strategy considered early in the planning process, but later discarded, was the sale of current water rights by entities not utilizing their full allowance. The proposal of this strategy resulted in only one willing potential participant, which would not have resulted in enough water to fulfill a need.

The North East Region (D) is taking a much closer look at strategies to meet the needs of smaller communities and districts. This area, traditionally with a large rural population, is concerned that these smaller areas have been overlooked in the past but have real needs that can be better addressed at this level of planning.

Conclusion

Interest in water resources and participation in water planning has increased dramatically as a result of Senate Bill 1. The results include increasing public involvement through establishment of the RWPGs, establishing a dialogue among participating state agencies and with stakeholders and raising public awareness through the RWPG public meetings and the resulting news articles and television exposure. Stakeholders now participate in regional planning as part of their job or level of interest, rather than reading about the state water policies and plans. Many more stakeholders are participating in the actual planning decisions than before Senate Bill 1.

Water patterns and trends for the state of Texas are now regionalized to a certain extent. Senate Bill 1 encourages all parts of the state to address their unique needs in more individual ways. Although the 1961 water plan indicated that planning had become too local and short-sighted, subsequent plans might have been considered too broad in scale and statewide in focus. With the passage of Senate Bill 1, the pendulum of water planning is somewhere in the middle.

Table 1. Proposed surface water management strategies and unique reservoir site designations

Regional Location	Selected Water Management Strategy	Recommended Reservoir Site	Approximate Firm Yield* (acre-feet/year)	Proposed Unique Sites for Reservoir Construction
Region C				
Red River and Titus counties	Marvin Nichols I (in Region D)		619,100	Marvin Nichols I (in Region D)
Fannin County	Lower Bois d'Arc aka New Bonham		123,000	Lower Bois d'Arc aka New Bonham
Cooke County	Muenster		4,700	Muenster
Freestone County			68,300	Tehuacana
Region D, North East Texas				
Gregg and Smith counties		Prairie Creek	17,215 to 115,000 (in phased development)	Prairie Creek
Red River and Titus counties		Marvin Nichols I	619,000	Marvin Nichols I
Delta and Lamar counties			129,700	George Parkhouse II
Smith, Upshur, and Wood counties			324,000	Waters Bluff
Harrison County			144,900	Little Cypress
Upshur and Wood counties			46,600	Big Sandy
Rains, Wood, and Van Zandt counties			95,630	Carl Estes
Gregg, Harrison, Panola, and Rusk counties			537,000	Carthage (in Region I)
Gregg, Rusk, and Smith counties			5,500	Kilgore II
Bowie County			No information	Barkman
Red River and Lamar counties			No information	Big Pine
Bowie County			35,840	Liberty Hills
Red River County			1,866	Pecan Bayou
Titus County			280,100	Marvin Nichols II
Delta and Hopkins counties			113,500	George Parkhouse I
Region G, Brazos				
Milam County	Little River		169,800	
Throckmorton and Shackelford counties	Breckenridge–Reynold's Bend		20,000	
Young and Stephens counties	South Bend		106,700	
Eastland and Throckmorton counties	Cisco, Throckmorton, Woodson		500, 200, 100 respectively	
Bosque, Limestone, and Somervell counties	Off-channel reservoirs		4,074	

(continued)

Table 1. *Continued*

Regional Location	Selected Water Management Strategy	Recommended Reservoir Site	Approximate Firm Yield* (acre-feet/year)	Proposed Unique Sites for Reservoir Construction
Falls County	Brushy Creek		2,000	
Brazos and Grimes counties	Millican–Bundic		73,580	
Region H				
Milam County	Little River (in Region G)		170,000	Little River (in Region G)
Austin County	Allen's Creek		99,650	Allen's Creek
Madison, Grimes, and Walker counties	Bedias		90,000	Bedias
Region I, East Texas				
Cherokee and Smith counties	Eastex		85,507	Eastex
Tyler, Angelina, Trinity, Polk, and Jasper counties			620,000	Rockland
Newton County			61,700	Big Cow Creek
Newton County and Beauregard Parish, Louisiana			440,000	Bon Weir
Panola, Harrison, Rusk, and Gregg counties			537,000	Carthage
Rusk, Gregg, and Smith counties			5,500	Kilgore
Smith and Rusk counties			3,500	Rabbit Creek
Rusk County			22,000	State Highway 322, Stage I
Rusk County			13,000	State Highway 322, Stage II
Panola County			39,131	Socagee
Panola County			280,000	Stateline
Cherokee County			105,966 (approximated)	Ponta
Anderson, Cherokee, and Houston counties			186,840 (approximated)	Fastrill (formerly Weches)
Region J				
	Johnson Creek		10,851 (average annual, not firm yield)	
Region K, Lower Colorado				
	Off-channel reservoirs		330,000 maximum	
Mills County				Mills County–5 sites
Region P, Lavaca				
Jackson County			30,000	Palmetto Bend II
Totals	17	2		39

* *Yields shown are approximate, subject to modification, and may not represent the actual firm yield.*

Senate Bill 1 has placed an emphasis on drought planning as a proactive and preventative measure. Although drought was a consideration in the past, the more severe case of drought of record is used to plan conservatively for future water supplies and needs. In some regions, particularly in the eastern part of the state, the standard approach of creating reservoir systems and drilling new wells to address water needs prevails. In the more arid central, western, and southern areas, slightly more innovative means of capturing water are being explored because much of the existing water is already committed. Increased implementation and acceptance of alternative technologies or methods such as desalination, conservation, wastewater reuse, and brush control are a continuation of the trend that began with recent water plans. Also, in nearly all regions, water is seen as a precious, limited commodity to be conserved, used, and reused. It seems that the geological principle "the present is the key to the past" has morphed slightly for water planning in Texas and has now become "the past is the key to the future."

References

Texas Board of Water Engineers. *A Plan for Meeting the 1980 Requirements of Texas.* Austin, May, 1961. Reprint, June, 1963.

Texas Natural Resource Conservation Commission. "Texas Public Water Systems Limiting Water Use to Avoid Shortages," table. Pers. comm., Mike Lannen, Austin, August 15, 2000.

Texas Water Development Board (TWDB). *The Texas Water Plan,* Austin: TWDB, November, 1968. Reprint, January, 1982.

———. *Summary of Historical Water Use.* Austin: TWDB, Water Resources Planning Division, 1980.

———. *Water for Texas: A Consensus-Based Update to the State Water Plan,* vol. 2: Technical Planning Appendix. Document GP-6-2. Austin: TWDB, 1997.

———. *Regional Water Planning Areas and Special Water Resources, Adopted Rules for: Regional Water Planning Grants, Regional Water Planning Guidelines.* State Water Planning Guidelines and Initial Coordinating Body Representatives. Austin: TWDB, March 11, 1998.

PART II

Regional Assessment

Although all of Texas faces a water crisis, the sixteen regions are sufficiently different from one another in geography, climate, and population to make any one solution unworkable. Each region has distinct issues and will require solutions that reflect this uniqueness. This section deals with some of the ways in which individual regions are approaching the coming shortages.

Lloyd V. Urban and A. Wayne Wyatt discuss the large semiarid region of the Panhandle and the Upper Colorado River (Regions A, O, and F), where water supplies originate mainly from the Ogallala aquifer and surface water that appears seasonally in playa lakes. This area is not extensively urbanized but must create a water plan that offers enough resources to meet its growing agricultural needs.

Richard A. Earl and Todd H. Votteler examine the San Antonio–Austin area, known as the Texas Hill Country. These cities use the Edwards and Trinity aquifers for their main water supply. The area suffers both from frequent droughts and from large floods, and difficulties are worsening with rising population. However, the region's main water problem is more entrenched in legality: several cities are competing for the same usage in a "use it or lose it" mentality.

The Coastal Bend region also faces frequent droughts, but C. Alan Berkebile and colleagues describe it as one of the Texas success stories. Historically, Corpus Christi relied on the Nueces River and some smaller aquifers, but these were not enough to support increases in population and agriculture. The response was developing more reservoirs, creating an aggressive conservation program, and facilitating interbasin transfers with other water suppliers, all before Senate Bill 1 was voted into place.

Region H, which includes the Houston area, also fights a dwindling water supply for a burgeoning population.

Four river basins and three aquifers are current water resources. However the pumping of groundwater causes subsidence of land and leads to further flood issues. Therefore Houston must switch most of its groundwater dependence to surface water sources. This region must also consider the problem of flood control by looking at large-scale channel improvements and the possibility of voluntary property buyouts for people who have settled in floodplain areas.

Glenn C. Clingenpeel's chapter is focused on the Dallas–Fort Worth water system, which is supplied by the Trinity River and its tributaries. The river, historically a polluted nightmare, is now relatively clean despite being heavily impacted by the urbanization and agriculture of the area. In this region issues revolve around water quality, not quantity, with emphasis on what can be done to ensure that the Trinity continues to stay clean.

CHAPTER 5

Water Resources of the Panhandle and Upper Colorado Regions of Texas

Lloyd V. Urban

Professor of Civil Engineering and Director

Water Resources Center, Texas Tech University

A. Wayne Wyatt

Manager

High Plains Underground Water Conservation District No. 1

Abstract

The Panhandle and Upper Colorado regions of Texas cover a vast area characterized by a predominantly semiarid climate, a relatively low population, and an economy based primarily on agriculture. The subject area is defined to include the seventy-four counties that form Senate Bill 1 planning regions A, O, and F. This combined area represents almost one-third of the entire state, extends from the Texas-Oklahoma border in the north to the Hill Country in the south, and includes portions of the Canadian, Red, Brazos, Colorado, and Rio Grande basins.

The overall area has prospered, but it has developed a thirst for water that has often exceeded nature's capacity to provide. Municipalities, industries, and agriculture have turned to the Ogallala and other aquifers and to the development of limited surface supplies in order to meet regional needs. Surface water authorities and underground water districts have been formed to protect and conserve the area's water resources. Throughout the area, significant quantities of both surface water and groundwater are transported over vast distances, primarily to meet municipal and industrial demands. This chapter presents an overview of the historic water resource use in the Panhandle and Upper Colorado regions of Texas, examines some water-related issues specific to the regions, and provides a view to the future as regional water planning groups respond to the requirements of Senate Bill 1.

Regional Descriptions

The Panhandle and Upper Colorado regions of Texas include all or parts of numerous aquifers and river basins. Because of the area's large size, climate, soils, and other natural features vary considerably. A contemporary political definition of the area was selected, and geographical and other—primarily water-related—descriptions may be utilized to form the basis for a discussion of the water resources of the area, past, present and future.

In 1997, the 75th Texas Legislature passed Senate Bill 1 (SB 1), a "bottom up" water planning process designed to ensure that the water needs of the state are met as Texas enters the twenty-first century. The Texas Water Development Board (TWDB) identified sixteen regional planning areas, established rules, and selected 270 individuals from eleven interest groups to serve as initial members of each regional water planning group (TWDB 2000). Region A (Panhandle Water Planning Area), Region O (Llano Estacado Region), and Region F form the overall area identified in this chapter as the Panhandle and Upper Colorado regions of Texas, although Region F includes a portion of the Rio Grande basin watershed (fig. 1). As shown in table 1, the total area of the three water planning regions is slightly over 80,000 square miles, or approximately 30 percent of the entire state, and the 2000 population is estimated to be 1,492,118, or approximately 7.1 percent of the state total (TWDB 2000).

The State of Texas has been divided into eleven natural regions classified on the basis of physiographic and biological differences (TPWD 2000). All or parts of six of these regions may be found in SB 1 regions A, O, and F.

Figure 1. Senate Bill 1 planning regions A, O, and F.

The three SB 1 regions lie within five of the fifteen major river basins designated by TWDB (1997), and all or parts of five of the state's nine major aquifers, along with over half of the twenty minor aquifers, may be found in the area.

SB 1 Region A

The Panhandle Water Planning Area consists of twenty-one counties: Armstrong, Carson, Childress, Collingsworth, Dallam, Donley, Gray, Hall, Hansford, Hartley, Hemphill, Hutchinson, Lipscomb, Moore, Ochiltree, Oldham, Potter, Randall, Roberts, Sherman, and Wheeler. Although it covers approximately 7.6 percent of the state, its 2000 population is estimated at only about 1.8 percent of that of the state. Regional population is expected to increase to 552,072 by 2050, with most of the increase occurring in larger communities and declining population expected in rural areas (TWDB 2000). The largest city in the region is Amarillo, with population estimated to be 177,644 in 2000, and the area includes seven other cities with population ranging between 2,500 and 10,000.

Major economic activities in Region A are agriculture and agribusiness, oil and gas operations, and wholesale and retail trade. Primary water-using activities include irrigation, petroleum refining, agricultural production, and food processing. With irrigation, the region produces 35 percent of the wheat, 49 percent of the corn, 14 percent of the grain sorghum, 74 percent of the swine, and 47 percent of the beef slaughter capacity in the state (PWPG 2000).

Approximately two-thirds of Region A is in the High Plains natural region, a relatively high plateau characterized by relatively flat terrain gradually sloping to the southwest. Nearly 5,000 playa lakes—shallow, round depressions that dot the landscape—form an important el-

Table 1. Demographic Data

	Region A	Region O	Region F	Combined Regions	Texas
Number of counties	21	21	32	74	254
Area, sq. mi.	19,742	20,294	40,054	80,090	266,807
Percent of state	7.6%	7.55%	15.0%	30.1%	
2000 Population (est.)	379,018	474,897	638,203	1,492,118	20,866,699
Percent of state	1.8%	2.3%	3.0%	7.15%	
2050 Population (est.)	552,072	586,156	921,907	2,060,135	39,619,648
Percent of state	1.4%	1.5%	2.3%	5.2%	

Source: Texas Water Development Board (2000).

Table 2. Estimated 2000 water demands (acre-feet)

	Region A	Region O	Region F	Combined Regions	Texas
Municipal	84,814	87,360	147,106	319,280	4,232,341
Irrigation	1,522,985	3,065,373	648,652	5,237,010	9,678,382
Industrial	63,810	59,782	61,232	184,824	2,656,906
Livestock	46,793	42,538	24,509	113,840	330,572
Total	1,718,402	3,255,053	881,499	5,854,954	16,898,201

Source: Texas Water Development Board (2000).

ement of surface hydrology and ecological diversity throughout the region. The Rolling Plains natural region cuts across the area along the Canadian River and also occurs in the southeast portion of the region, where it is separated from the High Plains natural region by the Caprock Escarpment. Precipitation ranges from about 22 inches along the eastern boundary to about 16 inches on the west and occurs primarily during the summer months (PWPG 2000).

Region A lies within the Canadian River and Red River basins. The Canadian River originates in New Mexico, traverses the Panhandle, and flows into Oklahoma from Hemphill County. Three major reservoirs for municipal water supply and recreation have been constructed in the Texas portion of the basin: Lake Meredith, Palo Duro Reservoir, and Rita Blanca Lake. The Red River basin is found in the southeast portion of Region A. Major reservoirs in the basin include Greenbelt Reservoir and Bivens Lake. Two major aquifers, the Ogallala and the Seymour, and four minor aquifers (Blaine, Rita Blanca, Whitehorse, and Dockum) serve as water sources for the region (PWPG 2000). Irrigation accounts for the bulk of current water demand in the region (table 2).

SB 1 Region O

The Llano Estacado Region is made up of twenty-one counties: Bailey, Briscoe, Castro, Cochran, Crosby, Dawson, Deaf Smith, Dickens, Floyd, Gaines, Garza, Hale, Hockley, Lamb, Lubbock, Lynn, Motley, Parmer, Swisher, Terry, and Yoakum. The region encompasses about 7.5 percent of the state and contains about 2.3 percent of the state's total population. Region O population is expected to reach 586,156 by 2050. Lubbock, with an estimated 2000 population of 204,026, is the largest city in the region, and ten other cities with population in excess of 5,000 persons are also located in the planning region (LERWPG 2000).

The primary economic base of Region O is agriculture.

Other significant contributors to the economy include oil and gas production, allied health, education, and agricultural processing. Approximately 60 percent of the state's cotton, 16 percent of its grain sorghum, and 25 percent of its corn are produced in the Llano Estacado Region. Irrigation accounts for the vast majority of the region's water use (LERWPG, 2000).

Approximately 80 percent of Region O lies within the High Plains natural region, and the Rolling Plains natural region constitutes the remainder. Elevation varies from about 1,900 feet in the southeast to about 4,300 feet in the northwest. Precipitation ranges from a high of about twenty-two inches per year in a portion of Crosby County to a low of sixteen inches per year in the southwestern portion of the region. Approximately fourteen thousand playa lakes provide the principal drainage for the High Plains portion of Region O (LERWPG 2000).

Region O includes the upstream parts of the Canadian, Red, Brazos, and Colorado basins. Major reservoirs include MacKenzie Reservoir in the Red River basin and Alan Henry and White River reservoirs in the Brazos River basin. Little surface water leaves the region. Two major aquifers (Ogallala and Seymour) and two minor aquifers (Edwards-Trinity and Dockum) supply water to the area (LERWPG 2000). As shown in table 2, irrigation accounts for most (nearly 95 percent) of the region's estimated 2000 water demand.

SB 1 Region F

The thirty-two counties of Region F are Andrews, Borden, Brown, Coke, Coleman, Concho, Crane, Crockett, Ector, Glasscock, Howard, Irion, Kimble, Loving, McCulloch, Martin, Mason, Menard, Midland, Mitchell, Pecos, Reagan, Reeves, Runnels, Schleicher, Scurry, Sterling, Sutton, Tom Green, Upton, Ward, and Winkler. The planning region is approximately the size of Regions A and O combined, or about 15 percent of the state's total area. The estimated 2000 population is about three percent of the state total and is expected to exceed 920,000 by 2050. Major cities and their 2000 estimated populations are Midland (109,885), Odessa (100,383), and San Angelo (99,750).

Although the largest employment sectors in Region F are the service industry, wholesale and retail trade, and the oil and gas industry, agriculture plays an extremely important role. The market value of crops and livestock in 1997 was almost $600 million, with livestock accounting for about 60 percent and crops accounting for the remainder of the total (RFWPG 2000).

Precipitation increases from west to east, ranging from just over ten inches per year in Reeves County to over twenty-eight inches per year in Brown County. Five of the state's eleven natural regions are found in Region F: High Plains, Rolling Plains, Trans-Pecos, Edwards Plateau, and Llano Uplift. As might be expected, the region is extremely diverse with respect to topography, soils, vegetation, and other natural features. The western half of it is underlain by the Permian Basin, well known for its oil and gas production.

Most of Region F is in the upper portion of the Colorado basin and in the Pecos portion of the Rio Grande basin; the remainder is in a small part of the Brazos basin. Nineteen major reservoirs have been constructed in the region, with sixteen in the Colorado basin and three in the Rio Grande basin. These reservoirs provide most of the region's municipal water supply. Major aquifers in the region are the Edwards-Trinity Plateau, Ogallala, and Cenozoic Pecos Alluvium. Eight minor aquifers provide additional supply: Dockum, Hickory, Lipan, Trinity, Ellenburger–San Saba, Marble Falls, Rustler, and the Capitan Reef Complex (RFWPG 2000). Table 2 shows that irrigation far outstrips all other demands in Region F, accounting for almost three-quarters of the total regional demand estimated for 2000.

Historical Perspective

The Panhandle and Upper Colorado regions have a long and rich history, beginning with archaeological evidence showing that Native Americans have been present in these regions since 11,500 B.P. (Handbook of Texas Online 2000a). Playas and ancient springs in the Panhandle and the Colorado, Pecos, and Concho rivers to the south provided water essential to plants and animals, thus becoming popular sites for hunting and camping.

In the High Plains, recorded history begins with Coronado's traverses of the area in 1541. Coronado found the region to be well populated by both bison and Native Americans, supported by playas, grass, and other features offering a relatively hospitable environment. A 150-year period of extensive Spanish exploration followed, but settlements, ranches, and missions were built primarily in New Mexico and what is now Central Texas. Although most of the Spaniards had been driven out of the region by the Comanche invasion of the 1700s, residents of Spanish New Mexico sought a peaceful coexistence and established a thriving trade with the Indians in the 1780s. Making use of the playas and springs as water sources, Comancheros (traders) developed a network of roads across the Llano Estacado and continued trading guns, blankets, tobacco, meat, slaves, and stolen cattle for almost a century (Murrah 1994).

In the early 1800s, the United States government sent explorers into the Great Plains, but their reports, unlike those of the Spaniards, described a barren wasteland, giving rise to the area being referred to as "the Great American Desert." To the south, Spanish missions of the 1700s gave way to the forts of the middle 1800s, providing staging areas for exploration and conquest to the lands lying to the north and west. The Civil War interrupted the exploration phase, but shortly thereafter, the campaign to defeat the "hostiles" began anew. Myths regarding the High Plains persisted until Colonel Ranald Mackenzie crossed the southern Llano Estacado in the 1870s and discovered the truth about the region's resources. By 1874, the military had ended Indian domination, and the westward push was on. By the mid-1880s, the once vast buffalo herds were gone, and the plains were full of cattle (Murrah 1994).

Although agriculture was profitable in wet years, long periods of drought took their toll on farmers and ranchers alike. In the High Plains, it was soon discovered that the solution often lay only a few feet beneath the ground: the water needs of both livestock and households could be met with hand-dug wells. Windmills, coming into general use after the Civil War, could be built or purchased from a growing list of manufacturers and could provide settlers with the means to sustain themselves during prolonged droughts (Baker 1976). By 1908, the first steam-driven irrigation system was constructed and the era of irrigated agriculture in the Texas High Plains had begun (Judd n.d.). The Texas Land and Development Company took advantage of the irrigation potential by drilling a well adjacent to the Santa Fe Depot in Plainview, ensuring that each prospective land buyer's first view would be of water gushing from the ground at 1,500 gallons per minute (Brunson 1970). By 1940, 2,180 irrigation wells had been drilled in the Texas High Plains (White et al. 1946). Growth accelerated after World War II and by the 1970s an estimated 71,000 wells were being used to irrigate approximately 6.4 million acres (Judd 1979). Groundwater use peaked in 1977 at 8.24 million acre-feet (High Plains Associates 1982).

In other parts of the Upper Colorado region, the influence of water also had a pronounced effect on settlement after the Civil War. San Angelo became a town as a result of Fort Concho, located at the confluence of the North Concho and the combined Middle and South branches (Handbook of Texas Online 2000b). Big Spring was named for the nearby large spring, well known to Indians, explorers, and cattlemen (Handbook of Texas Online 2000c). Throughout the Panhandle and Upper Colorado regions, a vast railroad network was established. Frequent water stops for the steam engines were necessary, and often wherever the train stopped was a convenient place to unload or take on shipments of cattle, passengers, or goods. Settlements followed, giving a possible answer to the frequently asked question, "Why on earth did they put a town *there*?"

The Ogallala

The High Plains of Texas are the southernmost extension of the Great Plains physiographic province of North America and extend approximately 300 hundred miles south of the Texas-Oklahoma line, covering about 35,000 square miles. About half the area is in cultivation and half is in grass and pasture (Urban 1992).

The High Plains aquifer system underlies most of the Texas High Plains, and the principal water-bearing unit of the system is the Ogallala formation. The Ogallala generally consists of layers of coarse-grained sand and gravel in the lower part, grading upward into fine clay, silt, and sand (Peckham and Ashworth 1993). A caliche layer known as the caprock occurs just beneath the surface of much of the area. The maximum thickness of the Ogallala formation is over 900 feet in Ochiltree County (on the Texas-Oklahoma border), and the saturated thickness ranges from only a few feet to over 500 feet, generally decreasing from north to south. Depth to the water table also varies greatly, ranging from a few feet to depths of 400 feet or more, and water moves slowly through the formation, generally toward the southeast. Water quality is generally good, with dissolved solids in the 300–1,000 mg/L

range and hardness in the "hard" category (Urban 1992). In recent years, the Ogallala has supplied irrigation water to about 4 million acres (TWDB 1997).

Throughout the early years of irrigation development, the supply of groundwater was thought to be inexhaustible, perhaps fed by Rocky Mountain snowmelt. Declining water levels and geologic and hydrologic studies disproved that theory, revealing that the Ogallala was indeed finite and, in fact, was replenished primarily by infiltration of precipitation on the surface (Peckham and Ashworth 1993). Estimates of the regional rate of recharge range from a few tenths of an inch to a few inches per year, and recharge is likely concentrated at playa lakes.

The Texas Board of Water Engineers was among the first to recognize and document declining water levels in the region. Maps were published in 1954 showing that declines of five to twenty-five feet were common during the fifteen-year period beginning in 1938 (Leggat 1954a). Furthermore, a follow-up board report indicated that drops of two to six feet occurred in the twelve-month period following the earlier report, with levels at some locations falling ten feet or more (Leggat 1954b). Subsequent studies showed further declines, and as the number of wells and pumping rates increased into the 1960s and '70s, predictions that the region would soon "run out of water" began to resonate. The average area-weighted water level drop in the High Plains aquifer in Texas was reported to be 33.7 feet from predevelopment to 1980 (U.S. Geological Survey 1995). However, with improvements in irrigation efficiency and overall management, those predictions have not been realized. The Texas Water Development Board (1997) recently reported that the total recoverable water in storage within the Ogallala, as calculated by a regional computer flow model, was 385 million acre-feet. Although down from 417 million acre-feet estimated in 1990, water table levels in several counties have stabilized, and a few have been recovering (Peckham and Ashworth 1993; *Cross Section* 2000).

Underground Water Conservation Districts

Recognizing the need for more effective groundwater management, the 51st Texas Legislature in 1949 authorized the establishment of underground water conservation districts to provide for the conservation, preservation, recharging, and prevention of waste of groundwater and to control subsidence. At present, there are twenty-two underground water conservation districts in operation in the three SB 1 regions under discussion. Region A districts include the Collingsworth County, Dallam County, Hemphill County, and High Plains Underground Water Conservation districts and the North Plains and Panhandle Groundwater districts. All or parts of eighteen counties of the region are included in these six districts (PWPG 2000).

In Region O, six districts are currently active: the High Plains, Sandy Land, Mesa, South Plains, Garza County, and Llano Estacado. All or parts of seventeen counties of the region are included in these districts (LERWPG 2000).

Parts or all of sixteen counties are included in the eleven underground water conservation districts in Region F: the Plateau, Sutton County, Glasscock County, Sterling County, Santa Rita, Permian Basin, Lipan-Kickapoo, Irion County, Hickory, Emerald, and Coke County districts. Ten of the districts in Region F form the West Texas Regional Ground Water Alliance, an organization that promotes the conservation, preservation, and beneficial use of water and related resources in the region (RFWPG 2000).

The High Plains Underground Water Conservation District No. 1 was the first district in the state created under the 1949 legislation. It was established in 1951 and headquartered in Lubbock, with all or parts of thirteen counties included in its jurisdiction. Additional territory has since been annexed; the district now consists of six full counties (Lubbock, Parmer, Cochran, Lynn, Hale, and Bailey) and parts of nine more counties (Armstrong, Castro, Crosby, Deaf Smith, Floyd, Hockley, Lamb, Potter, and Randall). District No. 1 has developed a management philosophy giving rise to a series of strategies. Through activities and rules aimed at issues such as well spacing, well permitting, production regulation, water level monitoring, data collection, and education, the district has developed a well-respected and often emulated water management program. Information is disseminated on its website, through special reports, and through its monthly newsletter, the *Cross Section,* which has a circulation of 6,737 with readership in all fifty states and fifty-three foreign countries. In addition, the district participates in the state's Agricultural Water Conservation Equipment Loan Program and has loaned over $15.3 million to area farmers and ranchers, who have used these loans to install more than 480 new, efficient center-pivot irrigation systems. Data collected from a network of observation wells in the district indicate that the average decline during the nine-year period from 1962 to 1970 was 2.5 feet per year.

During the 1970s, when irrigation peaked, the average annual decline was 1.42 feet. During the 1980s, a relatively wet decade, the average decline was reduced to 0.49 feet per year, and during the 1990s, which included a period of record drought, the drop averaged only 1.13 feet each year over the area.

Surface Water Development

Because surface water is rather limited in SB 1 planning regions A, O, and F, most of the available water from rivers and streams has been fully developed through various federal, state, and local projects and programs. These supplies are primarily managed through the several river authorities, water authorities, and surface water districts that operate within the regions. Major water providers in Region A are the Canadian River Municipal Water Authority (CRMWA), Greenbelt Municipal and Industrial Water Authority, and the City of Amarillo; the CRMWA, White River Municipal Water District, Mackenzie Municipal Water Authority, and City of Lubbock in Region O; and the Colorado River Municipal Water District (CRMWD) and Brown County Water Improvement District No. 1 in Region F. Additional water suppliers (e.g., municipalities and utilities) also provide significant amounts of water to users, principally in Region F.

The Canadian River Project

The Canadian River originates in the mountains of northeastern New Mexico and takes a 180-mile eastward path across the Texas Panhandle. With substantial flows cutting a broad valley (the "Canadian Breaks") some 400 to 500 feet deep through the alluvium of the Ogallala, the Canadian became the only stream on the Texas High Plains capable of large-scale development (Templer and Urban 1997). The Canadian River Project was authorized by Congress in 1950, and in 1953 the Texas Legislature authorized the Canadian River Municipal Water Authority (CRMWA) to distribute water from Lake Meredith to the eleven member cities: Amarillo, Borger, Pampa, Plainview, Lubbock, Slaton, Brownfield, Levelland, Lamesa, Tahoka, and O'Donnell. The U.S. Bureau of Reclamation began construction on the project in 1962 and completed Lake Meredith in 1965. The dam, located nine miles west of Borger, is 226 feet high and 6,380 feet long. The aqueduct system includes 322 miles of pipelines, ten pumping stations, and three regulating reservoirs, with water treatment plants at Amarillo, Plainview, Borger, and Lubbock. The CRMWA serves industry and over 450,000 municipal residents in the Canadian, Red, Brazos, and Colorado River basins, making the project one of Texas' best-known examples of successful interbasin transfer. To counter problems associated with extended drought and high salinity, CRMWA has acquired extensive groundwater rights in Roberts County located in Region A to reduce dependency on Lake Meredith and to improve water quality. In addition, a salinity control project has been initiated to improve the quality of water coming into Lake Meredith (CRMWA 2000).

Colorado River Municipal Water District (CRMWD)

By enacting legislation that was used as a model for subsequent municipal water districts, the Texas Legislature created the CRMWD in 1949 to provide water to the district's member cities of Odessa, Big Spring, and Snyder. (Handbook of Texas Online 2000d). The district has grown substantially over the years and currently owns, maintains, and operates ten dams and reservoirs as well as over six hundred miles of water transmission lines and twenty-one pump stations. In addition to its member cities, CRMWD supplies water to Midland, San Angelo, Stanton, Robert Lee, Grandfalls, Pyote, and Abilene. Three of the reservoirs are on the Colorado River: Lake J. B. Thomas, the E. V. Spence Reservoir, and the O. H. Ivie Reservoir. Historically, extended droughts have severely reduced quantity and quality of water in the district's reservoirs. The CRMWD operates several well fields, primarily used to supplement surface water deliveries during summer months. Another program involves diverting highly mineralized low flow from the Colorado River and Beals Creek, which would degrade water quality in Spence Reservoir. Instead, the otherwise undesirable water is delivered to oil companies for use in oil field secondary recovery operations (CRMWD 2000).

Playa Lakes

As noted in the initial description of SB 1 planning regions, playa lakes form an important part of the history, hydrology, and ecology of the Texas High Plains. These naturally occurring depressions provide the internal drainage for much of the region, concentrating stormwater runoff and forming lakes. Playa watersheds are essentially closed systems, with playa floors representing the deepest point of the watershed. In some locations, such as in the City of Lubbock, playas may fill and spill into adjacent basins, forming chains of lakes that are an integral part of local stormwater management systems. Most playas are ephemeral, holding water for a relatively short period after rainfall events.

Their origin has been the subject of speculation, studies, and extensive research programs, with everything including wallowing buffaloes, wind, chemistry, and natural geologic processes said to be responsible for their formation. Perhaps most, if not all of these factors may have influenced playa formation to some degree, and a recent study concluded that playas were formed from the integration of complex pedogenic, geomorphic, hydrochemical, and biological processes (Gustavson et al. 1995). Even the estimated number of playas in the state has varied, ranging from 15,000 to 30,000. In a recent study researchers at Texas Tech University used a Geographical Information Systems approach to analyze data from the Natural Resource Conservation Service and the U.S. Geological Survey to find and delineate 20,577 playa lakes in a sixty-five-county study area, which included virtually all of the Texas High Plains. Playa basins ranged in size from almost 850 acres in Ochiltree County to less that three-tenths of an acre in Glasscock County. The largest number of playas was found in Floyd County, with 1,721 individual lakes, and average size overall was about twenty-five acres (Fish et al. 1998).

Playas are important to the wildlife in the region. Nearly two hundred species of birds, nine species of amphibians, at least thirty-seven species of mammals, and several species of reptiles have been associated with playas. In the fall and spring, migratory waterfowl utilize playas during migration between wintering and summering grounds, and many—geese in particular—are utilizing them for wintering. Playas are also used as breeding and nesting areas for some species of waterfowl and provide important habitat for pheasants and other upland game. A total of 346 different types of plants is reported to have been found in playa basins (LERWPG 2000).

In addition to their importance to vegetation and wildlife, many playas concentrate stormwater runoff and account for a considerable amount of playa-focused recharge to the Ogallala (Mullican et al. 1997). In other cases, many playas that have tended to hold water for extended periods have been modified to encourage recharge, and others have been equipped with pumps to be used for supplemental irrigation or to recycle irrigation tailwater captured and concentrated there. Approximately thirty feedyards use playa basins and catchment ponds for feedlot runoff management (LERWPG 2000).

Weather Modification

Efforts to increase precipitation in the High Plains and Upper Colorado regions of Texas date back a hundred years or more. In 1891, General Robert Dyrenforth used explosive balloons and artillery in attempts to make rainclouds develop in Midland, and the experiments with dynamite exploded at four-minute intervals by C. W. Post in Lynn and Garza counties between 1910 and 1914 are still discussed today. After discovery in the 1940s that dry ice could be used to produce ice crystals in certain clouds, thereby enhancing precipitation, and the subsequent discovery that silver iodide could produce similar results, the stage was set for scientifically based rainmaking. Weather modification activities increased in the 1950s and '60s, and in 1967 the state adopted a statute to control cloud seeding operations. At that time, the Texas Water Development Board became responsible for licensing and permitting weather modification in the state. They were also responsible for performing research and development on weather modification technology. The Texas Natural Resource Conservation Commission now administers the license and permit program (Handbook of Texas Online 2000e).

At present, there are seven aircraft-type weather modification projects in operation in Texas, and three of them are located in the High Plains and Upper Colorado regions (LERWPG 2000). One of these, the CRMWD program, is the longest-running operational project in the state, having started in 1971. Primary goals for the program have been (1) to determine the feasibility of aerial application of silver iodide for precipitation enhancement, (2) to increase water supplies to Lake Thomas and Spence Reservoir, and (3) to increase rainfall over agricultural areas. CRMWD reports that precipitation analyses indicate a 35 percent increase for rain reporting stations in the fifteen-county target area, compared to only a 12 percent increase for reporting stations outside the target area. Further, the district reports a 44 percent increase in cotton yield in the seeded counties, a 37 percent increase for downwind counties, and a 6 percent increase for upwind counties in recent years (CRMWD 2000).

The High Plains Underground Water Conservation District No. 1 began a cloud seeding program in 1997. The program includes a target area covering 12,438 square miles at a total cost of about $517,000 per year, or 6.5 cents per acre per year. Results for the first three years of operation have been mixed but encouraging. The program is expected to continue for the foreseeable future (LEWRPG 2000). The West Texas Weather Modification Association program began in 1996 and covers all or parts of nine counties, primarily in the south portion of SB 1 Region F (RFWRPG 2000).

Future Water Resources Planning and Development

After assessing the population and water demand projections, SB 1 regional planning groups evaluated water supplies and water needs for various water user groups: municipal, industrial, steam-electric power, irrigation, mining, and livestock. Where needs were recognized, the planning groups began to identify opportunities for additional groundwater and surface water development. For communities in the High Plains, conventional groundwater development strategies to meet short-term needs consist primarily of locating and acquiring groundwater as near as possible to each city as the need arises. To provide for additional short-term and, to some extent, long-term regional needs, planners in SB 1 Region O will evaluate precipitation enhancement, brush control, desalination of brackish groundwater, water conservation, water reuse, irrigation application efficiency improvements, harvesting rainfall on farms, and secondary recovery of groundwater for possible application. Strategies being considered for meeting long-term needs include interconnection of municipal systems, industries, and feedlots to distribute available supplies efficiently from more distant sources; importation of water from areas of surplus; and advanced treatment of reclaimed water for potable uses.

In Region F, management strategies also include new groundwater well fields, water conservation, wastewater reuse, desalination, precipitation enhancement, and brush control. In addition, planners will consider changing to drought-tolerant crops, reallocation of reservoir storage, development of new surface water sources, and aquifer storage and recovery projects.

In Region A, strategies are focusing primarily on reducing irrigation demands with irrigation scheduling, changing crops and crop varieties, improved irrigation efficiency, and conservation tillage methods being considered. Precipitation enhancement is also included in the management options for reducing irrigation demands and improving dryland productivity.

Conclusions

While water resources in the Panhandle and Upper Colorado regions of Texas are limited, the citizens of the area have managed to make the best of what is available. Development of surface and groundwater supplies, often piping water over hundreds of miles, has transformed the area into one with major cities, significant manufacturing centers, and a rich agricultural economy—all vital to the future of Texas. Through effective management by municipalities, surface and underground water conservation districts, and other agencies, limitations of available water sources have been recognized and programs have been put into place to ensure that conservation and wise use practices are the order of the day. As SB 1 planning groups look to the twenty-first century, strategies for meeting anticipated needs of the citizens of the region are being developed with expectations that those future needs may be fully realized. It will not be a simple task, but it is one that is being taken very seriously by those who bear the responsibility of seeing that the job gets done.

References

Baker, T. L. "History of Water Supply Projects in the Southwest." In *Water Utilization Studies in the Dry Lands,* ed. R. M. Sweazy. International Center for Arid and Semi-Arid Land Studies. Lubbock: Texas Tech University, 1976.

Brunson, B. R. *The Texas Land and Development Company.* Austin: University of Texas Press, 1970.

CRMWA. 2000. Canadian River Municipal Water Authority. June 12, 2000. Available at http://www.crmwa.com/.

CRMWD. 2000. Colorado River Municipal Water District. June 12, 2000. Available at http://www.crmwd.org/.

Cross Section. "Ground Water Levels Declined 0.68 of a Foot Within District in 1999." High Plains Underground Water Conservation District No. 1, vol. 46, no. 4, 2000.

Fish, E. B., et al. *Playa Lakes Digital Database for the Texas Portion of the Playa Lakes Joint Venture Region* (CD-ROM). Technical Publication T-9-813. Lubbock: College of Agricultural Sciences and Natural Resources, Texas Tech University, 1998.

Gustavson, T. C., et al. *Origin and Development of Playa Basins, Sources of Recharge to the Ogallala Aquifer, Southern High Plains, Texas and New Mexico.* Report of Investigations no. 229. Austin: Bureau of Economic Geology, 1995.

Handbook of Texas Online. 2000a. Exploration. June 12, 2000. Available at http://www.tsha.utexas.edu/handbook/online/articles/view/EE/uzeuj.html.

———. 2000b. Concho River. June 12, 2000. Available at http://www.tsha.utexas.edu/handbook/online/articles/view/.

———. 2000c. Big Spring, Tx. June 12, 2000. Available at http://www.tsha.utexas.edu/handbook/online/articles/view/BB/heb9.html.

———. 2000d. Colorado River Municipal Water District. June 12, 2000. Available at http://www.tsha.utexas.edu/handbook/online/articles/view/CC/mwc4.html.

———. 2000e. Weather Modification. June 12, 2000. Available athttp://www.tsha.utexas.edu/handbook/online/articles/view/WW/ymwed.html.

High Plains Associates. *Six-State High Plains Ogallala Aquifer Regional Resources Study.* Austin: High Plains Associates, 1982.

Judd, P. F. *An Introduction to Water and Water Conservation with Emphasis on the High Plains of Texas.* Lubbock: High Plains Underground Water Conservation District No. 1, 1979.

Leggat, E. R. *Summary of Ground-Water Development in the Southern High Plains, Texas.* Board of Water Engineers Bulletin no. 5402. Austin, 1954a.

———. *Ground-Water Development in the Southern High Plain, Texas,* 1953. Board of Water Engineers Bulletin no. 5410. Austin, 1954b.

Llano Estacado Regional Water Planning Group (LERWPG). *Llano Estacado Regional Water Plan, Task 1: Description of the Planning Region.* Prepared by HDR Engineering, Inc., January, 2000.

Mullican, W. F., et al. *Playas and Recharge of the Ogallala Aquifer on the Southern High Plains of Texas: An Examination Using Numerical Techniques.* Report of Investigations no. 242. Austin: Bureau of Economic Geology, 1997.

Murrah, D. J. "Playas and the Exploration and Settlement of the Llano Estacado." In *Proceedings of the Playa Basin Symposium,* ed. L. V. Urban and A. W. Wyatt, 5–21. Lubbock: Texas Tech University, 1994.

Panhandle Water Planning Group (PWPG). *Task 1: Description of Region.* Prepared by Freese and Nichols, Inc., et al., January 14, 2000.

Peckham, D. S., and J. B. Ashworth. *The High Plains Aquifer System of Texas, 1980 to 1990: Overview and Projections.* Texas Water Development Board Report 341, 1993.

Region F Water Planning Group (RFWPG). *Task 1 Draft Report: Description of Region F.* Prepared by Freese and Nichols, Inc., et al., 2000.

Templer, O. W., and L. V. Urban. "Integrated Use of Surface and Groundwater on the High Plains of West Texas." In *Papers and Proceedings of the Applied Geography Conferences,* ed. F. A. Schoolmaster, 119–27. Vol. 20, 1997.

Texas Parks and Wildlife Department (TWPD). 2000. Natural Regions of Texas. June 12, 2000. Available at http://www/tpwd.state.tx.us/nature/tx-eco95.htm/.

Texas Water Development Board (TWDB). *Water for Texas: A*

Consensus-Based Update to the State Water Plan, vol. 2. Document GP-6-2. Austin: TWDB, 1997.

———. 2000. SB 1 Water Planning. June 12, 2000. Available at http://www.twdb.state.tx.us/wrp/home.htm.

U.S. Geological Survey. *Water-Level Changes in the High Plains Aquifer, 1980 to 1994.* U.S. Geological Survey Fact Sheet. FS-215-95, 1995.

Urban, L. V. "Texas High Plains." In *Groundwater Exploitation in the High Plains,* ed. D. E. Kromm and S. E. White, 204–23. University Press of Kansas, 1992.

White, W. N., et al. Groundwater in the High Plains of Texas. U.S. Geological Survey Water Supply Paper no. 889-F, 1946.

CHAPTER 6

Major Water Issues Facing South-Central Texas

Richard A. Earl and Todd H. Votteler

Department of Geography

Texas State University–San Marcos

Abstract

Juxtaposed between humid East Texas and arid West Texas, south-central Texas has the problems of both regions plus unique problems related to its explosive population growth and its dependence upon the limestone Edwards Aquifer. These regional characteristics placed in the framework of federal and state law have produced a contentious, aggressive struggle over the region's water supplies. Every decade or so there is a multiyear drought during which the surface water supply and groundwater recharge drop to less than half the average. With large areas of exposed bedrock and thin, clay-rich soils, combined with frequent twenty-four-hour storms bringing precipitation exceeding ten inches, floods with extraordinary unit discharge amounts devastate the region.

Reliance on the Edwards Aquifer and the constant threat of drought have forced changes in both surface and groundwater law. Endangered Species Act lawsuits mandated the creation of the Edwards Aquifer Authority (EAA) in the 1993 Senate Bill 1477, which requires management of the aquifer to protect species dependent upon Comal Springs and San Marcos Springs. To date, the EAA has not developed a plan to restrict pumping during droughts so as to ensure critical flows from the springs. Faced with limitations on its Edwards Aquifer water supply, water utilities, most notably those serving the City of San Antonio, have initiated steps to acquire surface water and groundwater from other sources. These efforts have triggered calls for restrictions on interbasin transfers, as contained in the 1997 Senate Bill 1, and calls for restrictions on pumping from other aquifers, most notably the Carrizo-Wilcox Aquifer. The ensuing scramble for water supplies has pitted city against city, rural people against urban residents, and river basin against river basin. An amelioration of the present situation will require changes in Texas water law to permit more thorough utilization of water marketing tools that are used in other western states, such as conjunctive use, dry year options, water salvaging, and prior appropriation of groundwater.

In this chapter we describe and analyze some of the major water resource issues facing the south-central Texas region. We intend to demonstrate that the unique characteristics of a region under intense population growth have produced conflicts and crises that can only be resolved by fundamental changes in traditionally held attitudes and legal frameworks.

The South-Central Texas Region

Intermediate between humid East Texas and arid West Texas, south-central Texas has the problems of both regions plus unique problems related to its explosive population growth and its dependence upon the limestone

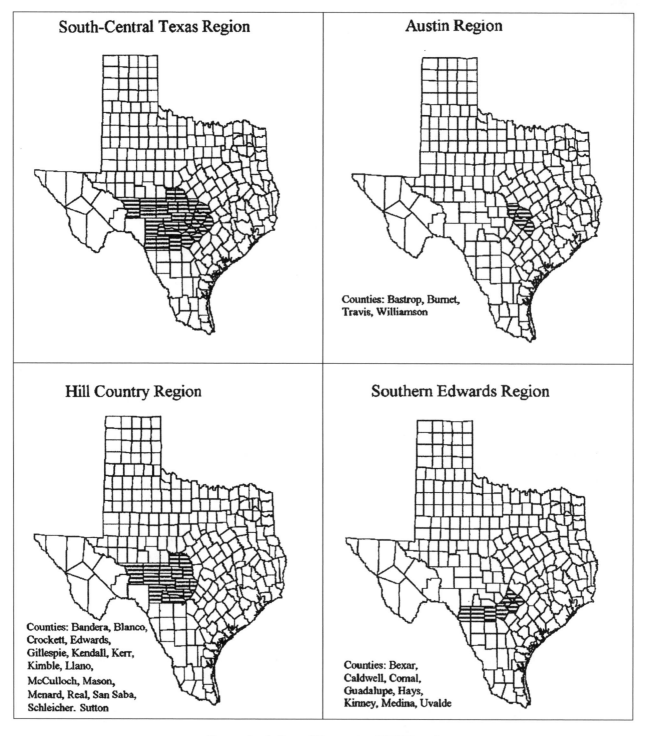

South-Central Texas Region

Austin Region

Counties: Bastrop, Burnet, Travis, Williamson

Hill Country Region

Counties: Bandera, Blanco, Crockett, Edwards, Gillespie, Kendall, Kerr, Kimble, Llano, McCulloch, Mason, Menard, Real, San Saba, Schleicher. Sutton

Southern Edwards Region

Counties: Bexar, Caldwell, Comal, Guadalupe, Hays, Kinney, Medina, Uvalde

Figure 1. South-Central Texas region (TWDB 1997).

Edwards Aquifer. These regional characteristics, placed in the framework of federal and state law, have produced a contentious, aggressive struggle over the region's water supplies. In drought years the area has less than half the average surface water supply and groundwater recharge.

The combination of large areas of exposed bedrock, thin, clay-rich soils, and frequent twenty-four-hour storms in which rainfall exceeds ten inches results in floods with extraordinary peak discharges ravaging the region.

For the purpose of this discussion, the south-central

Texas region is defined as the Texas Hill Country and the adjacent areas that receive its drainage. Most important, this region focuses upon the Austin–San Antonio urban corridor with its three million inhabitants. The region contains twenty-eight counties that constitute the "Austin Region," the "Hill Country Region," and the "Southern Edwards Region" of the 1997 state water plan, as shown in figure 1 (Texas Water Development Board 1997). Unfortunately, the Texas water planning regions that were created pursuant to Texas Senate Bill 1 (SB 1) in 1997 do not focus upon the Texas Hill Country and the Austin–San Antonio corridor. In the context of the regions created pursuant to SB 1, our study area contains parts of the SB 1 "South Central Texas," "Lower Colorado," "Plateau," and "Region F" shown in figure 2.

This region lies astride the Balcones Escarpment that separates the Texas Hill Country and Balcones Canyonlands landform districts of the Edwards Plateau (Fenneman 1931; 1938). The Balcones Escarpment breaks the Edwards Aquifer that underlies the Texas Hill Country and produces large springs along this topographic feature. Many of the major cities in the region, including Austin, San Marcos, New Braunfels, San Antonio, and Uvalde, were deliberately founded along the Balcones Escarpment at these spring sites (Brune 1975).

Explosive Sunbelt population growth has imposed serious demands on regional water resources and will do so increasingly. In 1960, the twenty-eight-county region had 1.2 million residents. Thirty years later, in 1990, it had doubled to 2.4 million, with a projected population of 6.7 million in 2050 (table 1; TWDB 1997). Between 1990 and 1998, spurred by booming high-tech industry, the Austin–San Marcos Metropolitan Statistical Area (MSA) was the fourth fastest growing large MSA in the United States (30.7 percent, with "large" defined as greater than 500,000). San Antonio was the twentieth fastest growing out of ninety-two large MSAs (16.1 percent; U.S. Bureau of the Census 1999).

Regional Water Supply

The spring sites where the Edwards Aquifer discharges along the Balcones Escarpment have been the locus of settlement in the region since the introduction of European culture, and in the case of San Marcos Springs, perhaps for ten thousand years or more (Shiner 1983). Both surface and groundwater sources are critical to the region. The region's climate straddles the boundary between dry climates (Koppen B) to the west and humid subtropical (Koppen Cfa) to the east. The region west of about 99°W has a subtropical semiarid climate, whereas the eastern part has a subhumid subtropical climate (Larkin and Bo-

Figure 2. The planning regions created pursuant to 1997 Texas Legislature SB 1 (TWDB 2000).

Table 1. Population in the south-central Texas region. For counties included, see figure 1.

Region	1960	% Total	1980	% Total	1990	% Total	2000	% Total	2030	% Total	2050	% Total
Texas	9,579,677		14,229,191		16,986,510		20,231,000		30,674,000		36,671,000	
Austin area	273,370	2.85	538,385	3.78	776,898	4.57	1,072,000	5.30	2,050,000	6.63	2,504,000	6.83
Hill Country area	86,543	0.90	116,436	0.82	136,119	0.80	173,000	0.86	213,000	0.69	240,000	0.65
Southern Edwards area	811,338	8.47	1,184,069	8.32	1,447,876	8.52	1,766,000	8.73	3,170,000	10.33	3,974,000	10.84
Region Total	1,171,251	12.22	1,838,890	12.92	2,360,893	13.09	3,011,000	14.88	5,433,000	17.71	6,718,000	18.32

Source: U.S. Bureau of the Census; Texas Water Development Board 1997.

mar 1983). Rather than a transitional climate between the two major climate types, the region irregularly swings between wetter than average and drier than average conditions. Because of this, regional water supply alternates between drought and flood conditions.

Understanding the extreme precipitation variability of the region is essential for understanding its water resources. "Average" precipitation and water supply values definitely do not signify "normal" conditions. For example, San Marcos has a long-term average annual precipitation of approximately 34 inches. Its wettest year was 1998 with 58.51 inches, which was immediately followed by its second driest year at 19.18 inches in 1999 (Sands 2000). As shown in table 2, San Antonio has a mean annual precipitation of 30.04 inches with a standard devia-

tion of 9.45 inches, which is 31 percent of the mean. This variability is nearly twice the world average variability for climates with similar precipitation amounts (Goudie and Wilkerson 1977). For San Antonio, during the last fifty years, 36 percent of the years have less than 25 inches (U.S. National Climate Data Center 2000).

The variability in the regional water supply is even greater than that of the precipitation. Runoff and groundwater recharge occur only after wetting the soil and evapotranspiration losses have occurred (Dunne and Leopold 1978). Consequently, when precipitation is low, negligible usable water is produced, whereas when there is above average precipitation, there is a disproportionate increase in surface and groundwater production (table 2). In years with between 60 and 80 percent of average precipitation,

Table 2. Precipitation, Edwards Aquifer recharge, and flow at Spring Branch of upper Guadalupe River

Year	Precipitation, San Antonio		Guadalupe River at Spring Branch			Edwards Recharge	
	inches	% mean	cfs	acre feet	% mean	acre feet	% mean
1950	19.86	66%	39	28,000	10%	200,000	27%
1951	24.44	81%	52	38,000	13%	140,000	19%
1952	26.24	87%	256	185,000	66%	276,000	38%
1953	17.56	58%	79	57,000	20%	168,000	23%
1954	13.70	46%	27	20,000	7%	162,000	22%
1955	18.18	61%	27	20,000	7%	192,000	26%
1956	14.31	48%	11	8,000	3%	44,000	6%
1957	48.83	163%	510	369,000	131%	1,143,000	155%
1958	39.69	132%	668	484,000	172%	1,711,000	232%
1959	24.50	82%	337	244,000	87%	690,000	94%
1960	29.76	99%	431	312,000	111%	825,000	112%
1961	26.47	88%	402	291,000	103%	717,000	97%
1962	23.90	80%	83	60,000	21%	239,000	32%
1963	18.65	62%	51	37,000	13%	171,000	23%
1964	31.88	106%	163	118,000	42%	413,000	56%
1965	36.65	122%	341	247,000	88%	624,000	85%
1966	21.44	71%	222	161,000	57%	615,000	84%
1967	29.26	97%	139	101,000	36%	467,000	63%
1968	30.40	101%	470	340,000	121%	885,000	120%
1969	31.42	105%	302	219,000	78%	611,000	83%
1970	22.74	76%	302	219,000	78%	662,000	90%
1971	31.80	106%	425	308,000	109%	925,000	126%
1972	31.49	105%	361	261,000	93%	756,000	103%
1973	52.28	174%	632	458,000	163%	1,487,000	202%
1974	37.00	123%	423	306,000	109%	659,000	90%
1975	25.67	85%	717	519,000	184%	973,000	132%
1976	39.13	130%	380	275,000	98%	894,000	121%

Guadalupe streamflow averages 44 percent of the fifty-year value, and Edwards recharge is only 51 percent of the average. Even including the Colorado River upstream of Lake Buchanan and the Guadalupe River upstream of Canyon Lake, virtually all of the streams in the region have gone completely dry during severe drought periods. Furthermore, the driest year has less than 20 percent of the long-term mean annual flow (table 3).

The persistence of dry conditions in the region limits the ability of reservoirs to provide water during lengthy droughts. Because of evaporation losses, a net value of two to three feet per year, and the need to meet permitted water demand, reservoirs can mitigate drought conditions for about a maximum of three years (Larkin and Bomar 1983). Because of this hydrologic reality, additional

reservoirs would have provided little if any additional water during the latter phases of long-term droughts such as occurred during 1950–56, 1962–66, and 1993–96.

Three major aquifers provide the region's groundwater supply. The Trinity aquifer supplies much of the Hill Country. The Carrizo-Wilcox Aquifer serves the eastern and southern portions of the region, and the Edwards Aquifer supplies the Balcones Escarpment region. Of these three, the most heavily utilized is the Edwards, which provides the sole water source for San Antonio, irrigation for approximately ninety thousand acres west of San Antonio, and a significant portion of the water supply for other cities along the Balcones Escarpment. The Edwards Aquifer is actually three hydrologically distinct aquifers: the northern segment, Barton Springs segment,

Table 2. *Continued*

Year	Precipitation, San Antonio		Guadalupe River at Spring Branch			Edwards Recharge	
	inches	% mean	cfs	acre feet	% mean	acre feet	% mean
1977	29.64	99%	544	394,000	140%	952,000	129%
1978	35.99	120%	650	471,000	167%	503,000	68%
1979	36.64	122%	766	555,000	197%	1,118,000	152%
1980	24.23	81%	225	163,000	58%	406,000	55%
1981	36.37	121%	791	573,000	203%	1,448,000	197%
1982	22.96	76%	224	162,000	58%	422,000	57%
1983	26.11	87%	162	117,000	42%	420,000	57%
1984	25.95	86%	106	77,000	27%	198,000	27%
1985	41.43	138%	680	492,000	175%	1,003,000	136%
1986	42.73	142%	628	455,000	162%	1,154,000	157%
1987	37.96	126%	1,319	955,000	339%	2,004,000	272%
1988	19.01	63%	283	205,000	73%	356,000	48%
1989	22.14	74%	118	85,000	30%	214,000	29%
1990	38.31	128%	292	211,000	75%	1,123,000	153%
1991	42.76	142%	629	455,000	162%	1,508,000	205%
1992	46.49	155%	1,461	1,058,000	376%	2,486,000	338%
1993	32.00	107%	278	201,000	72%	448,000	61%
1994	40.42	135%	256	185,000	66%	538,000	73%
1995	23.20	77%	256	185,000	66%	531,000	72%
1996	17.80	59%	168	122,000	43%	324,000	44%
1997	33.94	113%	1,086	786,000	279%	1,135,000	154%
1998	42.10	140%	498	361,000	128%	1,142,000	155%
1999	16.41	55%	170	123,000	44%	N/A	N/A
Mean	30.04		389	282,000		736,000	
Std. Dev.	9.45		317	230,000		520,000	
% Mean		31%	82%	82%			71%

Source: U.S. National Climate Data Center; U.S. Geological Society; Edwards Aquifer Authority.

Table 3. Mean annual flow, lowest daily flow, lowest yearly flow, and flood of record for selected streams in south-central Texas

Station Name and Number	Basin Area, sq. mi.	Mean Annual Flow, cfs	Mean Annual Flow, ac-ft	Lowest Daily Flow, cfs	Lowest Annual Flow, ac-ft	Flood of Record, cfs/year
Blanco River at Kyle, 08171300	412	158	114,000	0.0	3,000	139,000/1929
Colorado River at San Saba, 08147000	31,217	1,063	770,000	0.0	61,000	224,000/1938
Guadalupe River at Spring Branch, 08167500	1,315	197	143,000	0.0	9,000	160,000/1978
Llano River at Llano, 08151500	4,197	380	275,000	0.0	36,000	260,000/1997
Nueces River at Uvalde, 08192000	1,861	135	98,000	0.0	3,000	201,000/1996
Pedernales River at Johnson City, 08153500	901	197	143,000	0.0	3,000	441,000/1952
San Antonio River at San Antonio, 08178000	41.8	50.8	37,000	0.1	7,000	14,000/1998

Source: U.S. Geological Survey.

and San Antonio segment. Within each segment, extending in a north or northwest to south or southeasterly direction, there is a surface drainage or contributing zone, a surface water recharge zone, an artesian zone, and a zone of highly mineralized "bad water" (TWDB 1997). Over the last fifty years the largest of the three segments, the San Antonio, has had an average annual recharge of approximately 700,000 acre-feet, of which approximately 300,000 acre-feet discharges from Comal and San Marcos springs (table 2; U.S. Geological Survey). Because it is composed of porous, lower Cretaceous–age limestone, the Edwards Aquifer has high transmissivity and is highly susceptible to contamination and variability in recharge and pumping. These characteristics have led to attempts to protect its quality and springflow, thereby making it one of the aquifers most contested legally in the state.

Until recently, the limited population and irrigation agriculture of the Hill Country did not produce significant demands on the Trinity aquifer. This relatively deep aquifer, composed of a mix of lower Cretaceous–aged sedimentary rocks, has a large capacity but much slower response than the overlying Edwards Aquifer (TWDB 1997). The recent suburban "spillover" growth, largely west of Austin, has taxed the Trinity to the point of drying up residential wells, has forced the creation of a groundwater conservation district, and has led to the consideration of importing surface water from the Colorado River.

The southern- and easternmost of the major aquifers is the Carrizo-Wilcox, which is composed of Eocene-aged beach sandstone. Some portions of this aquifer have been heavily depleted, whereas other portions have maintained artesian flow. Indeed, artesian flow from this aquifer necessitated continuous pumping of the Aluminum Corporation of America (Alcoa) lignite mine near Rockdale. Recharge to this aquifer comes from both in situ infiltration and transmission losses from the rivers that cross this aquifer (TWDB 1997).

Flooding Hazards

The south-central Texas region is one of the most flood prone areas of the United States. Two major factors create this hazard. First, the Gulf of Mexico provides the region with a nearly infinite supply of very moist maritime tropical air. Second, the land surface of the region has low infiltration rates, producing high runoff rates, due to clay-rich, thin soils and exposed bedrock surfaces. Many stations with long-term records have twenty-four-hour amounts greater than 10 inches. According to the Lanning-Rush, Asquith, and Slade (1998), the maximum probable precipitation over a 100-square-mile drainage is a staggering 28 inches in twenty-four hours. This amount seems credible in light of the forty-eight-hour precipitation of 16 inches or greater over a 2,000-square-mile area in the storm of October, 1998; the 40 inches at Thrall (some 20 miles northeast of Austin) in 1921; and the 22 inches in three hours at D'Hanis (near Uvalde) in 1935 (Slade and Persky 1999; Slade 1986).

Historic occupation of the region has exacerbated the natural propensity toward flooding by reducing the vegetative cover through overgrazing and increasing impervious surfaces. Unit runoff amounts of over three inches per hour are possible, which produces huge flood discharges from seemingly small drainages (Asquith and Slade 1995). As shown in table 3, many of the streams have peak discharges five hundred to a thousand times their mean annual flow rate.

A major problem in dealing with this flood threat is the political pressure not to increase the magnitude of legally defined storm amounts. Increasing the legally defined storms would result in greater costs for drainage structures that developers would have to pay for and would limit the value of aesthetically attractive but flood-threatened land along streams. Consequently, the apparently low storm intensity values published in the 1961 *Rainfall Frequency Atlas* (Hershfield 1961) have largely been adhered to. As a result of employing these unrealistically low storm estimates, Federal Emergency Management Administration (FEMA) floodplain maps depicting the hundred-year and five-hundred-year floodplains have floodplain boundaries that are too narrow. For example, the event of October, 1998, the fourth largest flood in the last hundred years in San Marcos, flooded an area 50 percent larger than the official FEMA hundred-year floodplain (Adamitz 1999). In spite of the hydrologic real-

ity, efforts to increase floodplain limits have been successfully resisted (Hlott 1992).

Reliance on unrealistically low estimates of extreme rainfall events increases the risk not only of flash floods but also of "slow rise" floods. Precipitation in relatively distant headwaters produces flood waves that exceed the design capacity of flood detention structures and produce "spills" downstream. Such slow rise floods occurred downstream of the Colorado River below Austin in December, 1991–January, 1992 (U.S. National Weather Service 1995) and in the downstream reaches of the San Antonio and Guadalupe rivers in October, 1998 (Slade and Persky 1999).

Regional Water Use

As shown in table 4, regional water use will continue to increase in future years. The growth in water use paralleled the population growth until the 1980s, when cities in the region significantly expanded their conservation programs. The long-term trend is for water use to increase at a lower rate than population growth due to decreases in urban per capita use and the purchases of some agricultural and other rural water by large municipalities, most notably San Antonio. The population has grown so much, however, that even with municipal conservation, most regional water supplies, with the exception of the Colorado River, will be strained during drought periods and will force even more political and legal challenges to the legal framework controlling the region's water resources.

Table 4. Water use (acre-feet per year) in south-central Texas, 1990–2050

Region	1990	2010	2030	2050
Austin				
Mun. & Ind.	169,000	311,000	431,000	518,000
Agriculture	7,000	6,000	6,000	6,000
Total	176,000	317,000	438,000	524,000
Hill Country				
Mun. & Ind.	32,000	42,000	45,000	48,000
Agriculture	47,000	46,000	44,000	43,000
Total	79,000	88,000	89,000	91,000
Southern Edwards				
Mun. & Ind.	321,000	502,000	656,000	800,000
Agriculture	355,000	323,000	298,000	275,000
Total	676,000	825,000	954,000	1,075,000
Entire Region	931,000	1,230,000	1,481,000	1,690,000

Source: TWDB 1997

Legal Framework

Ultimately, all water resource issues, even natural events such as floods and droughts, involve legal matters. Federal law drives many of the legal restrictions involving water in Texas. In many instances, the state has passed laws to implement federal programs or mandates. This certainly is the case in south-central Texas, where the most severe restrictions on water use and water quality are driven by federal mandates. Independent state action has primarily focused upon long-term water supply and has been largely facilitated by the Texas Water Development Board; the various state water plans and the implementation of the 1997 SB 1 are prime examples. The Texas Natural Resource Conservation Commission (TNRCC) has the responsibility of permitting and managing the surface water of the state. As is explained in what follows, management of groundwater has been a difficult, contentious issue in the region, especially since the endangered species lawsuits initiated in 1992 forced the state to take a management rather than an advisory role in allocating the waters of the San Antonio section of the Edwards Aquifer.

Since the enactment of the Water Pollution Control Act in 1948, the federal government has taken an active role on water quality. The 1972 amendments to the Water Pollution Control Act created the National Pollution Discharge Elimination System (NPDES), which requires permits to discharge effluent into federally defined waterways. These requirements were tightened by the 1977 amendments, known as the Clean Water Act, and were expanded to nonpoint-source pollution by the 1987 amendments, known as the Water Quality Act. The federal Environmental Protection Agency (EPA), in its role as the primary implementation and enforcement agency for these laws, has issued a series of rules to bring about the objectives of these laws. The TNRCC has been the major cooperative state agency that has worked with the EPA to implement these mandates, which are included in the Texas Surface Water Quality Standards (TSWQS; see Texas Water Development Board 1992). The rivers of the state are divided into "stream segments" for the purpose of water quality management (Texas Water Commission 1989).

Expansion of EPA water quality rules in the 1990s has produced several significant impacts on the south-central Texas region. The EPA directed that the states generate lists of stream segments that do not meet the requisites for aquatic biota, and "swimable," "fishable" conditions. This list, known as the Clean Water Act section 303(d) list, includes a number of stream segments in south-central Texas (table 5; see TNRCC 1996). As a means to improve water quality, the TNRCC, under directives from the EPA, has established pollutant total maximum daily load (TMDL) standards, which are intended to define the maximum amount of pollutants that can be introduced and still have the stream meet the 303(d) standards (TNRCC 1999).

The expansion of NPDES in the 1987 Water Quality Act to include stormwater runoff from cities, industries, and construction sites will increasingly affect growth in the region. Phase 1 implementation of the Water Quality Act stormwater management applied to cities that had a population larger than a hundred thousand, requiring them to treat the first half inch of storm runoff. Phase 1 also applied to construction and industrial sites larger than five acres. Consequently, new construction in Austin and San Antonio had to incorporate stormwater treatment facilities that utilized approved "best management practices" (BMPs) for reducing pollutants in the runoff (TWDB 1992). More recently, the EPA has enacted Phase 2 rules that will require stormwater management for all entities with population larger than twenty thousand and for construction sites of between one and five acres, effective March 10, 2003. Not all of the details for these new rules have been finalized, but—not unexpectedly—they have caused major debate in the region due to the large number of entities that will be under the purview of these rules, including big state universities (U.S. EPA 2000).

In 1970, the state initiated steps to protect the water quality of the Edwards Aquifer. These initial steps placed minor restrictions on development. Lawsuits were filed under the federal Safe Drinking Water Act of 1974, and the state was forced to pass the "Edwards Rules" in 1991, which required land use restrictions for all three segments of the Edwards Aquifer. Among the major provisions of this law were requirements for minimum lot size, septic disposal methods, and petroleum storage tank restrictions within the recharge zone. In 1998, effective January 1, 1999, the TNRCC expanded these constraints to the contributing surface runoff zone within Williamson, Travis, Hays, Comal, Bexar, Medina, Uvalde, and Kinney counties (Rivera 1998).

With the exception of interstate rivers such as the Red and the Pecos, as well as the international Rio Grande, water use is covered by state law. Surface water in Texas is governed by the appropriative water rights doctrine common to most western states. Under this doctrine, water is

Table 5. Streams segments listed as not suitable for fishing, aquatic life, and/or contact recreation in South-Central Texas

Segment Number	Water Body Name	County	Comments
Streams listed due to high pathogens			
1217A	Rocky Creek	Burnet	Bacteria
1403	Lake Austin	Travis	Bacteria
1403A	Bull Creek	Travis	Bacteria
1414	Pedernales River	Blanco, Gillespie, Kimble, Travis	Bacteria
1427	Onion Creek	Hays, Travis	Bacteria
1427A	Slaughter Creek	Travis	Bacteria
1427B	Williamson Creek	Travis	Bacteria
1428	Colorado River below Town Lake	Bastrop, Travis	Bacteria
1428A	Boggy Creek	Travis	Bacteria
1428B	Walnut Creek	Travis	Bacteria
1428C	Gilleland Creek	Travis	Bacteria
1429A	Shoal Creek	Travis	Bacteria
1429B	Eanes Creek	Travis	Bacteria
1430	Barton Creek	Travis	Bacteria
1811A	Dry Comal Creek	Comal	Bacteria
1903	Medina River below Medina Diversion Lake	Bexar, Medina	Bacteria
1906	Lower Leon Creek	Bexar	Bacteria
1910	Salado Creek	Bexar	Bacteria
1911	Upper San Antonio River	Bexar	Bacteria
2110	Lower Sabinal River	Uvalde	Bacteria
2117	Frio River above Choke Canyon Reservoir	Uvalde	Bacteria
Streams listed due to chemical content			
1214	San Gabriel River	Williamson	Chloride
1427	Onion Creek	Hays, Travis	Sulfate, Total TDS
1814	Upper San Marcos	Hays	Sulfate
Streams listed due to depressed dissolved oxygen levels			
1217A	Rocky Creek	Burnet	
1403	Lake Austin	Travis	
1427	Onion Creek	Travis	
1806	Camp Meeting Creek	Kerr	
1815	Cyprus Creek	Hays	
1903	Medina River below Medina Diversion Lake	Bexar, Medina	
1906	Lower Leon Creek	Bexar	
1908	Upper Cibolo Creek	Comal, Kendall	
1910	Salado Creek	Bexar	
1913	Mid Cibolo Creek	Bexar, Comal, Guadalupe	
2113	Upper Frio River	Real, Uvalde	
2117	Frio River above Choke Canyon Reservoir	Uvalde	

Source: TNRCC 2000

held in trust by the state for the benefit of all the people, subject to a granted right to its use. Those who are "first in time" are "first in right" to take or divert water from a surface watercourse or reservoir and apply it to a beneficial use; they must "use it or lose it" (Kaiser 1987).

By relying on groundwater for 57 percent of its total supply, Texas is one of the most groundwater-dependent states. Historically, there has been almost no limit to groundwater withdrawals in Texas. Generally, groundwater in Texas is governed by the English common law concept known as the rule of capture, also known as the right of capture, the law of absolute ownership, and by other names. In accordance with this rule, underground water is the exclusive property of the owner of the overlying land, unless a state statute specifies otherwise. Remedies in tort law are unavailable to a landowner who has a well that is affected by someone else's pumping.

As coexisting legal frameworks, prior appropriation and the rule of capture can encourage incompatible behavior by water users depending upon the source. They contribute to the deleterious effects of droughts by treating ground- and surface water as separate legal entities. This separation ignores the fundamental hydrologic connection between them and provides no incentives for their efficient conjunctive use. "Three of the largest groundwater-using states—California, Nebraska, and Texas—do not allocate groundwater by the law of prior appropriation or acknowledge the potential for groundwater uses to deplete surface supplies. The net result is that state laws commonly allow groundwater overdraft— the depletion of an aquifer at a rate faster than the natural rate of recharge" (Western Water Policy Review Advisory Commission 1998).

In 1949, the Texas Legislature chose local groundwater districts with limited powers to prescribe spacing of wells as the preferred method for managing groundwater under the rule of capture. As late as 1997, the legislature reaffirmed this principle in Senate Bill 1 (SB 1 and HB 5, 75th Legislature, Regular Session). Between 1949 and 1999, only forty-two local groundwater districts covering a small percentage of the state had been created; in south-central Texas these included the Barton Springs Edwards Aquifer Authority, the Edwards Underground Water District/Edwards Aquifer Authority, Hill Country Underground Water Conservation District, and the Evergreen Underground Conservation District (*Sipriano et al. v. Great Spring Waters of America, Inc.,* concurring opinion [Tex. 1999]; Kaiser 1987).

Senate Bill 2 (SB 2), passed by the 77th Legislature (2001), created more than thirty new groundwater conservation districts, each with the authority to manage new groundwater permit applications based upon historic pumping and estimates of groundwater availability (Johnson 2003). Many of these new districts are defined and delimited by county boundaries and focus upon the Trinity Aquifer in Hays, Blanco, Kendall, Gillespie, Kerr, and Bandera counties (TWDB 2003b).

Prior to passage of SB 2, the Legislature had made only two exceptions to the rule of capture, each a response to different problems resulting from the overdraft of aquifers. In 1975, the Legislature created the Harris-Galveston Coastal Subsidence District to limit pumping from the Gulf Coast Aquifer because pumping had caused land to subside in portions of the area by as much as ten feet (Callaway 1985). The consitutionality of the newly created District was upheld in *Beckendorff v. Harris-Galveston Coastal Subsidence District* (558 S.W. 75 Tex. Civ. App.—Houston [14th Dist.] 1977).

The second example is the creation of the Edwards Aquifer Authority in 1993, which limited withdrawals in order to protect endangered species and to guarantee minimum flows of groundwater from Comal and San Marcos springs into the Guadalupe River. As a result of the judgment in *Sierra Club et al. v. Babbitt et al.,* the federal district court contributed to the end of the rule of capture in the Edwards Aquifer by forcing the legislature to create a pumping regulatory scheme.

Despite its adoption ninety-six years ago, the Texas Supreme Court acknowledged in 1978 that the rule of capture is in some respects "harsh and outmoded" and invited the legislature to provide "a more sensible rule" (*Friendswood Development Co. v. Smith-Southwest Industries,* 576 S.W.2d 21 [Tex. 1978]). Farther eastward, beyond the limits of the south-central Texas region, pumping of this aquifer by the Ozarka bottled water company caused wells on adjacent properties to go dry, which precipitated legal action that went all the way to the Texas Supreme Court (Fikac 1998). On May 6, 1999, the Texas Supreme Court unanimously decided in *Sipriano et al. v. Great Spring Waters of America, Inc.* (Ozarka) to retain the rule as the standard governing the use of groundwater. However, a concurring opinion in the Ozarka case by Justices Hecht and O'Neill concluded: "I would agree with the Court that it would be inappropriate to disrupt the processes created and encouraged by the 1997 legislation [Senate Bill 1] before they have had a chance to work. I concur in the view that, for now—but I think only for now—East should not be overruled" (*Sipriano et al. v.*

Great Spring Waters of America, Inc., concurring opinion [Tex. 1999]).

Under the rule of capture, gross misallocations of resources can occur. Much like the tragedy of the commons (Hardin 1968), each individual user of Edwards water who wished to maximize profits was compelled to increase consumption of water without limit, so long as such use was profitable or needed. For example, in 1991 the Living Waters Artesian Springs Farm, a catfish farm fifteen miles southwest of San Antonio, began using as much as 40 million gallons (123 acre-feet) of aquifer water per day to raise catfish, discharging the water directly into the Medina River (Texas House Research Organization 1994). At that time, on an annual basis, this usage equaled approximately 25 percent of the City of San Antonio's total water use from the aquifer (Illgner 1993). When the catfish farm was in operation, well levels in adjacent portions of the aquifer declined three to ten feet (Templer 1996). The catfish farm's water use demonstrated in a single example that the cumulative impacts of additional pumping could eventually lead to the overexploitation of the aquifer. The controversy over the catfish farmer's withdrawals drew attention to unrestricted pumping that might have gone unnoticed if many individuals had incrementally increased withdrawals by a similar total amount.

Edwards Aquifer Endangered Species Act Litigation

In 1991, the Sierra Club filed a suit in the U.S. District Court in Midland, Texas, alleging that the secretary of the interior and the U.S. Fish and Wildlife Service (USFWS) had allowed takings of endangered species by not ensuring a water level in the Edwards Aquifer adequate to sustain the flow of Comal and San Marcos springs. The Sierra Club, Guadalupe-Blanco River Authority, and other plaintiffs requested that the defendant, USFWS, be enjoined to restrict withdrawals from the Edwards Aquifer under certain conditions and to develop and implement recovery plans for certain endangered and threatened species found in the aquifer and at Comal and San Marcos springs (*Sierra Club et al. v. Lujan et al.,* No. MO-91-CA-69, 1993 WL 151353, [W.D. Tex. Feb. 1, 1993]). On February 1, 1993, the presiding Judge, Lucius Bunton, ruled in favor of the plaintiffs and required the USFWS to determine the minimum spring discharge requirements to avoid take and jeopardy of the listed species in both springs. According to Bunton's decision, if the Texas Leg-islature did not adopt a management plan to limit withdrawals from the aquifer by the end of its current session, the plaintiffs could return to the court and seek additional relief. The Sierra Club indicated that if they had to return to the district court, they would seek regulation of the aquifer by the USFWS, placing the aquifer under federal judicial control.

On May 30, 1993, one day before the deadline for threatened federal action, the Texas Legislature adopted Senate Bill 1477, creating a conservation and reclamation district named the Edwards Aquifer Authority (EAA). The EAA is to regulate groundwater withdrawals by modifying the rule of capture with a permit system in five counties and portions of three others. The authority replaced the Edwards Underground Water District, which at that time covered only three counties overlying the aquifer. Under SB 1477, withdrawals are eventually to be limited to 450,000 acre-feet before December 31, 2007, and 400,000 acre-feet thereafter, unless drought conditions require more severe restrictions (Ch. 626, 1993 Tex. Gen. Laws 2355, §1.14(b) and (c)). By December 31, 2012, "the authority [EAA] . . . shall ensure that . . . the continuous minimum springflows of the Comal Springs and the San Marcos Springs are maintained to protect endangered and threatened species to the extent required by federal law" (Ch. 626, 1993 Tex. Gen. Laws 2355, §1.14(h)). The EAA is specifically charged by SB 1477 with protecting threatened and endangered species (Act of May 30, 1993 73rd Leg., R.S., ch. 626, 1993 Tex. Gen. Laws 2355, §1.14(a)(6)).

The EAA is authorized to achieve the required limits on withdrawals by purchasing and retiring permitted withdrawal rights. Domestic and livestock pumping were excluded from the pumping caps, and agricultural irrigators were guaranteed two acre-feet of water per acre of irrigated cropland. The export of groundwater across county lines was limited.

Interbasin Transfers and the Scramble for Water

More than seventy surface water interbasin transfers existed in Texas as of 1998 (Hebert 1998). They are often characterized in terms of water "haves" in the wetter eastern half of Texas and "have-nots" in the drier western half of Texas; some in the east view these transfers as "state-imposed 'takings' to the areas of need"; furthermore, they feel as if these transfers could imperil future economic growth in East Texas (Hebert 1998). Provisions in SB 1 of

1997 make interbasin transfers more difficult than in the past but not impossible. One barrier in particular is the provision of a new section 11.085 of the Texas Water Code, which gives new interbasin transfers a "junior" priority within the basin of origin (Hebert 1998). Thus, a surface water right purchased in one basin for transfer to another does not retain its original priority date but becomes junior to all other rights in the basin of origin, such that an interbasin transfer cannot occur until all other senior permitted needs within the basin of origin are met. This discourages interbasin transfers, since such transfers are often initiated to meet demands outside the basin during droughts at a time when meeting needs within the basin of origin can also be difficult. However, the limits in SB 1 on interbasin transfers of water may apply only if the water right is sold; a term lease of water may not be subject to the required analytical process in the statute.

Interbasin transfers have long been considered an important water supply option for south-central Texas. The Colorado River has been considered a future water source for the Edwards Aquifer region since the 1968 Texas Water Plan. Previously, the Garwood Irrigation District sold 35,000 acre-feet of its Colorado River water right to Corpus Christi, which is outside the basin. On February 19, 1998, the Lower Colorado River Authority (LCRA) announced the purchase of the remaining 101,000 acre-feet water right held by the Garwood Irrigation District (Haurwitz 1998). In 1999, Austin purchased 75,000 acre-feet of this surplus. Austin, which does not use all of its current allocation, will have 325,000 acre-feet reserved, but it is not projected to use any of the additional 75,000 acre-feet until 2037 (Thornhill 1999). By 2050, Austin is projected to need all of it. The LCRA has expressed interest in selling water to San Antonio in the past. However, current LCRA policy is that no water will be sold to San Antonio (Thornhill 1999).

Alcoa Proposed Diversion to San Antonio

On December 30, 1998, the San Antonio Water System (SAWS) Board of Trustees approved a plan to pipe groundwater from the Simsboro aquifer (a formation within the Carrizo-Wilcox) at an Aluminum Company of America (Alcoa) lignite mining operation northeast of Austin near Rockdale (Needham 1998). As much as 90,000 acre-feet produced by Alcoa as it dewaters its mining area (about 50 percent of SAWS current annual withdrawals from the Edwards Aquifer) could be diverted annually through a pipeline across the Colorado and

Guadalupe River basins to San Antonio. The proposed diversion by Alcoa would not be subject to restrictions on interbasin transfers, which apply only to surface water. Alcoa could assure 40,000 to 60,000 acre-feet of water to San Antonio in seven years, if a maximum effort were made (Nevola 1999). A Bastrop County lignite mine could produce an additional 15,000 to 30,000 acre-feet in fifteen years (Nevola 1999). An analysis conducted for the Texas Water Development Board by the Bureau of Economic Geology (BEG) at the University of Texas reports that there is enough water in the Carrizo-Wilcox Aquifer to meet these withdrawals and current water needs, with additional water available for future use to the year 2050 (TWDB 1999). The BEG study found that over fifty years, the project could cause a maximum water-level decline in the aquifer of 260 feet in the vicinity of the areas of highest groundwater withdrawal (TWDB 1999).

Future Prospects

The exact direction for changes in Texas water law may be uncertain, but it is certain that south-central Texas will increasingly be faced with major water resources problems as its population soars. The rapid population growth will increase water demand on finite, largely unreliable sources. Population growth will force thirsty cities to develop creative means to tap rural water supplies without excessively alarming local residents. Population growth will increase runoff and add pressure to build on flood-threatened areas. Population growth will require enhanced, more expensive, wastewater treatment and will be associated with more stringent land use policies to reduce nonpoint-source pollution. Leaders and citizens in the region will need to acknowledge their critical water situation and work together to use its water resources effectively and efficiently.

References

Adamitz, Greg. "An Analysis of the October 1998 Flood and the 100 year FEMA Floodplain along the San Marcos River Using DOQQ Imagery." Directed Research Paper for Master's of Applied Geography, Department of Geography, Southwest Texas State University, San Marcos, 1999.

Asquith, W. H., and R. M. Slade, Jr. *Documented and Potential Extreme Peak Discharges and Relation between Potential Extreme Peak Discharges and Probable Maximum Flood Peak in Texas.* U.S. Geological Survey Water-Resources Investigations Report 95-4249, 1995.

Brune, Gunnar. *Major and Historical Springs of Texas.* Report 189. Austin: Texas Water Development Board, 1975.

Callaway, Rick. *Harris-Galveston Coastal Subsidence District: A Report on Its Creation, Powers, Limitations of Powers and Progress.* Houston: Butler and Binion, P.C., 1985.

Dunne, Thomas, and L. B. Leopold. *Water in Environmental Planning.* San Francisco.: W. H. Freeman and Company, 1978.

Earl, R. A., R. D. Benke, and K. Knaupp. "Analysis of the July 2002 Flood at the Canyon Dam Spillway, Guadalupe River, South-Central Texas." *Proceedings and Papers of the Applied Geography Conferences* 26 (2003): 371–79.

Edwards Aquifer Authority. *Edwards Aquifer Hydrogeologic Report for 1998.* San Antonio: Edwards Aquifer Authority, 1999.

Fenneman. *Physiography of the Western United States.* New York: McGraw-Hill, 1931.

———. *Physiography of the Eastern United States.* New York: McGraw-Hill, 1938.

Fikac, Peggy. "Ozark Water Pumping Case Bound for State Supreme Court." *Austin American-Statesman,* August 26, 1998, B11.

Goudie, Andrew, and John Wilkerson. *The Warm Desert Environment.* New York: Cambridge University Press, 1977.

Hardin, Garrett. "The Tragedy of the Commons." *Science* 162 (1968): 1243–44.

Haurwitz, Ralph. "LCRA Triples Its Water Rights." *Austin American-Statesman,* February 20, 1998, A1.

Hebert, A. T., Jr. "State Policy on Interbasin Transfers in Texas." In *Proceedings of 25th Water for Texas Conference, "Water Planning Strategies for Senate Bill 1," Texas Water Resources Institute,* Austin, December 1–2, 1998.

Hershfield, D. M. *Rainfall Frequency Atlas of the United States.* Technical Paper no. 40. Washington, D.C.: Weather Bureau, U.S. Department of Commerce, 1961.

Hlott, Debbie. "Hays Landowners Await Decision on Floodplain." *Austin American-Statesman,* November 16, 1992, B1, B4.

Illgner, Rick. "The Edwards Aquifer: Political Prisoner." Paper delivered at the 89th Annual Meeting of the Association of American Geographers, Atlanta, Georgia, 1993.

Johnson, R. S. "Groundwater Districts' Power." In *Proceedings of the CLE International Texas Water Law Conference,* Austin, Texas, October 2–3, 2003, 1–15.

Kaiser, R. A. *Handbook of Texas Water Law: Problems and Needs.* College Station: Texas Water Resources Institute, Texas A&M University, 1987.

Lanning-Rush, Jennifer, W. H. Asquith, and R. M. Slade, Jr. *Extreme Precipitation Depth for Texas, Excluding the Trans-Pecos Region.* U.S. Geological Survey Water-Resources Investigations Report 98-4099, 1998.

Larkin, T. J., and G. W. Bomar. *Climatic Atlas of Texas.* Report LP-192. Austin: Texas Department of Water Resources, 1983.

Needham, Jerry. "City Poised to Nail Down Major New Water Source." *San Antonio Express-News,* December 28, 1998, 8A.

Nevola, Roger. Attorney for the Aluminum Company of America and the Guadalupe-Blanco River Authority, interview by Todd Votteler, 1999.

Rivera, Dylan. "Rules on Edwards Aquifer Tightened." *Austin American-Statesman,* September 24, 1998, pp. A1, A19.

Sands, Steve, City of San Marcos. Weather Report for December 1999. San Marcos Public Utilities, San Marcos, Texas, 2000.

Shiner, J. L. "Large Springs and Early American Indians." *Plains Anthropologist* 29 (1983): 65–70.

Slade, R. M., Jr. "Large Rainstorms along the Balcones Escarpment in Central Texas." In *The Balcones Escarpment,* ed. P. L. Abbot and C. M. Woodruff, Jr., 15–20. Geological Society of America Annual Meeting, San Antonio, Texas, 1986.

Slade, R. M., Jr., and Kristie Persky. *Floods in the Guadalupe and San Antonio River Texas, October 1998.* U.S. Geological Survey Fact Sheet. FS-147-99, 1999.

Templer, Otis W. "Catfish as a Catalyst for Changing Texas Water Law." Paper delivered at the Forum of the Association for Arid Lands Studies, Lubbock, Texas, December, 1996.

Texas House Research Organization. "Regulating the Edwards Aquifer: A Status Report." Texas House of Representatives, Austin, 1994, 19, 73–78.

Texas Natural Resource Conservation Commission. "Texas Water Quality: A Summary of River Basin Assessments." SFR-46. TNRCC, Austin, 1996.

———. Draft "Water Quality Concerns." TNRCC, Austin, January 28, 1999.

———. Draft "Texas 2000 Clean Water Act Section 303(d) List." TNRCC, Austin, April 28, 2000.

Texas Water Commission. *Segment Identification Maps for Texas River and Coastal Basins.* Report LP 85-01. Austin: Texas Water Commission, 1989.

Texas Water Development Board (TWDB). *Water for Texas: Today and Tomorrow. Recommendations for the 1992 Update of the Texas Water Plan.* Document GP-6-1. Austin: TWDB, 1992.

———. *Water for Texas: A Consensus-Based Update to the State Water Plan.* Document no. GP-6-2. Austin: TWDB, 1997.

———. "Press Release: Texas Water Development Board Releases Carrizo-Wilcox Aquifer." TWDB, Austin, 1999.

———. Regional Water Planning Groups. At http://www.twdb .state.tx.us/wrp/reg-plan/images/maps/sb1map.gif, 2000.

Texas Water Development Board. *Water for Texas: Today and Tomorrow. Recommendations for the 1992 Update of the Texas Water Plan.* Document GP-6-1. Austin: TWDB, 1992.

———. *Water for Texas: A Consensus-Based Update to the State Water Plan.* Document GP-6-2. Austin: TWDB, 1997.

———. Press Release, "Texas Water Development Board Releases Carrizo-Wilcox Aquifer." Austin: TWDB, 1999.

———. Regional Water Planning Groups. At http://www.twdb .state.tx.us/wrp/reg-plan/images/maps/sb1map.gif, 2003a.

———. Groundwater Conservation Districts, Confirmed and Pending Confirmation. At http://twdb.state.tx.us/mapping/ maps/pdf/gcd, 2003b.

Thornhill, Paul. Lower Colorado River Authority, interview by Todd Votteler, 1999.

U.S. Bureau of the Census. Metropolitan area population estimates for July 1, 1998, and population change for July 1, 1997–July 1, 1998 and April 1, 1990–July 1, 1998. At http:// www.census.gov/population/estimates.metro-city/ ma98-01.txt, 1999.

———. City and County Data Book. Washington, D.C.: U.S. Government Printing Offfice, various years.

U.S. Environmental Protection Agency. Phase II of the NPDES Storm Water Program. At http://www.epa.gov/OWM/ sw?phase2/index.htm, 2000.

U.S. Geological Survey. Water Resources Data, Texas. U.S. Geological Survey, Austin, various years.

———. Flood Peaks, 2000. U.S. Geological Survey, Austin, Texas.

U.S. National Climate Data Center. Monthly Precipitation Data, 2000. At http://www.ncdc.noaa.gov/ol/ncdc.html.

U.S. National Weather Service. *Natural Disaster Survey Report: Disastrous Floods on the Trinity, Brazos, Colorado Rivers in Texas, December 1991–January 1992.* Washington, D.C.: Government Printing Office, 1995.

Votteler, T. H. "The Little Fish That Roared: The Endangered Species Act, State Groundwater Law, and Private Property Rights Collide over the Texas Edwards Aquifer." *Environmental Law* 28, no. 4, (1998): 845–80.

Western Water Policy Review Advisory Commission. *Water in the West: Challenge for the Next Century.* Western Water Policy Review Advisory Commission, 1998.

CHAPTER 7

The Present and Future Status
of Water in the Coastal Bend Area

C. Alan Berkebile, Karen K. Dodson, and Rick Hay

Center for Water Supply Studies

Texas A&M University–Corpus Christi

James A. Dodson

Nueces River Authority

Coastal Bend Division

Abstract

The Coastal Bend region of Texas (Corpus Christi and the surrounding area) has historically relied on the Nueces River for most of its water supplies. While the watershed of the Nueces River begins in the Edwards Plateau and runs southeastward to the Nueces–Corpus Christi Bay estuary on the Texas coast, much of the water supply for the Coastal Bend originates in the middle to lower portion of the river basin. Water management in this region—named the Wild Horse Desert by early settlers in the area—has focused on adapting to the drought and flood nature of the surface water resources and the limitations imposed on groundwater development by elevated levels of dissolved solids in readily accessible aquifers.

Responses to these natural constraints on water supply have included: the development of several large surface water reservoirs designed to capture and store infrequent flood flows for use during the inevitable drought periods; aggressive water conservation and drought management programs for municipal and industrial water use sectors to encourage effective and efficient use of the available water supplies; and recent interbasin transfers of water supplies from regions northeast of the Coastal Bend. The current Senate Bill 1 water planning program for the Coastal Bend region is building on a solid history of regional cooperation in the development of dependable, affordable, long-range water supplies.

In the summer of 1996, with South Texas in the grip of a drought that had started three years earlier, a congressional subcommittee convened a field hearing in Corpus Christi to examine the water supply situation. When called to testify, Mayor Mary Rhodes of Corpus Christi informed the members of the subcommittee that water providers in seven counties of the Coastal Bend area depended on water supplies from the City's two reservoirs in the Nueces River basin, and as of that date, the combined reservoir system storage was only 25.5 percent of total system capacity. Furthermore, projections of water storage levels based on the previous drought-of-record conditions revealed that the two reservoirs could be totally out of water within eighteen to twenty-four months. Mayor

Rhodes—noted for her dry wit—proceeded to inform the assembled congressmen that the early settlers of the lower Nueces River basin had called the area the Wild Horse Desert. "Now, that's a heckuva name for your watershed," she concluded.

While the 1996 water supply situation for the Coastal Bend was serious—as later hydrologic analysis indicated, it actually defined a new drought of record—the circumstances would have been far more critical if the region had not already been planning for new water supplies. Fortunately, this region of Texas has long recognized the natural constraints on water supply, given its setting in a portion of the state. Long-range water planning has been an almost constant activity so as to assure that dependable, affordable water supplies are available even during the inevitable droughts.

This chapter examines the history of water use, planning, and development in the Coastal Bend area. We look at what is currently being done to create an effective long-range water management plan and describe how that planning process depends heavily on new tools such as reservoir system simulation models and groundwater flow models to assess water availability under a range of management alternatives.

While there have been several instances over the last fifty years when the Coastal Bend region was almost caught short in keeping up with water demands, the region is looking ahead to the next fifty years as a time when the fruits of long-term planning are harvested even as the seeds of new water management strategies are being planted.

The Coastal Bend Region

The Coastal Bend region is generally considered to consist of the area surrounding the City of Corpus Christi, including Aransas, Bee, Brooks, Duval, Jim Wells, Kenedy, Kleberg, Live Oak, McMullen, Nueces, Refugio, and San Patricio counties. While Refugio County is not contained within the Coastal Bend planning region for current regional water planning under Senate Bill 1 (Texas Senate 1997), the area is significant in terms of providing a range of regional water management options for the conjunctive use of surface water and groundwater supplies. The eleven-county Senate Bill 1 regional water planning area is shown in figure 1.

This area of the state spans three unique ecosystem regions as defined by soils and vegetation: South Texas Brush Country to the west; Coastal Sand Plains to the

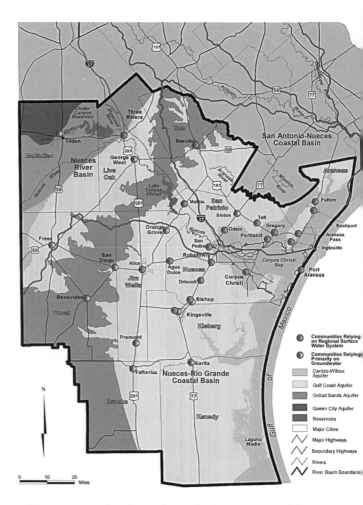

Figure 1. Water planning Region N, the eleven counties of the Coastal Bend (HDR Engineering, June, 2000).

south; and Gulf Coast Prairies and Marshes to the north. Annual rainfall amounts are typically exceeded by annual potential evapotranspiration by a factor of two to one. Rainfall decreases from east to west, as is reflected in differences in streamflow and vegetation across the region. For example, areas in the San Antonio–Nueces coastal basin tend to support larger, woody plant species, even outside riparian corridors, while the Nueces basin and the Nueces–Rio Grande coastal basin exhibit more brush species, except for limited amounts of riparian areas.

This part of the Texas Coast essentially sits atop the dividing line between the wetter parts of the state to the east and the more arid regions to the west. The Nueces estuary–Corpus Christi Bay system is on the cusp in terms of freshwater inflows. The bay systems to the north—even the Mission–Copano Bay system—tend to have significantly more freshwater inflows and flushing, whereas areas south of Corpus Christi receive so little fresh water that they tend to be hypersaline. The Corpus Christi Bay system receives most of its freshwater inflows from the Nueces River, and consequently it has experienced the effects of the same large-scale periodic events that drive the Nueces River streamflows; droughts and floods cause salinities in the bay to range from nearly fresh to hypersaline.

The major water demand areas are primarily municipal systems in the greater Corpus Christi area and large industrial users (manufacturing, steam-electric, mining) located along the Corpus Christi and La Quinta ship channels. Agriculture (irrigation and livestock) is the third largest category of water use in the region (fig. 2).

The Nueces River and its major tributaries, the Atascosa River and the Frio River, have been the primary sources of surface water supply for much of the municipal and industrial water use in the region. Streams like the Mission River and the Aransas River in the San Antonio–Nueces coastal basin have often measured large flood flows but have not been a source of reliable surface water supplies for municipal and industrial use. Streams in the Nueces–Rio Grande coastal basin are even more intermittent and unreliable in nature.

Some areas in the Coastal Bend region are dependent on groundwater supplies. Two major aquifers lie beneath the region: the Carrizo-Wilcox aquifer and the Gulf Coast aquifer. The Carrizo-Wilcox aquifer contains moderate to large amounts of fresh to slightly saline water. Although this aquifer reaches from the Rio Grande north into Arkansas, within the Coastal Bend region it underlies only parts of McMullen and Live Oak counties. In this downdip portion of the Carrizo-Wilcox aquifer, the water is softer and hotter (140° F) and contains higher amounts of dissolved solids than in updip portions of the aquifer. With the availability of more economical surface water and shallow groundwater supplies in the areas over the Carrizo-Wilcox aquifer in the Coastal Bend region, these deeper groundwater supplies remain virtually untapped.

The Gulf Coast aquifer underlies all counties within the Coastal Bend region and yields moderate to large amounts of both fresh and slightly saline water (fig. 3). Extending from northern Mexico to Florida, the Gulf Coast aquifer is made up of four aquifer units: Catahoula, Jasper, Evangeline, and Chicot. The Evangeline and Chicot aquifers are the uppermost water-bearing formations within the Gulf Coast aquifer system and, consequently, are the most commonly utilized. The Evangeline portion of the Gulf Coast aquifer contains the highly

transmissive Goliad Sands. The Chicot portion of the Gulf Coast aquifer comprises several different geologic formations, the Beaumont and Lissie formations being predominant in the Chicot aquifer within the Coastal Bend area. Artesian, or flowing, wells were common in the Coastal Bend area at one time, but as wells were left unplugged and additional pumping from the Gulf Coast aquifer occurred, water levels have declined and flowing wells are not as common as in the past.

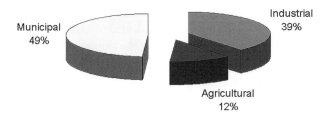

Figure 2. Water use in the Coastal Bend region, 1996 (HDR Engineering, June, 2000).

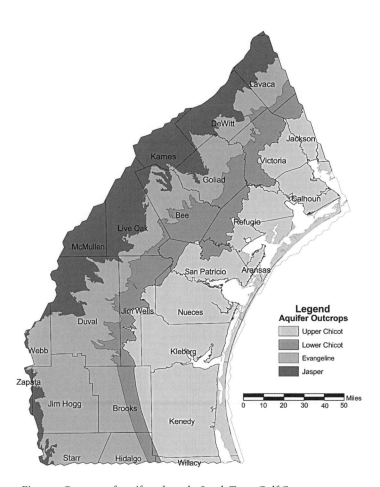

Figure 3. Outcrops of aquifers along the South Texas Gulf Coast (Hay 1999).

History of Water Use, Planning, and Development

Drought as a Call to Action, 1950s–1980s

Early water supplies in this region were extremely unreliable. Shallow wells produced limited quantities of generally poor quality water. Cisterns and small surface tanks went dry during droughts. It was not until the last several years of the nineteenth century that two major achievements in water supply for the region were made. The King Ranch, south of Corpus Christi, drilled its first successful deep artesian well in 1898, probably tapping the Goliad Sand. This proved the availability of groundwater of sufficient quality and quantity to support both livestock watering and some irrigation uses. At roughly the same time, a group of entrepreneurs constructed a small saltwater barrier dam on the tidal segment of the Nueces River about fifteen miles west of Corpus Christi. Utilizing a steam-driven pumping station and cast-iron piping, they began delivering fresh water from the newly created impoundment, called the Calallen Pool, into the City of Corpus Christi. This system later became Corpus Christi's first public water utility.

Demand for water in the Coastal Bend region has been primarily driven by the growth of the energy and petrochemical sectors. As oil and gas production increased, both groundwater and surface water use increased. Groundwater supported the mining and production activities, while surface water supported the refining and petrochemical manufacturing activities as well as the associated residential water use for the growing population of the region.

The City of Corpus Christi acquired large water rights in the Nueces River basin and then, in the 1930s, developed a reservoir near Mathis, some thirty miles west of Corpus Christi. Spurred by the drought of the late 1940s and early 1950s, Corpus Christi later built a new dam and larger reservoir at essentially the same location on the Nueces River. Wesley Seale Dam was completed in 1958, and by the 1960s, as population and water demand grew in communities around Corpus Christi, many of the groundwater supply systems began converting to surface water available from Lake Corpus Christi. The City of Corpus Christi gradually took on a role as a regional water provider.

Even at the time Wesley Seale Dam was being dedicated, community leaders expressed the need to continue the regional cooperation and planning that had made

Lake Corpus Christi a reality. It was estimated that the yield of Lake Corpus Christi could meet the area's growing needs for twenty-five years. Additional supplies would have to be developed within that time frame to assure a dependable, sustainable water supply for the region. Several state and federal surveys of potential reservoir sites had been conducted across Texas during the 1950s. These studies seemed to indicate that another reservoir could be built to develop additional water supplies within the Nueces River basin. By the early 1960s, efforts were under way in the Coastal Bend region to find the best site.

The process of finding the best site was contentious and time-consuming. Local, regional, state, and federal agencies argued about project sponsorship, water rights, site locations, and funding. Federal resource agencies, newly empowered by the landmark environmental legislation of the early 1970s, began to raise new questions about mitigation and endangered species. Opponents of the proposed project expressed concerns about the impact that building another reservoir in the Nueces basin would have on the Nueces estuary because of reduced freshwater inflows.

After a series of studies, the choice of sites was narrowed to two basic alternatives: Choke Canyon Reservoir on the Frio River near Three Rivers and the "R&M" Reservoir on the Nueces River between Lake Corpus Christi and Bluntzer. In a nonbinding referendum, voters in Corpus Christi supported the R&M site. However, with the potential of federal assistance available for construction at Choke Canyon, local, state, and federal leadership threw their support behind the site on the Frio River. Ultimately, the State of Texas issued a joint water rights permit for the Choke Canyon site to the City of Corpus Christi and the Nueces River Authority.

These two contesting sponsors then became the joint local sponsors of the project, which was built by the U.S. Bureau of Reclamation under congressional authorization. Federal interests in the recreation, fish, and wildlife benefits justified the federal government paying for a portion of the project costs.

Choke Canyon Reservoir was completed in 1982, just as the Coastal Bend area was going into another severe drought. Through 1983 and the first half of 1984, the drought in the Coastal Bend worsened as Choke Canyon sat basically empty, not providing any additional water supply. By the summer of 1984, the region was forced to implement severe drought management measures, including water rationing. As had been predicted in 1958, Lake Corpus Christi alone could only provide for the area's water needs for twenty-five years. The time-consuming process of developing the next source of supply for the Coastal Bend region resulted in the area getting caught a step short in assuring there would be a continuous, dependable supply of water available.

Fortunately, the drought broke in the fall of 1984, and due to a major tropical storm rainfall event in 1987, Choke Canyon Reservoir filled for the first time. But the lesson learned in 1984 gave rise to another series of studies evaluating the dependability of the new Choke Canyon–Lake Corpus Christi reservoir system. Estimates of the yield of the new system, and the water rights permits for its diversion and use, were based on hydrological studies and numerical calculations that had been done as early as the 1950s. Engineers and hydrologists had better, longer periods of records to work with by the late 1980s; more important, advances in hydrological modeling and numerical simulation provided better tools to analyze the interactions between the various components of the system.

Modeling Efforts Lead to Better Planning, 1990–1995

A new simulation model of the Nueces River basin was developed between 1989 and 1991 under a joint effort of the Texas Water Development Board, the Nueces River Authority, the Edwards Underground Water District (in San Antonio), and the City of Corpus Christi and its regional water partners. This model was used to assess the feasibility of building artificial recharge structures within the upper Nueces basin, to enhance the yield of the Edwards aquifer, and to measure the potential impact of these projects on downstream water rights like the Choke Canyon–Lake Corpus Christi permit. A more detailed version of the model was also developed for the lower Nueces River basin to reevaluate the yield of the Choke Canyon–Lake Corpus Christi reservoir system. This model had the capability to evaluate the impacts of various reservoir system operating policies, including the release of fresh water from the reservoir system to satisfy water rights permit conditions related to freshwater inflows to the Nueces estuary.

Use of the new model in reevaluating the firm annual yield of the Choke Canyon–Lake Corpus Christi reservoir system brought home the importance of not relaxing one's guard when it comes to water supplies. Choke Canyon Reservoir had originally been designed and permitted to provide 139,000 acre-feet per year of *additional, incremental* yield when operated in conjunction with

Lake Corpus Christi, which was estimated to be capable of producing 113,000 acre-feet per year on its own. Results of the new modeling indicated that rather than there being 252,000 acre-feet per year of firm annual yield available, the combined yield of the Choke Canyon–Lake Corpus Christi reservoir system might be as low as 153,000 acre-feet per year (HDR Engineering 1990).

With this new information, the region was suddenly facing yet another daunting task in identifying, evaluating, selecting, and developing new water supplies. Regional leaders lost no time in looking at alternatives; however, this time they recognized that the process would be occurring within a new context of environmental and regulatory issues. The old style of building projects first and then dealing with the environmental impacts after the fact was no longer an accepted practice. In the Coastal Bend, this meant looking at the process from an *integrated water resources management* approach rather than simply as a water supply development activity.

Given the significant decrease in the firm yield of the reservoir system, which appeared to be attributable to the freshwater inflow requirements for the Nueces estuary, regional water officials began to work with environmental and regulatory interests to try to craft a freshwater inflow operating plan that protected both the needs of the estuary and the region's water supply.

In 1991, a joint investigation sponsored by the Lavaca-Navidad River Authority, the Alamo Conservation and Reuse District, and the City of Corpus Christi studied additional water supplies for the cities of San Antonio and Corpus Christi. The study addressed the feasibility of transferring water from Lake Texana (Palmetto Bend Project), developing Stage 2 of the Palmetto Bend Project, and acquiring water from the Colorado River. The cost and efficiency of the diversion projects that would deliver the water to both cities were examined as well. The final recommendation of this study was to purchase the water from Lake Texana, obtain the Garwood Irrigation Company water rights in the Colorado River, and construct diversion structures to both San Antonio and Corpus Christi (HDR Engineering 1991).

In 1992, the Texas Water Development Board (TWDB) and the cities of Houston, Corpus Christi, and San Antonio initiated Phase I of the Trans-Texas Water Program to address water supply needs for each of these cities. The Corpus Christi service area was virtually the same as the Coastal Bend region, with the exceptions that Refugio and Atascosa counties were included in the study and Kenedy County was excluded. The City of Corpus Christi,

Port of Corpus Christi Authority, Corpus Christi Board of Trade, TWDB, and Lavaca-Navidad River Authority sponsored the Trans-Texas Water Program study for the Corpus Christi service area. The Phase I study compared long-term water demand (through 2050) with available water supplies, investigated sixteen options for additional water supply, and estimated the quantity of water available as well as the unit cost and the major environmental considerations for each option.

In Phase II of the study, twenty-two different water supply alternatives were evaluated. Combinations of these alternatives would be necessary to meet the projected need to develop 100,000 acre-feet per year of additional supply by the year 2050. The 1995 report on Phase II of the Trans-Texas Water Program study for the Corpus Christi service area recommended the incorporation of changes in the Lake Corpus Christi–Choke Canyon reservoir system operating policies and the 1995 Pass-Thru Agreed Order for freshwater inflows to the Nueces estuary (HDR Engineering 1995). The report also recommended additional water conservation practices and construction of pipelines to convey available water from Lake Texana and the Colorado River.

During this period, the City of Corpus Christi did more than just plan for future water supplies. Recognizing the urgency of the needs, the mayor of Corpus Christi assembled several regional water advisory groups to work on implementation issues, even as the planning studies were under way. Based on the recommendations of these groups, the City entered into a purchase option contract (1992), and then a purchase agreement (1993), with the Lavaca-Navidad River Authority for the purchase of up to 41,840 acre-feet per year of water from Lake Texana. The City also entered into an option contract with Garwood Irrigation District (1992) to acquire 35,000 acre-feet of the most senior water right on the Colorado River.

The Coastal Bend region recognized that acquiring and transferring water from other river basins would result in intense scrutiny of the way the region was using its existing water resources. Interests in the basins supplying the new waters questioned whether there was really a need for the water to be transferred at all. Often, water conservation could provide a means of reducing current and future demands significantly while providing an alternative to developing new water supplies. However, this was not the case in the Coastal Bend region.

Since water conservation and drought management had become such a way of life in the Coastal Bend, there was little room for large additional water savings. Per capita water use in the Coastal Bend from 1992 to 1995 was the lowest of any metropolitan area in Texas (HDR Engineering, July, 1999). A 1990 study of water use by industries in the region revealed that refineries in the Corpus Christi area used only one-third as much water per barrel of product throughput as did refineries on the upper Texas coast. In fact, the water efficiencies for refineries in the Coastal Bend were similar to those for refineries in chronically water short regions of California.

While a water conservation plan is implemented on a continuous basis, a drought management plan is something that is implemented only under certain conditions. Since 1987, the City of Corpus Christi's Water Conservation Plan has included a Drought Management Plan, which is to be implemented in four stages as drought conditions worsen; each stage includes measures designed to create additional reductions in water demand as the threat of water shortage increases. In Stages III and IV of the plan, both municipal and wholesale customers are subject to water allocation from the City of Corpus Christi. In turn, wholesale customers are responsible for imposing similar allocations on their customers. The plan also provides for the emergency pumping of groundwater from sixteen wells: twelve in the Gulf Coast aquifer, located in an area near Lake Corpus Christi, and four in the Carrizo aquifer, located on the Atascosa River near Campbellton.

Impact of the New Drought of Record and Senate Bill 1, 1996–2000

As Mayor Rhodes testified about the drought in the summer of 1996, the situation in the Coastal Bend once again become critical. The City of Corpus Christi and most other water providers in the region were in Stage II of their drought management plans and on the verge of implementing Stage III, including water rationing. Drought had sounded yet another call to action.

This time, action was swift; the City of Corpus Christi had already filed for the state water rights permit amendment necessary to take and transfer water from Lake Texana under the purchase agreement with the Lavaca-Navidad River Authority. In September, 1996, the Corpus Christi City Council voted to build a pipeline from Lake Texana to Corpus Christi that could deliver the water already being purchased. The challenge would involve designing, permitting, financing, acquiring right-of-way for, and constructing a 101-mile pipeline to provide access to the Lake Texana water *within two years*.

Fortunately, the earlier planning studies provided a jump start on the project. The Trans-Texas Water Program studies had included much of the preliminary evaluation of both the pipeline route and potential environmental issues associated with the right-of-way. The engineering cost estimates for the planning study proved to be detailed enough to provide a project budget of $135 million. The budget was used to structure a bond sale while actual engineering design work was being completed.

The interbasin transfer permit for the Lake Texana water was approved in October, 1996. However, the City still had the option to purchase the pending Garwood water rights. The pipeline project and the interbasin transfer strategy as a whole hinged on both sources of water being available. With the 75th Texas Legislature beginning its session in January of 1997, on the heels of the drought of 1996, the issue of water was surely to be at the top of the list of items for consideration. Legislative efforts to block the proposed interbasin transfers for the Coastal Bend region were anticipated.

The 75th Texas Legislature passed a major piece of water legislation—Senate Bill 1 (SB 1), enacting dozens of changes in wide areas of state water law. Major new requirements in SB 1 included stricter rules for interbasin transfer permit applications (the interbasin transfer permit for the Colorado River water rights purchased by the City of Corpus Christi was effectively grandfathered out of these new rules); new interbasin transfers would receive new priority dates on the water rights, based on the date of application (the junior rights provision—which also did not apply to the Colorado River water rights purchased by the City of Corpus Christi); nearly every water provider would be required to develop and file a water conservation and drought management plan; the State of Texas would develop and implement a statewide drought management program; and the state water planning process would become a regionally driven program wherein each region would be required to develop a long-range water management plan, which would then be submitted to the Texas Water Development Board for inclusion in the State Water Plan.

These changes in state water law have had a significant effect on the way the Coastal Bend region is addressing water planning. The Coastal Bend Regional Water Planning Program established under SB 1 is expanding the regional horizons. For the first time, groundwater resources in the Coastal Bend are receiving particular attention within the planning process, both in terms of protecting existing groundwater uses and in identifying methods of facilitating the integrated management of surface water and groundwater resources.

Unlike other regions of the state, where there is often only a single source of available water supply, there has been little conflict between the various constituents of water use in the Coastal Bend region because both surface water and groundwater supplies have been available. Furthermore, they have been effectively allocated between various uses by ability to pay. Throughout the period that the City of Corpus Christi expanded the regional surface water system to meet the needs of the major municipal and industrial water demands in the Coastal Bend region, groundwater supplies continued to meet the demands of most agricultural users at an affordable price. Communities in the more rural counties also found groundwater adequate and affordable to meet their limited municipal and industrial needs, although water quality concerns sometimes entered into the picture.

Current concerns focus on potential large-scale uses of groundwater in these areas, such as new demands driven by users outside the traditional groundwater constituency in the region. Maintaining groundwater availability and affordability is key to protecting the needs of those users in the Coastal Bend region who have no other affordable options but groundwater resources to meet their needs well into the foreseeable future.

Current and Future Water Supplies

The SB 1 regional water planning program relies on a comparison of available water supply with projected water demands to identify potential water needs in the region. The program then evaluates water management strategies to meet those identified water needs. The first step in the process is to develop estimates of water demand for each water user group over the fifty-year planning horizon (2000 through 2050).

Municipal water demand is primarily a function of population and per capita water use. In July, 1998, the Texas Water Development Board published population and water demand projections for each county in the state. The population projections are a consensus-based, most-likely scenario of growth, as determined by a Technical Advisory Committee consisting of state agencies, key interest groups, and the general public. The projections are based on recent and prospective growth trends and the committee's professional opinions. From this information, population projections were developed for

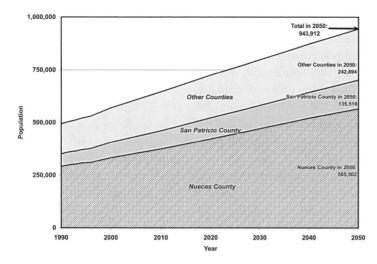

Figure 4. Total water demands for the Coastal Bend region through the year 2050 (HDR Engineering, June, 2000).

each county in the Coastal Bend region, with the data presented for each city within each county as well as for a "county—other" category used to capture those people living outside the cities. These projections were reviewed by each community in the region and, in several cases, were revised to reflect local demographic information that documented the need for changes in the original population projections.

Manufacturing, agricultural, mining, and steam-electric water demand estimates are generally a function of anticipated market and economic conditions in each sector. In the Coastal Bend region, manufacturing water use, like municipal water use, is projected to increase, while mining and irrigation water use is expected to decrease; livestock use and steam-electric use are anticipated to remain unchanged. Total projected water demand for the Coastal Bend region is shown in figure 4. While current water demands in the eleven counties in the Coastal Bend region are estimated to be 223,797 acre-feet per year, by the year 2050, total demand is anticipated to reach 309,754 acre-feet per year.

Methods to Determine Water Availability

Accurate estimates of current and future water availability are the other side of the equation used to evaluate water needs for the future. Prior to determining if any new supplies are necessary, current and anticipated water supplies must be compared to the projections of water demand. In the SB 1 regional water planning program, two computer simulation techniques were used to evaluate

water availability: surface water models and groundwater models.

Several hydrologic simulation models have been developed for the Nueces River basin over the last decade. The Nueces River Basin Model, originally developed in 1991 and updated in 1999, now covers a sixty-three-year historical period of hydrologic data for thirty control points throughout the basin. Operating on a monthly time-step, the model considers recharge to the Edwards aquifer, channel losses, water rights, and selected reservoir operating policies.

The Lower Nueces River Basin and Estuary Model is a more specialized, interactive modeling tool that can be used to simulate reservoir operations in the lower basin, compute the firm annual yield of the reservoir system, and provide information on inflows to the Nueces estuary. Hydrologic data for the five primary control points used in this model cover a sixty-four-year period, including the critical period of the new drought of record that occurred in the early months of 1997. This model is capable of simulating the effects of the Texana pipeline operation. The model can also be used to develop short- and long-range assessments of reservoir system reliability based on current storage, projected water demands, and the recurrence of historical hydrologic sequences. Reliability is measured in several terms: the probability of meeting water supply requirements; the probability of avoiding implementation of drought management measures; or the probability of maintaining desired lake levels (HDR Engineering, January, 1999). The Lower Nueces River Basin and Estuary Model has been used during SB 1 regional water planning to estimate the long-term yield of the Choke Canyon–Lake Corpus Christi–Lake Texana water supply system.

These two models were developed in the early 1990s specifically as tools to support regional planning efforts in the Coastal Bend. In 1997, SB 1 directed the Texas Natural Resource Conservation Commission (TNRCC) to develop surface water availability models for all river basins in Texas and to provide those models for use by the regional planning groups. The Water Availability Model (WAM) for the Nueces River basin was completed in 1999 and has been used to evaluate surface water availability for water rights in the Nueces River basin other than those associated with the Choke Canyon–Lake Corpus Christi reservoir system.

Scientific advances in groundwater modeling have stripped away many of the mysteries of groundwater availability. To be useful and accurate, however, these models require careful calibration, field verification, and hydrogeological expertise. While the Texas Water Development Board has used groundwater models in the past to make estimates of water availability, their estimates of groundwater availability for the aquifer systems in the Coastal Bend planning region were not considered suitable for current planning purposes. Instead, the Coastal Bend Regional Water Planning Group decided to develop a new groundwater flow model of the Gulf Coast aquifer in order to determine groundwater availability for the fifty-year planning horizon of the SB 1 regional water management plan. For that portion of the Coastal Bend region overlying the Carrizo-Wilcox aquifer, planners used a groundwater model that had been developed under several recent TWDB planning studies (HDR Engineering, June, 2000).

As part of the SB 1 planning effort, Hay (1999) developed a detailed regional model of the Gulf Coast aquifer using groundwater flow simulation software MODFLOW (McDonald and Harbaugh 1988). This three-dimensional numerical groundwater flow model was created to simulate steady-state predevelopment and developed flow in the Gulf Coast aquifer of the Texas Coastal Bend. The model consists of five layers with 10,000-foot grid spacing and extends from the Navidad River south to Willacy County and from the Gulf of Mexico inland to the up-dip limit of the Jasper aquifer. The following aquifer units are included in the model: Chicot aquifer (layers 1 and 2), Evangeline aquifer (layer 3), Burkeville-Lagarto confining unit (layer 4), and Jasper aquifer (layer 5). Horizontal hydraulic conductivity ranges from 1×10^{-4} ft/day to 7 ft/day in more permeable strata, while vertical hydraulic conductivity ranges from 1×10^{-4} ft/day to 0.275 ft/day. Information on formation tops, water levels, water quality, and aquifer characteristics was obtained by linking the model to an online database containing specifications on over twenty-five thousand wells in the area of interest.

Since there is no standard method or generally accepted practice for determining groundwater availability, the Coastal Bend RWPG decided to use local input in de-termining a comfortable level of aquifer drawdown that would provide the limits for various pumping scenarios to be tested using the model. A Groundwater Advisory Panel, consisting of RWPG members who represented groundwater interests and others who depend on groundwater for their livelihood, provided input to the groundwater modeling team regarding levels of aquifer drawdown that would be acceptable. The advisory panel's main concern was recognizing and protecting—through the fifty-year planning horizon—the future water needs of existing groundwater users in the planning region. As a result of these concerns, a fairly conservative criterion on acceptable drawdown levels was adopted and used to define the limits of water availability under the withdrawal scenarios tested with the model. This approach provided a method to translate the stakeholders' subjective values into numerical criteria that were then used to establish groundwater availability on a county-by-county basis.

Results of Water Availability Evaluations

Table 1 shows the results of the analysis of water availability for both surface water and groundwater sources that will be important to the Coastal Bend region. The totals in table 1 include all water sources that are presently under the control or ownership of water providers in the Coastal Bend region. This differs from the method of accounting for water availability in the SB 1 program, which would preclude sources such as the Colorado River water rights, owned by the City of Corpus Christi, from being shown as a currently available source of supply until the pipeline to convey the water to Corpus Christi is actually built. The numbers in table 1 assume that the pipeline to convey the water available under the Colorado River water rights will be built at the time the water is needed for use in the Corpus Christi area but do not include any other additional water supplies that could potentially be developed by the year 2050. Under this approach, the total amount of water currently available to the region is 355,025 acre-feet per

Table 1. Water available for the Coastal Bend region in acre-feet per year

Water Supply	Year					
	2000	2010	2020	2030	2040	2050
Surface water sources	269,718	266,858	263,998	261,138	258,278	255,418
Groundwater sources	85,307	85,307	85,307	85,307	85,307	85,307
Total supply	355,025	352,165	349,305	346,445	343,585	340,725

Source: HDR Engineering June, 2000.

year. This amount declines as sedimentation reduces reservoir capacities and, consequently, the firm annual yield of the Choke Canyon–Lake Corpus Christi reservoir system. By 2050, total water availability is estimated to decrease to 340,724 acre-feet per year.

Comparison of Water Demands with Water Supplies

On a regionwide basis, it would appear that there is sufficient water available to meet water demands through the fifty-year planning horizon; in the year 2050, total water demand is 309,754 acre-feet per year while total water supply is 340,724 acre-feet per year. However, these aggregate numbers for water availability mask some details that are important in determining whether there is actually water available for each water user in the region. Determining the amount of water available for each water user depends on a more detailed analysis of water needs as compared to water available by source of supply. Basically, not all water in the region is available for all users. This is particularly the case for to groundwater supplies, which are typically used on a very local basis. Groundwater may be available but not in the right location to provide for a particular need. Surface water supplies in the Coastal Bend, on the other hand, are widely distributed through the regional water supply system operated by the City of Corpus Christi and several major water wholesalers.

In the SB 1 planning program, the need for additional water supplies has been identified with respect to several water users within the region. In most cases, where future groundwater use is expected to exceed current well production capacities in existing systems, the need is simply for additional capacity to develop readily available groundwater resources. Some additional surface water supplies—beyond the Colorado River water rights—will probably be necessary to meet the long-term needs of the municipal and industrial water users now depending on the Choke Canyon–Lake Corpus Christi–Lake Texana water supply system. The amounts will be relatively small compared to those in many other regions of the state, but under the SB 1 planning program, a regional plan that identifies, evaluates, and recommends appropriate water management strategies to meet these needs should be in place by 2001.

Management Strategies for Sustainable Water Supply

Providing a sustainable, affordable water supply for the future of the Coastal Bend region will involve designing a plan that identifies appropriate water management strategies and lays out the framework for implementing those strategies over the planning horizon. *Appropriate water management strategies* extend current water supplies or provide dependable new water supplies at a fair cost and with a minimum of impact to the environment.

Current water sources are almost always the cheapest and easiest to access. However, there is often room for improvement in efficiency on both the supply side and the demand side of the water management equation. Water resources management focuses first on maximizing supplies from existing sources and on increasing the efficiency of existing water uses.

However, even with significant improvements in these areas, growth in demand will often require that new supplies be developed. When looking at potential water management strategies involving new sources, it makes great sense to look at the potential to utilize water supplies already developed but not being used to their full extent. This typically involves projects already built that have a surplus of water over the demands in their intended service areas. While these supplies may not be close to another demand center, the cost of transferring the water to a new service area may be less than other alternatives, and it is often the option with the least environmental impacts.

Groundwater management has typically been focused on identifying sustainable amounts of water that can be developed without seriously impacting the source aquifer. New water management strategies that involve the conjunctive management of groundwater and surface water supplies offers tremendous opportunities to get more than the sum of the parts when these two water resources are viewed in an integrated fashion.

Finally, vast new quantities of water supply may be available soon as improvements in membrane technologies provide access to large amounts of potable water supplies from brackish groundwater and surface water as well as seawater sources.

Conservation and Reuse to Make the Most of Available Supplies

Because of experiences in the droughts of the 1950s, '60s, and early '80s, the Coastal Bend region adopted water conservation practices that continue to result in significant reductions in water use as compared to most other parts of Texas. Throughout the 1990s, water use in the Coastal Bend region, on a per capita per day basis, was one of the lowest of any major metropolitan area in Texas—around 130 gallons per capita per day, as compared to a state average of 160 gallons per capita per day. Refineries in the Coastal Bend area produce a barrel of gasoline using only thirty gallons of water, compared to the ninety gallons of water used by refineries along the upper Texas coast to produce a barrel of gasoline.

To a certain extent, these water use efficiencies translated into a flattening of the water demand curve, pushing out into the future the point at which new water supplies should be available. Had this not been the case, the reduction in the firm annual yield of the Choke Canyon–Lake Corpus Christi reservoir system would have had more severe consequences at an earlier date. In fact, if water demand had grown as projected in some of the planning studies from the 1970s, the Coastal Bend region would have been short of water as early as 1990. Instead, conservation measures begun in the 1980s slowed the growth in demand so that the shortfall in supply did not become an acute factor until the new drought of record was being established in the 1996–97 period.

Success in water conservation is related to changing the behavior of water providers as well as water users. There are both supply side measures and demand side measures that can be effective in reducing water use in a community. The supply side focuses on increasing the efficiency in the areas under the control of the water provider, making sure that as far as possible, the full amount of water diverted from the source of supply is delivered to the customers of the system. This means accounting for all the water from the point of diversion to the point of use as well as identifying and correcting sources of loss, such as leaks in the diversion, treatment, and delivery systems, water uses that are not metered, and errors in metering systems. These measures have been implemented to a significant extent throughout water supply systems in the Coastal Bend region, resulting in considerable improvements in water system efficiencies.

On the demand side, water conservation measures focus on changing consumer behavior to instill a sense of stewardship that comes from recognizing the value of the resource and the need to make efficient use of available water supplies. This has been very effective in the Coastal Bend region, where the results of the voluntary, daily water conservation practices of residents and industries often rival the effects of mandatory drought management measures that are occasionally required in other parts of the state. While these daily water use efficiencies result in the low per capita water use found in the region, they do not appear to affect the regional economy the way mandatory water use restrictions can affect areas that must impose such measures.

Water reuse is a management measure that can achieve considerable water savings by substituting treated wastewater effluent for potable water supplies in many irrigation and industrial uses. However, water reuse in the Coastal Bend region is limited by the fact that wastewater effluents are a sizable and necessary source of freshwater inflows to local bays and estuaries. According to the freshwater inflow requirements associated with the Choke Canyon water rights permit, diverting wastewater effluent from current discharges into the Nueces estuary for purposes of a reuse project may mean that more water will have to be passed through the reservoir system to meet environmental water demands. This Catch 22 situation inhibits the consumptive reuse of water for most purposes.

Reservoir System Policies to Get More Water from Existing Sources

In the semiarid regions of Texas, reservoirs are basically designed to capture and store the infrequent flood flows for diversion and use during the more frequent periods of reduced flow (or, sometimes, no flow) that do not provide sufficient water to meet normal water demands. Storage is a precious resource in a highly variable hydrologic environment. How that storage is managed determines the amount of water that is available on a dependable basis through drought periods. However, reservoir system operating policies reflect the fact that multiple water management objectives often need to be satisfied and that maximizing firm annual yield is not always the only or the most important objective.

Environmental demands for instream flows and freshwater inflows to estuaries are two examples of reservoir operating considerations that can impact the ability of a reservoir to provide dependable water supplies. Other common operating considerations that may affect the dependable yield of a reservoir are honoring downstream senior water rights, providing adequate lake levels or streamflow for recreational interests, producing hydroelectric power, and preventing flooding. In the case of the Choke Canyon–Lake Corpus Christi–Lake Texana reservoir system that provides surface water supplies to the Coastal Bend region, the primary conflicts in terms of reservoir operations are the competing objectives of maximizing reservoir system yield while also meeting environmental and recreational water demands.

Often there are valid hydrologic reasons for operating a reservoir system in a manner that reduces both evaporative losses and delivery or channel losses, or that provides the most available storage in the reservoir with the greatest probability of receiving inflow events. It takes a carefully designed reservoir operating plan to optimize these factors in an effort to create the maximum reservoir yield while at the same time reducing potential conflicts, or failures, in terms of meeting other operating objectives, like providing freshwater inflows for the bays and estuaries or enhancing recreational opportunities.

The Choke Canyon–Lake Corpus Christi reservoir system faced a serious problem with respect to the effects of special conditions contained in the water rights permit for Choke Canyon Reservoir. The conditions were designed to ensure adequate freshwater inflows for the Nueces estuary. The first series of operating orders issued by the state to implement this special provision required the City of Corpus Christi, as the operator of the reservoir system, to release prescribed amounts of water from the reservoir system each month in an effort to meet what had been identified as the minimum freshwater inflow needs of the Nueces estuary. The amounts of these monthly releases were based on the monthly freshwater inflow needs. Less certain amounts of return flows were being discharged to the Nueces estuary from wastewater treatment plants throughout the region. The requirement to release stored water, even during periods of low reservoir system inflows, decreased the reservoir system firm annual yield by as much as 80,000 acre-feet per year, or 35 percent of the estimated 1990 firm annual yield (HDR Engineering 1990).

In order to honor the special condition regarding freshwater inflows for the Nueces estuary yet mitigate the impact it had on the reservoir system yield, water supply and environmental interests began working on a new freshwater inflow operating plan in 1992. By 1995, a plan had been developed and adopted that replaced the hard-and-fast monthly release requirements with a set of monthly freshwater inflow targets. These targets represent the desired freshwater inflow amounts, but the actual monthly freshwater inflow requirements are established by measuring the actual inflow into the Choke Canyon–Lake Corpus Christi reservoir system. If the monthly reservoir inflows are greater than the estuary inflow targets, then reservoir inflows up to the target amounts are passed through to the estuary. If the monthly reservoir inflows are less than the monthly estuary inflow target, then only the reservoir inflow amount is passed through to the estuary; there is no requirement to release any stored water from the reservoir to make up the difference. This pass-through operating plan mimics the natural variability in both streamflows and estuary inflows, while protecting the yield of the reservoir system to a much greater extent than did the original release plan.

Another factor that is considered in the current operating plan for the Choke Canyon–Lake Corpus Christi reservoir system is the recreational interests around Lake Corpus Christi. Although Lake Corpus Christi was constructed and financed as a water supply reservoir, the facility also provides an incidental benefit of considerable value to the local area around the reservoir—recreation. Recreational opportunities in Lake Corpus Christi are directly related to the reservoir levels. Recognizing this fact and the importance of the recreational use of Lake Corpus Christi, the operating plan adopted by the City of Corpus Christi in 1987 maintains a certain minimum level for Lake Corpus Christi by transferring water from Choke Canyon Reservoir. This is not a maximum yield operating plan, but it was selected as an operating policy for as long as the regional water demand is less than the firm yield of the reservoir system. Maximum reservoir system yield would be obtained by operating solely out of Lake Corpus Christi until it is practically empty before transferring any water from Choke Canyon Reservoir.

Recently, the complexity of the situation has been greatly increased by the fact that Choke Canyon and Lake Corpus Christi are now part of a three-reservoir system created by the delivery of water supplies from Lake Texana. The operating policies of the Choke Canyon–Lake Corpus Christi reservoir system are being reevaluated to determine if new operating policies could potentially provide a greater overall yield in light of the way the water from Lake Texana is being delivered on a regular basis.

Another management strategy being considered is a way of addressing an old problem that has a major impact on the yield of the Choke Canyon–Lake Corpus Christi reservoir system—delivery or channel losses in the reach between the two reservoirs. Investigations have documented that as much as 30 percent of the water released from Choke Canyon Reservoir for transfer to Lake Corpus Christi, for diversion either there or downstream in the Corpus Christi area, is lost to the underlying aquifer or consumed by evapotranspiration en route. Studies indicate that construction of a pipeline capable of conveying most of the water that would be involved in these transfers could increase the Choke Canyon–Lake Corpus Christi reservoir system yield by approximately 30,000 acre-feet per year, or about 15 percent of the current yield (HDR Engineering, June, 2000).

Interbasin Transfers to Move Water between Regions

Water is not always evenly distributed between sources and demands. Areas of Texas, primarily the eastern portions of the state, are blessed with more abundant rainfall and generally have much more water available than the semiarid to arid regions of West Texas. However, even within areas that have relatively abundant water supplies, the facilities to store and divert available water resources are not always within the same region or river basin as the point of demand. For example, the City of Dallas has more water supplies originating in sources outside the Trinity basin than it does within that basin. Statewide, there are more than eighty permitted interbasin transfers that help to distribute water more efficiently between sources and demands.

As early as the 1950s, the Coastal Bend region recognized that there were limits to the amount of dependable water supplies it would be possible to develop from the Nueces River basin. At the time Wesley Seale Dam was under construction on the Nueces River, federal and state water planners informed interests in the Coastal Bend region of the likelihood that one more reservoir could be built within the basin and that beyond this next source of water from within the basin, new water supplies would need to come from sources outside it.

Almost immediately after Choke Canyon Reservoir was completed in 1982, creating the second and perhaps last major reservoir in the Nueces River basin, the Coastal Bend region experienced a severe drought. With no additional water supply being realized from the new reservoir and the water levels in Lake Corpus Christi plummeting, regional water planners looked to another new reservoir that offered available water supply even during the drought in the Nueces basin. Lake Texana, completed on the Navidad River in Jackson County in 1979, had a permitted firm annual yield of 75,000 acre-feet. However, water demand in the service area for the new reservoir had not materialized as originally projected, and surplus water was available for municipal and industrial water supply.

In 1984, as the drought in the Nueces River basin resulted in the implementation of water rationing in the Coastal Bend area, the City of Corpus Christi entered into a short-term water purchase agreement with the Lavaca-Navidad River Authority (LNRA) for water from Lake Texana. The concept was to utilize existing out-of-service natural gas pipelines to transfer water 101 miles from Lake Texana to the Corpus Christi area. The State of Texas authorized a term permit for this proposed interbasin transfer. The drought broke in late 1984, and the plan was never put into action, but the concept of using water from Lake Texana remained a viable option.

The concept of interbasin transfers from Lake Texana and other sources to the northeast of the Corpus Christi area suddenly became extremely important in the early 1990s as the Coastal Bend discovered that the dependable yield from the Choke Canyon–Lake Corpus Christi reservoir system was not nearly as great as originally estimated. In addition to the Lake Texana water supplies, the Coastal Bend began to look at potential sources of water from the Colorado River basin. One of the largest senior water rights on the Colorado River was held by a privately owned irrigation operation, the Garwood Irrigation Company.

In 1992, the City of Corpus Christi entered into an option agreement with the LNRA for the annual purchase of up to 41,840 acre-feet of water from Lake Texana. Discussions between the City of Corpus Christi and the Garwood Irrigation Company began in 1990, and by 1992 the City also entered into an option agreement for the purchase of 35,000 acre-feet per year of the Garwood Irrigation Company's water right. Final purchase of these water rights was contingent upon the successful amendment of the Garwood permit to change the use of this portion of the water right from irrigation to municipal and industrial and to authorize the transfer of the 35,000 acre-feet for use within the Corpus Christi service area. Rather than buying the water right as is, the City of Corpus Christi wanted assurances that the water it was acquiring could actually be transferred and used as intended in the Corpus Christi service area. Although the original Garwood permit authorized an interbasin transfer for irrigation purposes—most of the authorized irrigation service area was actually outside the Colorado River basin in the adjoining Navidad River basin—the issue of moving this amount of water out of the Colorado basin to the Corpus Christi area for municipal and industrial use was known to be controversial.

These two option contracts set the stage for the investigation of a wide range of water supply options for the Coastal Bend region under the Trans-Texas Water Planning Program that took place between 1992 and 1995. By 1993, the Phase I interim report on the Trans-Texas study provided enough information to compare most of the options on the basis of the amount of dependable yield available, the cost per unit of dependable yield, and relative environmental impacts. Analysis of all the options showed that the interbasin transfers from Lake Texana and the Colorado River would be the most dependable, affordable water of any significant quantity that the Coastal Bend might have available in the near future.

Based on this initial evaluation, the City of Corpus Christi made the decision in 1993 to exercise the Lake Texana water purchase option, while retaining an ongoing option on the Garwood water rights to pursue further a favorable permit amendment for the interbasin transfer from the Colorado River. The Lavaca-Navidad River Authority filed an application for the interbasin transfer from Lake Texana to the Corpus Christi service area and went through a relatively brief (one-year) process of administrative hearings that resulted in a permit being issued.

While the drought of 1996 brought attention to statewide water problems and motivated lawmakers to introduce Senate Bill 1, in the Coastal Bend area the impacts of the drought on the Choke Canyon–Lake Corpus Christi reservoir system caused so much concern that the decision to build the pipeline from Lake Texana to Corpus Christi was immediately taken. The period originally anticipated for the project had been 2005–2007, but the City of Corpus Christi now entered into agreements with the Nueces River Authority (NRA) and the Port of Corpus Christi Authority to build a 101-mile water delivery system that would transport water from Lake Texana to the City's Stevens Water Treatment Plant in Calallen. Under these agreements, the City guaranteed the repayment of bonds sold by NRA to fund the pipeline design, right-of-way acquisition, and pipeline construction; NRA engaged the port authority to manage the entire project. LNRA had previously agreed to finance and construct facilities on Lake Texana properties as part of the original water purchase and conveyance agreement with the City.

Under this extremely effective regional partnership arrangement, a 101-mile concrete and steel pipeline of sixty-four-inch internal diameter, capable of delivering 107,800 acre-feet per year, was designed, manufactured, and installed within almost exactly two years. All of the more than fifteen thousand joints of pressure pipe were actually laid within one twelve-month period. The route involved nine major stream crossings, two of which were done by directional drilling, including one that now stands as the longest, largest diameter directional boring successfully completed in the United States. Three pump stations were constructed: a primary pump station at Lake Texana and two booster stations along the route.

On September 29, 1998, the Lake Texana to Corpus Christi pipeline was dedicated as the Mary Rhodes Memorial Pipeline in honor of Mayor Mary Rhodes, who championed the project during her tenure in office and who died shortly after the first joints of pipe were laid in June, 1997.

While the Mary Rhodes Pipeline project sailed along, obtaining the interbasin transfer approval for the Garwood water rights was another matter. Under the purchase option agreement, the Garwood Irrigation Company was to file the application and pursue the amendment with the support of the City of Corpus Christi. Only if Garwood were granted an acceptable permit amendment was the City obligated to conclude the purchase of the 35,000 acre-feet per year of Colorado River water rights.

Garwood filed the application for the amendment in January, 1997, just as the 75th Texas Legislature convened. Closely following the 1996 drought, this legislative session was to address the problem of water as a primary goal. Because of the strong, organized opposition to the Garwood water rights transfer, there was great concern that legislative initiatives would further restrict the ability of the Coastal Bend region to secure the interbasin transfer permit for the Garwood water.

The concern was well founded. The 75th Legislature passed Senate Bill 1, which contained several new requirements making interbasin transfers much more difficult and less dependable. Fortunately, the legislature was sympathetic to the needs in the Coastal Bend area for additional water supplies and to its reasonable and far-sighted efforts to develop new supplies on the basis of willing seller–willing buyer transactions like the Lake Texana and Garwood transfers. The Garwood transaction was exempted from any of the new provisions of Senate Bill 1, allowing it to go through the permitting process under the rules in effect prior to the new application requirements in SB 1 and to retain the 1900 priority date.

Even with the legislative grandfathering of the Garwood interbasin transfer application, the administrative process was marked by considerable opposition from interests in the Colorado River basin, particularly from the Lower Colorado River Authority (LCRA) and the City of Austin. However, by July, 1998, LCRA was negotiating with Garwood Irrigation Company for the remaining part of the Garwood water right. When the two parties signed a purchase contract, one of the contract provisions was that LCRA would withdraw its opposition to the Corpus Christi purchase and interbasin transfer. Further, if for any reason the Corpus Christi transfer were not approved, then Garwood would not sell to LCRA. As a result, concerns within the Colorado River basin about the Corpus Christi purchase of the Garwood water rights were mollified, and almost all protests were withdrawn.

On October 7, 1998, TNRCC approved the Garwood interbasin diversion. Thus, within a period of less than ten years, Corpus Christi and the Coastal Bend region proved that with planning and cooperation, water supplies for the future of the region could be secured and that, even in today's regulatory climate, it was possible to go from planning to pumping in record time.

Groundwater Management, an Integrated Approach

Groundwater resources in South Texas have not historically been considered adequate for large-scale municipal and industrial use, but recent changes in laws governing surface water use in Texas have created more impetus to investigate groundwater availability and conjunctive management of surface and groundwater supplies.

Conjunctive Management—the integrated management of groundwater and surface water resources—has been a buzzword in Texas for a long time, but few opportunities have existed to put the concept into practice. The perception of the separate nature of surface water and groundwater supplies has generally dictated that these two water resources be managed separately. However, whether the water is considered surface water or groundwater depends only on the location of water in the hydrological cycle. With the understanding of the interconnected nature of surface and groundwater, the Coastal Bend region has begun integrating conjunctive management strategies into a water planning philosophy. This philosophy emphasizes the most efficient use of water resources to ensure that the future water demands for South Texas are met.

The Texana pipeline changed the face of water resources management in the Coastal Bend region. It did more than merely make possible the transfer of water from other surface water sources; it opened the door to conjunctive management opportunities. The SB 1 regional planning study for the Coastal Bend area used a combination of surface water models and groundwater models to investigate opportunities for conjunctive management, including aquifer storage and recovery and the use of groundwater to firm up surface water rights.

The entire route of the Texana pipeline is roughly parallel to the trend of the Gulf Coast aquifer and, in many areas, crosses through portions of the aquifer where groundwater availability modeling has revealed the potential for significant yields of groundwater. Dodson (1997) developed and calibrated a MODFLOW (McDonald and Harbaugh 1988) numerical groundwater model that was used to simulate the effects of groundwater withdrawals on aquifer conditions in Refugio County. The model simulates the impact of different well-field configurations and various pumping rates—from 10,000 to 60,000 acre-feet per year—on water levels in the Gulf Coast aquifer. Based on results of these model runs, it appears that up to 30,000 acre-feet per year could be available on a dependable-yield basis from the Gulf Coast aquifer in Refugio County.

Municipal water supply systems in Refugio County include wells currently producing water that exceeds state and federal drinking water standards for chlorides (TNRCC 1997; Guadalupe-Blanco River Authority 1994). In order to meet drinking water standards, these communities will either need to implement some form of treatment (demineralization) or need to abandon these wells and replace them with new wells. Optionally, wells that might be developed to supply the regional water supply system via the Texana pipeline could also provide better quality groundwater to the communities of Refugio and Woodsboro. In this case, the cost of the new wells would be shared by users of the regional system, not just water users in Refugio and Woodsboro.

In 1997, the Texas Legislature passed Senate Bill 1, and the Texas Water Development Board initiated the regional water planning process called for in this historic water legislation. Refugio County was included in the South Central Texas regional planning area rather than the Coastal Bend region. However, it appears that Refugio County groundwater may still play a pivotal role in the long-term water management plans of these two adjacent regions.

The South Central Texas Regional Water Planning Group is currently evaluating five alternative regional water management plans. One of the plans is based on the joint development of water supplies with several other planning areas, including the Lower Colorado, the Lavaca, and the Coastal Bend planning regions. The plan involves both surface water and groundwater sources being transferred between several supply and demand points across South Texas, with conveyance systems of rivers and pipelines. One of the largest sources of water being considered for transfer in the Inter-Regional Plan is about 80,000 acre-feet per year of run-of-the-river water rights on the Guadalupe River, which could be diverted at the saltwater barrier just below the confluence of the Guadalupe and San Antonio rivers.

The Inter-Regional Plan calls for the use of groundwater from Refugio County to firm up these run-of-the-river water rights during drought-of-record conditions when the surface water would not be fully available. With the current priority date for these surface waters, up to 34,000 acre-feet of groundwater would have to be pumped during the worst year of the drought of record in order to assure the continued full delivery of the 80,000 acre-feet per year (HDR Engineering, June, 2000).

Aquifer storage and recovery (ASR) is a water management technique being investigated in the Coastal Bend region in terms of both inter-regional and local water management strategies. ASR employs pumping treated surface water into wells when there is excess water available (storage), then later withdrawing (recovering) the water during periods when the surface water is in short supply. While further investigations would be necessary to define particular sites better, the general characteristics of the Gulf Coast aquifer and the availability of nearby run-of-the-river water rights would appear to support the development of an ASR system in the Refugio County area. The Texana pipeline could convey water from these surface water sources, when available, to a location in Refugio County. After relocation, the water would be treated and used for aquifer replenishment and then recovered and put back into the Texana pipeline during drought periods when the less dependable surface water rights would not be able to provide water to meet demands.

This conjunctive management of surface and groundwater supplies may be a practical method of increasing the overall dependability of a regional water system. At a more local level, SB 1 planning in the Coastal Bend also includes ASR studies for the Rockport and Driscoll areas. Municipal water supply systems often encounter periodic increases in water demand due to the influx of tourists or increased lawn irrigation during the summer. ASR may be used to meet these additional demands on the water supply system without having to build new well capacity, surface water treatment capacity, or trunk line capacity. In these cases, during the low demand periods, excess treated water is stored in the aquifer at a point accessible to the city's distribution system and is then used as an additional supply of treated water to meet seasonal peaks in demand. ASR may prove to be a viable water management strategy to make more efficient use of available water supplies, thus avoiding the need to develop new supplies to meet a periodic water demand situation.

As interest increases in managing or regulating groundwater withdrawals, the detailed model of the Gulf Coast aquifer (Hay 1999) can provide a tool for groundwater management activities throughout the region. The calibrated and verified Gulf Coast aquifer groundwater flow model can be used to provide information on groundwater availability, the effects of various well spacing and pumping scenarios, seawater intrusion rates, and leakage of poor quality water between aquifers.

Desalination, the Next Horizon

Desalination of seawater has been implemented to produce potable water in energy-rich but water-poor areas, such as portions of the Middle East, for many years. However, in most areas with other water supply options, seawater desalination has not been economically viable until recently. Advances in reverse osmosis (RO) membrane technology and desalination process systems are decreasing costs to a point where the large-scale production of potable water from seawater is becoming a reasonable alternative for some areas. Also, finished water regulatory requirements are becoming more stringent, and population growth continues in areas with limited freshwater resources, such the Texas coast.

Texas leads the nation in population growth and the 2000 Census will likely show Texas with more than 20 million people. With this rate of population growth, stretching water treatment strategies to include desalination is occurring statewide. Desalination of brackish water or seawater in Texas has the potential to expand the resources available for producing potable water. Due to excess salinity, large amounts of brackish ground- and surface water and a virtually limitless supply of seawater are not suitable for drinking unless treated.

The Coastal Bend region has focused recent studies around membrane technologies and has removed distillation processes from consideration due to their energy requirements translating into high costs in this part of the world. RO and electrodialysis reversal (EDR) systems are the primary membrane treatment options to desalinate brackish water. Reverse osmosis is the only viable membrane treatment option to desalinate seawater. Process selection includes the consideration of water quality, treatment objectives, and costs.

RO offers several advantages over EDR, including control of dissolved organic constituents and pathogenic microorganisms. Due to the potential for cost savings, EDR has a treatment niche for waters not requiring the removal of these constituents and for waters that require removal of less than 3,000 mg/L of total dissolved solids.

A survey of desalination plants operating in Texas indicates that the majority of membrane desalination plants are RO systems treating brackish groundwater. However, both RO and EDR systems are currently being used to treat inland brackish surface water in Texas. No seawater desalination plants exist in the state, and few are operational in the United States. However, two contracts awarded in 1999 highlight the potential for low-cost seawater desalination. One contract, known as the Tampa Bay Water Desalination Project, is being closely examined by the Coastal Bend region.

The majority of drinking water RO systems operating in the United States use groundwater as their source. Groundwater sources generally have low turbidity, and the primary treatment objective is the removal of total dissolved solids. Therefore, typically the only pretreatment required involves addition of acid and scale inhibitor and use of cartridge filtration. Surface water requires more stringent monitoring than groundwater because of the variables that can influence pretreatment. Surface water requires more pretreatment due to seasonal variations, which can produce significant levels of suspended solids and biological matter in the source water. For low turbidity surface water sources, in addition to the acid and scale inhibitor and cartridge filtration required for pretreatment ahead of the membranes, coagulant ahead of media filtration may also be required. In cases where the surface water source is highly turbid, full conventional treatment (coagulation/flocculation, sedimentation, media filtration) is required before the chemical addition and cartridge filtration. Due to the extensive pretreatment requirements, therefore, treatment of brackish surface water may be more expensive than treatment of groundwater.

The Coastal Bend region borders the Gulf of Mexico, a system known by its users as very salty. This reality introduces the major drawbacks for use of seawater desalination in Texas. First, other water resources, such as brackish surface and groundwater, are cheaper to treat. The high costs associated with seawater desalination may be mitigated, however, when seawater desalination is co-located with a power plant. Co-locating the two can provide opportunities for sharing intake, outfall, and permitting costs. Further, the increased-temperature effluent can be used to lower treatment costs by increasing the reverse osmosis membrane flux rate. In a deregulated power environment there may also be some savings in power costs due to decreased power distribution costs.

Second, the requirement for high salt rejection and higher than normal osmotic pressure limits seawater reverse osmosis systems to 35 to 50 percent recoveries. Therefore, the discharged reject water, known as concentrate, is generally 50 to 100 percent greater in total dissolved solids than the raw water. Disposal of this concentrate into a system known for areas of hypersalinity may be prohibited due to negative environmental impacts. For example, the Laguna Madre, which extends from near Corpus Christi to near Brownsville, is one of only four estuaries in the world that regularly exhibit hypersaline conditions (greater than 33,000 mg/L; HDR Engineering, May, 2000).

Summary and Conclusions

The Coastal Bend region has learned from the lessons it has experienced over the last century of water resources development. Planning is the key to being prepared for the surprises inherent in the variable climate that characterizes the region. Planning, however, must be followed with implementation. Experience has shown that in spite of adequate planning, if management strategies are not implemented on a timely basis, there is still the risk of getting caught short on the continuing path to sustainable water supplies.

In this new century, management strategies for the Coastal Bend region will focus on resource conservation and protection as well as the innovative, conjunctive management of both surface water and groundwater resources. New horizons will include the increased application of membrane technologies to desalinate brackish groundwater, brackish surface water, and even seawater. Using this approach to water resources management, the Coastal Bend region should continue to enjoy the benefits of a reliable, affordable water supply and a healthy environment that provides a high quality of life for current and future residents.

Acknowledgments

The authors wish to thank several individuals with HDR Engineering, Inc., of Austin, Texas, for their contributions to the body of knowledge about water resources management in the Coastal Bend region. Ken Choffel,

Sam Vaugh, Kelly Payne, Larry Land, Bryan Black, and Mark Graves have been instrumental in developing the information and tools that have made regional water planning such a success in this area.

References

Dodson, K. K. "Identifying Underutilized Groundwater Resources in the Coastal Bend Region of Texas." Master's thesis in Environmental Science, Texas A&M University–Corpus Christi, 1997.

Guadalupe-Blanco River Authority. "City of Woodsboro, Texas Water Quality Study." Report to the City of Woodsboro, 1994.

Hay, R. G. "A Numerical Groundwater Flow Model of the Gulf Coast Aquifer Along the South Texas Gulf Coast." Master's thesis in Environmental Science, Texas A&M University–Corpus Christi, 1999.

HDR Engineering. *Regional Water Supply Planning Study of the Nueces River Basin*, vol. 1: *Executive Summary*. Report to the Nueces River Authority, City of Corpus Christi, Edwards Underground Water District, South Texas Water Authority, and Texas Water Development Board, 1990.

———. *Regional Water Planning Study: Cost Update for Palmetto Bend Stage 2, Yield Enhancement Alternative for Lake Texana, and Palmetto Bend Stage 2*. Report to the Lavaca-Navidad River Authority, Alamo Conservation and Reuse District, and City of Corpus Christi, 1991.

———. *Trans-Texas Water Program, Corpus Christi Study Area, Phase II Report*. Vol. 2: *Technical Report*. Report to the City of Corpus Christi, Port of Corpus Christi Authority, Corpus Christi Board of Trade, Texas Water Development Board, and Lavaca-Navidad River Authority, 1995.

———. *Water Supply Update for the Corpus Christi Service Area*. Report to the City of Corpus Christi Water Department, January, 1999.

———. *Water Conservation Plan for the City of Corpus Christi*. HDR Engineering Report to the City of Corpus Christi, July, 1999.

———. *Desalination for Texas Water Supply*. Draft Report to the Texas Water Development Board, Nueces River Authority, Central Power and Light Company, City of Corpus Christi, and San Patricio Municipal Water District, May, 2000.

———. *Coastal Bend Regional Water Management Plan*. Draft Report to the Coastal Bend Regional Water Planning Group, June, 2000.

McDonald, M. G., and A. W. Harbaugh. *A Modular Three-Dimensional Finite-Difference Ground-Water Flow Model*. U.S. Geological Survey Techniques of Water-Resources Investigations Report 06-A1. 1988.

Texas Natural Resource Conservation Commission (TNRCC). TNRCC database for Refugio County; water quality compliance records, well logs, well location information, water levels, and well records. 1997.

Texas Senate. Senate Bill 1. Act of June 19, 1997, 75th Legislature, regular session. *Vernon's Texas Session Laws,* ch. 1010. 1997.

CHAPTER 8

Houston Water Issues

Philip B. Bedient, Hanadi S. Rifai, Monica P. Suarez, Rik M. Hovinga, and Burke Nixon

Department of Environmental Science and Engineering

Rice University (Bedient, Hovinga, Nixon)

Department of Civil and Environmental Engineering

University of Houston (Rifai, Suarez)

Abstract

The City of Houston, Gulf Coast Water Authority, San Jacinto River Authority, Trinity River Authority, and Brazos River Authority currently provide 6 percent of the total surface water supply available to Region H. Other surface water sources provide 10 percent of the total surface water supply and are projected to provide 12 percent by 2050.

In order to curb future subsidence and to protect shallow groundwater quality in Region H, groundwater usage from the Chicot, Evangeline, and Jasper aquifers will be reduced from the current 29 percent to approximately 24 percent of the total water usage over the 2000–2050 period. Numerical groundwater availability models of major aquifers in Texas are being utilized to make a correct assessment of groundwater usage.

Management strategies for the future, such as water transfers, water redistributions, and new surface water reservoirs for the Brazos River Authority, Gulf Coast Water Authority, and San Jacinto River Authority are considered necessary to sustain future water demands. The Trinity River Authority is expected to supply water to the City of Houston. Future water supply strategies will have to include the need of sufficient freshwater inflows to the bay systems to protect the critical estuary habitat.

Flat topography and the rapid expansion of urban development within floodplains have resulted in flooding problems well beyond the boundaries represented on current floodplain maps. The decade of the nineties generated a number of large flood events and associated damage to the region. Small-scale structural flood control options for highly urbanized watersheds in Region H are often insufficient, forcing the use of more complex options such as large-scale channel improvements or of nonstructural alternatives like voluntary property buyouts.

The Houston Region (Region H), one of the sixteen regional water planning groups established by Texas Water Development Board (TWDB), is located in the Brazos, Trinity, San Jacinto, and Neches river basins and the Brazos-Colorado, San Jacinto–Brazos, Neches-Trinity, and Trinity-San Jacinto coastal basins (fig. 1). Region H comprises approximately thirteen thousand square miles and encompasses parts of three main river basins in southeast Texas: the Trinity, San Jacinto, and Brazos. This chapter summarizes the findings from recent studies from the Region H Water Planning Group (2000) and is organized into three sections that address groundwater issues, surface water supplies, and flooding issues.

The area is dominated by the presence of the City of Houston, fourth largest city in the United States and one of the major municipal users in Texas. In 2000, municipal

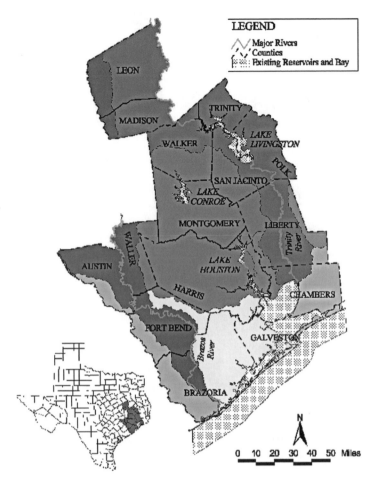

Figure 1. Region H reservoirs and river basins.

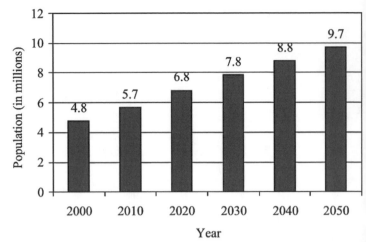

Figure 2. Projected population growth for Region H (RHWPG 2000).

the problem of water shortage between 2000 and 2050 involves the development of new surface water reservoirs on the Brazos River and strategic interbasin transfers of water within the Brazos, San Jacinto, and Trinity basins.

Population growth for the next five decades will be the key factor in the determination of projected future municipal water needs, in combination with the estimates of per capita water use and water conservation assumptions. Consequently, the water requirements for Region H are projected to increase from 2.25 million acre-feet per year (ac-ft/yr) in 2000 to over 3.18 million ac-ft/yr in 2050 (table 1). Municipal and industrial water requirements are expected to increase throughout the planning period. Irrigation water demands are expected to remain constant for Region H except for Brazoria County, where they are expected to decrease. Water requirements for livestock production are also projected to remain constant within Region H.

water use accounted for 40 percent, industrial water use for 37 percent, and irrigated agriculture for 23 percent of Region H water use. The complexity of water use in the area is quite high and requires unique solutions, especially as the region's population is expected to more than double over the next fifty years (fig. 2). The primary solution to

Table 1. Projected water use for Region H, in acre-feet per year

Year	2000		2030		2050	
Municipal water use	897,209	39.9%	1,263,941	45.6%	1,485,639	46.6%
Manufacturing	708,113	31.5%	874,028	31.5%	1,048,194	32.9%
Irrigation	501,053	22.3%	474,102	17.1%	471,679	14.8%
S.E. power cooling	95,100	4.2%	116,100	4.2%	135,000	4.2%
Mining	33,826	1.5%	31,242	1.1%	35,243	1.1%
Livestock	13,038	0.6%	13,038	0.5%	13,038	0.4%
Total water requirements	2,248,339		2,772,451		3,188,793	

Source: RHWPG 2000.

Present Status of Groundwater in the Houston Region

Groundwater use currently comprises 33 percent of all water used in the region; however, by year 2050 groundwater use is projected to comprise only 17 percent (TWDB 1997). Groundwater within the Houston-Galveston area is predominantly withdrawn from the Gulf Coast aquifer system, specifically from the Chicot and Evangeline aquifers (Harris-Galveston Coastal Subsidence District [HGCSD] 1998).

Hydrogeology

The Gulf Coast aquifer is a leaky artesian aquifer system that consists of interbedded clays, silts, sands, and gravels hydrologically connected. Four major components form the system: the Catahoula, Jasper, Evangeline, and Chicot aquifers (from deepest to shallowest). Not all formations are present throughout the system. Maximum total sand thickness varies between seven hundred feet in the south and thirteen hundred feet in the northern part (TWDB 1997).

The Chicot and Evangeline aquifers are composed of discontinuous deposits of sand, silt, and clay that thicken to the southeast (Williams and Ranzau 1985). The Chicot aquifer, or upper component of the Gulf Coast aquifer system, consists of the Lissie, Willis, Bentley, Montgomery, and Beaumont formations and overlying alluvial deposits (TWDB 1997). The Evangeline aquifer in the Houston area is composed of the Pliocene Goliad Sand Formation and the Miocene Fleming Formation (HGCSD 1998). These deposits are present in subparallel bands that strike from southwest to northeast and thicken downdip in the southeast (Noble 1997).

The Chicot and Evangeline aquifers are composed of thick unconsolidated sediments with high permeability, containing water under artesian head (HGCSD 1998). These sediments are generally found above a depth of about twenty-four feet. The outcrop area of the formations is approximately parallel to the coastline, and the formations dip to the southeast (fig. 3). The hydraulic conductivity of the Chicot aquifer is up to twice as high as that of the Evangeline aquifer, whereas the transmissivity of the two aquifers is fairly similar (HGCSD 1998). Estimated transmissivity of the Chicot aquifer ranges from 3,000 to 25,000 ft^2/d, while the estimated transmissivity of the Evangeline aquifer varies between 3,000 and 15,000 ft^2/d (Meyer and Carr 1979). The Evangeline aquifer is generally thicker than the Chicot, which explains its higher transmissivity despite having lower hydraulic conductivity.

The Jasper aquifer, which underlies the Chicot and Evangeline, has not historically been used as a groundwater source in Harris, Galveston, and Fort Bend counties; however, it is widely used in Montgomery County. The major reason the Jasper aquifer has not been utilized in some counties is the depth of the aquifer and the drilling costs associated with accessing it for water supply (HGCSD 1998).

A large part of the recharge zone for the Chicot and Evangeline aquifers is located north of Harris, Galveston, and Fort Bend counties. The primary recharge area for the Chicot aquifer is located in Harris and southern Montgomery counties, while the main recharge area for the Evangeline aquifer is located in Austin, Grimes, and Waller counties (Fort Bend Subsidence District 1998; HGCSD 1998). Based upon the upper bound for the 1953–90 recharge record and the 1953–95 extended period of record, the United States Geological Survey (USGS) estimated average annual recharge in outcrops in the Chicot and Evangeline aquifers in the Houston area to be approximately six inches per year (Noble 1997). However, the USGS points out that due to uncertainty with some of the assumptions used in calculating recharge, this is not a definitive rate.

Recharge was estimated by the TWDB to be 302,700 acre-feet per year in Harris and Galveston counties and 74,381 acre-feet per year in Fort Bend County (TWDB 1998).

Artificial recharge of the aquifers by seepage from the surface has not been determined to be feasible due to the

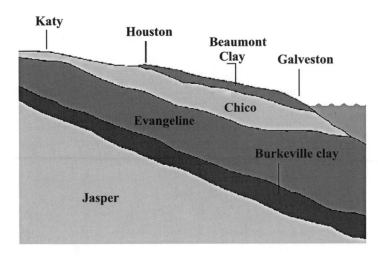

Figure 3. Gulf Coast aquifer cross section (Source: HGCSD 1998).

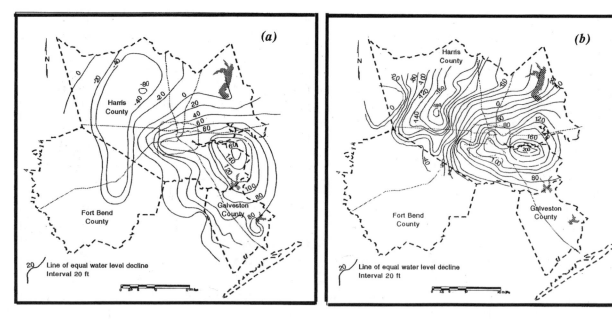

Figure 4. Groundwater level changes in the Houston-Galveston counties, 1977–99; (a) Chicot aquifer, (b) Evangeline aquifer (Coplin et al. 1999b).

slow groundwater flow rate (sixty feet per year) and the presence of Beaumont Clay Formations that prevent filtration. The Harris-Galveston and Fort Bend subsidence districts are evaluating artificial recharge to the aquifers. However, injection of recharge water generates concerns regarding groundwater quality and economic issues.

Groundwater Levels

The USGS has historically analyzed water levels in the Gulf Coast aquifer. A joint effort between the Harris-Galveston Coastal Subsidence District (HGCSD), Fort Bend Subsidence District (FBSD), USGS, and the City of Houston allows monitoring of five hundred wells within Fort Bend, Galveston, and Harris counties. The water table in this region varies between approximately ten and thirty feet below land surface. In general, water table measurements have shown no long-term trends since groundwater development has begun (HGCSD 1998). Water level changes in the Chicot and Evangeline aquifers (as in all artesian aquifers) are a function of changes in potentiometric pressure and are significantly influenced by groundwater withdrawal. Water levels in this region are the result of coalescing cones of depression originating from groundwater withdrawal (HGCSD 1998). Figures 4 and 5 show the changes in potentiometric surface in the region as illustrated by the USGS (Coplin et al.

1999a, 1999b). As seen in figures 4 and 5, water level rises have occurred in the eastern and central regions of HGCSD, while significant declines have occurred in the western area of Harris County and the northeastern part of the FBSD.

Although water levels continued declining in certain areas during 1980–90, the rate of decline has decreased when compared to historical trends because of increased use of available surface water supplies. Water table decline in the Chicot aquifer occurred in five isolated areas in western Harris and northeastern Fort Bend counties during this period. Declines in the Evangeline aquifer also occurred but at a faster rate than in the shallower Chicot. In northwest Harris County, a fifty-foot decline in water level occurred over approximately a third of the area between 1980 and 1990 (TWDB 1997).

Groundwater Use

The Harris-Galveston and Fort Bend subsidence districts have compiled historical data and determined water demands for their regulatory jurisdictions since 1976 and 1989, respectively. Table 2 presents groundwater use by regulatory area in Harris and Galveston counties, while table 3 contains the water pumpage by region in Fort Bend County. It can be seen in table 2 that regulatory areas 1, 2, and 3 (see fig. 6) have experienced a significant decrease in

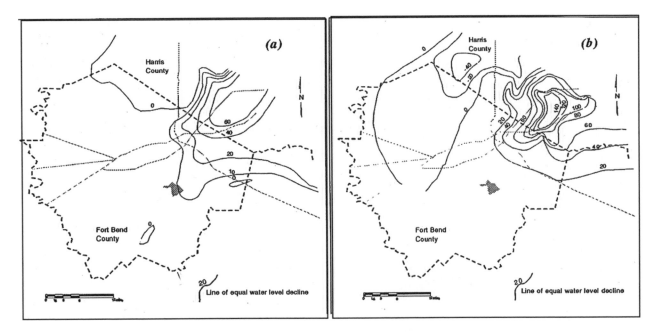

Figure 5. Groundwater level changes in Fort Bend County, 1990–99; (a) Chicot aquifer, (b) Evangeline aquifer (Coplin et al. 1999a).

Table 2. Groundwater use by regulatory area in Harris-Galveston counties (in million gallons per day)

Year	1976	1978	1980	1982	1984	1986	1988	1990	1992	1994	1996	1997
Area 1	139.4	71.7	55.2	37.7	30.2	25.1	22.4	17.2	10.5	11.4	11.4	11.2
Area 2	115.4	113.2	99.5	95.4	80.9	67.0	64.6	65.7	41.6	39.3	33.6	32.5
Area 3	43.6	54.1	58.1	54.9	49.2	51.5	47.2	50.3	29.9	25.8	16.8	12.1
Subtotal	298.4	239.0	212.8	188.0	160.3	143.6	134.2	133.2	82.0	76.5	61.8	55.8
Area 4	23.8	33.0	39.7	51.7	53.0	56.8	59.4	62.3	58.2	62.3	70.4	63.4
Area 5	2.8	4.2	5.2	5.1	5.8	6.1	8.7	8.2	7.9	7.4	9.7	8.1
Area 6	82.3	101.4	123.5	133.3	127.8	131.6	135.6	131.3	130.5	143.4	151.3	134.4
Area 7	48.5	45.7	49.6	49.2	35.9	25.9	39.8	34.1	28.3	29.5	33.6	27.3
Subtotal	157.4	184.3	218.0	239.3	222.5	220.4	243.5	235.9	224.9	242.6	265.0	233.2
Total	455.8	423.3	430.8	427.3	382.8	364.0	377.7	369.1	306.9	319.1	326.8	289.0

Source: HGCSD 1998.

Note: For area locations, see figure 6.

Table 3. Groundwater use by region in Fort Bend County (in million gallons per day)

Year	1990	1991	1992	1993	1994	1995	1996	1997
Northeast Region	29.9	29.3	29.0	29.0	28.9	29.9	32.1	28.9
Northwest Region	14.1	11.0	10.9	10.1	11.9	14.9	15.7	14.5
Southern Region	18.6	16.1	16.2	16.2	19.1	17.9	19.5	17.9
Total	62.6	56.4	56.1	55.3	59.9	62.7	67.3	61.3

Source: FBSD 1998.

Note: For region locations, see figure 6.

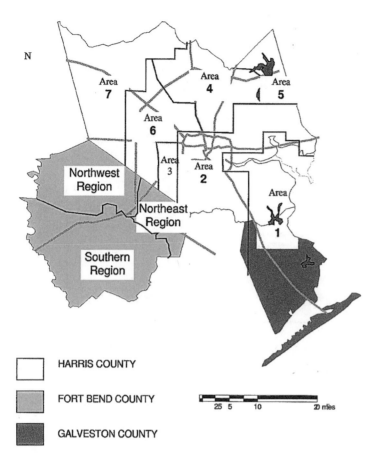

N

Area 7

Area 4

Area 5

Area 6

Area 3

Area 2

Area 1

Northwest Region

Northeast Region

Southern Region

HARRIS COUNTY

FORT BEND COUNTY

GALVESTON COUNTY

25 5   10   20 miles

Figure 6. Harris-Galveston regulatory areas and Fort Bend regions for groundwater use.

accounted for 36 percent, and industrial accounted for 12 percent. The greater Houston metropolitan area is the largest municipal user, with an average well yield of about sixteen hundred gallons per minute (TWDB 1997).

Annual availability of groundwater for the Gulf Coast aquifer is determined through the implementation of a computer model that simulates the aquifer's response to changes in injection and pumpage and predicts water levels and flows under potential future conditions. The TWDB has performed hydraulic modeling of the Gulf Coast aquifer to estimate the potential groundwater availability in the Chicot and Evangeline aquifers in the Houston-Galveston area and Fort Bend County. This model was updated in 1990 and will be updated under the Groundwater Availability Model (GAM) initiative within the next two years. The 1990 version of the model (see table 4) reported a perpetual annual effective recharge for the Gulf Coast aquifer of 302,700 acre-feet per year in Harris and Galveston counties and of 74,381 acre-feet per year in Fort Bend County (270 and 66 million gallons per day, respectively; HGCSD 1998; FBSD 1998). These estimates, however, need to be reevaluated for the following reasons: "A definitive delineation of groundwater availability by county using the TWDB modeling method is difficult to assess due to local variable aquifer characteristics (sand thickness, transmissivity, etc)," and the "actual recorded water-level declines in the Houston area have dropped up to 350 feet below the land surface and subsidence continues to occur" (TWDB 1997).

Shallow Groundwater Contamination

Groundwater contamination cases in water wells and monitoring wells are reported by the Texas Natural Resource Conservation Commission (TNRCC), the Railroad Commission of Texas, and the groundwater conservation districts that make up the Texas Alliance of Groundwater Districts (Texas Groundwater Protection Committee 1999).

There have been over 1,252 reported cases of groundwater contamination. These were identified by release detection monitoring in the TNRCC's petroleum storage tank program. More than half the cases are still awaiting confirmation of contamination, and only about 10 percent of the sites are in corrective action planning, while less than 20 percent of the sites did not require further action. It is safe to say that groundwater cleanup remains a challenge that requires speeding up the cleanup process and optimizing the available resources while protecting

the amount of water pumpage; this is due mainly to an increase of surface water usage in order to reduce subsidence. In regulatory areas 4 through 7, groundwater usage has increased as a result of growth (HGCSD 1998). The groundwater usage in Fort Bend County has increased as a direct result of population growth, as is shown in table 3. As of 1996, 61 percent of groundwater pumpage in the district was used for municipal purposes, a 14 percent increase over 1990 municipal usage. Most of this increase occurred in the northeastern part of the district, due to urbanization in that area causing a shift from irrigation to municipal use. The decrease in groundwater pumpage in 1997 is an anomaly and was a result of above average rainfall in the region (FBSD 1998).

Groundwater Availability

The total pumpage from the Gulf Coast aquifer was approximately 1.1 million acre-feet in 1994; municipal pumpage accounted for 51 percent of the total, irrigation

Table 4. Aquifer recharge and groundwater availability (acre-feet per year)

| Basin | Recharge | Groundwater Availability | | | | | |
		1980–1989	1990–1999	2000–2009	2010–2019	2020–2029	2030
Harris[a]							
Trinity-San Jacinto Basin	16,886	16,886	16,886	16,886	16,886	16,886	16,886
San Jacinto Basin	235,429	235,429	235,429	235,429	235,429	235,429	235,429
San Jacinto-Brazos Basin	28,185	28,185	28,185	28,185	28,185	28,185	28,185
Harris County Total	280,500	280,500	280,500	280,500	280,500	280,500	280,500
Galveston[a]							
Neches-Trinity Basin	1,389	1,389	1,389	1,389	1,389	1,389	1,389
San Jacinto-Brazos Basin	20,811	20,811	20,811	20,811	20,811	20,811	20,811
Galveston County Total	22,200	22,200	22,200	22,200	22,200	22,200	22,200
Fort Bend[b]							
San Jacinto Basin	10,210	10,210	10,210	10,210	10,210	10,210	10,210
San Jacinto-Brazos Basin	20,583	20,583	20,583	20,583	20,583	20,583	20,583
Brazos Basin	34,017	38,669	38,669	38,669	38,669	38,669	34,017
Brazos-Colorado Basin	9,571	9,571	9,571	9,571	9,571	9,571	9,571
Fort Bend County Total	74,381	79,033	79,033	79,033	79,033	79,033	74,381
Total Three Counties	377,081	377,081	377,081	377,081	377,081	377,081	377,081

Sources: a. HGCSD 1998, b. FBSD 1998.

human health and the environment (Texas Groundwater Protection Committee 1999).

Water Quality

Although there is some shallow groundwater contamination, the groundwater from the deeper Chicot and Evangeline aquifers continues to be of relatively high quality and, in most cases, requires only secondary disinfection before transmission to users (HGCSD 1998). For most of the region, the water is fresh, containing less than 1,000 mg/L of total dissolved solids. The water quality in the Chicot and Evangeline aquifers may be threatened by subsidence and downward transport of contamination from shallow aquifers. However, at present time there is not a clear analysis of historical data showing a correlation between subsidence and degraded groundwater quality in the Chicot and Evangeline aquifers.

Subsidence as a Management Issue

The Houston Area has experienced a significant decrease in land surface levels due to declines in water levels in the Chicot and Evangeline aquifers. Figure 7 shows historical land surface subsidence in Harris, Galveston, and Fort Bend counties between 1906 and 1995. Lowering of the potentiometric levels in these confined aquifers decreases the water pressure holding up the overlying sediments. This causes the clay content of the confined aquifers to compress, resulting in ground level subsidence (HGCSD 1998). As seen in figure 7, subsidence in the Houston area is most critical in areas along Galveston Bay, where the land surface has sunk as much as ten feet since 1906, causing serious flooding.

In response to historical water level declines, the Harris-Galveston Coastal Subsidence District was created in 1975 to regulate groundwater withdrawals in order to prevent subsidence and its associated problems. The district's 1992 management plan requires the gradual conversion from groundwater to surface water supplies to meet demands, so that by the year 2030, at most 24 percent of total water use will be obtained from groundwater. As a result, the City of Houston is using mostly surface water (90 percent) for municipal supply; hence the water levels in the Chicot and Evangeline aquifers have bounced back in parts of southeast Harris County and northern Galveston County. Nevertheless, data indicate that continued groundwater pumpage in the northwestern Harris County would result in additional water level declines (TWDB 1997).

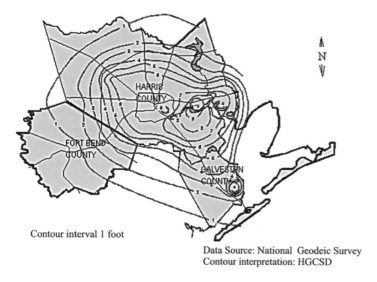

Contour interval 1 foot

Data Source: National Geodeic Survey
Contour interpretation: HGCSD

*Figure 7. Subsidence in the Houston area between 1906 and 1995
(HGCSD 1998).*

Management Issues and Regional Water Planning

In 1997, the Texas Legislature passed Senate Bill 1, which directs sweeping changes in the way of conducting water resources planning in Texas (Trans-Texas Water Program Southeast Area 1998). This bill requires water master planning at the regional level for the entire state. Starting in 2000, the State Water Plan will be composed of the plans from sixteen regions. These plans must determine regional water needs and available supplies; analyze various methods of meeting the water needs; involve the public (stakeholders) in the decision-making process; and acknowledge competing needs and equity issues. The two groundwater conservation districts currently operating in the Houston area (HGCSD and FBSD) have filed comprehensive management plans with the TNRCC. Plans from other conservation districts in the region are under way.

Finally, during the 76th legislative session, the Texas Legislature approved initial funding for the Groundwater Availability Modeling (GAM) program. The purpose of the GAM program is to provide reliable and timely information on groundwater availability to the citizens of Texas in order to ensure adequate supplies, or recognize inadequate supplies, over a fifty-year planning period. Numerical groundwater flow models of the major aquifers in Texas will be used to make this assessment of groundwater availability. The expectation is that GAM will (1) include substantial stakeholder input; (2) result in standardized, thoroughly documented, and publicly available numerical groundwater flow models and sup-

port data; and (3) provide predictions of groundwater availability through 2050 based on current projections of groundwater demands during drought-of-record conditions. GAM will provide the tools to evaluate water management strategies in regional water plans and groundwater conservation district management plans.

Surface Water Issues for the Houston Region

Of the sixteen regions defined by Senate Bill 1 in 1997, Houston is located in Region H (fig. 1). The region is located along the upper Texas coast and consists of fifteen counties: Austin, Brazoria, Chambers, Fort Bend, Galveston, Harris, Leon, Liberty, Madison, Montgomery, the western part of Polk, San Jacinto, the western part of Trinity, Walker, and Waller. Region H encompasses parts of three major river basins and four coastal basins in southeast Texas.

Current and Projected Supply

Surface water resources in Region H are located within the Brazos, San Jacinto, and Trinity river basins, the Lower Neches basin, and the coastal basins. The major sources of surface water supply for Region H are provided by Lake Houston (168,000 ac-ft/yr) and Lake Conroe (99,950 ac-ft/yr) within the San Jacinto River basin and Lake Livingston (1,321,279 ac-ft/yr) within the lower Trinity River basin.

The total amount of water supply (groundwater and surface water) available to Region H from existing water sources for the year 2000 is 3.69 million ac-ft/yr; of that amount, about 71 percent is surface water. By the year 2050, the available total water supply will be 3.46 million ac-ft/yr, of which approximately 76 percent will consist of surface water. The reduction in supply from 2000 to 2030 (table 5) is due to a decrease in availability of groundwater as restrictions on use of groundwater are implemented to reduce and ultimately prevent subsidence.

The five major water providers (MWP) for Region H presented in table 5 are the Brazos River Authority (BRA), City of Houston, Gulf Coast Water Authority (GCWA), San Jacinto River Authority (SJRA), and Trinity River Authority (TRA). These major water providers supply 61 percent of the total water necessitates to Region H in 2000, which will increase to 64 percent in 2030 and 2050.

Water Management Strategies

As shown in table 6, water transfers, water redistributions, and new surface water reservoirs will be of pivotal

Table 5. Projected water supply for Region H (acre-feet per year)

Provider	2000	2030	2050
BRA	104,625	104,625	104,625
City of Houston			
Groundwater	145,479	100,643	99,345
Surface water	1,258,829	1,258,829	1,258,829
GCWA	210,850	210,850	210,850
SJRA			
Groundwater	12,181	18,001	18,001
Surface water	143,921	143,921	143,921
TRA	380,479	380,479	380,479
Other Sources/Providers			
Groundwater	898,826	709,914	711,212
Surface water	531,494	531,717	531,773
Total	3,686,684	3,458,979	3,459,035

Source: RHWPG 2000.

importance to the sustainability of future water demands in Region H. Irrigation conservation ($60–$80 per ac-ft) will be of high importance for Brazoria County, Fort Bend County, and to some extent Waller County. The construction of new surface water reservoirs will relieve many of the major water providers and contribute significantly to the increasing water demand. Possible new surface water reservoirs (fig. 8) involve Allens Creek Reservoir ($121 per ac-ft, yields 99,650 ac-ft/yr, located in Austin County); Little River Reservoir ($160 per ac-ft, 169,800 ac-ft/yr, Milam County); and Bedias Reservoir ($112 per ac-ft, 90,700 ac-ft/yr, Grimes, Walker, and Madison counties). Wastewater reclamation ($299 per ac-ft) will make up a small to medium fraction of the future water supply for the City of Houston.

The Brazos River Authority and the Gulf Coast Water Authority will have to execute serious management strategies in order to sustain current and future water demands (table 6). The San Jacinto River Authority will have to employ management strategies to accommodate increased water demands for the year 2030 and thereafter. The City of Houston has a sufficient water supply up to the year 2040 but will need to execute water management strategies before 2050. The Trinity River Authority has an abundant water supply and is expected to provide water to the City of Houston.

Galveston Bay Freshwater Inflows

To ensure freshwater inflow for Galveston Bay, the Galveston Bay Freshwater Inflows Group (GBFIG) has been

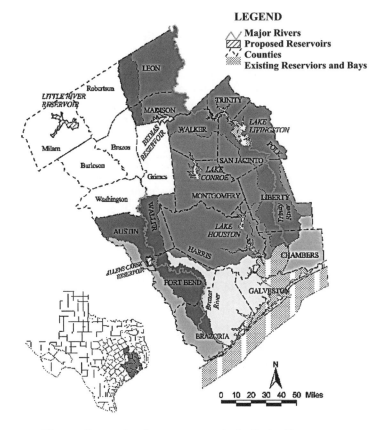

LEGEND
- Major Rivers
- Proposed Reservoirs
- Counties
- Existing Reservoirs and Bays

Figure 8. Proposed surface water reservoirs for Region H.

charged to develop management strategies. In order to yield maximum productivity in the bay, the Texas Parks and Wildlife Department recommends a freshwater inflow of 5.2 million acre-feet per year. GBFIG constructed a schedule of target flows in which the maximum produc-

Table 6. Water supply balances and strategies for the five major water providers (acre-feet per year)

Major Water Provider	Management Strategy	2000	2010	2020	2030	2040	2050
BRA	Balance without strategies	−48,573	−89,544	−107,392	−135,860	−173,649	−216,704
	Municipal conservation	0	762	3,008	4,101	4,302	5,207
	Irrigation conservation	0	29,332	43,581	43,581	43,581	43,581
	Redistributions/Transfers	60,500	60,500	60,377	60,218	60,038	58,589
	Allens Creek Reservoir	0	0	29,900	29,900	29,900	29,900
	Little River Reservoir	0	0	0	85,000	85,000	85,000
	Balance	11,927	1,050	29,474	86,940	49,172	5,573
City of Houston	Balance without strategies	515,639	394,117	174,907	88,414	9,728	−76,380
	Municipal conservation	98	7,763	17,055	16,783	13,652	13,366
	Allens Creek Reservoir	0	0	69,750	69,750	69,750	69,750
	Wastewater reclamation	0	90,700	90,700	90,700	90,700	90,700
	Redistributions/Transfers	0	200,000	200,000	200,000	200,000	177,000
	Balance	515,737	692,580	552,412	465,647	383,830	274,435
GCWA	Balance without strategies	−11,393	−11,919	−18,767	−34,631	−59,087	−85,440
	Municipal conservation	92	840	1,676	2,676	2,858	3,682
	Little River Reservoir	0	0	0	44,800	44,800	44,800
	Redistributions/Transfers	18,000	18,000	18,000	18,000	18,000	41,000
	Balance	6,699	6,921	909	30,845	6,571	4,042
SJRA	Balance without strategies	56,495	34,876	5,045	−19,222	−47,003	−74,602
	Municipal conservation	0	2,632	5,080	6,175	6,586	7,707
	Redistributions/Transfers	0	0	0	75,000	75,000	75,000
	Balance	56,495	37,509	10,125	61,953	34,583	8,105
TRA	Balance without strategies	278,220	273,421	271,891	260,925	259,129	255,392
	Municipal conservation	0	0	0	579	451	531
	Bedias Reservoir	0	0	0	15,700	15,700	15,700
	Redistributions/Transfers	0	−200,000	−200,000	−200,000	−200,000	−200,000
	Balance	278,220	73,421	71,891	77,204	75,280	71,623
Total MWPs	Balance without strategies	790,388	600,951	325,684	159,626	−10,882	−197,734
	Balance with strategies	869,078	811,481	664,811	722,589	549,436	363,778

Source: RHWPG 2000.

tivity of the bay occurs in at least 50 percent of future years. To guarantee good health and productivity in the Galveston Bay, the quantity, quality, frequency (variation of inflow per month), and location of inflows must be and are considered in the planning.

Flooding and Floodplain Development in Houston

A number of areas in southeast Texas, particularly near Houston, have dense urban development within and around established hundred-year floodplains. An enormous increase in population over the last thirty years, mainly in the Houston metropolitan area, has led to this development, which in turn has greatly increased the potential for urban runoff and associated flooding problems. During the boom of the 1970s, prior to the recognition of the effects of urbanization on flooding and the establishment of Federal Emergency Management Agency (FEMA) regulations for Harris County, many developments were allowed inside floodplain areas. The City of Houston and Harris County are ranked high—third and fourth—on the national list of areas most prone to repetitive property loss claims (RPL) under the National Flood Insurance Program (NFIP). While RPLs account for only 2 percent of all properties in the United

States, they claimed 40 percent of all payments between 1978 and 1995. During that time, more than half of the NFIP payments were made in Louisiana and Texas (National Wildlife Federation 1998).

Clay soils, intense rainfalls, and flat topography result in a natural tendency for large floodplains throughout the region. The clay soils of the region have little potential for infiltration, allowing only 0.01 to 0.1 inches infiltration per hour and causing most of the rainfall to become runoff. The intense rainfalls can drop as much as 6.8 inches of rain in a span of three hours, or 12.5 inches in twenty-four hours. These rainfall totals represent the hundred-year storms for the durations indicated. When such quantities of water fall on compact clay soils, in a topographically flat area, the result is an extensive floodplain. This is compounded with the effects of urbanization, which increases the runoff due to impervious cover, such as buildings and parking lots, and reduces the travel time for runoff to reach the receiving stream. The increase in runoff and decrease in travel time often results in a large increase in the quantity of water in the receiving stream when the flow peaks, forcing the runoff to exceed the banks of local creeks and bayous.

Susceptibility to flood damage around the watersheds of this region is significantly greater today than it was a few decades ago. As the National Wildlife Federation notes in *Higher Ground*, "the physical geography [of this region], combined with rapid development, has expanded flooding problems well beyond the boundaries represented on floodplain maps." As long as population growth and development in Region H continue at their current rate, and development practices do not consider downstream floodplain effects, flooding will continue to expand and create long-term problems.

Major Watersheds and Bayous

Brays Bayou offers a typical example of how development affects the floodplains within a watershed in the Houston area. The Brays Bayou watershed covers a 129-square-mile area in southwest Harris County and has been the subject of many hydrologic studies relating to flooding and flood control (Bedient and Huber 1992; Hoblit et al. 1999; Bedient et al. 2000). The main channel of the watershed extends thirty-one miles from east Fort Bend County directly through southwest Houston before flowing into the Houston Ship Channel. When the main bayou was channelized in the 1950s, it was designed to accommodate flows exceeding a hundred-year rainfall

event. Due to years of urban expansion since the 1970s in Houston, the Brays Bayou channel is no longer able to contain a ten-year rainfall event. More than 90 percent of the watershed has now been urbanized, including an estimated thirty thousand structures inside the hundred-year floodplain. A hundred-year flood event on Brays Bayou would result in approximately $1.8 billion in damage (Harris County Flood Control District [HCFCD] 2000a).

The Harris Gully watershed, which drains into Brays Bayou, is located in a highly developed area in central Houston that is home to Rice University and the Texas Medical Center (TMC), the largest medical center in the United States, as well as a large number of associated businesses, homes, and a museum district. Due to the high level of urbanization, many of these homes and institutions are susceptible to flooding during heavy storm events. Opportunities for structural flood control options, such as detention ponds or diversion in the Harris Gully watershed, are limited, and these control options may not be able to prevent damage for greater than ten-year rainfall events. A real-time flood alert system (FAS) has been designed for the area. The FAS uses NEXRAD radar rainfall estimates from the National Weather Service to estimate flooding potential for the TMC. The NEXRAD rainfall estimates have been calibrated to rain gauge measurements and are transformed to flooding potential of the Brays Bayou at the TMC location (Bedient et al. 1998, 2000; Hoblit et al. 1999). The FAS has provided the TMC with a powerful early warning system for overbank flooding of Brays Bayou.

The Clear Creek watershed drains approximately 260 square miles of land, including parts of four counties (Harris, Brazoria, Galveston, and Fort Bend) and part or all of sixteen cities, including Houston and Friendswood. Clear Creek includes one of the few remaining stretches of pristine bayou waterways in southeast Texas, and to preserve this environmental asset, a solution to Clear Creek flood problems must involve much more than simply straightening and widening the main channel. Nearly thirteen thousand acres of land in the watershed are inside the hundred-year floodplain, and hurricane surges in Galveston Bay, located at lower end of the watershed, further impact water levels in the floodplain. A Corps of Engineers study from 1982 estimated that flooding along Clear Creek would cause $6.6 million in damage each year under existing conditions for this area. The estimated damages have increased since 1982 due to development in the watershed.

Projects continue to be proposed and will eventually be implemented on Brays Bayou and Clear Creek watersheds as well as on White Oak, Sims, and Greens bayous. These bayous remain relatively unmanageable at this time, and no project to date has produced significant flood protection along any of them. However, a number of new projects are planned that may produce positive results compared to projects of the past.

Brays Bayou Federal Project

Brays Bayou has been the focus of an ongoing project known as the Brays Bayou Federal Project, which will have significant effects on flooding in southwest Houston (HCFCD 2000a, 2000b). The project is divided into two major parts: upstream and downstream. The study for the upstream project was completed in 1988 and some construction began in 1994. This part of the ongoing project consists of the excavation of channel modifications to Brays Bayou and addition of three major stormwater detention basins upstream of the Sam Houston Tollway (Beltway 8). According to the Harris County Flood Control District, the detention basins will provide approximately 8,100 acre-feet of storage volume along the upstream section of the Brays Bayou. A 3.7-mile stretch of the channel located between Old Westheimer Road and State Highway 6 will also be enlarged. As of July, 2001, about 98 percent of the 520 acres for the detention basins had been acquired, and excavation was in progress. Construction for the upstream element has an estimated completion date of 2008. This part of the project will cost $200 million to build and will provide hundred-year flood protection along Brays Bayou between the Sam Houston Tollway and State Highway 6.

The study and analysis of the second element of the Brays Bayou Federal Project, the downstream element, has only recently been completed. The study sought to find a more effective alternative to a diversion element that was originally suggested in 1985. After a long process of formulating and then rejecting or altering flood control plans, a final approach has been agreed upon by the public and HCFCD. The plan is expected to reduce residential and business flooding and to minimize project cost.

The HCFCD plan involves the enlargement of seventeen miles of the channel from the mouth of the Brays Bayou at the ship channel to Fondren Road, in order to increase the flow-carrying capacity of the channel. A second feature of the plan is a detention basin of 1,865 acre-feet along Willow Waterhole, a tributary of Brays Bayou. This basin will help detain runoff and reduce the peak flows of Brays Bayou. A third feature of the plan is the replacement of fourteen bridges spanning Brays Bayou, including on State Highway 288, and the extension of an additional seventeen bridges. As of July, 2001, four of fifty-five tracts had been purchased for the detention area, and channel design was in the preliminary stages. Construction is scheduled to begin in 2006. It will cost about $242 million, providing fifty-year flood protection between the ship channel and the West Sam Houston Tollway.

Community input played a large part in the planning stages of the project. As a result, the project will incorporate extensive aesthetic, environmental, and recreational improvements. The upstream element includes attractive detention layouts, including playing fields, trails, landscaping, and the planting of twenty thousand trees and shrubs. Some detention areas will include wet bottom marshes to improve water quality and to create wetland habitats. The detention area just upstream of the West Sam Houston Tollway will be a Harris County Precinct Three park. During the planning of the downstream element, several public meetings and coordination with the Brays Bayou Citizens Advisory Committee provided a substantial voice to community concerns. In the downstream reach, the Willow Waterhole Detention Basin will also incorporate wetlands and park and recreation features, though the exact design is not yet complete.

The entire Brays Bayou Federal Project should be completed around 2012. It will significantly reduce flood elevations along Brays Bayou, bringing the number of homes in the hundred-year floodplain down from thirty thousand to seventeen hundred. The total cost is projected to be $437 million, reducing flood damages by about $98 million per year. This amounts to a net benefit of $62 million per year.

Clear Creek Watershed

As early as 1968, the pristine waterways of Clear Creek in southern Harris County had been increasingly encroached upon by urbanization. Developments inside the floodplains continue to increase, impacting natural floodplains and leaving the Clear Creek watershed highly vulnerable to flooding. In addition, Clear Creek is unique in that it contains a fifteen-mile stretch of natural bayou with little development along the banks.

The Friendswood area is located upstream of this stretch of natural bayou, and is listed tenth on the RPL list from the Higher Ground report (National Wildlife Federation 1998). The Clear Creek Federal Flood Control Project is attempting to alleviate this flooding problem in the best way possible. The Corps originally planned a $100 million flood control channelization plan but commenced a restudy in 1996, due to opposition from public interest groups. These groups were concerned that such a plan would devastate one of the few natural freshwater bayou systems left in the Houston area. One year later, HCFCD offered an alternative plan, which was also structurally based, although with a reduced depth and width of the channel and reduced cost.

The Corps is currently in the process of developing a General Reevaluation Report that will consider the HCFCD plan and other options. The Corps is collecting new hydrologic and hydraulic data as well as considering nonstructural buyout options such as those directed by Challenge 2000. However, in the spring of 2000, a report issued by Washington-based Taxpayers for Common Sense and the National Wildlife Federation stated that the Corps has not seriously considered the buyout and relocation option. The report named the Clear Creek Federal Flood Control Project as one of the nation's twenty-five most wasteful and environmentally damaging water projects, making any project on Clear Creek subject to increased public scrutiny.

A flood control plan that includes property buyouts has been advanced and may cost much less than current structural plans. This plan would preserve the important wetlands resources of the area while still providing hundred-year flood protection (Benavides et al. 2000). The proposed solution would combine limited channelization with buyout of the most flood-prone properties.

Major Floods of the Past Decade

A handful of major storms that struck southeast Texas in the past decade have been reminders of the realities of intense flooding and of the importance of controlling this flooding. A massive flooding event struck southeast Texas on October 14–19, 1994, with two days of heavy rain (up to twenty-five inches in some areas) that produced widespread flooding over much of the region including Harris County. More than twenty-two thousand homes were flooded, and the damage to homes, bridges, and agriculture was estimated at over $900 million. Tragically, seventeen lives were lost as a result of the flood, and more than ten thousand people were displaced from their homes. The storm produced record lake levels at Lakes Conroe, Houston, and Livingston, with Livingston reaching a record high release flow of 110,000 cubic feet per second. The storm also ruptured fuel pipelines on the San Jacinto

River, which produced a massive, dangerous "river of fire" along the river. Another major storm occurred in September, 1998. Tropical Storm Frances came in from the Gulf of Mexico, inundating Harris County and other counties with flood-producing rainfalls. Significant rains began on September 10, and by daybreak September 11, significant flooding was occurring in Harris County and the City of Houston. Many homes in Jersey Village and Woodland Trails in northwest Houston along White Oak Bayou were flooded as White Oak Bayou experienced major overbank flooding. Massive problems occurred and many school children were trapped in buses or at school because the rising waters peaked early in the morning. Many of the flooded areas in White Oak Bayou had never flooded before this event. Flood damage in Houston and surrounding counties totaled more than $286 million.

Repetitive Flood Losses

According to *Higher Ground,* Texas has $36 billion worth of property in hundred-year floodplains. The majority of these properties are located in the southeast Texas region. There is a significant lack of floodplain zoning in the counties surrounding the Houston area, allowing major development in floodplains and even in floodways. Although fewer homes in Houston and Harris County flood at any particular time compared to other areas in the nation, *Higher Ground* notes that the homes that do flood will often flood "several times a year during almost any season." Seven of the top twenty-five repetitive flood loss communities (ranked by payments) are located in the Houston-Galveston region (see table 7).

Of the top two hundred single family homes with NFIP payments exceeding the building value, more than half are located in three communities in the Houston area: fifty-seven in Harris County, thirty-six in Houston, and eighteen in Friendswood. This exorbitant amount of repetitive loss has served to deplete our nation's flood insurance funds without providing solutions for or permanently alleviating any flooding problems. The data clearly show that many of the houses that claim repetitive losses should never have been built in the floodplain in the first place and that other management options (i.e., buyout) may prove useful as a permanent flood solution.

The Buyout Option

While not widespread, the buyout/relocation option is increasingly becoming a successful alternative to struc-

Table 7. Top 200 repetitive loss communities ranked by payments

Community	U.S. Rank	Repetitive Loss Properties	Total Payment
City of Houston	3	2030	$114,118,850
Harris County	4	1651	$97,400,994
Montgomery County	6	577	$33,629,140
City of Friendswood	10	314	$29,384,522
Galveston County	16	650	$20,076,944
Brazoria County	21	499	$16,523,302
City of Pasadena	24	242	$14,070,937

Source: Repetitive loss properties data from NWF 1999.

tural flood control and repetitive insurance funding. *Higher Ground* urges the nation to treat floodplains for what they are and not as areas meant for urban (and suburban) development. The report notes that voluntary buyouts are "not only an investment in averting disaster, but they also enhance urban and rural environments and provide meaningful help to people living in high-risk floodplains . . . at the same time, they move us toward a crucial goal of reclaiming the floodplains' natural and beneficial functions." While some floodplains in Houston are far too developed with permanent institutions to implement buyouts and relocations, many of Houston's residential areas that lie vulnerably within the floodplain might be ideal for this option.

Previous efforts at structural flood control on Houston's creeks and bayous were not only ineffective in their attempts to restrain the floods but were also costly and environmentally destructive. The channelization examples on Brays Bayou and White Oak Bayou show how large channel projects attracted more development into a protected floodplain, creating a flood-prone area once again. In the case of Brays Bayou, the county is in the process of enlarging and expanding a flood control project that was clearly under-designed at the time it was built. But with the watershed currently over 90 percent developed, no further development impacts will occur to reduce capacity in the future.

Clear Creek and White Oak Bayou are farther from any permanent flood control solution than Brays Bayou. It is possible that nonstructural approaches will be considered and implemented for these watersheds. It is becoming increasingly clear that buyouts could be a more practical and effective way to contend with flood damage, especially in areas such as Friendswood. However, the main concern in implementing buyouts is the shortage of funding to advance buyout and relocation programs.

Conclusion

Region H comprises approximately thirteen thousand square miles and encompasses parts of three main river basins in southeast Texas: the Trinity, San Jacinto, and Brazos. The area is dominated by the presence of the City of Houston, fourth largest city in the United States, which is one of the major municipal users in Texas. The predominant solution to the projected water shortage between 2000 and 2050 is the development of new reservoirs on the Brazos and Trinity rivers and interbasin transfers of water within the Brazos, San Jacinto, and Trinity basins.

Groundwater use for the region has declined since the 1970s and will continue to decline as proposed surface water reservoirs come on line. Some areas of the region have had a significant decrease in pumpage of groundwater since the 1970s, while other areas have shown an increase in pumpage. Subsidence is clearly correlated to groundwater withdrawals in the overall region and is a growing issue, especially in the north and northwest part of Harris County. In order to reduce and prevent subsidence, groundwater will have to be replaced with surface water for municipal and other use. Water demands will continue to grow, over the next fifty years, as the population is expected to more than double.

Finally, flooding and floodplain issues in the region are described in some detail, with specific examples from Brays Bayou and Clear Creek highlighted. Brays Bayou, which is now one of the most flood-prone areas in the City of Houston, will undergo a massive federal project over the next decade to bring flood protection back to the hundred-year level. Correct flood protection solutions for Clear Creek will be difficult to implement due to complex interacting issues involving riparian habitat, urbanization in floodplains, and the conservation of wildlife habitat. Alternative measures such as buyouts are recommended.

References

Bedient, P. B., B. C. Hoblit, D.C. Gladwell, and B. E. Vieux. "NEXRAD Radar for Flood Prediction in Houston." *ASCE Journal of Hydrologic Engineering* 5, no. 3 (2000): 269–77.

Bedient, P. B., and A. Holder, et al. "Flood Prediction Manual for Brays Bayou." Prepared for the Texas Medical Center, 1998.

Bedient, P. B., and W. C. Huber. *Hydrology and Floodplain Analysis,* 2nd ed. New York: Addison-Wesley Publishing Company, 1992.

Benavides, J. A., et al. "A Sustainable Approach for the Clear Creek Watershed." Presented at the ASCE Spring Meeting, Austin, Tex., April, 2000.

Coplin, L. S., H. X. Santos, and D. W. Brown. "Water-Level Altitudes 1999 and Water-Level Changes 1990–99 and 1998–99 in the Chicot and Evangeline Aquifers, Fort Bend County and Adjacent Areas, Texas." Open File Report 99-177, U.S. Geological Survey (Reston, Va.), City of Houston, and Harris-Galveston Coastal Subsidence District, 1999a.

Coplin, L. S., H. X. Santos, and J. W. West. "Water-Level Altitudes 1999, Water-Level Changes 1977–99 and 1998–99, and Compaction 1973–98 in the Chicot and Evangeline Aquifers, Houston-Galveston Region, Texas." Open File Report 99-178, U.S. Geological Survey (Reston, Va.), City of Houston, and Harris-Galveston Coastal Subsidence District, 1999b.

Fort Bend Subsidence District. "Groundwater Management Plan." Houston, 1998.

Harris County Flood Control District (HCFCD). Brays Bayou Federal Project Report, 2000a.

———. Brays Bayou Flood Damage Reduction Plan, 2000b.

Harris-Galveston Coastal Subsidence District (HGCSD). "Groundwater Management Plan." Houston, 1998.

Hoblit, B., B. Vieux, A. Holder, and P. Bedient. "Predicting with Precision" *Civil Engineering Magazine* (November, 1999): 40–43.

Meyer, W. R., and J. E. Carr. "A Digital Model for Simulation of Groundwater Hydrology in the Houston Area, Texas." Report LP-103, Texas Department of Water Resources, 1979.

National Wildlife Federation. *Higher Ground: A Report on Voluntary Property Buyouts in the Nation's Floodplains.* Washington, D.C.: National Wildlife Federation, 1998.

Noble, J. E. "Estimated Rate of Recharge in Outcrops of the Chicot and Evangeline Aquifers near Houston, Texas." Fact Sheet FS-97-179, U.S. Geological Survey, Reston, Va., 1997.

Region H Water Planning Group. "Initially Prepared Plan," prepared by Brown and Root and Turner Collie and Braden, 2000. At http://www.twdb.state.tx.us/assistance/rwpg/main-docs/reg-plan-index.htm.

Texas Groundwater Protection Committee. "Joint Groundwater Monitoring and Contamination Report, 1998." SFR-56/98, Texas Natural Resource Conservation Commission, Austin, 1999.

Texas Water Development Board (TWDB). *Water for Texas: A Consensus-Based Update to the State Water Plan.* Document GP-6-2. Austin: TWDB, 1997.

———. "Groundwater Database." At http://www.twdb.state.tx.us/data/waterwells/well_info.html.

Trans-Texas Water Program Southeast Area. "Phase II Report." 1998.

Williams, J. F. I., and C. E. Ranzau, Jr. "Approximate Water-Level Changes in Wells in the Chicot and Evangeline Aquifers, 1977–1985, and Measured Compaction 1973–85, in the Houston-Galveston Region, Texas." Open File Report 85-158, U.S. Geological Survey, Reston, Va., 1985.

CHAPTER 9

Status and Trends
of North-Central Texas Water Resources

The Integrity of the Trinity River

Glenn C. Clingenpeel

Trinity River Authority

Abstract

The upper Trinity River basin is heavily impacted from a variety of sources including urbanization, construction of reservoirs, and agriculture. All of these issues severely affect the water quality and physical and biological integrity of the Trinity River, its reservoirs, and tributaries. Although municipal wastewater treatment plants were found to cause elevated levels of nutrients in receiving streams throughout the upper basin, the magnitude of their impact on biological integrity is difficult to determine. However, in some cases, the impact may be positive. Impacts from agriculture were found to be most significant in the Blackland Prairie ecoregion, which has the greatest amount of cultivated land. Rangeland was found to have the least impact. The most significant impacts from agriculture on a regional basis were seen in reservoirs, which receive large loads of water quality constituents such as pesticides during rainy months. Impacts from urbanization include physical modifications and heavy management of stream and river channels for flood control; stormwater runoff from residential, commercial, and industrial areas; and discharges from municipal wastewater treatment plants. Of these three types of urban impacts, those involving the physical modification of stream channels are expected to have the greatest impact on biological integrity, while stormwater runoff is expected to have the greatest impact on use attainability based on human health concerns. Point sources from municipal dischargers are expected, under the conditions observed during this study, to have the least effect on use attainability.

The Trinity River, which stretches some seven hundred miles from its headwaters near the Red River in North-Central Texas down to Galveston Bay, is arguably one of the most important river systems in Texas in that it supplies water to just under half the population of the state. And yet, the image that comes to mind when one thinks of the Trinity is not that of a healthy, life-giving river system. Rather, to many, the image is one of a polluted river clogged with trash. Although no longer accurate, this image and the reputation of the river can be traced back to the late 1800s, when large amounts of untreated, or undertreated, sewage from municipal and industrial sources were dumped directly into the river. The result was a septic river devoid of oxygen and thus of most aquatic life. In a report of the State Health Department of Texas dated October, 1924, to June, 1925, J. G. Burr of the Game, Fish, and Oyster Commission wrote of the Trinity River: "The flow below Dallas for many miles does not impress one as being that of a river. A stench from its inky surface putrescent with the oxidizing processes to which the shadows of overarching trees add Stygian blackness and the suggestion of some mythological river of death. With this burden of filth the purifying agencies of the stream are prostrated. . . . A thing of beauty is thus transformed into one of hideous danger."

This situation persisted through much of the 1900s, finally improving during the 1960s. Since that time the river has experienced tremendous improvements in water quality and is now in many areas a healthy river system. Impressively, this improvement has been realized in spite of the fact that the Dallas–Fort Worth area has experienced one of the highest growth rates in the nation, with the population burgeoning to its current level of around five million. This increase in population has resulted in numerous water quality issues. Among these are concerns arising from discharges of treated municipal effluent and urban runoff. In addition, the Trinity River basin has a significant amount of both animal and crop-related agriculture. Of particular interest are the cultivated fields of

the Blackland Prairie ecoregion, which stretches across the center of the basin. Understanding each of these factors is of obvious importance in assessing both the water quality and the physical and biological integrity of the upper Trinity River basin.

Methods

The basin was divided into three major water quality regions, each with distinct characteristics or economic factors thought to influence the aforementioned three measures of integrity most heavily. The water quality regions are the Western Forks, Central Forks–Blackland Prairie, and the Upper Main Stem. Figure 1 shows the locations of these regions, along with their major water bodies. Figure 2 shows the locations of ecoregions in reference to the water quality regions.

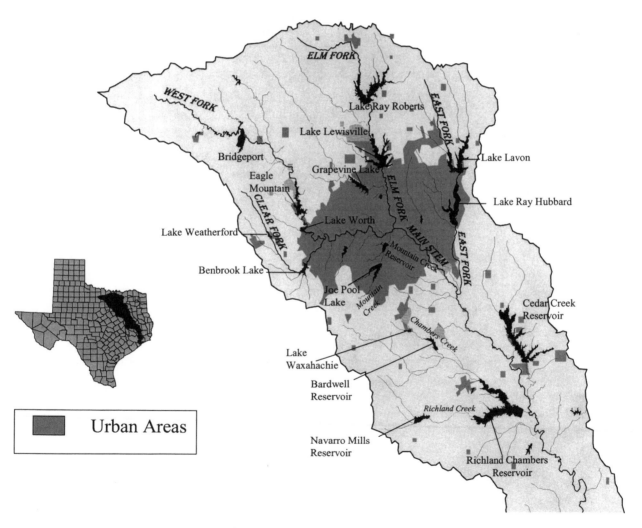

Figure 1. Upper Trinity River water bodies.

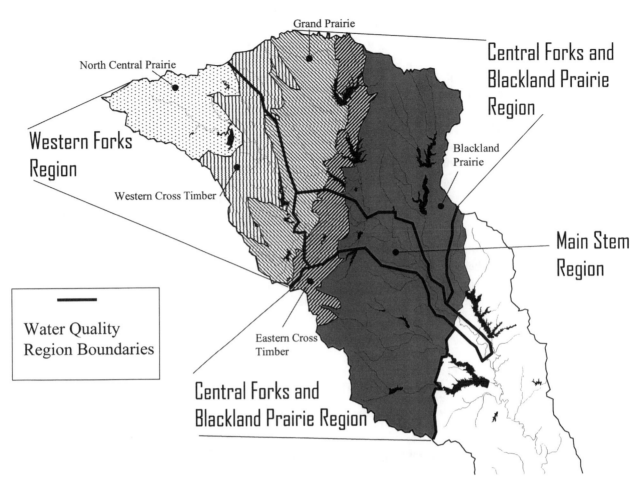

Figure 2. Ecoregions and water quality regions of the upper Trinity.

The Western Forks region encompasses the northwestern portions of the basin, including the Clear and West forks. The Central Forks–Blackland Prairie region includes the Elm Fork, East Fork, and the remainder of the Blackland Prairie ecoregion outside the Dallas–Fort Worth metroplex. The third of the three regions, the Upper Main Stem, encompasses the most heavily urbanized areas within the basin, including the Dallas–Fort Worth metroplex. The water quality and the physical and biological integrity of each of these regions were examined. Although water quality data were plentiful, data concerning both biological and physical integrity were extremely limited.

Water quality integrity was evaluated by examining a set of common parameters in each region. Data for this exercise were obtained from a large, ten-year multiagency database of over 380,000 records. The database was compiled from various sources, and quality was assured. Time series graphs of nineteen important water quality vari-ables were then created for key sites throughout the study area. More than fourteen hundred graphs were made in this fashion. Parameters evaluated and discussed here were limited to those deemed of greatest interest, capable of providing information concerning known or suspected water quality issues. In addition to the time series graphs, box plots were created at key locations within each sub-watershed and arranged on a single graph in hydrologic order, so that water quality changes within each subwa-tershed could be identified. In this fashion, water quality in the basin was analyzed both temporally and spatially.

Although conventional water quality variables were used within each region in a systematic evaluation of wa-ter quality, other variables such as pesticides or other non-conventional parameters are also discussed. Data for non-conventional parameters were obtained from sources other than the Trinity River Authority's (TRA) water quality database. The biological and physical integrity of each region were evaluated using a much sparser data set.

This consisted of data from one or two sample locations within each region. Personal knowledge of the area was combined with these data to make estimations of physical and biological integrity.

The Western Forks Region

Of the three water quality regions, the Western Forks has the least development, and that which has occurred is largely restricted to the lower portions of both forks. The major agricultural activity in this region is cattle production, although some cropland does exist.

Dissolved oxygen values in both forks display a similar pattern of low concentrations in the upper reaches followed by an increase to a relatively constant median value of around 9 mg/L. Dissolved oxygen concentrations in the Clear Fork are significantly lower than in the West Fork. Tenth percentile dissolved oxygen concentrations, against which stream standards are compared, are below the 5 mg/L prescribed for this region (fig. 3). This indicates that the segment is not meeting its designated use as supportive of high aquatic life. As the uppermost

portions of both the Clear Fork and West Fork are intermittent, it is suspected that the lower dissolved oxygen levels seen at these stations are a result of low flow conditions. This is supported by dissolved oxygen saturation data for measurements taken at two locations on the Clear Fork: FM 51 above Lake Weatherford (site 11062, fig. 4) and IH-20 below Lake Weatherford. Measurements at both sites were taken in pools that had flow entering and exiting at all times. The site at FM 51 receives no flow from point sources, and during dry summer months it is believed to be fed by a spring approximately one mile upstream. Intensive diurnal sampling at a frequency of once per month over the course of a year demonstrated a dramatic decrease in dissolved oxygen levels beginning in June of 1999 and persisting through February of the next year. Similar but less dramatic declines are noted every summer since 1993. An identical situation was noted for site 11060 below the lake. This site receives flow from water seeping through the Lake Weatherford dam as well as from a small municipal plant treating effluent from the town of Willow Park. Neither of these flows is significant, however, and it is believed that low flow during the

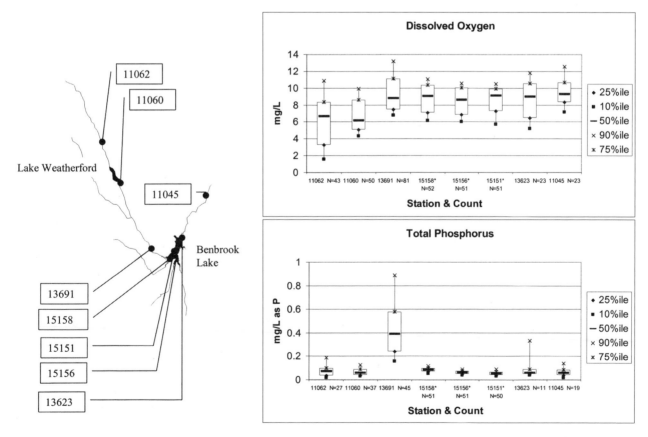

Figure 3. Dissolved oxygen and total phosphorus concentrations in the Clear Fork, Trinity River.

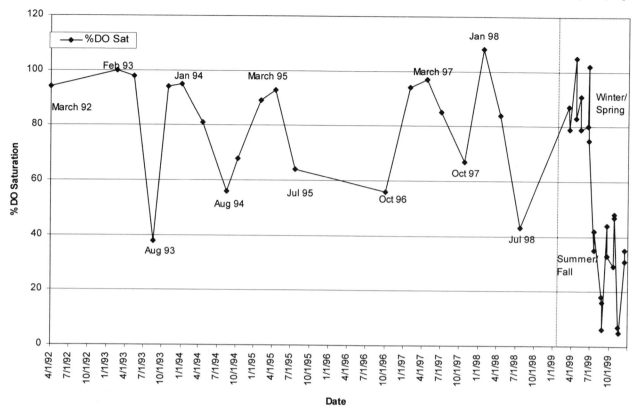

Figure 4. Dissolved oxygen saturation graph of data from Clear Fork station 11062 above Lake Weatherford at FM 51.

drought conditions of 1999 led to the low dissolved oxygen saturation levels observed during that time. Examination of scatter plots of nutrient concentrations (orthophosphate, total phosphorus, and total Kjeldahl nitrogen) indicated that nutrients have not been excessive at this site and are, therefore, not believed to be causing, or significantly contributing to, the dissolved oxygen deficit. Chlorophyll-*a* concentrations were also low at this site, with an average concentration of 4.2 μg/L. It is therefore proposed that once flow reaches some definable critical low, dissolved oxygen begins to be removed by naturally occurring oxygen demanding substances (e.g., leaf litter). Due to the high temperatures and stagnant condition of the water, re-aeration occurs only very slowly via diffusion, causing low dissolved oxygen concentrations.

Looking at total phosphorus concentrations (fig. 3) along the reach, a trend toward higher concentrations is noted as one progresses downstream. The higher levels at the farthest downstream site above Lake Benbrook (13691) can be attributed to point sources, namely municipal

outfalls from the cities of Weatherford and Aledo. During much of the year, treated effluent from these point sources constitutes most of the water in the Clear Fork below Lake Weatherford. However, dissolved oxygen concentrations at this location seem to indicate that the point sources have a net positive effect on water quality, as dissolved oxygen saturation is much higher at this site than at any of the less impacted sites upstream. There is evidence of eutrophication at this site, as dissolved oxygen saturation values frequently topped 140 percent and on two occasions climbed above 160 percent.

In the West Fork of the Trinity River an almost reverse trend is seen in total nitrogen and phosphorus concentrations, with higher values occurring at the uppermost site and dropping as one moves downstream. Mean total nitrogen and phosphorus concentrations at this upper site were 1.4 mg/L and 0.24 mg/L, respectively. The higher concentrations at the upper site, while not as high as values seen downstream from municipal discharges, are somewhat surprising. There are no known point sources in the upper West Fork that could account for the observed levels of nitrogen and phosphorus. These higher concentrations must, therefore, be a result of natural and/or agricultural sources. The erodible nature of soils in this area may help to explain these elevated levels. The fact that the concentrations are reduced with downstream movement is explained by the presence of Lake Bridgeport, which, like all reservoirs, effectively traps most nutrients.

Unfortunately, few data exist concerning the physical and biological integrity of this region. However, last year a receiving water assessment was conducted on a small tributary near Eagle Mountain Lake. The study was conducted on Walnut Creek, which receives treated effluent from the city of Springtown. Receiving water assessments examine the physical and biological status of streams in order to determine the level of aquatic life they support. This study concluded that the stream supports high aquatic life use. Although not entirely indicative of the region as a whole, the study does suggest that the physical, chemical, and biological integrity is good; buttressing this is the fact that little development has occurred in this region. The greatest impacts were observed in the Clear Fork above Benbrook and were a result of municipal point sources. For this reason, the reach between Lake Weatherford and Lake Benbrook is an obvious exception to the preceding statement concerning water quality integrity. The point sources discussed affect both the water quality and physical integrity of the river. The physical integrity is affected via the fact that the point sources provide a constant source of flow, even in times when the river would historically have gone dry. Because of this situation and because dissolved oxygen values tend to drop to extremely low levels during summer flows, it is possible that the point sources could be having a net positive effect. A comparison of the health of aquatic communities above and below the point sources would help in making this determination. On the other hand, water quality data are present in good quantity. Future efforts to understand the water quality integrity of the region better should therefore focus on confirming that the low dissolved oxygen levels seen in the upper portions of both the Clear and West forks are due to low flow conditions and not a result of introduced oxygen-demanding substances. Future sampling should also be tailored to determine the source of the high nutrient levels seen in the upper West Fork, though this may also be accomplished via a more intensive survey of historical data and by attempting to locate potential sources, such as concentrated animal feeding operations.

The Central Forks and Blackland Prairie

Of the three upper Trinity River basin water quality regions, the Central Forks and Blackland Prairies is the largest. It encompasses the Elm Fork, East Fork, Mountain Creek, and Richland and Chambers creeks. These four forks and tributaries of the Trinity are all heavily influenced by the Blackland Prairie ecosystem within which they are located.

The Elm Fork begins near the Red River to the northwest of the city of Gainesville. It then flows south through Lake Ray Roberts and Lake Lewisville. From there it flows almost due south through the heavily urbanized suburbs of Lewisville and North Dallas before emptying into the West Fork. The Elm Fork provides drinking water for several cities, including Gainesville, Denton, Dallas, Irving, and Lewisville and is, therefore, an important source of water for the upper basin. Figure 5 is a box plot diagram of dissolved oxygen along the Elm Fork. According to this figure, the upper reaches through Lake Lewisville (site TR78) confirm the segment's designated use as supportive of high aquatic life. However, below the lake the data indicate that the segment is not supporting this use. An investigation into the situation by the city of Dallas led to the discovery that the low dissolved oxygen values were a result of deep-water releases from the Lewisville dam, which have subsequently been stopped.

Examining nutrient concentrations in the Elm Fork via total phosphorus concentrations show a dramatic increase below the city of Gainesville (fig. 5). This increase is a result of municipal discharge from the city. However, despite the increase in nutrients, no significant increases in chlorophyll-a concentrations were observed. Although both sites immediately above and below the city exceeded the Texas Commission on Environmental Quality's (TCEQ) segment-specific screening level for chlorophyll-a concentrations of 14 μg/L, thus indicating a potential problem, there are no known significant anthropogenic impacts above Gainesville. In addition, nutrient concentrations above the city were found to approximate concentrations *typical* of unimpacted sites elsewhere in the basin. The chlorophyll-a concentrations below the city cannot, therefore, be directly attributed to the increased nutrient loading resulting from the municipal discharge. Furthermore, concentrations of all other parameters examined below Gainesville, including dissolved oxygen, indicate that this reach complies with its designated use as supportive of high aquatic life. Accordingly, although the impact from the city of Gainesville is significant, it cannot,

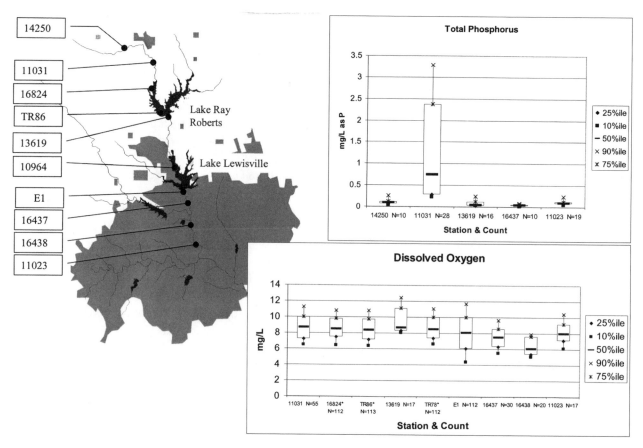

Figure 5. Dissolved oxygen and total phosphorus concentrations in the Elm Fork, Trinity River.

with the data at hand, be said to be negative. As one moves down the Elm Fork and through Lakes Ray Roberts and Lewisville, the elevated levels of nutrients are quickly reduced. No other elevated levels of nutrients are noted downstream from there, despite the influence of heavy urbanization south of Lake Lewisville and discharges from several municipal treatment plants. This is believed to be a result of the high quality of releases from Lake Lewisville, which dilute point- and nonpoint-source impacts. The East Fork, situated entirely within the Blackland Prairie ecoregion, begins to the northwest of Lake Lavon. It continues south through Lake Ray Hubbard, eventually reaching the main stem of the Trinity River below Dallas.

The East Fork is similar to the Elm in that it is also impacted by both agriculture and urbanization. The primary land use in the upper East Fork is cropland, with urbanization predominant in the lower portion below Lake Lavon.

Dissolved oxygen concentrations in the upper East Fork demonstrate the same general trend as seen in the West Fork and Clear Fork, with lower concentrations at the uppermost sample sites, followed by a rapid rise to a

more or less constant level. Dissolved oxygen concentrations in the lower East Fork below Ray Hubbard show a gradual decrease to levels that indicate the segment's failure to meet its designated use as supportive of intermediate aquatic life (fig. 6). Dissolved oxygen concentrations recover somewhat at the next station downstream, creating a sag. Total phosphorus concentrations immediately below Lake Ray Hubbard jump to a median value of 3.7 mg/L, gradually dropping to a median concentration of 0.94 mg/L at Highway 175. Chlorophyll-*a* values are also elevated, with an average value of 14 µg/L and maximum values exceeding 30 µg/L. These are among the highest concentrations seen in the basin. In addition to elevated nutrient concentrations, concentrations of both chloride and sulfate violate site-specific stream standards. The reason for the severity of the impacts seen here, which can be attributed to point sources, remains somewhat of a question. One possible answer lies in a cumulative effect resulting from the close proximity of several large wastewater treatment plants in this segment.

Mountain and Chambers creeks are both located

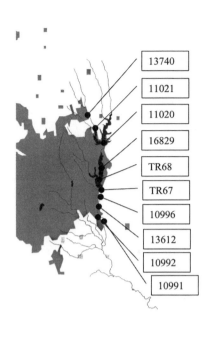

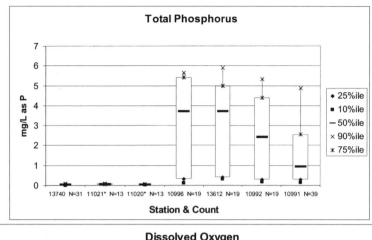

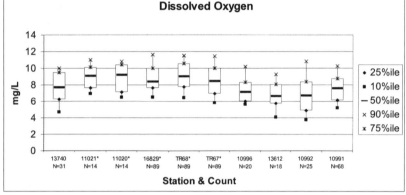

Figure 6. Dissolved oxygen and total phosphorus concentrations in the East Fork, Trinity River.

south of the Dallas–Fort Worth area in the heart of the Blackland Prairie ecoregion. The primary impact in both of these watersheds is from crop production. Dissolved oxygen data indicate that Mountain Creek above Joe Pool Lake is supporting its designated use. However, dissolved oxygen data from Chambers Creek at FM 1126 indicate that the stream at this site is not supporting its use. As is the case in upper portions of the Clear Fork and West Fork, it is believed that the failure to meet minimum stream standards requirements is a result of low flow. A close examination of the data shows that most of the low dissolved oxygen values occur during the summer to late fall period.

Nutrient concentrations from these watersheds were found to be relatively low, with an average total phosphorus concentration in Mountain Creek at FM 157 (site 13622) of 0.092 mg/L and 0.095 mg/L at Chambers Creek and FM 1126 (10977). This can be compared to an average concentration of 0.12 mg/L measured in the Elm Fork above Gainesville and 0.085 mg/L measured in the Clear Fork above Lake Weatherford. At both reference sites, no

significant anthropogenic impacts are expected to exist. According to these results, crop agriculture does not seem to be affecting nutrient concentrations. The United States Geological Survey (USGS), however, found that about three quarters of all nitrogen carried by the Trinity River originates from agricultural sources (Puckett 1994). It is believed that the majority of nitrogen originating from agricultural sources enters waterways during rainy months. Although concentrations in the streams carrying these nutrients may not be as high as those seen downstream from municipal discharges, the total mass loading from agricultural areas is much greater. As reservoirs fill primarily with stormwater runoff, it is logical that agricultural sources have the greatest impact upon their water quality. As agriculture is believed to contribute the majority of nutrients carried through the Trinity, reservoirs in agricultural areas should have higher levels of nutrients than in other areas. In an effort to examine impacts from agricultural sources, major reservoirs within the basin that have been noted to contain high levels of Atrazine were identified on an ecoregion map (fig. 7).

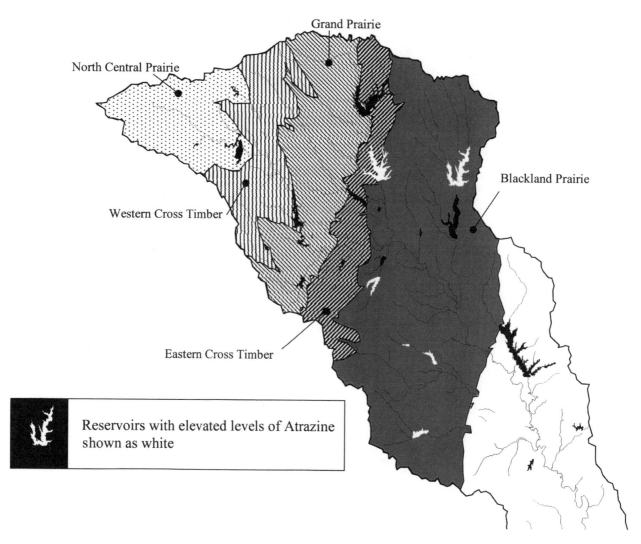

Figure 7. Reservoirs with elevated levels of Atrazine.

Atrazine is a common herbicide used on row crops such as corn, wheat, and sorghum and is also found in many "weed and feed" products widely used in residential areas. It should be noted that every reservoir with high concentrations is located in the Blackland Prairie ecoregion. The exception is Richland Chambers Reservoir, which has a watershed lying almost exclusively within the Blackland Prairie ecoregion. In this region, reservoirs not noted as having elevated concentrations of Atrazine have the greatest amount of urbanization in their watersheds and, therefore, less runoff from agricultural sources. This indicates that agricultural land is the predominant source for this contaminant in reservoirs.

A receiving water assessment performed on the Elm Fork above Gainesville in the Grand Prairie ecoregion found the area supportive of high aquatic life (Huther

1995). It is therefore expected that other undeveloped streams in the Grand Prairie and possibly Eastern Cross Timbers ecoregion have similar high biological and physical integrity. Unfortunately, the effects on the biological integrity of the municipal effluent discharged into the upper Elm Fork are not known. A similar study conducted by the USGS on Chambers Creek (USGS 1998b) found that the creek has been severely impacted and that the fishery has been degraded. It is likely that other streams and tributaries within the Blackland Prairie ecoregion have been similarly impacted via agricultural activities.

Main Stem

The upper main stem water quality region stretches from the Lake Worth dam in Fort Worth to Highway 22 east of

Corsicana. Of all the water quality regions, none has been more obviously impacted than the upper main stem. This river segment has suffered from urbanization in and around the Dallas–Fort Worth area since settlement of the region around 1862. From that time to the 1960s, the river received large amounts of untreated or undertreated sewage, resulting in the "mythological river of death" Burr so eloquently described.

Significant improvements in water quality were realized during the 1970s and 1980s following the Upper Trinity River Basin Comprehensive Sewage Plan of 1971 and federal pollution control laws enacted around the same time. These measures resulted in significant improvements being made to large area dischargers, who continued upgrading their plants as new technologies became available. At the same time, the population of the Dallas–Fort Worth area was burgeoning and creating even greater quantities of treated effluent to be discharged into the Trinity. Figure 8 shows the steady increases in municipal wastewater discharge from the Dallas–Fort Worth area from 1975 to 1995. The graph also shows total pounds of biochemical oxygen demanding substances (BOD) released with the discharges, which are seen to have decreased instead of increased. The effect these improvements in wastewater treatment made in water quality can be seen in figure 9, which shows average daily dissolved oxygen values from the Trinity River at Rosser below Dallas.

Average dissolved oxygen concentrations of more recent data, 1990 through 1999, indicate that the segment is supporting high aquatic life use. Tenth percentile dissolved oxygen concentrations at eight stations from the West Fork above Fort Worth to Highway 22 well below Dallas were all above 5 mg/L, and only one station, south Loop 12 below Dallas, had a tenth percentile value below 6 mg/L. Although apparently not significantly affecting dissolved oxygen concentrations, impacts from Dallas–Fort Worth municipal discharges on nutrient concentrations is significant (fig. 10). Chloride and sulfate concentrations are also elevated as a result of point sources, peaking at Beltline Road (station 11081) and IH-30 (station 10936). However, neither constituent was noted to be in violation of stream standards for this reach. Somewhat surprisingly, chlorophyll-*a* concentrations appear much higher in the West Fork above the large Dallas–Fort Worth municipal dischargers than below them. Concentrations of chlorophyll-*a* at Beach Street in Fort Worth averaged 16.1 μg/L, with 57 percent of measurements exceeding the TRNCC screening level of 13.7 μg/L, as compared to an

average of 6.8 μg/L at South Loop 12. It is believed that the higher concentrations of chlorophyll-*a* in the West Fork are a result of the physical conditions at that location. The river in that area is shallow and slow moving, with little if any canopy cover. This allows excellent light penetration, which fuels algal growth. This observation lends further support to the hypothesis that light, and not nutrients, is limiting to algal growth in the Trinity River. This situation appears to hold true even when nutrients are present at background concentrations. Accordingly, it does not appear that the nutrient enrichment occurring as a result of Dallas–Fort Worth area municipal dischargers is affecting chlorophyll-*a* production in the main stem.

Impacts from nonpoint sources, namely stormwater runoff from urbanized areas, also affect the main stem and associated water bodies. In fact, every one of the seg-

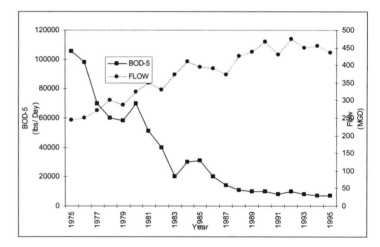

Figure 8. Flow and BOD from Dallas–Fort Worth area dischargers.

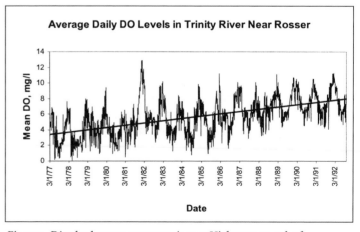

Figure 9. Dissolved oxygen concentrations at Highway 34 south of Dallas, 1977–92. (NCTCOG)

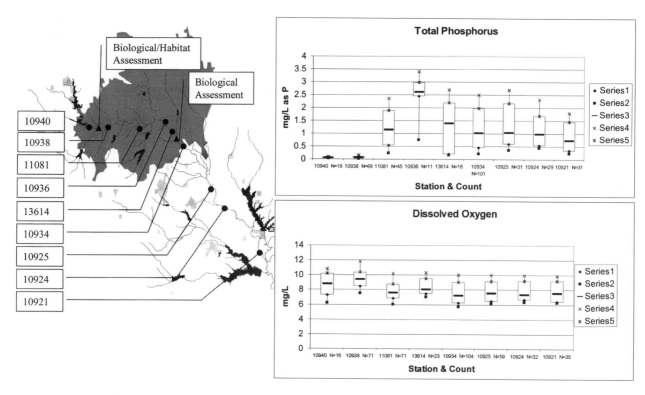

Figure 10. Dissolved oxygen and total phosphorus concentrations in the main stem, Trinity River.

ments in this water quality region that has been listed as not meeting its designated use, or for which the Texas Department of Health has issued a fishing ban, is believed to be impaired due to urban runoff. Of particular concern are legacy pollutants and pesticides used in urban areas, such as chlordane and PCBs. These pollutants have been found in fish tissue and sediments at concentrations sufficient to cause the respective segment to be listed as impaired by the TCEQ. In particular, residential areas seem to have the greatest impact; a 1998 study by the USGS (1998a) found chlordane, although banned since 1988, in 22 percent of all samples collected in residential areas. Dieldrin, banned for agricultural use, was found in 9 percent of samples. Diazanon, although not directly linked to use impairment in any area waters, was detected with greatest frequency, occurring in 93 percent of samples. Another USGS study conducted in 1997 (Moring 1997) found greater concentrations and occurrences of organic contaminants in urban than in nonurban sediments and fish tissue, further demonstrating the significant impact urban nonpoint sources have on water quality.

In terms of the physical and biological integrity of this region, it is obvious that the river has been severely impacted and that biological communities have suffered. In addition to the water quality impacts already discussed, the river has undergone many physical modifications, having been channelized and leveed through much of the Dallas–Fort Worth area. Municipal discharges also affect the physical integrity of the river by providing constant flow, even during extreme drought conditions when none would otherwise exist. During their 1992–95 assessment, the USGS National Water Quality Assessment (NAWQA) program evaluated habitat and biological communities at a reach along the West Fork above Fort Worth. The study found that the reach was an example of a "highly altered stream characterized by incised and leveed channels, low density of vegetation in the riparian zones, and unstable streamflow characteristics" (USGS 1992). It was concluded that these factors, in addition to possible others such as water quality, have degraded the fish communities in that reach. Although no directly comparable work has been performed on the Trinity River below Dallas, three separate studies were conducted between 1972 and 1995 in order to characterize fish communities in that area. The first, conducted by the Texas Parks and Wildlife Department during the years 1972–74, found a total of four species; a second study conducted by TPWD in 1987 found a total of eleven species. A third study, conducted by USGS personnel in conjunction with their 1993–95 NAWQA program, collected a total of twenty-five species (USGS 1998b). Among the species collected during the 1993–95 NAWQA study were several tolerant species (USGS 1998b). This prompted the USGS to conclude that the area is returning to a more natural condition. Unfortunately, there are few biological data from the main stem in either Dallas or Fort Worth. A year-long quarterly toxicity study was, however, conducted by TRA's Clean Rivers Program from March, 1999, to February, 2000. The study used water and sediment samples collected at Beltline Road in Irving and examined them for toxicity to *C. dubia*. One of the whole water samples was found to be lethally toxic, although none of the remaining three samples or sediment elutriate taken the same day as the toxic water sample had any effect.

Summary and Conclusions

Examining and interpreting water quality data and information from various sources concerning the integrity of the upper Trinity River indicate that the area is heavily impacted from a variety of different sources. These sources include crop agriculture, urbanization, and effluent from municipal wastewater treatment plants. Municipal wastewater treatment plant discharges have significant effects on nutrient concentrations and in some cases on dissolved salts. No direct evidence was found to suggest that these elevated nutrient levels are causing any impairments to designated uses. Furthermore, chlorophyll-*a* concentrations appear to be much more dependent upon light penetration than on nutrients. However, point sources in the East Fork appear to be responsible for apparent use impairment via sulfate concentrations. Most of the data considered were several years old. Accordingly, it was not possible to determine whether the segment is still failing to meet its designated use as supportive of intermediate aquatic life. It is not clear why this segment experiences apparent use impairment when other effluent-dominated streams do not.

In some cases, as is suspected of occurring in the Clear Fork, it is possible that point sources have a positive effect on habitat. This may apply to most small tributaries in the upper basin that are either intermittent or experience annual dry weather low flows. However, the habitat created or ameliorated in such a fashion represents an artificial situation. Furthermore, certain constituents in the effluent, or combinations of them, may create stresses causing a shift in aquatic community structures toward tolerant and or non-native species. Future work should be undertaken to determine exactly what impacts point sources have on biological integrity.

Examination of routine water quality data failed to indicate significant impacts or use impairment due to agriculture. However, a review of reservoirs known to have elevated levels of Atrazine, and their location in relation to the heavily cultivated Blackland Prairie ecoregion, showed a clear relationship between the two. This relationship is believed to be characteristic of impacts from agriculture, which appear to be the predominant influence upon water quality in reservoirs. A more thorough examination of historical water quality data concerning the seasonality of agricultural impacts would be helpful.

Urbanization in and around the Dallas–Fort Worth metroplex has had the greatest impact on the water integrity of the region. Although significant improvements have been made, the effects are lingering and severe. Stormwater runoff has affected the water quality of the area and has caused use impairments for human health and safety. Although the cause of the toxicity seen in the Trinity at Beltline Road remains unknown, it is possible that toxicants from nonpoint sources, perhaps combined with stressors from municipal effluent, are to blame. Channelization, leveeing, and management of vegetation in the flood plans of the Trinity River throughout the Dallas–Fort Worth area has significantly affected the physical integrity of the river, causing a loss of valuable habitat. This is believed to be the most significant contributor to degradation of biological integrity of the area. Despite these habitat impacts, no aquatic life use impairments exist in this region, according to the Clean Water Act §305(b) report or §303(d) list of impaired waters. These aforementioned measures of determining use support, however, do not consider the type of biological data collected by the USGS NAWQA program on the West Fork. Despite this fact, an effort should be made to collect more biological data throughout the upper main stem so that a proper assessment of the biological integrity of the region can be made.

The improvements that have been made in water quality in the Trinity River are often hidden within the shadows of the memory of its polluted past. Despite the relative health of the river in many locations compared to its historic condition, there are numerous issues yet to be resolved. Perhaps foremost among these is a need to understand better the true effect of the myriad impacts that occur in the Trinity River basin. So doing will enable more specific countermeasures to be taken in the future, ensuring that the different uses of the river, from aquatic life to contact recreation and human health, will be supported throughout the basin. Furthermore, it is essential for the standards that are put in place to be based upon sound science and that in our striving to achieve them, the uses they are meant to maintain will ultimately be protected.

References

Huther, Bruce. Receiving Water Assessment of the Elm Fork of the Trinity River above Gainesville in Cooke County, Texas. Unpublished. 1995.

———. Receiving Water Assessment of Spring Creek in Tarrant County, Texas. Unpublished. 1998.

Moring, J. B. *Occurrences and Distribution of Organochlorine Compounds in Biological Tissue and Bed Sediment from Streams in the Trinity River Basin, Texas, 1992–93.* U.S. Geological Survey Water-Resources Investigations Report 97-4057, 1997.

Puckett, L. J. *Nonpoint and Point Sources of Nitrogen in Major Watersheds of the United States.* U.S. Geological Survey Water-Resources Investigations Report 94-4001, 1994.

U.S. Geological Survey (USGS). "Urban Stormwater Quality, Event-Mean Concentrations, and Estimates of Stormwater Pollutant Loads," Dallas–Fort Worth area, Texas, 1992–93. U.S. Geological Survey Water Resources Investigations Report 98-4185, 1998a.

———. "Water Quality in the Trinity River Basin," Texas, 1992–95. U.S. Geological Survey Circular 1171, 1998b.

PART III

Climate

and Water Quantity

Many factors enter into the climate and water content of an area, making it impossible to study one region without taking a global view. This next section examines the world's weather as it affects the Texas region and offers some creative solutions in terms of water conservation and the use of dams.

In the first paper Jurgen Schmandt asks the question: Will the world have enough water for the next twenty-five years? He examines the overall meteorological situation and gives a positive prediction for the future. However, he quickly points out that this conclusion is misleading. Many of the individual regions either already are or will soon become areas of water stress or water scarcity. The number of these regions will continue to grow.

Gerald R. North follows these ideas with an examination of global warming. He discusses the causes of this condition and points out the effects of temperature pat-terns on the hydrological cycle. In semiarid regions, like Texas, the increased temperature will mean that evaporation will quickly outstrip precipitation. Thus more severe droughts are likely.

The next chapter relates to these ideas by discussing how highly episodic the Texas rainfall is, particularly farther away from the Gulf of Mexico. However, accurate precipitation forecasting is essential for proper water management. Therefore, David R. Legates suggests the use of real-time monitoring of climatological conditions rather than depending on an "annual mean" number for water resource management.

Kent M. McGregor's contribution deals with the global event known as El Niño/Southern Oscillation (ENSO). He notes that an ENSO event is associated with a greater likelihood of flooding in Texas, while the opposite event, La Niña, is associated with drought conditions. Although these occurrences are variable in their duration and effects, water resource managers could use the knowledge to benefit water planning.

Groeger, Kelley, and Martin address the implications of Texas' extreme climatic variability for the state's reservoir ecosystems. They suggest that flow is a crucial factor: while a warming climate may in the future influence Texas reservoirs, they argue, variability of flow may be much more important.

Douglas F. Welsh examines the use of specialized landscaping to help in water conservation. He points out the seven principles used in xeriscaping so that landscapers can cultivate beautiful gardens without excess use of irrigation. Significant amounts of water could be saved if water-stressed areas avoided planting water-rich shrubbery.

Finally, Anne Chin and Jean Ann Bowman take a look at a specific water management system: the Somerville Dam built across Yegua Creek in the 1960s. Since that time, dam construction in the United States has decreased due to the effects of such structures on downstream habitats. However, the Somerville Dam succeeded in easing the severe flooding that plagued the south-central area of Texas in the early twentieth century, and it created a reservoir and recreation area that acts as a large income source as well as water supply for the region.

CHAPTER 10

Will We Have Enough Water?

An Overview

Jurgen Schmandt

Houston Advanced Research Center and the University of Texas at Austin

Abstract

At the turn of the century, one often hears the comment that water scarcity will compete with oil as a cause for international and regional conflicts in the twenty-first century. How real is the danger? To put things into perspective, I shall review existing estimates of available freshwater supplies at global and regional levels. Using the concepts of water stress and water scarcity, I then identify regions that are subject to these conditions. I conclude with options for doing more with less in water-scarce environments.

The Global Picture

Ninety-seven percent of the world's water is stored in the oceans. Because ocean water is saline, it cannot be used for drinking or irrigation. Fresh water, the remaining 3 percent, amounts to 35 million km³. Yet, 99.7 percent of fresh water is stored in polar ice sheets or deep underground aquifers that are not accessible or where access is too expensive for human use. Usable fresh water in rivers and lakes amounts to less than 100,000 km³. This represents only 0.26 percent of the total amount of fresh water on earth (Shiklomanov 2000, p. 160).

Fossil fuels are nonrenewable. Fresh water exists in two forms: static, or stored for long time periods, and dynamic, or replenished at yearly or seasonal intervals. Static water has a full renewal period ranging from decades to millennia. It is stored in large lakes, aquifers, or glaciers. Depletion of static water causes economic and eco-

logical damage, and restoration takes tens or hundreds of years, if it can be done at all. Postel (1999) estimates that the overuse of groundwater amounts to 200 km³/year, with the most serious overpumping occurring in India, the United States, the Mediterranean countries, and China. This practice is unsustainable and has begun to cause harm in places as varied as Yemen, the Ogallala, or the Paso del Norte on the U.S.-Mexico border.

Renewable water is the principal resource for supporting human life and activities. But renewable water in lakes and rivers is equally important for supporting water ecosystems. Prudent water management, therefore, must consider both and keep water use within the range of renewable resources. How does water get renewed and how much can we expect to have available each year?

The amount of renewable water available varies from year to year. The best data set available covers the period 1921–85. During this time, the amount of renewable water showed annual variations of about 7 percent (Shiklomanov 2000, p. 176). Shiklomanov's revised estimate of renewable water varies between 39,780 and 44,780 km³/year, for an annual average of 43,000 km³.

Renewable water is produced through the process of evaporation and precipitation. Solar heating evaporates water from sea and land—505,000 km³ from the oceans and 72,000 km³/year from the continents. Precipitation returns 458,000 km³/year to the sea and 119,000 km³/year to land. Because less water falls on the oceans than is lost to evaporation, the difference, an estimated 43,000 km³/year, is transferred to land. These 43,000 km³ are "new" waters that run off into rivers, streams, and lakes and

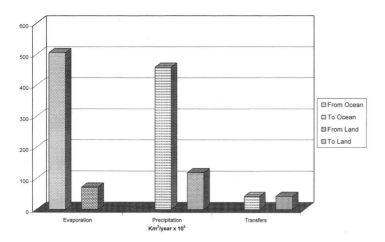

Figure 1. Nature's water cycle (km³/year × 10³).

recharge renewable aquifers. This is the water available to meet the yearly water demands of wildlife, vegetation, and human beings (fig. 1).

With a world population of six billion, an average of 43,000 km³ of new water translates to 7,200 m³/year available for each person. Current per capita withdrawals in North America, the region with the highest consumption in the world, amount to 1,692 m³/year. United Nations demographers predict that world population, using the most likely medium-fertility variant, will peak at 9.4 billion by 2050 and then begin to decline gradually (United Nations 1998). If the world of 2050 used as much water as we do today in North America, this would still give us each 4,600 m³/year. On a global scale, therefore, there seems to be enough water for all of us.

While these numbers may be useful for a first comparison of supply and demand for the world as a whole, they are highly misleading. In order to guide water managers, estimates must consider the water needed to maintain the ecological system, make informed assumptions about the drivers of future supply and demand, and most important, take into account differences between water-poor and water-rich regions. We may also want to pause when considering the rate of change over time. For example, per capita availability of fresh water was 17,000 m³ in 1950—more than twice the current amount (National Research Council 1999, p. 90).

A recent review article by Peter Gleick identifies twenty-six global water assessments since 1967 (Gleick 2000a). Most projections use a time horizon of twenty to fifty years into the future, with one outlier attempting a seventy-five-year forecast. This suggests that water planners differ from most managers of natural resources by

considering the longer term. But how useful are the results? To find the answer we must understand how global forecasts are made and what they project.

Water assessments compare water resources (supply) to water use (demand). The term *water use* is not defined consistently. The most widely followed convention distinguishes between two kinds of water use: water withdrawal and water consumption. *Water withdrawal* refers to water removed from a source and used for human needs. Some of this water may be returned to the original source in more or less acceptable quality for reuse. The terms *water consumption* or *consumptive use,* in contrast, refer to water withdrawn from a source and not returned to the source (Gleick 2000a, p. 38). Assessments simply reporting water use are useless unless they specify what exactly the term covers.

Early assessments arrived at predictions of future water demand by simply extrapolating two measures of water use in different parts of the world—use per person and use per irrigated acre of land. Recent studies use a larger number of demand categories: drinking water, industry, agriculture, and ecosystem functions. These categories are often further divided into areas such as irrigated, non-irrigated agriculture, and livestock. Some studies also take into account water losses such as evaporation in reservoirs. One assessment (Shiklomanov 2000, p. 165) explicitly considers climate change but concludes that regional impacts on precipitation and runoff remain uncertain and that projections up to 2025 can safely ignore possible changes resulting from climate change. Over time, assumptions about future needs have also become more sophisticated, moving from simple "business-as-usual" projections to alternative development and technology scenarios. The most recent assessment, conducted by the World Water Commission for the 21st Century, estimates demand and supply in 2025 under three different scenarios: business-as-usual, more efficient water use relying on markets and technology, and value and lifestyle changes that lead to a more sustainable world (World Water Commission for the 21st Century 2000; Rijsberman 2000). Finally, the quality and resolution of water statistics and the computing power to process large amounts of data have improved. As a result, today's assessments often begin with watershed-based data sets, which are then aggregated into national, regional, and global assessments.

Yet water statistics in many parts of the world remain deficient and seriously limit the accuracy of forecasts. Some data are not collected, some are not reliable, and some are kept secret. "Analysts should not assume that increasing model or scenario sophistication will lead to more accurate forecasts" (Gleick 2000a, p. 28). This warning must not be forgotten.

While drawing several conclusions from his review, Gleick claims early projections vastly overestimated future demand, as they simply extrapolated current trends into the future. Furthermore, as assessment methodology has improved, water demand projections now recognize and incorporate two significant reasons for lower demand. On the positive side, improvements in using water more efficiently reduce the need for additional water. On the negative side, slow economic development in parts of the world delayed increasing demand for water. As a result, actual water withdrawals in the mid-1990s were only half of what they had been projected thirty years ago to become. Recognizing these factors, the world's most experienced author of global water assessments now predicts water withdrawals in 2025 that are lower than his own estimates for 2000 made in 1974 (Shiklomanov 2000). Per capita demand for water rose until the mid-eighties and has since declined. In the United States, water withdrawals in 1995 were 10 percent less than in 1980.

Table 1 summarizes estimates of water withdrawal and consumption by the major world water assessments Gleick reviews. The decline in estimates of future demand over time should be noted. This is due to improved assessment methodologies and data, improved efficiency in water use, and slower than anticipated development in parts of the world. Only time will tell if projections made today similarly overestimate future demand. Even between recent assessments, large differences in estimated water use remain. Seckler, writing in 1998, projects withdrawals in 2025 that are similar to actual withdrawals in 1995 (Seckler et al. 1998). His result is based on the assumption that irrigation water is used more efficiently throughout the world. Shiklomanov (2000), making more cautious assumptions about future improvements, predicts a 72 percent increase in water use between 1995 and 2025.

Shiklomanov's article is a preview of the most ambitious global water assessment to date. The full results will be published later this year (Shiklomanov et al., forthcoming). Several important improvements in data availability and study methodology are incorporated in the as-

Table 1. Global water use projections 1974–2000 and actual use 1995 (km³/year)

Author/Year	Assumption/Base	Forecast Year	Withdrawal Total	Withdrawal Irrigation	Consumption Total
Group 1: 1974–87					
1a L'ovich 1974/79	Business-as-usual	2000	12,770	4,400	6,350
1b L'ovich 1974/79	Rational use	2000	6,825	3,950	6,335
2a Falkenmark/Lindh 1974	No wastewater reuse	2000	8,380		
2b Falkenmark/Lindh 1974	Wastewater reuse	2000	6,030		
2c Falkenmark/Lindh 1974	No wastewater reuse	2015	10,840	5,850	
2d Falkenmark/Lindh 1974	Wastewater reuse	2015	7,885	5,850	
3 De Mare 1976	Business-as-usual	2000	6,080		
4 Shiklomanov 1987/93	Business-as-usual	2000	5,186		2,893
Group II: 1990–2000					
5 WRI 1990	3% Increase/year	2000	4,660		2,700
6 Gleick 1997	Sustainability criteria	2025	4,270	2,930	
7a Shiklomanov 1998	Increased efficiency	2000	3,927	2,560	2,329
7b Shiklomanov 1998	Increased efficiency	2025	5,137	3,097	2,818
8a Alcamo 1997	Medium water use	2025	4,580	1,724	
8b Alcamo 1997	Medium water use	2075	9,496	1,826	
9a Seckler 1998	Business-as-usual	2025	4,596	3,376	
9b Seckler 1998	Irrigation efficiency	2025	3,625	2,432	
10 Shiklomanov 2000	Use since 1960	2025	5,235	3,189	2,764
Withdrawal 1995	Shiklomanov 2000		3,790	2,507	2,074

Sources: Compiled from Rijsberman 2000, Gleick 2000a, Gleick 2000b, and Shiklomanov 2000.

sessment. Approaches and findings are summarized in the following paragraphs.

The study is part of the International Hydrological Programme IV of UNESCO and was prepared by the State Hydrological Institute in St. Petersburg (Russia). The assessment incorporates careful evaluation of long-term historical water supply and demand data from all parts of the world. Previous assessments used limited historical data as a benchmark for their projections. Shiklomanov's world data set allows him to estimate water supply and demand during the sixty-plus-year period from 1921 to 1985. The data were compiled from measurements at twenty-five hundred hydrological sites throughout the world. The sites are part of the world hydrological network. However, recent data for the years after 1985 could not be obtained for parts of Africa, Asia, and South America. Values for these years had to be calculated from meteorological data (precipitation and air temperature) with the aid of correlation models and hydrological analogy methods. After evaluating the historical record, the study team selected the period from 1960 to 1985 for developing past water use trend lines. These were calculated for twenty-six "natural economic regions," three to eight regions for each continent. Regions tend to be vast, varying in size from one to eight million square kilometers. Areas making up the regions share two characteristics: homogeneous natural conditions and a similar level of economic development. North America, for example, is divided into three regions: Canada, the United States, and Central America.

Shiklomanov's projections up to 2025 are the result of combining the following parameters: historical trend line, population growth, social and economic development, and improvements in using water more efficiently.

Shiklomanov finds that water withdrawals and consumption increased 70 percent over the last thirty-five years. In 1960, 2,000 km^3 were withdrawn. In 1995, withdrawals rose to 3,765 km^3 and 2,070 km^3 (61 percent) were consumed. Sixty-six percent of all withdrawals and 85 percent of consumption were used by agriculture. Asia accounted for 59 percent of total withdrawals and 67 percent of water consumption. Future world water withdrawal is estimated to increase by 10–12 percent each decade and will reach 5,235 km^3 by 2025—a 1.38-fold increase. Water consumption will increase slightly less, at 1.33 times the current rate.

The volume of water withdrawn in 1995, at the global scale, amounts to 8.4 percent of available (i.e., renewable) water resources. This number will increase to 12 percent by 2025. For the world as a whole, these numbers do not suggest a crisis. As a matter of fact, some hydrologists deride the notion of a looming world water crisis. Robert Ambroggi states: "The total quantity of water on earth exceeds all conceivable needs of the human population." Unfortunately, the numbers come out very differently when the large regional differences in availability of water resources are considered.

Water in the Regions

While water at the global scale may be abundant, it is often limited, highly variable, and uncertain at the regional scale. Water distribution is extremely uneven. Average annual precipitation varies between nothing and ten meters. Multiyear, annual, and seasonal shortfalls in precipitation and runoff are common.

Regional water assessments are best when they measure conditions within individual catchments or watersheds. Global assessments stress the importance of regional variations and increasingly use basin-specific data. But they must aggregate data to large regional scales, such as continents or very large regions within continents. Even so, they are useful in identifying major trouble spots, areas already experiencing water stress, and those that have water stress pending at some point during this century.

Table 2 presents the regional water withdrawal estimates made by the same global water assessments reviewed in the previous section. The withdrawal data are by continent with one exception. Until 1990 the Soviet Union was counted as a separate region. Since then, water withdrawn in Russia and the other succession states of the USSR have been incorporated into Europe and Asia, according to geographical location. With this adjustment, the prominence of water withdrawals in Asia has become more pronounced—more than four times the volume withdrawn in North America and six times that in Europe. However, these numbers become meaningful only when they are placed in the context of regional water availability and human presence.

The volume of water available in a region is a function of climate and climate variation. How much of it is withdrawn and consumed is determined by population density and level of development. Combining these factors provides a metric to distinguish between water-rich and water-poor regions. Rosegrant (1997), following others before him, distinguishes between two levels of insufficient water supply. *Water stress* is present when annual per capita water availability is limited to 1,000 to 1,600 m^3.

Table 2. Regional water withdrawal projections 1974–2000 and actual use 1995 (km³/year)

Author/Year	Assumption/Base	Forecast Year	Europe	Asia	USSR	Africa	North America	South America	Australia & Oceania	Total
Group 1: 1974–87										
1a Ľovich 1974/79	Business-as-usual	2000								12,770
1b Ľovich 1974/79	Rational use	2000								6,825
2a Falkenmark/Lindh 1974	No wastewater reuse	2000	741	4,826	430	1,044	437	859	46	8,383
2b Falkenmark/Lindh 1974	Wastewater reuse	2000	536	3,465	312	742	317	616	33	6,021
2c Falkenmark/Lindh 1974	No wastewater reuse	2015								10840
2d Falkenmark/Lindh 1974	Wastewater reuse	2015								7,885
3 De Mare 1976	Business-as-usual	2000	405	3,140	640	520	1,025	290	60	6,080
4 Shiklomanov 1987/93	Business-as-usual	2000	444	3,140	229	314	795	216	47	8,186
Group II: 1990–2000										
5 WRI 1990	3% Increase/year	2000	404	2,160	533	289	946	293	35	4,660
6 Gleick 1997	Sustainability criteria	2025								
7a Shiklomanov 1998	Increased efficiency	2000	534	2,245		230	705	180	33	3,927
7b Shiklomanov 1998	Increased efficiency	2025	619	3,104		331	786	257	40	5,138
8a Alcamo 1997	Medium water use	2025								4,580
8b Alcamo 1997	Medium water use	2075								9,946
9a Seckler 1998	Business-as-usual	2025								4,569
9b Seckler 1998	Irrigation efficiency	2025								3,625
10 Shiklomanov 2000	Use since 1960	2025	559	3,254		337	786	260	40	5,235
				2,231	219					
Withdrawal 1995	Shiklomanov 2000		455				686	167	30	3,765

Sources: Compiled from Rijsberman 2000, Gleick 2000a, Gleick 2000b, and Shiklomanov 2000.

Water scarcity reigns when people have less than 1,000 m³ to meet their needs. Currently, twenty-eight countries, with a total population of 338 million, are water stressed. Of these, twenty are water scarce. Rosegrant predicts that water shortages will increase dramatically in the future, expanding the number of water-stressed countries to about fifty by 2025.

Shiklomanov uses six categories to characterize regional water availability—from catastrophically low (less than 1,000 m³ per person/year) to very high (more than 20,000 m³ per person/year). He finds that 35 percent of the world population is living under conditions of low or catastrophically low freshwater availability. By 2025, 30–35 percent of the world population is expected to live in areas with catastrophically low water availability.

Strzepek et al. (2000) use the demand/supply ratio as a proxy for water-related stress on nature and people. If the ratio is less than 0.1, the region experiences no stress. Low stress, stress, and high stress regions have demand/supply ratios of 0.1–02, 02–04, and greater than 04, respectively. These values are calculated for eighteen regions, using assessment results of the World Water Vision 2000 exercise (Rijsberman 2000). The population in water stress is then calculated. As a final step, the population at risk of hunger is also calculated. The regions with the largest populations exposed to water stress are South Asia (including India, Pakistan, and Bangladesh), China, the Middle East, North Africa, and Western Europe. Water stress was present in all of these regions in 1995 and will significantly increase (except for Western Europe) by 2025. The number of people at risk of hunger is also high in South Asia and China, suggesting that these regions will have to deal with water and food scarcity simultaneously. The total number of people living in water-stressed regions was 1.9 billion in 1995 and is estimated to be 3.4 billion in 2025. This last number assumes a business-as-usual development path. Under a more normative view of a sustainable world based on value and lifestyle changes, the 2025 number of people under water stress would be 2.8 billion.

The assessments of regional water needs of the human population in the preceding discussion combine human domestic needs with water needed for the production of food. Water needed for food varies greatly, depending on the kind of diet (vegetarian or meat) people consume. It is useful, therefore, to consider human domestic needs alone. Various organizations (World Bank, World Health Organization, and U.S. Agency for International Development) have set a standard between twenty and forty liters per capita per day to meet needs for drinking water and sanitation. Gleick (2000b, p. 11) adds water needed for bathing and food preparation (not production) and arrives at a basic needs standard of fifty liters per person per day. He reports that 2.2 billion people live in sixty-two countries that do not meet this standard, and in most cases this is not a result of water availability but of it not reaching the people who need it.

Conclusion

The water problem of the future is not one of water availability per se. The problem we face is regional, and within water-scarce and water-stressed regions it is social, economic, and political. It is unlikely that increased supplies, massive new water projects, or new technologies will provide the necessary solutions. For example, we should not expect to move water around the globe as we have done in the case of petroleum. To a limited extent this will happen indirectly. Lester Brown et al. (1999) report that even today, North Africa and the Middle East are increasingly forced to feed their people by importing food. Importing a ton of wheat is equivalent to importing a thousand tons of water. But the real solution to regional water stress and scarcity must come from improvements in water infrastructure, water efficiency, and management.

In March of 2000, at the World Water Forum held at the Hague, Ismael Serageldin presented the recommendations of the World Water Commission for the twenty-first century (World Water Commission for Water in the 21st Century 2000). Serageldin pointed out that invest-

ments in water infrastructure projects rarely recover more than 35 percent of their costs. To meet the water needs of nine billion people by the middle of the century, massive investments are needed to build and maintain water supply and treatment systems. The commission estimates that $180 billion per year are needed. At present, the countries of the world invest $70 billion each year. The commission believes that the needed funds require a massive increase in private investment. To provide the needed incentives, the central recommendation is to move rapidly toward full cost pricing of water services. Public funds, under the new policy, would be used for two purposes: research and water assistance to the poor. Governments and international lending institutions would no longer subsidize water projects. Their most ambitious new task would be to ensure that poor people have access to water. A possible model for accomplishing this goal is based on Chile's example of issuing water stamps. Water stamps would work like food stamps, which have long been used to improve access to food by the poor. The commission's water vision for the new century advocates privatization and water stamps as the key strategies in solving the growing water problems of water-scarce and water-stressed countries.

Ken Frederick, in a World Bank report, endorses the need for managing water as an economic good (Frederick 1992). The cost of using water has to be borne by users in order for the resource to be used efficiently. This translates into a shift from supply to demand management of water. Demand management includes the right to transfer water among alternative uses in response to changing supply and demand conditions. For Frederick, the division of labor between the private and public sectors would be structured as follows: prices and markets must become the primary tools of managing water demand; government would define and enforce property rights and regulate the prices and profits of monopolistic suppliers; government would also require and oversee comprehensive basinwide water resource planning as a guide to investment decisions.

This brings us back from the large scale—the world, continents, and mega regions—to the smaller scale of the watershed. Global assessments, as I have tried to show, provide increasingly useful information on the ratio between renewable water and used water. They can also pinpoint large trouble spots. But they are of limited usefulness for the local water manager. They treat the entire North American continent, for example, as a single water-rich region. But we all know that west of the hundredth meridian the declining supply of water and the rapidly increasing human population are on a collision course. The assessments reviewed in this chapter provide limited guidance for the water manager in the Delaware or the Rio Grande basins. For this a much closer look is needed.

References

Brown, L., C. Flavin, and H. French. Chapter 7, "Feeding Nine Billion," *State of the World*. New York: Norton, 1999.

Clarke, R. *Water: The International Crisis*. Cambridge, Mass: MIT Press, 1993.

Cosgrove, W. J., and F. R. Rijsberman. *Making Water Everybody's Business*. London: Earthscan Publications, 2000.

Frederick, K. D. *Balancing Water Demands with Supplies: The Role of Management in a World of Increasing Scarcity*. Washington, D.C.: World Bank, 1992.

Gleick, P. H. *Water in Crisis*. New York: Oxford University Press, 1993.

Gleick, P. H. "Water Futures: A Review of Global Water Resources Projections." In *World Water Scenarios: Analyses*, ed. F. R. Rijsberman, 27–45. London: Earthscan Publications, 2000a.

Gleick, P. H. *The World's Water 2000–2001*. Washington, D.C: Island Press, 2000b.

National Research Council. *Our Common Journey: A Transition toward Sustainability*. Washington, D.C: National Academy Press, 1999.

Postel, S. *Pillar of Sand: Can the Irrigation Miracle Last?* New York: Norton, 1999.

Rijsberman, F. R., ed. *World Water Scenarios: Analyses*. London: Earthscan Publications, 2000.

Rosegrant, M. W. *Water Resources in the Twenty-First Century*. Washington, D.C.: International Food Policy Research Institute, 1997.

Seckler, D., U. Amarsinghe, D. Molden, R. de Silva, and R. Barker. *World Water Demand and Supply, 1990–2025: Scenarios and Issues*. Research Report 19, International Water Management Institute, Colombo, Sri Lanka, 1998.

Shiklomanov, I. "World Water Resources and Water Use: Present Assessment and Outlook for 2025." In *World Water Scenarios: Analyses*, ed. F. R. Rijsberman, 160–203. London: Earthscan Publications, 2000.

Shiklomanov, I., and S. C. Rodda. *World Water Resources at the Beginning of the 21st Century*. Cambridge: Cambridge University Press, 2003.

Strzepek, K. M., A. Holt, E. Kemp-Benedit, P. Raskin, G. Gallopin, and F. Rijsberman. "Regionalization and Implications of the World Water Scenarios." In *World Water Scenarios: Analyses*, ed. F. R. Rijsberman, 120–59. London: Earthscan Publications, 2000.

United Nations, Population Division of the Department of Economic and Social Affairs. *World Population Projections to 2150*. New York: United Nations, 1998.

Serageldin, I. *Toward Sustainable Management of Water Resources*. Washington, D.C.: World Bank, 1995.

Uitto, J. I., and J. Schneider. *Freshwater Resources in Arid Lands*. United Nations New York: University Press, 1997.

World Water Commission for Water in the 21st Century. "A Water Secure World: Vision for Water, Life, and the Environment. Commission Report." World Water Council, 2000.

CHAPTER 11

Water and Climate Change in the Twenty-first Century

Gerald R. North

Department of Atmospheric Sciences

Texas A&M University

Abstract

According to a distinguished international group of experts on climate change, we can expect the globe to warm significantly over the next century—in fact, several times the warming experienced over the last century. The hydrological cycle as well as the temperature field will be affected. It is likely that the rate of the hydrological cycle will increase, but the local effects may be quite variable. Climate models are not particularly reliable in pinning down the exact locations of deficits or surpluses, but several models suggest that in the Texas region, evaporation rates will outstrip precipitation increases. This could mean serious changes in the availability of water for Texas applications.

Global Warming

A crude definition of climate is that it is a statistical summary of weather. For example, at a particular station it might be the arithmetic average over time of the temperature and of other meteorological variables. In addition, we might include some measure of variability; for example, if the statistics are normally distributed, we could include the variance. More comprehensive definitions might include covariances with other stations or other variables and lagged temporal correlations. All of these statistics form a space-time multivariate probability density function, the parameters of which define the climate. When climate changes, these defining parameters change.

The major question we must ask is whether the warming of 0.6°C over the last century came about because of a change in the climate parameters or whether it is a fluke, merely a member of a fixed distribution of weather variates. Complicating matters is the fact that the weather system (including the "weather" of the ocean currents) moves very slowly to fill out its normal distribution. It may take hundreds of years to do this, in which case the possibility of a fluke is enhanced, given only a data string of finite length. But should the climate be changing?

The elementary answer to this is yes. Simple but convincing theories of climate suggest that increasing the concentration of greenhouse gases will cause the global average temperature to go up. There is ample empirical evidence that the greenhouse gases in the atmosphere, primarily carbon dioxide (CO_2), are increasing steadily and that these increases are likely to be anthropogenic.

Traditional Theory

The greenhouse theory of global warming can be explained in simple terms as follows. First, almost all solar radiation is absorbed at the ground, heating it. Heat is removed from the ground by infrared radiation in the vertical, evaporation of water, and convection of sensible heat in the vertical. Infrared radiation to space originates at the surface, from infrared emitters in the warm air above and from cloud tops. The air above is cooler than the surface. A greenhouse gas such as carbon dioxide absorbs and emits radiation in the infrared. Carbon dioxide is well mixed in the atmosphere, and if its concentration is increased, it will effectively emit to space at a higher altitude than before. Since the atmospheric temperature steadily decreases as a function of altitude, the emitted radiation from the carbon dioxide will be from a cooler source, and therefore it will cool the planet less than at the reduced concentration. This lowered cooling rate will have to be compensated for by a warming of the atmosphere at the level of the emission. The simplest theories accomplish this by raising the temperature of the whole column of air, including the surface. In most climate models the doubling of concentration of carbon dioxide leads to a warming of the globe of about 2 to 4°C.

Greenhouse Gases

The most abundant greenhouse gas is water vapor. It is also the most powerful, since it absorbs strongly all across the infrared spectrum, where most radiation from our planet is concentrated. Water vapor is naturally occurring and is quite variable, mostly concentrating in the lowest one or two kilometers of the atmosphere. We do not normally consider water vapor as one of the anthropogenic greenhouse gases, but it is likely to change under changing climatic conditions in reaction to responses to other stimuli. For example, if the planet were to warm, conventional wisdom suggests that the amount of water vapor in the air column would increase, leading to a "thickening" of the greenhouse and therefore an amplification of the warming brought about by the primary driver. In most climate models this amplification is roughly a factor of two.

The greenhouse gases considered anthropogenic are carbon dioxide, primarily generated by the burning of fossil fuels, land clearing, and various industrial processes; nitrous oxide (N_2O), which originates from agricultural practices; and methane (CH_4), which originates from various anthropogenic sources such as natural gas leaks, rice paddies, etc. The first two of these gases have adjustment times in the atmosphere of hundreds of years, while that of methane is only a few years. Effectively, we are pumping these gases into the atmosphere much faster than they can be reabsorbed into the natural system.

Evidence for the Warming

There is empirical evidence that the globe has warmed significantly over the last hundred years, lending strength to the greenhouse theory. Not only do surface instrument records show this warming, but there are ancillary measures such as melting permafrost, shrinking mountain glaciers, and decreasing snow cover.

Climate Models

The equations governing the movement of the atmosphere and ocean can be approximately solved by numerical procedures implemented on supercomputers. These models have been studied extensively over the last forty years, first in weather forecasting, then as climate simulators over the last twenty-five years. Models for ocean and atmospheric simulation evolved separately and were joined together in the late 1980s. The late 1990s produced fairly satisfactory coupled atmosphere-ocean general circulation models (AOGCMs). These models can now reproduce the seasonal cycle and the correct circulation statistics and can even simulate the climate change over the last century with some degree of satisfaction. While the models do these things with such fidelity that it is hard to ignore them, there is still considerable disagreement among them as to what the next century's climate will be like.

The IPCC's Third Assessment Report

The Intergovernmental Panel on Climate Change (IPCC) is a group under the auspices of the United Nations charged with publishing the results of research on climate change every five years in an effort to report to the public. The first report was published in 1990 (First Assessment Report, FAR), the Second Assessment Report (SAR) was published in 1995, and now the Third Assessment Report (TAR) is about to be published by Cambridge University Press in April of 2001. The process of gathering the information that goes into such a report is conducted over a period of several years before publication. Literally hundreds of scientists gather in numerous meetings to address individual aspects of the problem, and they eventually arrive at a draft of the final document. After drafts of the chapters are written, they are distributed to hundreds of other scientists for anonymous review. The final product represents (in my opinion) the most up to date and accurate thinking on the problem. It is not perfect, but there does not seem to be a better way to do this job.

The Globe Is Warming

Perhaps the most important observation is that data indicate that the earth has been warming over the last century. The instrumental record is more certain now than it was five years ago, and it indicates that the global average temperature is up by about 0.6°C over the last century. The warmest decade of the past century was the 1990s, with 1998 being the warmest year on record. Several groups have analyzed new proxy data from ice cores and other sources suggesting that the twentieth century is unique in its abrupt warming compared to other centuries during the last millennium. Over the last few decades, where upper air data are available, there are indications that air temperature has increased significantly throughout the lowest eight kilometers of the atmosphere. Snow- and ice-covered areas have been decreasing significantly. Sea level has increased 0.1 to 0.2 meters. Heavy precipitation events may have increased in middle latitudes. At the same time some variables have not changed significantly, such as the number of Atlantic hurricanes.

Greenhouse Gases Are Increasing

Greenhouse gas concentrations are up. For example, carbon dioxide is up 31 percent since the beginning of the Industrial Revolution, taken here to be 1750. About three quarters of this increase is thought to be attributable to fossil fuel burning, but other sources include clearing of land and various industrial processes. The rate of increase of carbon dioxide is rather variable, from 0.9 to 2.8 parts per million per year. Methane (CH_4) has increased 151 percent over this same period, and about half of its increase is presumed to be anthropogenic. Nitrous oxide is up 17 percent. The chlorofluorocarbons (CFCs) have increased enormously, but their rate has dropped in the last few years due to the Montreal Protocol.

Aerosols and Natural Forcings

Since the industrial revolution, aerosols (small particles suspended in the air) have been increasing due to human activities (smokestacks, auto exhausts, etc.). These tiny particulates can cause changes in climate in several ways. Most are sulfate aerosols derived from fossil fuel burning.

These aerosols, for the most part, should cause a cooling effect on the atmosphere because they reflect solar radiation back to space before it can heat the air and surface. Some aerosols come from biomass burning, and these can have a mixed effect, both reflecting solar radiation back to space and absorbing the solar rays providing a heat source for the surrounding air. Finally, aerosols can modify the formation of clouds, the droplets of which are formed on these tiny bits of solid or liquid matter. This latter is called the *indirect aerosol effect* and is currently rather poorly understood, although some models purport to include it, albeit crudely.

Some other natural forcings include volcanic eruptions, which often spread a veil of aerosols in the stratosphere, screening out sunlight, as with the anthropogenic aerosols. Volcanic aerosols (mostly composed of sulfur compounds and adsorbed water) tend to remain in the stratosphere for a year or two before falling out harmlessly. The climatic effect can be quite dramatic. For example, after the eruption of Mount Pinatubo in the early 1990s, the globe cooled temporarily by nearly 1°C. Hence, volcanic activity can lead to punctuated coolings of rather large magnitude and lasting for a few years. When bunched together, they can cause a prolonged lowering of the global average temperature.

Other natural forcings include the effects of solar variability. It is now well established that the total radiation flux from the sun has a variation following the nearly periodic eleven-year solar cycle. The amplitude of this cycle is about 0.1 percent in luminosity, and attempts have been made to detect this very faint signal in the climate system response, with mixed results but some reasons for optimism (North and Wu 2001). Theoretically, the sun has been increasing its luminosity over the century, but the most popular theories indicate that this stimulus to global warming may be only a small fraction of that expected on the basis of the greenhouse effect. I take the theory of a brightening sun to be rather speculative at this point.

Climate Model Confidence Has Increased

There is a general feeling in the community that our confidence in climate models has improved over the last five years. For example, there has been better appreciation of the many processes involved. A number of field programs have collected and analyzed data over this period, and new data have come from satellite observing systems such as the Tropical Rainfall Measuring Mission. Our ability to simulate the present seasonal cycle and such features as El Niño has increased significantly. In addition, there have been some successful simulations of past climates. Even with this increase in our confidence, climate models still exhibit about a 50 percent range of uncertainty in their prediction of the response of the global average temperature due to a doubling of CO_2.

Evidence for Attribution

There has been considerable activity over the last five years in the area of detecting climate response signals in the instrumental data stream of surface temperatures collected over the last fifty and one hundred years. Done properly, this allows us to attribute the climate change to various inducing agents, including greenhouse gases, anthropogenic aerosols, volcanic activity, and solar variation. The results are based upon climate model simulations lasting thousands of years, thus establishing the level and patterns of natural variability ("noise," in this application). Then an *ensemble* of runs with prescribed forcings is used to establish the expected responses or signal patterns from each of the forcings. One then passes the data through this detection filter and comes up with an estimate of the signal strengths in the data and their statistical uncertainty. The results from several groups are consistently showing that the greenhouse gas signal is very significant at better than the 95 percent confidence level, and so is that for the volcanic responses. The results are significant for the aerosol contribution over the last fifty years. Solar cycle response is still marginal at about the 75 percent confidence level.

Human Activities in the Present Century

The adjustment times for different greenhouse gases differ. In particular, it is important to realize that the times for adjustment of the atmospheric concentration of CO_2 and N_2O are roughly hundreds of years. This means that after pumping an overload of CO_2 into the air, it will take some two hundred years for the atmosphere to adjust itself back to its normal equilibrium level of this gas. The same holds for N_2O. On the other hand, it has been pointed out that methane has a much faster equilibration time, and taking action on reducing methane emissions is likely to have a quick response and might be part of an important greenhouse reduction strategy.

Temperatures and Sea Level Are to Rise

Because of the long time constants of the greenhouse gases, and because of the long time constants of the slower components of the system (e.g., world oceans and continental ice sheets), these slowly responding parts of the system take a long time to "catch up" with the current radiation balance or imbalance. They will cause the system's temperature field to lag behind the current imbalance. Thus, even if we make a change in our greenhouse gas emission rates, they will lag behind in responding to the changes, and warming may well continue for hundreds of years. In fact, sea level would surely continue rising as the excess heat spreads throughout the world ocean and causes the thermal expansion that leads to most of the expected sea level rise.

More Understanding Needed

Finally, the report suggests that continued research is needed to gain a more complete understanding of the system. I will not elaborate here, but it is clear that better and faster computers are essential, along with the continued deployment of global observing systems that can provide data used to confront the models.

Model Simulations of Future Climate

As part of the IPCC TAR process, a team was asked to provide model scenarios of future emissions of greenhouse gases and aerosols. This activity was termed the Summary Report of Emissions Scenarios (SRES). These scenarios were for a range of different assumptions about different societal evolution types. Some types were based on energy-conserving strategies, while others relied on strict market principles. The scenarios were not meant to be representative of any kind of statistical distribution; they were simply a set of guiding principles to see the range of possibilities. These emissions scenarios were then fed into a model to see how the climate forcings would come out (e.g., gas concentrations). Once the forcings were obtained as a function of time, the climate models could be used to simulate the future climates. While the models provided some detailed information about regional climate change, there was enough difference between models to suggest that for the present purposes, the global average values would be sufficient (fig. 1).

Considering the whole envelope of climate responses,

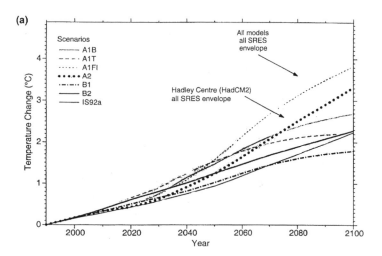

(a)

Figure 1. *Modeled responses in the global average temperature by the Hadley Centre Model and an envelope of other models for a representative group of emission scenarios.*

we might expect a global average warming of between 1.5 and 4.5°C. The models also indicate an increase of the global hydrological cycle.

On a regional basis there are a few robust results. For example, the temperature change is amplified toward the poles by a factor of two or three. In the low latitudes it is diminished by a slight amount. The temperature change in the neighborhood of Texas can be taken to be that of the global average without too much error. There are also some regional precipitation effects in the tropics, but these are not likely to be important for our present purposes.

Application to Future Texas Climate

So what can we deduce from all this information about the future climate of Texas? I think it is reasonable to suppose that the climate *will* change and that in Texas we can expect a warming of 1.5 to 4.5°C (3 to about 8°F) over the next century. It is disturbing that the range is so great, since the bottom of this range is rather benign and the top of it is disastrous. There are many reasons for the range of

uncertainty (North 1995), but that aside, let us concentrate on what might be in store for Texas.

As already indicated, we might expect the annual average temperature of Texas to go up by something like the global average temperature's rise. While this will cause us to use much more energy to cool ourselves in summer, it will have a far greater effect on water supplies because of the exponential dependence of evaporation rates on surface temperature. I believe we can state with a fair degree of certainty that evaporation rates will increase. This means that lakes and other surface waters and wet soil will evaporate and evapotranspirate to the extent that Texas rivers will not be like they are today. Some may not make it to the Gulf as they do now. On the other hand, the total hydrological cycle may increase, but it may not resemble that of today, perhaps showing more downpours and flooding. A key uncertainty is El Niño. Our climate models are beginning to have El Niño events in their simulations, but they are not as yet realistic. I expect that in a few years we will have more definitive answers about whether El Niño frequency and intensity will increase with a warming world. El Niño plays such a key role in Texas water supplies that it will be important to see how this turns out.

In summary, I believe that Texas climate will be warming steadily over the next century, leading to an increase of sea level of roughly 0.1 to 0.2 m, temperatures increasing 1.5 to 4.5°C, and surface water supplies endangered by a dramatic increase in evaporation rates.

References

North, Gerald. "Climate Change and the Texas Region." In *The Changing Climate of Texas,* ed. J. Norwine, J. Giardino, G. North, and J. Valdés, 7–21. College Station: Texas A&M University Press, 1995.

Watson, Robert, John Houghton, and Ding Yihui, eds. *Third Assessment Report on Climate Change.* Cambridge: Cambridge University Press, 2001.

Watson, Robert, John Houghton, and Ding Yihui, eds. *Climate Change: Summary for Policymakers and Technical Summary of Working Group I Report.* Cambridge: Cambridge University Press, 1991.

CHAPTER 12

Climate and Water

Precipitation, Evapotranspiration, and Hydroclimatological Aspects

David R. Legates

University of Delaware

Abstract

The highly variable nature of the hydrologic cycle across Texas is demonstrated using both historical data and examples taken from a real-time hydroclimatological monitoring system. In particular, the spatial and temporal variability in precipitation, potential and actual evapotranspiration, and soil moisture are mapped for the state of Texas. It is concluded that given the highly variable nature of Texas' climate, Texas is clearly an excellent laboratory for examining, studying, and monitoring hydroclimatic variability. Real-time monitoring and forecasting of hydroclimatological conditions is therefore essential for adequate water resource management and planning across the entire state.

Texas climate exhibits a wide range of weather processes and patterns. From the humid southeast to the arid Panhandle, the hydroclimatological diversity of the state is striking, influenced as it is by both the moist Gulf of Mexico and the dry mountains of the southern Rockies. However, the high spatial and temporal variability that characterizes the hydroclimate of Texas is not often conveyed in maps of mean annual precipitation or evapotranspiration (combined water loss from soil evaporation and plant transpiration). Precipitation events are often episodic, with daily rainfall totals that in some areas occasionally exceed ten inches, making flooding commonplace. Although precipitation amounts decrease as the

distance from the Gulf of Mexico increases, precipitation variability becomes more extreme and more important. Precipitation in western Texas, in contrast to the humid southeast, can be so sparse that droughts, both widespread and localized, are not uncommon.

Given that precipitation provides the input to the surface water balance, the variability of Texas precipitation leads to significant irregularities in soil moisture, evapotranspiration, streamflow, and runoff. Agriculture and other economic activities are affected and challenged by the highly inconstant nature of these hydroclimate variables.

The Annually Averaged Texas Hydroclimate

Mean annual precipitation, potential and actual evapotranspiration, and runoff were computed for Texas, portions of adjacent states, and Mexico (fig. 1). Long-term mean monthly air temperature and precipitation data for nearly one thousand stations (333 in Texas) were obtained from the Legates' (1987) global station archive. A simple Thornthwaite-style water balance (Thornthwaite 1948) was computed for each station and the resulting annual fields were mapped. Precipitation gauge measurement biases were estimated and removed from the precipitation data (Legates 1987), and Hamon's (1963) method was used to estimate potential evapotranspiration. Hamon's method was selected since it has relatively small overall bias for large-scale computations of the terrestrial water balance (Vörösmarty et al. 1998) and is preferable to the Thornthwaite potential evapotranspiration method

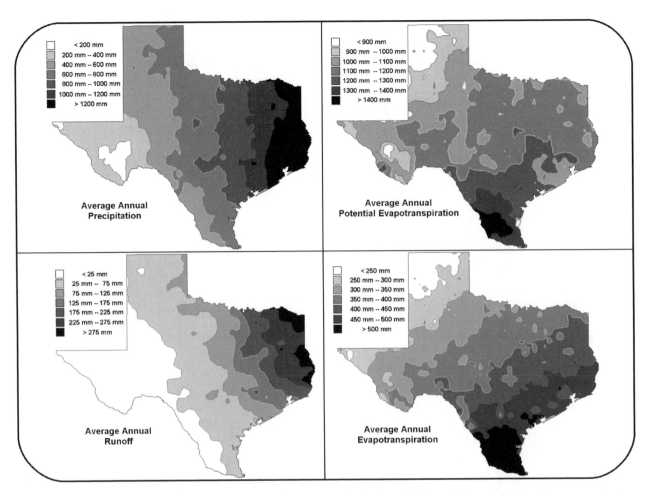

Figure 1. Average annual precipitation (top left), potential evapotranspiration (top right), runoff (bottom left), and evapotranspiration (bottom right) computed for Texas using long-term mean monthly data taken from Legates (1987).

when gauge bias adjustments have been included (Legates and Mather 1992).

Area-preserving splines were used to interpolate temporally the monthly precipitation and air temperature data to thirty pseudo-days per month; precipitation then was assumed to fall on every fifth day, to simulate the passage of synoptic systems. Soil moisture resistance was assumed to decrease linearly to zero after the soil water content fell below 70 percent and field capacity (FC) was specified by

$$FC = 1110 + 10\,\lambda + 10\,(33 - \phi)\ (\text{in mm depth})\quad(1)$$

where λ is the station longitude (negative longitude for the western hemisphere) and ϕ is the station latitude (both in degrees). This allows for a gradual change in field capacity from a maximum of about 200 mm along the

Gulf coast to a minimum of 60 mm in West Texas and the Texas Panhandle.

Depicting precipitation, potential and actual evapotranspiration, and runoff, the maps in figure 1 show precipitation (moisture supply) as exhibiting a strong longitudinal gradient, with precipitation across the state decreasing dramatically to the west. Potential evapotranspiration (moisture demand), which is tightly coupled to both the solar input (latitude) and elevation, decreases from the southeast toward the northwest. Moisture surplus, or runoff, is strongly coupled to the precipitation, as is to be expected. Finally, the actual evapotranspiration—moisture transferred from the land surface to the atmosphere—is a function of the difference between the moisture availability (including its timing) and the moisture demand. Isolines in figure 1 have not been smoothed to indicate the relative spatial variability of these fields.

Inter- and Intra-Annual Variability

Inter-annual (between years) and intra-annual (within year) variability are important features of the hydroclimate of Texas that are not evident from simple annual evaluations. As already noted, the climate in Texas is highly variable, making floods and droughts commonplace. As a result, actual conditions across the state can vary markedly from the patterns depicted in figure 1.

To examine the inter- and intra-annual variability in these hydroclimate variables, data from 1970 through 1999 were used to compute January and July extremes (maximum and minimum) and averages for four stations located in a cross section of Texas between 31.0°N and 33.5°N latitude (table 1). This small subset of data available for the state illustrates considerable inter-annual variability. Both potential and actual evapotranspiration peak in the summer, owing to the dependence of potential evapotranspiration on the solar input, while precipitation and runoff also exhibit significant month-to-month variability.

Substantial intra-annual variability also can be seen in all four variables (table 1). In particular, the highly variable nature of precipitation (precipitation totals can be as much as five times the long-term average) can lead to years in which substantial flooding occurs (significant runoff), or years where a drought prevails (low runoff and actual evapotranspiration). Clearly, the highly variable nature of precipitation and, to a lesser extent, potential evapotranspiration across the state mean that hydroclimate conditions can be misleading and often do not adequately represent the true intra-annual variability of Texas climate.

Summary

Using both historical data and examples from a real-time hydroclimatological monitoring system, this chapter has

Table 1. Average and extremes of monthly totals of precipitation (P), potential evapotranspiration (PE), evapotranspiration (ET), and runoff (R), computed from a thirty-year time series (1970–99). All values are in millimeters.

		Wink Winkler Co.			Munday Knox Co.			McGregor McLennan Co.			Lufkin Angelina Co.		
		min.	avg.	max.	min.	avg.	max.	min.	avg.	max.	min.	avg.	max.
Jan.	P	0	57	308	0	60	240	1	61	193	18	121	338
	PE	29	35	41	24	35	42	27	38	47	29	43	57
	ET	2	20	40	8	25	37	19	34	45	28	43	57
	R	0	24	295	0	19	230	1	25	188	18	78	318
Apr.	P	0	16	121	3	47	190	5	75	180	8	79	173
	PE	79	94	114	76	93	117	77	94	117	81	100	118
	ET	3	27	69	15	55	91	26	71	93	38	80	112
	R	0	1	112	3	7	109	5	12	118	8	14	156
Jul.	P	0	50	150	0	43	134	0	51	338	0	66	155
	PE	170	206	243	176	218	265	183	213	243	190	203	243
	ET	4	46	109	5	48	103	10	55	152	23	73	140
	R	0	3	135	0	1	130	0	7	332	0	1	125
Oct.	P	0	39	143	0	68	211	10	95	260	11	111	395
	PE	67	86	100	64	90	108	70	95	116	72	95	110
	ET	4	34	83	5	45	81	8	50	106	23	59	104
	R	0	3	134	0	13	201	10	19	206	11	31	395
Longitude		103.20°W			99.62°W			97.40°W			94.45°W		

examined the spatial and temporal variability in precipitation, potential and actual evapotranspiration, and soil moisture for the state of Texas. Given the highly variable nature of the climate of Texas, however, real-time monitoring and forecasting of hydroclimatological conditions is essential for adequate water resource management and planning. In light of these issues, Texas is clearly an excellent laboratory for examining, studying, and monitoring hydroclimatic variability.

Acknowledgment

Computational assistance by Kathleen A. Felter is greatly appreciated.

References

Hamon, W. R. "Computation of Direct Runoff Amounts from Storm Rainfall." *Int. Assoc. Sci. Hydrol. Publ.* 63 (1963): 52–62.

Legates, D. R. "A Climatology of Global Precipitation." *Publ. Climatol.* 40, no. 10 (1987). 84 pp.

Legates, D. R., and J. R. Mather. "An Evaluation of the Average Annual Global Water Balance." *Geogr. Rev.* 82 (1992): 253–67.

Thornthwaite, C. W. "An Approach toward a Rational Classification of Climate." *Geogr. Rev.* 38 (1948): 55–94.

Vörösmarty, C. J., C. A. Federer, and A. L. Schloss. "Potential Evaporation Functions Compared on U.S. Watersheds: Possible Implications for Global-Scale Water Balance and Terrestrial Ecosystem Modeling." *J. Hydrol.* 207 (1998): 147–69.

CHAPTER 13

The El Niño/Southern Oscillation and Impacts on Climate Anomalies in Texas

Kent M. McGregor

Department of Geography

University of North Texas

Abstract

El Niño/Southern Oscillation (ENSO) events are important contributors to climatic anomalies in Texas and the southwestern United States. El Niño events are associated with enhanced precipitation in Texas during the spring and winter months. La Niña events are associated with drought conditions. Thus, conditions in the Pacific may be used as indicators of future climatic anomalies in the Southwest. As science progresses and future ENSO events can be predicted with longer lead times, seasonal forecasts and perhaps even climatic forecasts become possible. The potential benefits for water resources planning are immense; therefore, the best use of such forecast information becomes a serious question.

El Niño/Southern Oscillation (ENSO) events have been closely linked to precipitation and other climatic anomalies around the world. The very intense 1997–98 event caused devastation around the world, and the resulting media coverage sharply focused public attention on the phenomenon. El Niño has become both a household name and one of the most studied topics in the atmospheric sciences, second only to global warming.

El Niño causes a reversal of the usual pressure pattern across the equatorial Pacific Ocean. The usual arrangement is for low pressure in the western Pacific (Indonesia) and high pressure in the eastern Pacific (Peru). El Niño events refer to an unusual warming of tropical waters off the west coast of South America. Since the warming starts in late December, it is named El Niño after the arrival of the Christ child. This warming causes profound changes in weather across the tropical Pacific. The normally dry coastal deserts of Peru and Chile receive torrential rains. Meanwhile, Indonesia and Australia suffer severe drought. Since El Niño involves a flip-flop of the normal weather patterns, these phenomena are also called the Southern Oscillation. The two terms are frequently combined and abbreviated to ENSO. In addition, there is the opposite phase or anti–El Niño phenomenon called La Niña. As the abnormally warm water fades, it is often replaced by unusually cool waters. This event is called a La Niña. Many, but not all, El Niño events are followed by La Niña events. La Niña is actually an intensification of the normal pattern that results in more rain in the western Pacific and stronger trade winds. Because of the difference in sea surface temperatures, El Niño events are called warm phase and La Niña events are called cold phase. Both events have been linked to climate anomalies throughout the world.

ENSO is important to the earth's climatic system because it is the single largest source of inter-annual variability. In addition, a better understanding of ENSO has profound implications for the question of global warming (Zebiak 1999). There is at least some credible evidence that ENSO events have become more frequent and extreme in the last hundred years. Certainly the 1982–83 events and the 1997–98 events stand out as the most extreme on record. Paleoclimatic studies indicate that

ENSO has been around for at least five thousand years, and there is some scientific conjecture that the time frame is much longer. Many sources of paleoclimatic information—tree rings, cores from ice and coral, marine sediments and certain fossil organisms preserved in these sediments—indicate that ENSO-like oscillations have operated for thousands of years in the tropics. In addition, there is ample evidence that the connections extend well outside the tropics (Diaz and Markgraf 1992). One of the strongest such associations is with northern Mexico and the southern tier of the United States, including Texas.

However, the scientific community has conducted research on ENSO for only about twenty years. Modern research on ENSO began in the 1920s when Sir Gilbert Walker (1936) first identified the opposite relationship of atmospheric pressure across the equatorial Pacific. Walker named this the southern oscillation. Later, the data collected during the International Geophysical Year of 1957–58 allowed Jacob Bjerknes (1966) to explain the relationship of atmospheric pressure to sea surface temperatures (SSTs). The El Niño event of 1972–73 finally captured the attention of the scientific community. The events in the 1970s defined the canonical form—that is, the sequence of oceanic and atmospheric events that is typical of a developing and then maturing event. This canonical form became the standard to which other events were compared. Nevertheless the very strong 1982–83 event was well under way before scientists took notice. It was not predicted in advance, and as it developed it did not follow the canonical form. Zebiak (1999) made the first actual prediction for the 1986–87 event. The event did not appear quite on time, but it did appear, and it was forecast by a computer model. The forecasts in the early 1990s missed the mark in many cases because of the unusual conditions at the time. In fact, if one looks at sea surface temperatures from the central Pacific, it looks like one long, three- to four-year event. If one looks at the SSTs from the eastern Pacific, it looks like three independent events. Finally, the 1997–98 event was predicted in advance but not with significant lead time. The 1990s taught the research community that ENSO events come in many forms (Zebiak 1999).

Atmospheric Processes and Linkage to Texas Precipitation Anomalies

What are the atmospheric processes that link ENSO to climatic anomalies in Texas and surrounding regions? In the wake of the 1982–83 event, Philander (1989) provided an excellent overview of the ENSO phenomenon and its impact. This event was the strongest of the century until that time. Even so, it caught scientists flat-footed, and it was well under way before scientists were certain it was happening. Rasmusson (1985) noted the unusual arrangement of the Rossby wave train across the Pacific, which resulted in a strong area of low pressure over the southeastern United States. The subtropical jet in the eastern Pacific strengthened and extended farther east than usual. The result was unusual rains across the entire southern United States, from California to Florida.

One of the common consequences of an El Niño event is strong winter storms that batter the West Coast. Higgins and colleagues (2000) described the physical causes for the intensification of the subtropical jet stream that carries Pacific moisture and storms into the West Coast. In response to the more uniform pattern of heating in the tropics during El Niño, the winter jet streams tend to be more zonally (west to east) uniform and extend farther east than normal. For North America there is a significant strengthening of the subtropical jet stream. This enhancement of the so called "pineapple express" is responsible for increased precipitation in Texas during warm ENSO events.

Woodhouse (1997) focused on the Sonoran desert region using a number of indices of atmospheric circulation, including the Southern Oscillation Index (SOI) and the Pacific/North American (PNA) index. Using principal components analysis (with rotation), two components explained 63 percent of the variance in rainy days. The first related to ENSO and the other related to PNA. These two indices may not be strictly independent, but the results clearly demonstrate the influence of Pacific conditions on precipitation patterns in this part of the world.

Ting and Wang (1997) explored the variation in summer precipitation in the Great Plains. They found that ENSO events clearly impacted the area in both wet and dry years. However, the SSTs in the North Pacific had an even stronger influence by setting up a wave train that brought more storms into the region during wet years. They claimed that the interaction of the two modes could reinforce each other, contributing to anomalous events (1988), or cancel each other, also leading to anomalous events (1983). Trenberth, Branstator, and Arkin (1988) and Namias (1991) linked the 1988 Middle West drought to La Niña conditions in the Pacific. The 1988 La Niña event was relatively short-lived but intense while it lasted. It was the worst drought in fifty years in the Midwest.

Finally Mo, Paegle, and Higgins (1997) also investigated wet and dry events during the summer in the central United States. They observed that heavy summer precipitation in the central United States coincided with less precipitation to the south. Wet events were preceded by a strengthening of the westerlies from 30° to 40°N, and the low level jet coming from the south also strengthened and brought moisture into the central United States. During dry years, a different pattern prevailed with more easterly winds in the subtropics that were nonconducive to transportation of moisture into the central United States. This situation was also linked to a northward shift in the intertropical convergence zone. The increased strength of the Hadley circulation resulted in stronger subsidence over the southeastern United States. This is consistent with a drier Texas during cold events. Ropelewski and Halpert (1989) found that the Gulf of Mexico and northern Mexico region displayed a tendency for below median precipitation during cold ENSO events for the October to April season.

How do these conditions affect Texas? It is important to remember that no two ENSO events are exactly the same; they differ in strength and length. Also, the position of abnormally warm or cool pools of water in the Pacific is different with each event and therefore affects atmospheric circulation differently. In Texas, it appears that the recent El Niño events have brought rain (and flooding), while La Niña events are associated with drier conditions.

Examples of ENSO Events Impacting Texas and the Southwest

Inspection of the record of ENSO events and unusual weather conditions in Texas reveals a number of seemingly direct links. Three droughts early in the twentieth century (1909–11, 1916–17, and 1924–25) occurred with persistent La Niña conditions in the Pacific. The 1930s Dust Bowl drought ended with the 1940 El Niño. Interestingly, the Dust Bowl drought occurred during a time when the Pacific was relatively quiet, 1931–39. In contrast, the early 1950s witnessed a drought as severe as the Dust Bowl drought of the 1930s. During 1954–56 there was an extremely persistent La Niña (cold event) in the Pacific. Then a strong El Niño (warm event) developed in March and April of 1957. The torrential spring rains of 1957 brought the 1950s drought to an abrupt end and brought some of the worst flooding in the state's history. It was estimated that these storms generated 38 million acre-feet of runoff, and virtually every river in the state was at flood

stage for most of the three months of April, May, and June, 1957 (Texas Board of Water Engineers 1957).

The recent record shows that a strong El Niño (warm event) tends to result in abnormally high amounts of rainfall in Texas, especially during the winter and spring. The 1982–83 event brought twice the normal rainfall to extreme West Texas and positive precipitation anomalies in the remainder of the state. This was also true with the 1991–92 event. The association was demonstrated again in 1997–98 with heavy rainfall and the resultant flooding in Texas.

This event was followed by a remarkably pesky La Niña event that began in spring of 1998 and lasted until spring of 2000. One curious detail of this cold event was that the cooler waters were confined to the central Pacific. They did not extend eastward to the coastal areas of Peru. The result was actually higher than normal precipitation in western South America when the usual La Niña expectation calls for reduced precipitation. Meanwhile, the usual La Niña pattern prevailed in Texas as severe drought engulfed the southwestern United States and Mexico.

Additional investigations have shown the impact of ENSO events on Texas precipitation. Stahle and Cleaveland (1988) found evidence of cyclical phenomena based on tree ring measures in the 1698–1980 Texas drought record. Their procedures involved using tree rings to predict the value of the June Palmer Drought Severity Index (PDSI). Stewart (1995) expanded on their findings by correlating Pacific conditions with the reconstructed June PDSI values. The strength of the correlation was weak but still highly significant. Finally, NOAA's Climate Prediction Center analyzed precipitation patterns in Texas for nine warm ENSO events during the twentieth century. They found that strong El Niños bring 120 to 180 percent of normal precipitation from December to March.

Thus there is ample evidence in the literature that ENSO events impact Texas and the surrounding areas through a number of atmospheric processes and that this has been the case for hundreds of years. All of the recent El Niños (1983, 1987, 1991, 1994, 1997–98) have brought increased precipitation to Texas, especially in the winter and spring. The drought of 1999 was connected to an extremely persistent La Niña event.

The Science of Climate Prediction

The payoffs of El Niño research are potentially very large, not only in economic terms based on the value of forecasts but also in our understanding of the climate system.

While vast strides have been made in the ability to forecast weather a few days ahead, accurate climate forecasts for the next season or the next year remained elusive. A knowledge of ENSO has changed that to some small degree. Currently, the situation in the Pacific is routinely used by the Climate Prediction Center in its seasonal forecasts for individual states. An example might deal with the phase on an ENSO event. Is the event at its peak or in a valley, given the processes that typically occur? For example, warm ocean temperatures in the central tropical Pacific in October would indicate that an El Niño is under way, and the probability is 70 percent that precipitation in the Gulf Coast states will be higher than normal during the following winter. Since there is a two- to four-month lag between the beginning of an El Niño and subsequent impacts on the southwestern United States, this translates into a kind of seasonal predictability. Thus, one could take actions based on a climatic prediction for the coming season. A more thorough understanding of ENSO offers the possibility of turning the dream of annual climatic prediction into a reality. The models are improving as understanding of ENSO improves.

For example, Zebiak (1999, 12–14) claimed that predicting the beginning of the 1997–98 event with significant lead time was an outright failure. However, a subsequent analysis of the model revealed two ways to improve the lead time. The first was to include data on winds from environmental satellites. The original information was based on ship reports. The second was to include sea level data. Progress has accelerated due to a vastly improved observational system in the tropical Pacific (consisting of buoys and environmental satellites) and advances in understanding of ENSO processes. Thus improved models can potentially result in practical prediction.

There is also some predictive power in the global climate models. These models were developed to simulate the climatic dynamics of the earth. They are also used to investigate the effect of perturbations on the climate system. The most obvious example is the increase in carbon dioxide and other heat-absorbing gasses. However, because of their global scale, GCMs are poor in showing the details of regional processes. As ENSO models and regional models of other oscillations become better linked, there is tremendous potential for practical prediction a year ahead. George Philander has said that "at present climate forecasting is in its infancy, it is where weather prediction was a half century ago. . . . We are at the beginning of a new era that promises rich rewards" (quoted in Glantz 1996, 154). Glantz concluded that forecasting El Niño will be science's gift to the twenty-first century.

The Application of Climate Information

Assuming that future climate predictions can be made with some reasonable degree of accuracy (Stern and Easterling 1999), how can that information be best utilized? Pielke (2000) says forecasting should be viewed as a process involving prediction, communication, and decision. Sarachick (1999) suggests a kind of end-to-end forecasting, in which the information is put into the most usable form for a particular application. This includes evaluating the results of the actions taken based on the forecast information. Glantz (1996) makes the distinction between the wholesaling and retailing of ENSO information. Wholesaling is done by the scientific community to policy makers, educators, and the public. Retailing involves much more detail and requires identifying, sector by sector, activity by activity, if and how ENSO information might be helpful in decision making. The 1997–98 event provides a good illustration of these processes. While the beginning of the event in 1997 was not well forecast, once it was under way, its consequences were forecast and decision makers were able to take anticipatory mitigation actions. For example, agricultural losses during the 1982–83 event in California were $2.2 billion (adjusted dollars). In contrast, the losses during the 1997–98 event were about $1.1 billion or about half. The cost of the mitigation measures was about $165 million. The California state government assembled a mitigation team to determine which agency should take what measures in anticipation of the impacts (Pielke 2000).

In spite of some successes, ENSO and other climate forecasts (where one is forecasting for a season or a year ahead) will, of necessity, be expressed in probabilities. Note that in terms of decision making, this changes the decision process from one based on uncertainty to one based on risk. In an uncertain situation, the decision maker does not have enough information even to assess probabilities. When more information becomes available, and the decision maker can express the future in probabilities, then the previous uncertainty becomes one of risk. Knowing that the probability of an El Niño next winter is 75 percent does not guarantee that it will really happen. The chances remain that one out of four times, it will not happen. Even if it does, the results may be different from those anticipated. The 1976–77 event is the best example. Normally El Niños bring strong winter storms and floods to California. The 1976–77 event brought the worst drought in more than fifty years. It did not bring milder winter temperatures to the Midwest but rather the coldest winter in a hundred years. As a Yakima, Washington, water superintendent said in 1977, "A forecast is a forecast, not a guarantee" (Glantz 1996, 150).

Another aspect that must be included is the specificity of the prediction. This applies to the future course of events, the timing or sequence of events, and geographic location included. For example, the prediction that is valid for the southern tier of the United States may not prove to be as reliable for a smaller region like a state. This is the classic scale problem. If the forecast is too specific, then the result is inevitably a decrease in forecast skill. This is summarized in a very ancient rule of prophecy, "It doth not profit the prophet to be too specific."

Since the science of climate forecasting is in its infancy, there have been a only a few events with which to evaluate the effectiveness of the forecast. When forecasting weather, one knows how good or bad the forecast was a few days later. In the course of a year, one might make a hundred separate forecasts, all of which can be evaluated during the same length of time. However, there would be only one climate forecast and perhaps four seasonal forecasts to evaluate in the same period. Thus, long experience is necessary with climate forecasts to establish probabilities, determine skill, and evaluate the remaining uncertainties.

Conclusions and Recommendations for Texas

Not all climate anomalies are caused by ENSO, and all ENSOs do not behave in the same way. Perhaps there is too much of a tendency to view these events in black and white terms. If El Niño brings rain, La Niña must bring drought. ENSO events come in a multiplicity of forms and have a multiplicity of impacts. However, the overall associations do indicate certain prudent courses of action and research needs. Warm El Niño events tend to bring enhanced precipitation to Texas in the winter and spring. It would be useful to know how this varies given the type or strength of the event. A related topic deals with the transition into and out of ENSO events or the transition from warm event to cold event.

The El Niño events of the twentieth century have resulted in a 120–180 percent increase in precipitation during the winter and spring in Texas. Also, some of the wettest years on record were El Niño years. Since much of

the recharge to groundwater aquifers and substantial increases in streamflow necessary to replenish reservoirs occur during these infrequent pluvial episodes, they are of major importance for Texas. The droughts of La Niña summers place increased demand on the available water resources. These topics provide fertile areas for future research.

References

Bjerknes, J. "A Possible Response of the Atmosphere Hadley Circulation to Equatorial Anomalies of Ocean Temperature." *Tellus* 8 (1996): 820–29.

Cleaveland, M. K., K. F. Cook, and D. W. Stahle. "Secular Variability of the Southern Oscillation Detected in Tree-Ring Data from Mexico and the Southern United States." In *El Niño: Historical and Paleoclimatic Aspects of the Southern Oscillation*, ed. H. F. Diaz and V. Markgraf, 271–92. Cambridge: Cambridge University Press, 1992.

Climate Prediction Center. Available at http://www.cpc.ncep.noaa.gov/.

Diaz, H. F., and V. Markgraf, eds. *El Niño: Historical and Paleoclimatic Aspects of the Southern Oscillation*. Cambridge: Cambridge University Press, 1992.

Glantz, M. H. *Currents of Change: El Niño's Impact on Climate and Society*. Cambridge: Cambridge University Press, 1996.

Higgins, R. W., J. K. E. Schemm, W. Shi, and A. Leetmaa. "Extreme Precipitation Events in the Western United States Related to Tropical Forcing." *Journal of Climate* 13 (2000): 793–820.

Mo, K. C., J. N. Paegle, and R. W. Higgins. "Atmospheric Processes Associated with Summer Floods and Droughts in the Central United States." *Journal of Climate* 10 (1997): 3028–46.

Namias, J. "Spring and Summer 1988 Drought over the Contiguous United States: Causes and Prediction." *Journal of Climate* 4 (1991): 54–65.

Pielke, R. A., Jr. "Implications for Forecast Value and the Future of Climate Services." In *El Niño 1997–1998: Climate Event of the Century*, ed. S. A. Chagnon, 179–82. Oxford: Oxford University Press, 2000.

Philander, S. G. H. "El Niño and La Niña." *American Scientist* 77 (1989): 451–59.

Rasmusson, E. M. "El Niño and Variations in Climate." *American Scientist* 73 (1985): 168–77.

Ropelewski, C. "The Great El Niño of 1997–98: Impacts on Precipitation and Temperature." *Consequences* 5, no. 2 (1999): 17–25.

Ropelewski, C. F., and M. S. Halpert. "Precipitation Patterns Associated with the High Index Phase of the Southern Oscillation." *Journal of Climate* 2 (1989): 268–84.

Sarachik, E. S. "The Application of Climate Information." *Consequences* 5, no. 2 (1999): 59–74.

Stahle, D. W., and M. K. Cleaveland. "Texas Drought History Reconstructed and Analyzed from 1698 to 1980." *Journal of Climate* 1 (1988): 27–36.

Stewart, R. H. "Predictability of Texas Rainfall Patterns on Time Scales of Six to Twelve Months: A Review." In *The Changing Climate of Texas: Predictability and Implications for the Future*, ed. J. Norwine, J. R. Giardino, G. R. North, and J. B. Valdés, 38–47. College Station: Cartographics, Texas A&M University Press, 1995.

Stern, P. C., and W. E. Easterling (eds.). *Making Climate Forecasts Matter.* Washington D.C.: National Research Council, National Academy Press. 1999. Available at http://www.nap.edu/.

Texas Board of Water Engineers. *Texas Floods of April, May, and June 1957.* 1957.

Ting, M., and H. Wang. "Summertime U.S. Precipitation Variability and Its Relation to Pacific Sea Surface Temperature." *Journal of Climate* 10 (1997): 1853–73.

Trenberth, K. E., G. W. Branstator, and P. A. Arkin. "Origins of the 1988 North American Drought." *Science* 242 (1988): 1640–45.

Walker, G. T. "Seasonal Weather and Its Prediction." *Smithsonian Institute Annual Report,* 1936, 117–38.

Woodhouse, C. A. "Winter Climate and Atmospheric Circulation Patterns in the Sonoran Desert Region, USA." *International Journal of Climatology* 17 (1997): 859–73.

Zebiak, S. "El Niño and the Science of Climate Prediction." *Consequences* 5, no. 2 (1999): 3–15.

CHAPTER 14

Influence of Climatic Variability on Texas Reservoirs

Alan W. Groeger, Bruce G. Kelley, and Joe Martin

Aquatic Biology, Department of Biology

Texas State University–San Marcos

Abstract

Climatic variability in Texas is often extreme, and this has large implications for the reservoir ecosystems found here. Using patterns observed in two reservoirs from the Guadalupe River basin on the Edwards Plateau and south-central Texas, we examine the influence of air temperature and flowthrough on these ecosystems. Flow, generally one of the most unpredictable physical state variables that ecologists confront, is extreme in Texas. Flow is important in structuring these ecosystems and the resultant water quality, and inter-annual variability makes predictions about these systems difficult.

Reservoirs represent an extremely valuable resource to the state of Texas as the major source for surface water supply as well as for a number of other important uses. The physical, chemical, and biological characteristics of the water found within and downstream of these reservoirs is important in determining the usability and value of the water and the ecosystem itself. Not only do these characteristics vary with location within the state (Ground and Groeger 1994), but they can vary drastically between years at a single location. Climate is a key factor influencing this variability in reservoirs, and one of the repeating themes in recent work on the climate of Texas (e.g., North 1995) was the large inter-annual variability in climate throughout the state. In this chapter we focus on the influence of climatic variability on two reservoirs located on the

Guadalupe River; we have seen similar effects in other Central Texas reservoirs and expect these to be of great potential importance throughout the state.

Reservoirs

Texas reservoirs are best classified as subtropical lakes (Hutchinson 1957; following Yoshimura 1936) or those where the surface waters are never less than 4°C, there is a large annual variation in surface temperature, there is a strong thermal gradient if a deep water column is present, and one annual mixing period occurs in the winter. Canyon Reservoir is a relatively large and deep Texas reservoir. At its conservation pool (277 m asl) it has a surface area and volume of 33.4 km² and 4.71×10^8 m³. The dam drains from a fixed depth release at 236 m asl. The drainage basin area upstream of the reservoir is 3,709 km², and mean and maximum depths are 14.3 and 48 m. Lake Dunlap, about fifty river kilometers downstream of Canyon, is much smaller, with surface area of 1.7 km² and mean depth of 4.4 m. Dunlap is within and downstream of New Braunfels and has much higher nutrient inputs and urban influence than does Canyon Reservoir.

Climatic Variability in the Edwards Plateau and South-Central Texas

Aspects of the local climate that have the greatest influence on surface water resources include air temperature, precipitation, and runoff. Focusing on the Guadalupe

Table 1. Climatic characteristics in the Guadalupe River drainage basin upstream of Canyon Reservoir over the history of the reservoir, 1969–99

	Annual Air Temperature (°C)	Annual Winter Temperature (°C)	Annual Precipitation (cm)	Annual Discharge (cms)
Mean (Median)	18.5 (18.5)	9.6 (9.6)	92.9 (89.3)	13.9 (10.8)
Range	17.4–19.6	7.1–2.0	47.4–163.0	3.0–41.1
CV (%)	2.8	12.6	28.5	68.7

Note: CV = coefficient of variation.

River basin directly upstream of Canyon Reservoir, we have used data from the Boerne weather station and Spring Branch flow gauge (U.S. Geologic Service hydrologic index station 8167500) to examine the local climate and its variability. Inter-annual variation in mean air temperature is low in this area relative to the other climatic factors (table 1), though variation is much greater during the winter than at other seasons. Another interesting trend is that there have been no winters with mean temperatures in the lowest quartile since the winter of 1987–88 (fig. 1), or there have been eleven consecutive years without a cold winter.

Precipitation and river discharge have been higher over the history of the reservoir than the long-term means for this area (Bomar 1983; USGS flow data). Inter-annual variability in these two characteristics is extremely high. The coefficient of variation (CV) of greater than 28 percent for precipitation compares quite well to those found immediately to the south in Texas (Norwine 1995). Norwine found these CVs to be among the highest in the world for regions of similar annual precipitation. River discharge (the expression of runoff from an upstream watershed measured as flow at a location in the river) is a direct function of precipitation. In spite of this close relationship between these two variables, inter-annual variability in discharge is much higher. This is apparently due to the relationship between precipitation event intervals and the moisture content of the basin in determining runoff production (Ward 1995). The CV of discharge for this river would place it among the very highest for perennial rivers in the continental United States (Poff and Ward 1989).

Influence of Air Temperature on Reservoirs

Inflowing river temperatures and near-surface water temperatures for Canyon Reservoir can be predicted with great confidence from air temperatures ($R^2 = 0.95$ and 0.96, respectively, for predicting daily inflow and daily near-surface temperatures, Groeger and Bass, manuscript submitted). Air temperature has generally been found to be an excellent predictor of stream temperatures (Stefan and Preud'homme 1993) and lake surface temperatures (Shuter et al. 1983) throughout North America. This general relationship should therefore be applicable to predicting these temperatures in most Texas reservoirs.

The relationship between air temperature and deep-water temperature is much weaker and complex, due to these waters being isolated from atmospheric influence during the warmer months in reservoirs that become thermally stratified. Air temperature during the period when the water column of the reservoir is isothermal, or essentially mixing from top to bottom in the winter, is a fairly good predictor of the deep-water temperatures. Mean winter air temperature is a reasonable predictor of

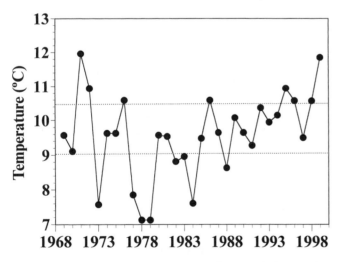

Figure 1. Mean winter temperatures (°C) over the history of Canyon Reservoir (from the winter of 1968–69 through 1998–99). The dashed lines represent the first and third quartiles for the winter temperature distribution.

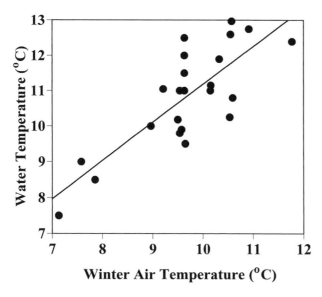

Figure 2. Relationship between February water temperatures at a depth of 30 m in Canyon Reservoir and the mean winter temperature for that winter.

the temperature of these waters in February in Canyon Reservoir (fig. 2). A similar influence of winter air temperatures on a subtropical lake in the Middle East has been observed (Hambright et al. 1994).

The temperature of these deeper waters at the end of the winter is important for a number of reasons: (1) It determines the initial temperature of hypolimnetic waters for the following stratification period. This will determine the maximum quantity of oxygen that these waters will hold. When the water is colder, there is more dissolved oxygen, and it lasts longer into the stratified period. For example, if we compare the coldest and warmest February temperatures from Canyon Reservoir, 7.5 and 12.97°C, the difference in saturation concentrations is 12 and 10.5 mg O_2/L, respectively. (2) Biological activity is directly influenced by temperature. The rate of oxygen consumption is approximately doubled at an increase of 10°C; thus not only does the warmer winter water start with less oxygen, but the oxygen is consumed more quickly. Fish reproduction and growth are also closely tied to water temperature, and spring is commonly an important season in the life cycle of many Texas fish. (3) The greater the difference in temperature from the surface to the bottom of the water column, the stronger the density gradient between these zones. The stronger the gradient is, the more it retards mixing of nutrients from the bottom up into the surface waters.

Influence of Flow on Reservoirs

Because of the extreme nature of flows through Canyon Reservoir, year-to-year variability in water residence time is high, ranging from 0.3 to 4.6 years (Groeger and Tietjen 1998). One of the primary influences this has on both the structuring and functioning of this ecosystem is to control the temperature of the hypolimnion. Once the reservoir thermally stratifies (this process generally begins in March), the cold winter water in the hypolimnion is isolated from the atmospheric influences that heat the surface waters or the epilimnion. Throughout the summer, warm upstream water flows into the reservoir and the colder hypolimnetic waters are released from the bottom. Therefore the hypolimnion warms throughout the summer (unlike a deep natural lake), and the rate of warming is dependent on how much water is released (fig. 3). During the driest of years, when the winter hypolimnion is not entirely drained, river temperatures in the tailwaters are as low as 12°C in August. In the wettest years, these winter waters may be lost downstream quite rapidly, and August tailwater temperatures may exceed 24°C. We suggest that this extreme inter-annual variability in seasonal temperatures is much greater than for almost any unregulated stretch of river in Texas and has important impli-

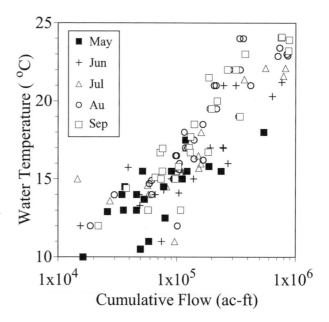

Figure 3. Relationship between water temperature at 30 m in Canyon Reservoir during the May through September period and the cumulative water outflow from the reservoir from March 1 through September. Water temperatures are from near-dam profiles from 1971 through 1999.

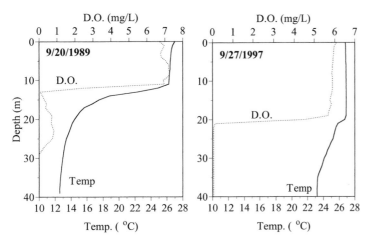

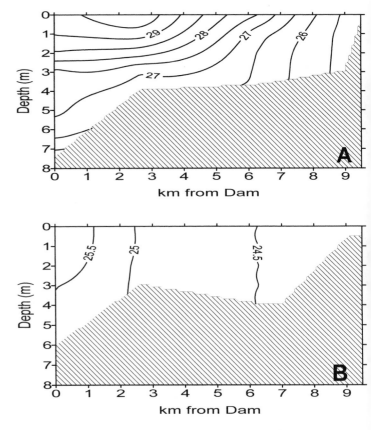

Figure 4. Vertical profiles at a near-dam station in Canyon Reservoir during 1989 (dry year) and 1997 (wet year).

Figure 5. Longitudinal cross sections of temperature in Lake Dunlap reservoir; (A) the dry year of 1999, (B) the wet year of 1992. The x-axis is the distance moving upstream from the dam (0 represents the location of the dam).

cations for this segment of the river ecosystem. It also seems to have a large impact on the put-and-take trout fishery found in this stretch of the river.

This year-to-year difference in inflows and outflows also has a tremendous impact on various aspects of the reservoir ecosystem itself. The relatively rapid turnover and warming of hypolimnetic waters during wetter years leads to a more rapid exhaustion of dissolved oxygen and accompanying decline in redox potential, disappearance of cool-water habitat, and decreased water column stability. Vertical profiles relatively late in the growing season for a dry year (1989) and wet year (1997, fig. 4) show some of these patterns quite well. In 1989 there was a classic thermal stratification with three distinct regions of the water column (the upper well-mixed waters or epilimnion; a deep, cold hypolimnion; and the metalimnion in between with a very strong thermal gradient) and dissolved oxygen still present in the upper waters of the hypolimnion. In 1997 the stratification was much weaker, with a much deeper epilimnion, and oxygen was essentially depleted completely from the deep waters. During wet years the deepening of the epilimnion occurs at a much faster rate during the summer, and fall turnover of the water column occurs much earlier than during drier years.

The influence of variable flows is often more dramatic on smaller reservoirs with shorter water residence times. Lake Dunlap is greatly influenced by the rate of water flowthrough. In the relatively dry August of 1999, the reservoir was distinctly stratified during a period when it had a water residence time of 6.6 days (fig. 5A), with the horizontal isotherms showing the formation of a distinct epilimnion near the dam. At the dam, chlorophyll-*a* concentrations near the surface were greater than 20 μg/L (characteristic of a eutrophic ecosystem), and the bottom waters had low oxygen concentrations. During a wetter August in 1992 (fig. 5B), when the reservoir had a residence time of 2.6 days, the isotherms were vertical, or there was no stratification. At the dam on this date, chlorophyll-a concentrations near the surface were less than 5 μg/L (characteristic of a much less productive ecosystem), and the entire water column had high concentrations of oxygen. During the summer of the wet year this reservoir ecosystem was structured in a completely different manner.

Conclusions

Climatic variability in Texas should preclude water policy makers and managers from making some of their decisions based on long-term annual means or one time measurements—year-to-year variability needs to be factored into many of their considerations. This variability in our climate may be growing (Norwine 1995), which will make the projections more difficult. While water quantity may be the more pressing question, the quality of that water must also be considered. A warming climate will have important implications for the structure and function of Texas reservoirs in the future, but variability of flows may be much more important.

Acknowledgments

We would like to thank all the students who have helped us collect these data over the years. We would also like to thank the Army Corps of Engineers and Guadalupe-Blanco River Authority (GBRA) for sharing their data with us. The Texas Natural Resource Conservation Commission and GBRA have funded our work on Lake Dunlap.

References

Bomar, G. W. *Texas Weather*. Austin: University of Texas Press, 1983.

Groeger, A. W., and T. E. Tietjen. "Hydrological and Thermal Regime in a Subtropical Reservoir." *Internat. Rev. Hydrobiol.* 83 (1998): 83–92.

Ground, T. A., and A. W. Groeger. "Chemical Classification and Trophic Characteristics of Texas Reservoirs." *Lake and Res. Manage.* 10 (1994): 189–201.

Hambright, K. D., M. Gophen, and S. Serruya. "Influence of Long-term Climatic Changes on the Stratification of a Sub-tropical, Warm Monomictic Lake." *Limnol. Oceanogr.* 39 (1994): 1233–42.

Hutchinson, G. E. *A Treatise on Limnology*, vol. 1. New York: John Wiley & Sons, 1957.

North, G. R. "Climate Change and Texas." In *The Changing Climate of Texas: Predictions and Implications for the Future*, ed. J. Norwine, J. R. Giardino, G. R. North, and J. B. Valdés, 7–12. College Station: Cartographics, Texas A&M University, 1995.

Norwine, J. "The Regional Climate of South Texas: Patterns and Trends." In *The Changing Climate of Texas: Predictions and Implications for the Future*, ed. J. Norwine, J. R. Giardino, G. R. North, and J. B. Valdés, 138–54. College Station: Cartographics, Texas A&M University, 1995.

Poff, N. L., and J. V. Ward. "Implications of Streamflow Variability and Predictability for Lotic Community Structure: A Regional Analysis of Streamflow Patterns." *Can. J. Fish. Aquat. Sci.* 46 (1989): 1805–18.

Shuter, B. J., D. A. Schlesinger, and A. P. Zimmerman. "Empirical Predictors of Annual Surface Water Temperature Cycles in North American Lakes." *Can. J. Fish. Aquat. Sci.* 40 (1983): 1838–45.

Stefan, H. G., and E. B. Preud'homme. "Stream Temperature Estimation from Air Temperature." *Wat. Res. Bull.* 29 (1993): 27–45.

Ward, G. "Response of Texas Water Budget to Climatological Forcing." In *The Changing Climate of Texas: Predictions and Implications for the Future*, ed. J. Norwine, J. R. Giardino, G. R. North, and J. B. Valdés, 264–84. College Station: Cartographics, Texas A&M University, 1995.

Yoshimura, S. "A Contribution to the Deep Water Temperatures of Japanese Lakes. Part 1: Summer Temperatures." *Jap. J. Astr. Geophys.* 13 (1936): 61–120.

CHAPTER 15

Landscape Water Conservation through Xeriscape

Douglas F. Welsh

Professor and Extension Horticulturist

Texas Cooperative Extension

Texas A&M University System

Abstract

Xeriscape is quality landscaping that conserves water and protects the environment; it is not cactus and rocks, skulls-and-crossed-bones landscaping. Xeriscape emerged in 1981 in an effort by the Denver Water Board and local green industry representatives to begin managing the demand for water. It incorporates seven basic principles that lead to water and cost saving. Xeriscape has become a successful means by which a community's water demand can be reduced through educating landscape owners and managers about proper design and maintenance of beautiful, water-wise landscapes.

The easiest way to define xeriscape landscaping is to identify what it is not. Xeriscape is not cactus and rocks, skulls-and-crossed-bones landscaping. Xeriscape *is quality landscaping that conserves water and protects the environment*—beautiful, colorful landscapes that adorn the pages of magazines like *Southern Living, Sunset,* and *Better Homes and Gardens.*

Xeriscape is not just for the desert regions of the nation. It is commonplace in water-rich regions such as Atlanta, South Florida, and Long Island.

All xeriscapes do not look alike. Xeriscape is a continuum in water use, ranging from lush yet water-efficient landscape to more moderately planted, lower-water-requirement landscape. A posh hotel and resort demands a vibrant landscape, but it can still be a xeriscape. A public library or school requires a much less elaborate landscape, and it too can be a xeriscape.

Xeriscape emerged in 1981 in an effort by the Denver Water Board and local green industry representatives to begin managing the *demand* for water versus the earlier philosophy of managing only supply (continuous expansion of water supplies to meet any demand). Booming populations, seasonal drought, and increased restrictions on water resource development are common concerns confronting municipal water suppliers in many regions of the nation. Xeriscape has become a successful means by which a community's water demand can be reduced through educating landscape owners and managers about proper design and maintenance of quality, water-wise landscapes.

Local ordinances and even state laws now encourage the adoption of xeriscape principles. In California, state law AB325 requires that municipalities adopt city ordinances addressing landscape water conservation. In Florida and Texas, state laws require that all state-owned buildings be xeriscape landscaped. Model ordinances have been written by water suppliers and districts for use by municipalities and developers. Each of these ordinances and laws further encourages the supports and adoption of xeriscape as the state of the art in landscaping.

Xeriscape incorporates seven basic principles that lead to saving of water and cost:

Planning and design
Soil analysis
Appropriate plant selection
Practical turf areas
Efficient irrigation
Use of mulches
Appropriate maintenance

Planning and Design

Developing a landscape plan is the first and most important step in a successful xeriscape. A properly planned xeriscape takes into account the regional and microclimatic conditions of the site, existing vegetation and topographical conditions, the intended use and desires of the property owner, and the zoning or grouping of plant materials by their water needs. A landscape plan also allows landscaping to be done in phases.

Soil Analysis

Soils vary from site to site and even within a given site. A soil analysis based on random sampling provides information that enables proper selection of plants and any soil amendments needed. When appropriate, soil amendments can enhance the health and growing capabilities of the landscape by improving drainage, moisture penetration, and the soil's water-holding capacity.

Appropriate Plant Selection

Plant selection should be based on the plants' adaptability to the landscape area, the effect desired, and the ultimate size, color, and texture of the plants. Plants should be arranged to achieve the aesthetic effect desired and grouped in accordance with their respective water needs. Most plants have a place in a xeriscape. Maximum water conservation can be achieved by selecting those plants that require a minimal amount of supplemental watering.

Practical Turf Areas

The type and location of turf areas should be selected in the same manner as all other plantings. Turf should not be treated as a fill-in material but rather as a planned element of the xeriscape. Since most turf varieties require supplemental watering at frequencies different than the other types of landscaping plants, turf should be placed so that it can be irrigated separately. While turf areas provide practical and aesthetic benefits in a landscape, how and where they are used can result in a significant reduction in the use of irrigation water.

Efficient Irrigation

Watering only when plants need water and watering deeply encourages deeper root growth, resulting in a healthier and more drought-tolerant landscape. If a landscape requires regular watering and an irrigation system is desired, the system should be well planned and managed properly in order to conserve water. Great strides are now being made in landscape irrigation, which can increase irrigation efficiency significantly.

Use of Mulches

Mulches applied and maintained at appropriate depths in planting beds assist soils in retaining moisture, reduce weed growth, and prevent erosion. Mulched areas can also be used where conditions are not adequate for or conducive to growing quality turf or groundcovers. Commonly used mulches include bark chips, pine straw, nut shells, small gravel, and shredded landscape clippings.

Appropriate Maintenance

Proper landscape and irrigation maintenance will preserve and enhance a quality xeriscape. When the first six principles have been followed, maintenance of a xeriscape is easier and less time-consuming than otherwise. Because a xeriscape is more adapted to local conditions and uses a minimal amount of water, less fertilizer, pesticides, and other chemicals are needed to maintain the landscape.

Water is the life blood of planet earth and should be a vital concern for everyone. Implementing the xeriscape principles will help ensure water supplies for future generations.

CHAPTER 16

Changes in Flow Regime following Dam Construction, Yegua Creek, South-Central Texas

Anne Chin

Department of Geography

Texas A&M University

Jean Ann Bowman

Texas Engineering Experiment Station

Texas A&M University

Abstract

Yegua Creek is one of the principal tributaries of the Brazos River in south-central Texas. It is an important water supply source for the Brazos River Authority, the region's largest holder of water rights. Despite its regional importance, however, the flow regimen along Yegua Creek has not been thoroughly examined since the 1960s, when Somerville Dam was constructed for flood control and water supply. This chapter reviews the history of flooding and dam construction on Yegua Creek and examines the effects of flow regulation on streamflow characteristics. Analysis of sixty-eight years of streamflow data (1924–91) indicates that flood peaks and flooding potential have decreased in the period following dam construction, as expected. The distribution of monthly flows has also changed, resulting in a more equitable flow regime. These results show that dam construction has had a notable impact on the hydrology of Yegua Creek. They also provide insights for assessing the present and future water resources of Texas.

Yegua Creek occupies portions of Burleson, Lee, Milam, Washington, and Williamson counties in south-central Texas. The upper basin consists of East Yegua Creek, Middle Yegua Creek, and West Yegua Creek, which drain areas of 155, 278, and 274 mi^2 (402, 720, 710 km^2), respectively (fig. 1). The main Yegua Creek is formed by the confluence of East Yegua Creek and Middle Yegua Creek at a point just west of the town of Somerville. Downstream of Somerville, Davidson Creek enters from the north (drainage area 207 mi^2; 536 km^2) and contributes a large portion of the runoff from the lower basin. Yegua Creek continues to flow east until it empties into the Brazos River. Because water in the Brazos is tightly controlled by the Brazos River Authority, a state-authorized agency charged with purchasing water rights and leasing them to water users (Bowman 1993), Yegua Creek is of broad regional interest in the context of water supply and water rights.

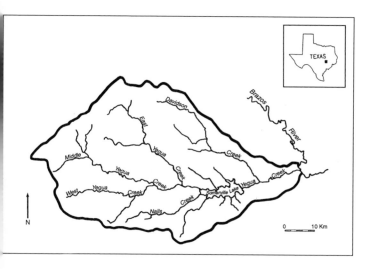

Figure 1. Yegua Creek drainage basin.

Figure 2. Somerville Dam and Lake, with gauging station monitoring lake levels. The top of the dam (a road) is at the right edge of photograph.

Yegua Creek is also of interest to researchers and students seeking to understand the fundamental connection between natural ecosystems and human activities. Although Middle Yegua Creek is designated as one of six least disturbed streams in Texas (Twidwell and Davis 1989), with agriculture dominating land use in the basin, the region has experienced increased demand for water as a result of urban development over the last thirty years. Anticipating future population growth, and recognizing the fact that Yegua Creek and its tributaries were prone to extended dry periods punctuated by erratic flood events, the U.S. Army Corps of Engineers (USACE) dammed the creek in the 1960s and built a reservoir for the purposes of flood control and water supply. The combination of land uses, along with the dam that created Somerville Lake (figs. 1, 2), has created a landscape with aspects of both natural and managed ecosystems.

Despite its regional importance and academic interest, Yegua Creek has not been examined in detail since the construction of Somerville dam, and the effects of the dam remain incompletely understood. The purpose of this work is to outline the history of flooding on Yegua Creek, review the background for the construction of Somerville Dam, and evaluate the effects of the dam on flow regimes. Historical accounts were compiled from source material located in collections and archives held by Texas A&M University, the USACE, the Brazos River Authority, the Burleson County Historical Society (BCHS), the *Burleson County Citizen-Tribune,* and the Harriet P. Woodson Memorial Library in Caldwell, Texas. Data for the flow analysis were kindly provided by the Fort Worth

office of the USACE, including historic mean daily flows for the entire period of record from three U.S. Geological Survey (USGS) automated stream gauging stations along Yegua Creek and its tributaries.

This chapter is organized into four parts. The first is a brief description of the physical setting of the Yegua Creek basin, including climate, geology, and vegetation. The second part outlines the history of flooding on Yegua Creek. Part three reviews the planning and construction of Somerville Dam, including political and economic considerations that went into decision making. Part four reports on the analysis of the streamflow data and focuses on the changes in flow regime following dam construction.

Physical Setting

The Yegua Creek basin is representative of others in the south-central Texas region in terms of climate, geology and hydrology, and vegetation. The climate is humid subtropical. Annual temperature averages 68.4°F (20.2°C), although maximum temperatures often exceed 100°F (38°C) in the summer and minimum winter temperatures can drop below 20°F (−7°C). Annual precipitation averages about 39 inches (991 mm), with April being the wettest month. Precipitation is evenly distributed throughout the year, although dry periods are common in July and January (Larkin and Bomar 1983).

The geology of the Yegua Creek area is dominated by the Wilcox group (Paleocene-Eocene age) and the Claiborne and Jackson groups (Eocene ages; Kelly 1955). Consisting chiefly of silt and clay accumulations, and thick layers of sands and shales, these formations are well suited for groundwater storage. The sands of the Claiborne and Wilcox groups are the principal water-bearing units of the Carrizo-Wilcox aquifer. The Simsboro Formation (part of the Wilcox group), in particular, provides the source of water for nearby cities including Bastrop, Elgin, College Station, and Bryan (Thorikildsen and Price 1991).

Vegetation in the Yegua Creek basin is classified as post oak savannah (Correll and Johnston 1979). At one time, this plant community was grassland with scattered groves of post oaks. However, as people settled in the area and plowed up prairies, the post oak spread laterally, and savannahs turned into woodlands (Kutac and Caran 1994). The dominant species in the upland communities are *Quercus stellata* (post oak) and *Q. marilandica* (blackjack oak). Shrubs such as *Ilex vomitoria* (yaupon) are also commonly found with the oaks. Riparian communities along Yegua Creek and its tributaries include *Cephalanthus occidentalis* (buttonbush), *Planera aquatica* (water elm), *Ulmus occidentalis* (cedar elm), and *Carya aquatica* (water hickory).

History of Flooding

Before records were kept in the early part of the twentieth century, no firm data existed to relate frequency and magnitude of flood events on Yegua Creek. Flooding certainly occurred, but the impact may have been minimal as population was sparse until 1883, when the earliest platting of properties in the town of Somerville occurred. Floodplain utilization in the late nineteenth century was dominated by cotton production (USACE 1961a). However, as more areas became cultivated, runoff into Yegua Creek probably increased, along with flooding potential.

The earliest recorded devastating flood in the area occurred from June 27 to July 1, 1899, and caused extensive damage. According to the *Caldwell News-Chronicle* (June 30, 1899), "the Yegua is just all over the country, having been over three miles in width Wednesday before the worst of the flood came. The Santa Fe [Railroad] has suffered severely. . . . The damage in this county to roads, bridges, fences and crops is almost incalculable." The damage was in fact calculated a few days later—$4 million to $5 million (*Caldwell News-Chronicle*, July 7, 1899).

The largest flood in the first half of the twentieth century occurred in 1913, when a storm originating in Central Texas pummeled the region between December 1 and 5.

This event was reportedly more devastating than the flood of 1899 (BCHS 1980). Peak discharge was estimated at 82,000 cubic feet per second (USACE 1960a). The *Burleson County Ledger* (December 12, 1913) reported:

The worst flood in the history of the Brazos and Yegua Rivers was the one in the past two weeks. . . . The waters began to rise as a result of the heavy rains all up both streams and by Tuesday morning both were spreading all over the country. The alarm was given but those in the Brazos bottom depended on the levee for protection, and before they were aware of their danger [they] were being surrounded by water coming from the Yegua where it empties into the Brazos . . . and to add to their peril the levee began to break, letting in a wall of water some four feet high which rushed down on them with only a short warning, and they were forced to act quick in order to save themselves by taking refuge on top of houses, in gin houses, in trees and any place they could. The water was several feet higher than the former flood of 1899 and damage . . . and loss of life will be much greater.

Besides the 1913 event, forty-two other floods along Yegua Creek were reported between 1912 and 1958 (Clouse 1972). Although none approached the magnitude of the 1913 flood (table 1), they nevertheless caused significant economic impact. For example, an estimated 70 percent of agricultural crops were destroyed during the 1957 flood (*Burleson County Citizen*, May 3, 1957). Floods also threatened livestock operations, which were becoming increasingly important along the floodplain as cotton production waned. Furthermore, floods were potentially

Table 1. Floods on Yegua Creek, recorded at Somerville gauge; peak discharge for 1913 flood is estimated

Date	Peak Discharge (cfs)
December, 1913	82,000
April, 1926	34,600
May, 1929	41,200
May, 1936	23,500
July, 1940	56,800
August, 1947	29,600
April, 1957	17,300

Source: USACE 1960a.

devastating for significant corporate interests, especially those of the Santa Fe Railroad. Because the railroad had purchased the Texas Tie and Lumber Preserving Company in 1905 (renamed the Santa Fe Tie and Lumber Preserving Company; Clouse 1972; BCHS 1980), not only was its ability to move cargo through Somerville threatened by floods, but so was its sizable investment in the lumber treatment plant.

Somerville Dam

The significant economic impacts brought on by floods on Yegua Creek demanded relief, and local leaders started to rumble about a dam in the late 1930s. These leaders were also concerned about the declining population in Somerville at that time, and they had hoped that a reservoir would create recreational and economic opportunities that would help stabilize the community (Schaffer 1974). Thus, as funding became available from the federal New Deal public works program, the Somerville community, like others elsewhere in Texas and across the country, proposed the construction of a flood and water conservation reservoir. The U.S. Army Corps of Engineers began initial planning for reservoirs in Texas as early as the 1930s. However, these plans were interrupted by World War II, and it was not until after the war, when Texas politicians ascended to positions of national prominence, particularly to Congress, that Texas was able to get its reservoirs.

Political Details

Many politicians and civic leaders were instrumental in getting the legislation passed for the construction of Somerville Dam. The political positions of Sam Rayburn, Lyndon Johnson, and Homer Thornberry were especially critical. Rayburn served as speaker of the House of Representatives from 1940 to 1957; Lyndon Johnson was representative for Texas' 10th District, then senator, vice president, and president of the United States. Thornberry was the representative from Texas' 10th District who shepherded the legislation through Congress. (A road leading to the dam is named in Thornberry's honor.) It was these men and other members of Congress whom a group of a hundred or so civic and business leaders from Burleson and Washington counties lobbied. Among these leaders was Clint Lewis, a native and one-time sheriff of Burleson County who had worked as a "special officer" for the

Figure 3. A granite monument at Somerville Dam honors the leaders responsible for creating Lake Somerville.

Santa Fe for two years before returning to Burleson County in 1950 to wage a successful campaign to become county judge (*Burleson County Citizen-Tribune,* October 15, 1998). Lewis was the last of the survivors of the group of civic leaders responsible for creating Lake Somerville; he passed away in October, 1998. A monument erected at Somerville Dam pays tribute to these individuals (fig. 3).

The Somerville Dam was approved on September 3, 1954, and authorized by Congress in the Flood Control Act (Public Law 780, 83d Congress, 2d Session), in accordance with the Plan of Improvement, as outlined in House Document No. 535 (81st Congress, 2d Session; USACE 1960a). The Public Works Appropriation Act of 1959 authorized the U.S. Army Corps of Engineers to initiate advance planning. The act was approved on September 2, 1958 (Public Law 85-863); the Advice of Allotment C-126 was dated October 6, 1958.

Planning and Construction

Several key issues had to be addressed before construction of the dam could begin. The first was the purpose of the reservoir—should it serve the sole purpose of flood control or include water conservation capacities? Cost estimates were produced for both configurations: $11,100,000 for a flood control reservoir, and $12,500,000 for a dual-purpose structure (USACE 1960b). Given that the water conservation capacity could be gained for minimal additional expenditure, the Corps of Engineers decided on the latter. Although the initial House Document No. 535 had

Table 2. Somerville reservoir size and capacity. Data from USACE.

	Elevation (feet-amsl)	Area (acres)	Capacity (acre-feet)
Top of dam	280.0	47,400	1,267,400
Max. design water surface	274.5	39,800	1,028,800
Spillway crest	258.0	24,400	507,500
Top of conservation pool			
initial	238.0	11,460	160,100
after 50 yrs sedimentation	238.0	10,900	143,900
Max. tailwater	244.0		
Streambed	200.0		
Flood control storage[a]			
initial			347,400
after 50 yrs sedimentation			337,700
Sedimentation storage			25,900

a. *The flood control storage space is that portion of the lake between the top of the conservation pool at elevation 238 feet and the spillway crest at 258 feet.*

allowed for only 38,800 acre-feet of conservation storage, the State of Texas argued for more, and the storage capacity was increased to 143,900 acre-feet (table 2) when the Brazos River Authority proposed acquisition of conservation storage space at Somerville (USACE 1960a.). On May 10, 1962, the secretary of the army approved a contract authorizing the Brazos River Authority to control and distribute waters within Somerville Lake (Lapotka 1979).

The second question was where to construct the dam, and the USACE made two cost estimates in this regard as well. The estimated cost for the dam at the present location (mile 20.0 on Yegua Creek) was $12,197,000, whereas the cost at an alternate location (mile 21.3 on the creek) was higher, at $14,664,000 (USACE 1960b). It simply cost more to acquire land, transport materials, and to design and build the dam and spillway at the second location, so the first was chosen. As it was, Somerville Dam was an expensive project. Dam construction alone required the acquisition of some ninety tracts of land (2,961 acres) at a cost of greater than $800,000 (USACE 1961a); land acquisition for the entire project totaled more than $5,000,000 (USACE 1961b). Some 170 families and businesses were also displaced (*Burleson County Citizen*, September 20, 1962). By June, 1961, the estimated cost of the project had increased to $16,900,000; final figures indicate a total federal expenditure of approximately $27,916,000 (Schaffer 1974; Texas State Historical Association 1996).

The third issue concerned the level of sediment storage and flood protection. Based on an estimated sediment inflow rate of 515 acre-feet per year into the reservoir, the Corps of Engineers had projected a need for

25,500 acre-feet of sediment storage for fifty years. This figure was consistent with the original estimated storage of 25,900 acre-feet in the initial plans (table 2), although these figures may have been overestimates, as recent calculations showed a sedimentation rate of only 263 acre-feet per year in the first twenty-eight years of dam operation (Brazos River Authority 1995; Wooten 1997). Finally, decisions were made to design the dam to accommodate the fifty-year flood (USACE 1960a). This level of impoundment was expected to protect more than 9,000 acres of land along Yegua Creek as well as an estimated 887,000 acres adjacent to the Brazos River downstream (USACE 1972).

Once these major issues were resolved, preparations and construction began. More than five thousand people attended the official ground-breaking ceremonies on September 22, 1962, including Vice President Lyndon B. Johnson and his wife, Lady Bird (Clouse 1972). President Kennedy, who had been scheduled to be in Houston the day before the ceremony, was reported to have considered attending (*Burleson County Citizen*, September 3, 1962). At the event, Johnson and Representative Thornberry symbolically turned the first spades of dirt with gold-plated shovels (*Burleson County Citizen*, September, 27, 1962). Actual construction began in January, 1963, and four years later, on January 3, 1967, H. H. "Hub" Baker, a landowner along Yegua Creek, turned the control wheels that closed the dam gates to start impounding water (BCHS 1980). Somerville Dam was officially completed on October 27, 1967 (table 3) and dedicated on May 17, 1968 (Buckner et al. 1981). Johnson, now President, sent a

Table 3. Dimensions of Somerville dam, spillway, and outlet works. Data from USACE.

Dam

Type	rolled earth fill
Length, total	26,175 ft
Length, dam	20,210 ft
Length, dike	4,715 ft
Height, above stream bed	80 ft
Width, crown, embankment	20 ft
Width, crown, dike	34 ft

Spillway

Type	ogee weir
Crest elevation, amsl	258 ft
Length at crest, net	1,250 ft
Control	None

Outlet Works

Type	gate controlled conduit
Dimensions	10 ft diameter
Elevation of inverts, amsl	206 ft
Control	two 5 ft × 10 ft tractor-type gates

telegram which was read from the speaker's platform at the dedication ceremony.

Somerville Lake

The impoundment of Yegua Creek by Somerville Dam created Somerville Lake, and it has had a profound effect on the region. Somerville Lake has provided excellent recreational and commercial opportunities, including fishing, boating, hiking, and camping (fig. 4). At a normal lake pool elevation of 238 feet above mean sea level, the lake encompasses an area of 11,460 acres (table 2) with a shoreline of eighty-five miles. There are three parks along the shoreline that are operated by the Corps of Engineers: Overlook Park, Rocky Creek Park, and Yegua Creek Park. The State of Texas, through the Texas Parks and Wildlife Department, administers the Lake Somerville State Park Complex, which consists of the Birch Creek Unit, Nails Creek Unit, and Lake Somerville Wildlife Management Area/Trailway. The City of Somerville manages an additional city park (Welch Park), while private individuals operate the Lake Somerville Marina and the Big Creek

Figure 4. Boating activities at Lake Somerville.

Park Marina. Millions of tourism dollars have flowed into the local economy as more than three million visitors a year have taken advantage of these recreational opportunities (Lapotka 1979). Additionally, surrounding communities have benefited from stabilized water supplies provided by the lake. Major consumers of the reservoir's conservation water include the city of Brenham and farmers within the lower Brazos River.

Changes in Flow Regime

Although Somerville Dam has had a visible impact on the region in terms of recreation and water conservation, the resulting changes in the downstream flow regime of Yegua Creek have not been quantified (fig. 5). The pre-dam hydrology was documented as part of the dam design in a U.S. Army Corps of Engineers internal memorandum (USACE 1960a), but it has not been revisited since that time. In the remaining sections of this paper, the flow regimes before and after dam construction are compared. The analysis focuses on changes in annual and monthly flows and also on changes in the rating curves (stage-discharge relationship) for Yegua Creek.

Data and Methods

Discharge (or streamflow) records are available for three continuous gauging stations including the main Yegua Creek near the Somerville Dam site (1924–91) and the middle and east branches of Yegua Creek. However, since gauging stations were installed for the middle and east branches of the creek *after* dam construction and therefore do not provide information about those portions of the stream before the dam was built, only data from the main Yegua Creek station are considered here. There are approximately forty-three years of pre-dam flow records (1924 to part of 1966) and twenty-five years of post-dam data (part of 1966 to 1991).

Daily flow values were sorted in the data record from which mean flow and peak flow were identified. Mean annual discharge, mean monthly discharge, and monthly minimum and maximum discharge were then plotted for

Figure 5. Yegua Creek downstream of Somerville Dam. Photo taken from top of dam. People can be seen fishing.

the periods before and after dam construction to reveal trends. Stage data (height of water surface) were also available, corresponding with annual peak flows; discharge and stage were plotted in rating curves for the two periods. Because there were often years in which secondary events were actually larger than the peak event of another year, and thus an analysis using only annual peaks (known as the annual series) may be deceptive, the partial duration series was evaluated in addition to the annual series (Linsley et al. 1982). The partial duration series includes all flood events having a magnitude greater than an arbitrary minimum base value, so that in a given year, there could be several large floods included in the analysis. In this case, the partial duration series was constructed using a minimum base value of 1,000 cubic feet per second (cfs). Therefore, all flood events greater than 1,000 cfs were included in the analysis, not just the single largest event each year.

Results

Figure 6 shows the annual peak flows for the periods before (a) and after (b) dam construction. The effect of the dam on peak flows of the main Yegua Creek is clearly evident in that annual peaks are greatly moderated following dam construction, as would be expected. The mean annual peak flow in the pre-dam period was 11,064 cfs, compared to 1,623 cfs in the post-dam period, and there are no floods greater than 5,000 cfs following dam closure (fig. 6b). Somerville Dam has therefore completely eliminated large floods on Yegua Creek.

Monthly mean discharge in the pre- and post-dam periods is shown in figure 7 (a and b). Data for a total of 509 months were available for the pre-dam period, and 299 months for the post-dam period were analyzed. The effect of the dam on monthly mean flows is similarly evident in the diminished flows shown in figure 7b. The average monthly mean flow for the pre-dam period was about 290 cfs, compared to the post-dam average of 272 cfs. The difference between the two periods is even more evident when the month-to-month variances in mean monthly flow are compared. The variance is much greater in the pre-dam period; the pre-dam standard deviation is 546 cfs, compared to 428 cfs for the post-dam period. The flow regime of Yegua Creek is thus more consistent in the years following impoundment.

Figures 8 and 9 present the pre- and post-dam comparisons for monthly maximum and minimum dis-

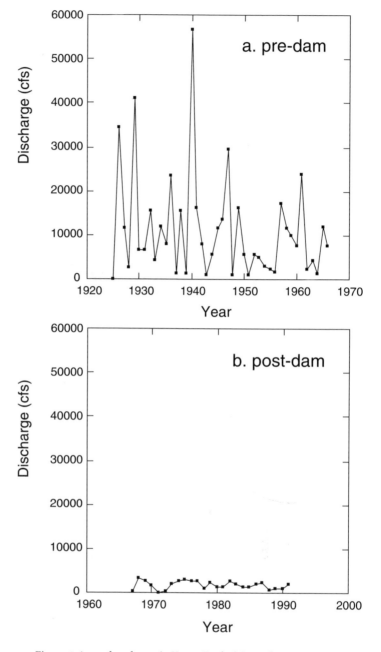

Figure 6. Annual peaks, main Yegua Creek; (a) pre-dam, (b) post-dam.

charge. Similar to the situation with annual peak flows, the moderation of monthly maximum discharge by Somerville Dam is evident. Average monthly maximum discharge in the pre-dam period (fig. 8a) was 1,871 cfs, compared to 578 cfs in the post-dam period (fig. 8b.) Variance in monthly maximums is also lower in the post-dam period; a standard deviation of 4,281 cfs in the pre-dam

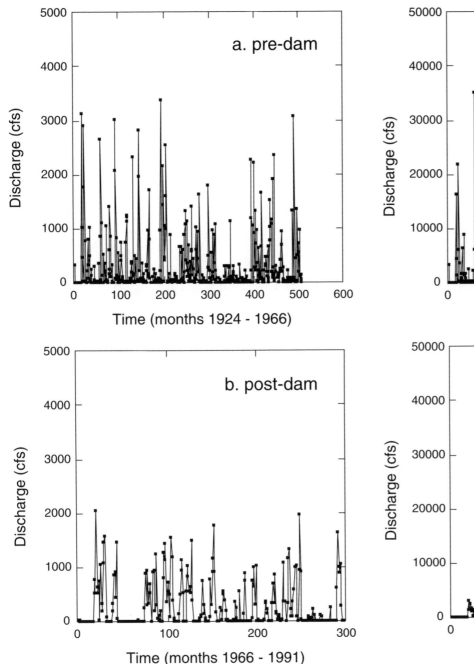

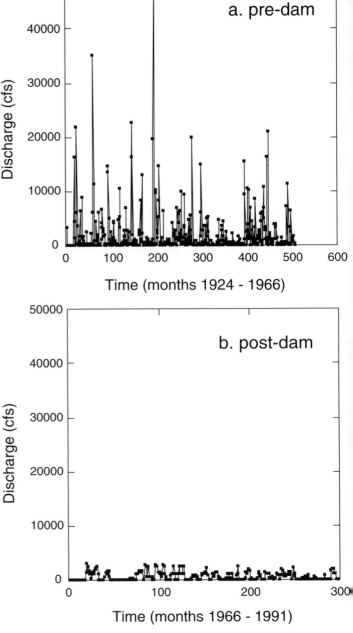

Figure 7. Monthly mean discharge; (a) pre-dam, (b) post-dam.

Figure 8. Monthly maximum discharge; (a) pre-dam, (b) post-dam.

period (nearly four times the magnitude of the mean) was calculated, compared to 751 cfs (not even twice the magnitude of the mean) for the second period.

Patterns in the monthly minimum discharge also show the effects of flow regulation (figs. 9a and b). Pre-dam monthly minimums are lower on average than post-dam

monthly minimums, indicating that, as would be expected, controlled releases from the dam were better able to sustain a minimum in-stream flow rate during periods of low precipitation. Extended periods of little or no flow are evident in the pre-dam data, indicating that the stream was intermittent in years with below-average pre-

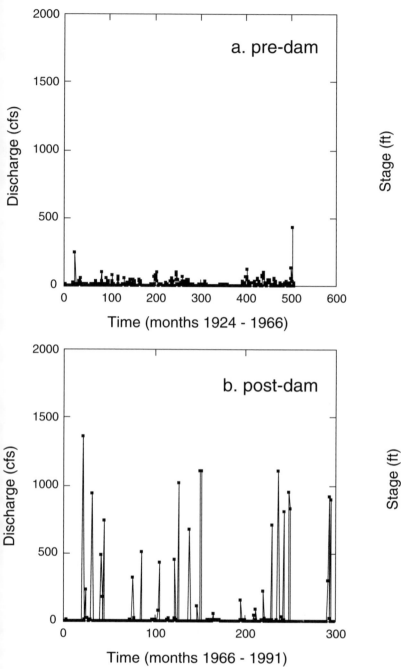

Figure 9. Monthly minimum discharge; (a) pre-dam, (b) post-dam.

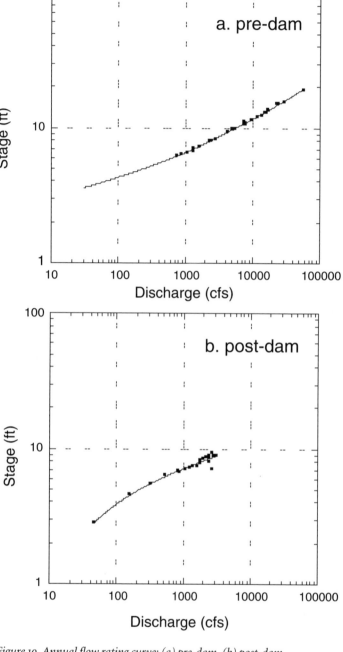

Figure 10. Annual flow rating curve; (a) pre-dam, (b) post-dam.

cipitation. Average monthly minimum flow before impoundment was 12 cfs, with a standard deviation of 28 cfs. Average monthly minimum flow following dam construction was 58 cfs, although the standard deviation in the post-dam period is higher at 210 cfs.

Flow rating curves are presented for the pre- and post-

dam years using both the annual flood series (fig. 10) and the partial duration series (fig. 11). Pre-dam peak flows using the annual series (fig. 10a) range from 20 to 80,000 cfs, corresponding to stages of 2 to 20 feet, whereas post-dam peak flows (fig. 10b) range from 20 to 4,000 cfs, with corresponding stages of only 2 to 9 feet. Similarly, the par-

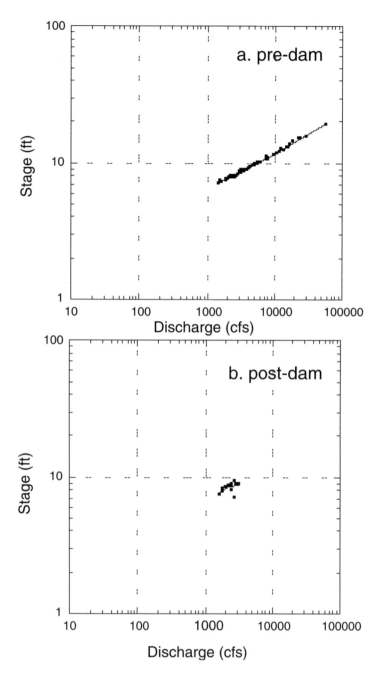

Figure 11. Partial duration flow rating curve; (a) pre-dam, (b) post-dam.

tial duration rating curves show that peak flows range from 1,000 to 80,000 cfs with stages varying from 7 to 20 feet before impoundment (fig. 11a). In the years following dam construction, in contrast, peak flow and stage values are shown to cluster around the moderate ranges of 1,000 to 4,000 cfs and 7 to 9 feet, respectively (fig. 11b). Thus, the partial duration series analysis reveals far more flood

events of moderate magnitude and also indicates that the overall flood magnitudes are lower after dam construction. These results support the conclusion that Somerville Dam has been effective in mitigating high flows.

Summary and Conclusions

Taken as a whole, analysis of streamflow characteristics indicates that the construction of Somerville Dam has had two primary effects on the hydrology of Yegua Creek. First, the dam has greatly mitigated high flows and eliminated large floods; flood magnitudes in the years following dam closure have not approached the peaks experienced in the early part of the twentieth century. Second, flow regulation has redistributed the flows with the effect of maintaining larger and more consistent minimum flows during periods of low rainfall. In short, flow regulation by Somerville Dam has produced a more equitable flow regime on Yegua Creek.

As one of the numerous dams built in the 1960s, during a period of accelerated dam construction in the Texas Gulf region and elsewhere in the country (Ramos 1995; Graf 1999), Somerville Dam has apparently achieved its multipurpose goals of flood control, municipal water supply, and recreation. However, despite these successes, it remains unclear how dam construction may have impacted other biophysical systems downstream, such as the ecology, vegetation (Jennings 1999), and geomorphology (Chin et al. 2002). The environmental effects of dams have become obvious only recently and thus have captured academic attention in recent years (Hunt 1988; Church 1995), because reservoir storage has generally been in place only two to three decades (Graf 1999). As the dam building era comes to an end in Texas and elsewhere in the nation (Graf 1999, 2001), and as dams are increasingly targeted for retirement due to high environmental costs (Task Committee on Guidelines for Retirement of Dams 1997), it becomes important to assess and register the downstream impacts of Somerville Dam in a way that would facilitate decision making. This chapter lays the groundwork for further research in this regard.

Acknowledgments

The research in this chapter is part of a larger project to examine the hydrology and geomorphology of Yegua Creek. The project is conducted in a series of graduate fluvial geomorphology courses taught by the senior author in the Department of Geography at Texas A&M University. Numerous participants in the courses have contributed background materials and useful data to this project. Christopher Lockwood, Laura Musacchio, and Mei-Shin Lin, in particular, gathered much of the historical and background information for this chapter. The following individuals provided valuable assistance in locating the data: Emmitt Attaway, Jon Cole, and Steven Tilney (U.S. Army Corps of Engineers), Pat Beavers (Harriet P. Woodson Memorial Library), Billy Giesenschlag (Burleson County Historical Society), the staff of the *Burleson County Citizen-Tribune*, and the staff of the Cushing Memorial Library at Texas A&M University. Frances Crate provided valuable discussion during many field visits to Yegua Creek as well as helpful comments on a draft of this paper. Daniel Harris produced figure 1.

References

Bowman, J. "Reallocating Texas' Water: Slicing up the Leftover Pie." *Texas Water Resour.* 19, no. 4. College Station: Texas Water Resources Institute, 1993.

Brazos River Authority. "Lake Sedimentation Surveys Using New Technology Increase Yield by More than 38,000 Acre-Feet of Water per Year." In *Brazos Basin Update*. Waco, Tex.: Brazos River Authority, 1995.

Buckner, H. D., E. R. Carrillo, and H. Davidson. "Water Resources Data, Water Year 1981." Water Resources Division, USGS, Dept. of the Interior, Austin, Texas, 1981.

Burleson County Historical Society (BCHS). *Astride the Old San Antonio Road*. Caldwell, Tex.: Burleson County Historical Society, 1980.

Chin A., D. L. Harris, T. H. Trice, and J. L. Given. "Adjustment of Stream Channel Capacity following Dam Closure, Yegua Creek, Texas." *Journ. of the Amer. Water Resources Assoc.* 38, no. 6 (2002): 1521–31.

Church, M. "Geomorphic Response to River Flow Regulation: Case Studies and Time-Scales." *Regulated Rivers: Res. and Management* 11 (1995): 3–22.

Clouse, J. V. *The History of Somerville, Somerville, Burleson County, Texas: 1895–1972*. Huntsville: Educational Service Center, 1972.

Correll, D. S., and M. C. Johnston. *Manual of the Vascular Plants of Texas*. Richardson: University of Texas at Dallas, 1979.

Graf, W. L. "Dam Nation: A Geographic Census of American Dams and Their Large-Scale Hydrologic Impacts." *Water Resour. Res.* 35, no.4 (1999): 1305–11.

———. "Damage Control: Dams and the Physical Integrity of America's Rivers." *Annals of the Assoc. of Amer. Geographers* 91 (2001): 1–27.

Hunt, C. "Down by the River: The Impact of Federal Water Projects and Policies on Biological Diversity." Washington, D.C.: Island Press, 1988.

Jennings, S. "Implications of Stream Impoundment on Yegua Creek, Texas." *Journ. of Environ. Systems* 27, no. 4 (1999): 299–316.

Kelly, T. E. Geology of North-Central Burleson County, Texas. Master's Thesis, Texas A&M University, College Station, 1955.

Kutac, E. A., and S. C. Caran. *Birds and Other Wildlife of South Central Texas*. Austin: University of Texas Press, 1994.

Lapotka, G. Development of Recreational Second-Home Subdivisons at Lake Somerville, Texas: A Case Study Analysis. Master's Thesis, Texas A&M University, College Station, 1979.

Larkin, T. J., and G. W. Bomar. *Climatic Atlas of Texas*. Report LP-192. Austin: Texas Department of Water Resources, 1983.

Linsley, R. K., J. B. Franzini, and J. L. Paulhus. *Hydrology For Engineers*. New York: McGraw-Hill, 1982.

Ramos, M. G. *Texas Almanac (1996–1997)*. Dallas: Dallas Morning News, 1995.

Schaffer, R. C. "Sociological Analysis of Dam Impact: A Study of Twenty-Two Large Dams in Texas." In *Reservoir Impact Study*, E. Cook (principle investigator), Final Rept. to the Office of Water Resour. Res., U.S. Dept. Interior. College Station: Texas A&M University, 1974.

Task Committee on Guidelines for Retirement of Dams. *Guidelines for Retirement of Dams and Hydroelectric Facilities*. New York: American Society of Civil Engineers, 1997.

Texas State Historical Association. *The New Handbook of Texas*, vol. 5. Austin: Texas State Historical Association, 1996.

Thorikildsen, D., and R. D. Price. *Ground-Water Resources of the Carrizo-Wilcox Aquifer in the Central Texas Region*. Publication 332. Austin: Texas Water Development Board, 1991.

Twidwell, S. R., and J. R. Davis. *An Assessment of Six Least Disturbed Unclassified Texas Streams*. Austin: Texas Water Commission, 1989.

U.S. Army Corps of Engineers. "Design Memorandum No. 1 on Somerville Reservoir, Yegua Creek, Texas: Hydrology." U.S. Army Engineers District, Fort Worth, Texas. 1960a.

———. "Design Memorandum No.2 on Somerville Reservoir, Yegua Creek, Texas: Site Selection." U.S. Army Engineers District, Fort Worth, Texas, 1960b.

———. "Design Memorandum No. 3 on Somerville Reservoir, Yegua Creek, Texas: Real Estate, Part I, Lands for Construction Area." U.S. Army Engineers District, Fort Worth, Texas, 1961a.

———. "Design Memorandum No. 5 on Somerville Reservoir, Yegua Creek, Texas: General." U.S. Army Engineers District, Fort Worth, Texas, 1961b.

———. "Map of Somerville Dam and Lake." U.S. Army Engineers District, Fort Worth, Texas, 1972.

Wooten, S. Predicting Reservoir Sedimentation. Master's thesis, Texas A&M University, College Station, 1997.

PART IV

Water Quality

With all the demands and impacts on the state's water resources, it is prudent to ask about water quality. Chemicals in pesticides and fertilizers, landfill contamination, and wastewater runoff all have the potential of adversely affecting the quality of an area's drinking water. Therefore, any plans developed to increase water quantity must also include a serious look at quality. While the scale of these presentations is more focused than those of the first three sections, they are mostly summaries of current, cutting-edge research vital to water-related topics.

Robert D. Larsen and Ronald J. Stephenson examine the presence of closed municipal solid waste landfills and their proximity to nearby potable water supplies. They discuss the mapping of such landfills across the state and the creation of a First Alert! risk assessment program to monitor possible contamination.

Michael G. Messina and R. Scott Beasley look at forest management and its impact on local water sources. Forests are seen as pristine areas but their management, including harvesting, soil preparation and planting, and the use of beneficial chemicals could cause changes in the local surface water supply.

One case study involves the Barton Springs region, which supplies a large portion of Austin's drinking water. Martha A. Turner and David A. Johns investigate this area as a potential situation where overdeveloped urbanization is altering the local water supply. Although not at dangerous levels, the changes they found in the area's groundwater warrant further monitoring.

Ric Jensen examines the question of whether research funds from the Texas Water Resource Institute (TWRI) are being fairly distributed to Texas universities with water research programs. He demonstrates that the TWRI, although based at Texas A&M University, has successfully distributed funds to most of the other universities with significant water programs. He also points out that TWRI's newsletter, *New Waves,* publishes research-related articles from many university sources, whether they are supported by TWRI funding or not. This newsletter accurately reflects concerns in water management issues today.

The last chapter, by Edmond R. McCarthy, Jr., and Michael A. Gershon, discusses the idea of reuse or recycled water as a conservation measure. They review the viable yet expensive options of direct reuse water and indirect reuse water in industry and irrigation. They indicate some of the legal problems in obtaining permits for utilization of reuse water, which make it difficult to promote the concept to water managers.

CHAPTER 17

Using a Geographic Information System to Identify Impacts from 4,200 Closed Municipal Solid Waste Landfills

Robert D. Larsen and Ronald J. Stephenson

Department of Geography

Texas State University–San Marcos

Abstract

Our work on the inventory of closed municipal landfills, as required by the Texas Legislature, began in August of 1995 and continued under an interagency contract between the Texas Natural Resource Conservation Commission and Texas State University until September of 1999.

In this inventory, nearly 4,200 closed municipal solid waste landfills (CMSWLFs) have been mapped in ArcView and an ARC/INFO-based Geographic Information System (GIS) using secondary information sources. Field verification of original databases was completed by twenty-four regional councils of government, and determination of exact CMSWLF boundaries, wherever adequate data are available, is ongoing.

Additional GIS data layers were added to the closed landfill layer to give the inventory greater power as a versatile analytical and decision-making tool. These layers include location and attribute information on public water supply intakes, public schools, hospitals, colonias, municipal utility districts, surface hydrography, aquifers, etc. The proximity of closed landfills to such uses and features could pose significant risk potential from leachate excursions.

This chapter is focused on identification, location, and investigation of the spatial relationship of the 188 public water supply intakes that our research indicates are located within one thousand feet of 151 CMWSLFs. Interactive GIS procedures and their application in risk assessment relating to existing and future potable water supplies are discussed.

Under Subtitle D amendments to the Resource Conservation and Recovery Act (RCRA), several requirements were implemented to increase landfill safety and instill public confidence in landfills as the primary alternative in the integrated waste management system. Similar rules were adopted by the Texas Natural Resource Conservation Commission (TNRCC) to establish new standards for landfill location, design, construction and operation, closure, and postclosure care to protect public health, safety, and the environment. However, the closed and abandoned landfill sites operating prior to Subtitle D changes, and often before Texas instituted its permitting regulations, typically did not have liners, impermeable covers, or monitoring wells to detect potential groundwater contamination and off-site gas migrations. Also, many landfills were poorly located, with communities often using old sand and gravel borrow pits, ravines, and floodplains for their sites. In fact, such landfill locations were recommended because of their position in "marginal-value" lands where leachate would rapidly dissipate into its surroundings.

Because of several specific problems relating to closed municipal landfills, including the abandonment of an apartment complex and a school, together with potential health and safety problems associated with historic landfill practices, the 73rd Texas Legislature enacted House Bill 2537. The main features of this bill established requirements for the inventory and recording of locations of closed and abandoned municipal solid waste landfills. They also established the permitting of development over such closed landfill units. In addition, HB 2537 called for the state's twenty-four councils of governments (COGs) to submit the information on those closed site locations to the county clerks for recording on county land deeds. Because mainly point-information was obtained, these data were not deed-recordable.

Process Used in Conducting the Closed Landfill Inventory

In 1995, the TNRCC contracted with Southwest Texas State University (SWT) to do an initial inventory of all closed municipal solid waste landfills (CMSWLFs), to determine the location and general characteristics of all known sites. The initial inventory was completed on August 31, 1999. SWT personnel were able to document nearly 4,200 closed landfills throughout the state using secondary sources of information. The TNRCC provided initial data, and landfill site locations were geo-coded and entered into a Geographic Information System (GIS). ArcView and ARC/INFO GIS software were used for the inventory. The ArcView software permitted the overlaying of various base map layers such as roads, hydrography, and political boundaries. A GIS provides users with the ability to view tabular sets of data in a spatial context. Also, these geographically referenced data can be viewed from different scale perspectives and analyzed by themselves or with one or more different overlays. The results of these data manipulation and analysis efforts can be output as tabular reports, maps, graphics, or numerical summaries.

The sites in the inventory consisted of landfills that were permitted, had applied for a permit, were illegal, or were grandfathered into the records when the permitting process began in the mid-1970s under the Texas Department of Health. Also included were those sites that never intended to be permitted, operating as unauthorized, unpermitted facilities.

Data verification involved both internal and external validity checks. Internal validity checks were based on the assumption that the TNRCC coordinates were reliable, but locations were queried to see if the landfills were in the correct county. External validity checks involved review of landfill location maps by the twenty-four COGs and subsequent verification by local government officials. All records relating to closed municipal landfills in the TNRCC archives in Austin were reviewed, and a preliminary draft atlas of the closed landfills was compiled and sent to all COGs and TNRCC district offices for verification and/or correction. Final atlases were produced from verified maps and attribute files for each COG region. A composite atlas of the entire state, consisting of eighteen hundred maps in traditional and digital formats and nearly five thousand pages of attribute files, was produced for the TNRCC.

Uses of the Closed Landfill Inventory

A question that needs to be addressed is: Do these landfills pose a problem to public health, safety, and the state's environment? Closed and abandoned municipal landfills may be generating leachate that is moving off-site and that may contaminate groundwater and/or surface water. These concerns are magnified since the land that was once used as landfills may subsequently have been developed with other land uses.

Although the initial SWT inventory was completed, it did not give the needed geographic and scientific information to determine which landfill sites are or may be a threat to health, safety, or the environment. It was necessary to acquire additional data on such elements as the location of public water supply intakes, aquifers, floodplains, etc., and, using relational database analysis, to compare these data to the locations of CMSWLFs already found in the inventory. By using the ArcView GIS to make comparisons of the locations of selected land uses and sensitive environments with data in the closed landfill inventory, it is possible to determine the proximity of selected features to closed and abandoned landfills and if there may be existing or potential problem areas. It is then possible to establish additional criteria and procedures for conducting risk assessments that can be focused on those particular sites determined to be of immediate concern.

Based on the innovative structure of the closed landfill inventory, and the unique capabilities of the GIS that was used to process those data, the closed landfill inventory has been used as an extremely powerful research tool. Databases in GIS can be assembled in a variety of different geographic regions and scales—for example, by COG, county, city, legislative district, municipal utility districts (MUDs), water control and improvement districts, or public water supply districts. The ability to assemble databases in such a variety of ways provides enormous amounts of information to legislators, decision makers, and service providers at almost any government level or to the private sector.

In this research GIS was used to overlay closed municipal solid waste landfill data upon the more than sixteen thousand sites in the public water supply intake (PWSI) data set. In this way it was determined which, if any, surface or groundwater supply intakes were in close proximity to closed landfills. Additional site-specific research could then be conducted on those intakes situated near closed landfills. This research would investigate such factors as the intake's hydrogeology, well depth, presence of an aquiclude or aquitard, the number of people served, activity status of a well, and indications of water quality problems evident from sampling records.

Also, the closed landfill and U.S. Geological Survey (USGS) digital aquifer data sets could be overlaid to identify potential health risks associated with possible contaminated aquifer-sourced drinking water supplies. Proximity of wastes to potable drinking water supplies could be determined. Investigators could then evaluate water quality sampling records for each PWSI located proximal to a CMSWLF and thereby ascertain which, if any, contaminants are present. Regional health records could also be evaluated if necessary. These procedures are extremely important since the focus of the Wellhead Protection Program of the Federal Safe Drinking Water Act has shifted to the 1996 amendments establishing the Source Water Assessment and Protection Program (SWAP). Under these changes, the emphasis has evolved from vulnerability to

susceptibility, wherein data such as closed landfill locations will be required of the states.

We have developed a risk assessment methodology—FirstAlert! Risk Assessment Procedure (FARAP)—that uses an analysis of the closed landfill inventory and related data sets to rank CMSWLF sites as to potential problems and possible remediation status. The ranking is based on conflicts of land use, sites containing hazardous wastes, shallow depth to ground- or surface water supplies, proximity to public water supply intakes, and similar considerations.

Highlights of Findings of the Closed Landfill Inventory

Despite the vast land area of Texas, statistically it is quite probable that some of the more than 16,000 surface and groundwater PWSIs are going to be found in close proximity to the nearly 4,200 CMSWLFs. These geographically proximal sitings are enhanced by several factors. People typically access their water supplies and dispose of their wastes near to themselves; Texas is a highly urbanized state; and historically, waste disposal was encouraged on nearby "marginal" lands such as wetlands, floodplains, along riverbanks, and in areas of rugged topography etched by water erosion. Of the more than 16,000 PWSIs on record, 615 are surface water sourced, while 15,751 tap groundwater resources.

A summary of water sources in "close" proximity to CMSWLFs is presented in tables 1 and 2. In table 1, the groundwater source data are categorized by distance separating PWSIs and CMSWLFs and by depth of well. Although there may be intervening protective or mitigating factors such as aquicludes, sound well casings, or a small number of customers for the water source, depth of the

Table 1. Number of groundwater source public water supply intakes (PWSIs) by depth and by proximity to CMSWLFs

| Well Depth | Distance between PWSI and CMSWLFs | | | |
	< 500 feet	501–1,000 feet	1,000 feet to 1/4 mile	Totals
< 100 feet	7*	6*	17	30
101–250 feet	4*	19*	19	42
251–500 feet	12	32	20	64
501–1,000 feet	15	32	20	67
> 1,000 feet	8	17	21	46
	N = 46	N = 106	N = 97	N = 249

*These sites should receive initial research consideration.

Table 2. Number of surface water public water supply intakes (PWSIs) by proximity to CMSWLFs

Distance	Number
< 500 feet	N = 0
500–1,000 feet	N = 5
1,001 feet to 1/4 mile	N = 2
1/4 mile to 3 miles	N = 364
Total	N = 371

water source is an important initial consideration in any impact analysis. Analysis of our data identifies thirty shallow wells (less than one hundred feet deep) located within one-fourth of a mile of CMSWLFs. A total of 249 groundwater PWSIs of all depths are within the one-fourth-mile range. More site-specific research should be targeted to these relationships. FARAP identifies which factors and sources of information are most pertinent.

About 8 percent of all CMSWLFs in Texas lie within one-fourth of a mile of streams. While over one-half of the surface PWSIs appear to lie within three miles of a CMSWLF, it must be noted that many of the PWSIs are upstream of the CMSWLFs and as such are not susceptible to contamination from that source. It is our intent to investigate further the relative positioning of the phenomena and to conduct a First Alert!-type risk assessment on those relationships where the PWSI is within three miles downstream from a CMSWLF.

There are 288 CMSWLFs that are located over the Edwards aquifer. This designated sole-source aquifer supplies potable water to many communities along the Interstate 35 highway corridor, the largest being San Antonio and its Bexar County suburbs. Of the 288 CMSWLFs over the entire Edwards aquifer, 222 are situated in Bexar County alone. There are 275 groundwater PWSIs in the same area. It should be noted that these are public water supply intakes, and private water sources are not included. Again, a site-specific FirstAlert!-type risk assessment is necessary to evaluate properly the current or potential contamination problems associated with these relationships.

Conclusions and Future Research

During the 76th Texas legislative session, House Bill 2537 was substantially revised by Senate Bill 1447. Now under Texas Health and Safety Code, regional waste management plans prepared and maintained by the COGs are re-

quired to include an inventory of closed municipal solid waste landfill units. This inventory must include the location of such units, the current owners of the land on which the former landfill units were located, and the current use of the land. The exact boundaries of each former landfill unit, or the best approximation of each unit's boundaries, must be inventoried, mapped, and deed-recorded by the county clerk. Where exact boundaries of a former landfill unit are known, the COG shall also notify the owner of the land of its former use. The records shall be made available by the county clerk for public inspection.

The Department of Geography at SWT is currently under contract to six of the COGs to complete the latest legislative inventory requirements by August 31, 2001. The remaining COGs are either completing the inventory internally or contracting with consulting firms. The results of this latest inventory will be the development of more accurate information on CMSWLF boundaries rather than simple point-data. Also, land ownership and current land use data will be important additions in helping determine the extent of potential public and private water supply contaminants from CMSWLFs.

Sources of Data and Information

Cooperating federal agencies included the U.S. Department of Agriculture, Soil Conservation Service; U.S. Department of Commerce, Bureau of the Census; U.S. Department of Health, Education and Welfare; and U.S. Treasury Department, Resolution Trust Corporation. Cooperating state agencies that provided information included the Texas Natural Resource Conservation Commission; Texas Department of Health; Texas Water Commission; Texas Department of Transportation; Texas Department of Community Affairs; and Texas Natural Resource Information System. Cooperating regional or county agencies included the Lower Colorado River Authority; Harris County Pollution Control Department; municipal utility districts; water control and improvement districts; and councils of governments.

Of particular importance have been three sources of information: House Bill 2537, 73rd Texas Legislature; Senate Bill 1447, 76th Texas Legislature; and the "Source Water Assessment and Protection Program Strategy" prepared in 1999 by the state's Source Water Assessment and Protection Team in the Water Permits and Resource Management Division of the Public Drinking Water Section.

CHAPTER 18

Nonpoint-Source Pollution from Silviculture in Texas

Michael G. Messina

Department of Forest Science

Texas A&M University

R. Scott Beasley

Arthur Temple College of Forestry

Stephen F. Austin State University

Abstract

Forest management can potentially influence water quality through activities ranging from simple alteration of the water cycle by cutting trees to the addition of chemicals designed to augment forest productivity. This chapter examines the impacts of common silvicultural practices on water quality in East Texas and the southern United States. We begin with an examination of the effects of site manipulation from harvesting through site preparation and planting on such physical water characteristics as total suspended solids (primarily sediment) and then discuss possible impacts from the use of fertilizers and pesticides on chemical water characteristics. We finish with recommendations for minimizing or eliminating off-site impacts from forest management. Major summary points are:

- If silvicultural manipulations are carefully conducted, water quality impacts are relatively minor and of short duration, especially when compared to sediment losses from construction and row-crop agriculture.

- Established forests protect and rebuild the soil resource and yield high quality water.

- It is only during the harvest and regeneration stage that soils are disturbed and exposed.

- In recent years, harvesting has increasingly involved the creation of streamside management zones, even along ephemeral streams.

- In general, forestry use of pesticides poses a low pollution risk to groundwater due to its dispersed nature, low frequency of application, and low rates.

- The greatest potential chemical hazard to groundwater comes from handling concentrates (transport of formulations; storage; spilling during mixing; and loading, disposal, and rinsing of containers), not from operational application of dilute mixtures.

- Most forestry use of pesticides is confined to small-scale watersheds containing ephemeral or intermittent streams.

- *Forestry pesticides have not been identified in surface or groundwater at sufficiently high concentrations to impair drinking water quality.*
- *Avoiding direct chemical application to water will generally preclude water contamination.*

The quality of water draining from forests has always been of concern to professional foresters for a variety of reasons. Minimizing soil and nutrients lost to runoff is essential to sustaining forest productivity. Furthermore, many watersheds supplying municipal drinking water are either forested or contain water that has passed through forested ecosystems. Forests are often viewed by the general public as being relatively pristine and are highly valued for recreation. Forests are also home to many wildlife species, including some listed as threatened or endangered. Many national and state parks are surrounded by managed forests, and the headwaters of most of America's major river systems are in forested areas.

Modern forest management has intensified in many areas through increased use of mechanical harvesting, site preparation, and planting as well as elevated use of chemicals, particularly herbicides. Forested environments have a number of characteristics that may affect water quality. Many forested areas have higher slopes than surrounding land, and they sometimes have shallower soils with a high infiltration capacity, low pH, and high organic matter content. These characteristics may make forests either a source or a sink for sediment and chemicals, with the critical difference dependent upon both natural features and management practices.

The importance of the water quality impacts of forestry practices was highlighted by the highly controversial and recently aborted Total Maximum Daily Load (TMDL) proposal by the Environmental Protection Agency (EPA) that would have classified forestry as a point-source of water pollution, rather than nonpoint, as it has been for decades. If adopted, this would have meant much more stringent regulation of forestry practices under the Clean Water Act. Federal permits would have been required by all forest landowners for management activities such as reforestation and construction of firelines if they impacted a water quality limited stream. Therefore, it is critical to examine available data pertaining to off-site export of sediment and chemicals from forests under active management.

In this chapter we examine the impacts of common silvicultural practices on water quality in East Texas. Due to a paucity of data unique to that region and also due to the general similarity between East Texas and much of the southern United States, data from other areas are reviewed as necessary. We begin with an examination of the effects of site manipulation from harvesting through site preparation and planting on such physical water characteristics as total suspended solids (primarily sediment), going on to discuss possible impacts from the use of fertilizers and pesticides on chemical water characteristics. We finish with recommendations for minimizing or eliminating off-site impacts from forest management.

Water Quality Effects of Physical Site Manipulations

Pollution can be characterized as a resource out of place. Sediment is a good example. Forest soils provide a valuable reservoir of moisture and nutrients to sustain the growth of trees and associated organisms. Yet when soil particles are detached and transported to streams by flowing or falling water—that is, the process of sedimentation—they lose their useful function and become a liability. Sediment clogs culverts and bridges, destroys habitat for aquatic organisms, and reduces the capacity of streams to support fisheries and recreation. Furthermore, the productivity of forest ecosystems may be significantly reduced if erosion and sedimentation are severe or prolonged.

Undisturbed forests, whether natural or artificially regenerated, yield high quality water. Plant canopies absorb energy of falling rain, and layers of organic debris on the forest floor promote infiltration. Percolation of water through the soil profile is enhanced by the presence of macropores created by organic residues, animal and insect burrows, and the growth, death, and decay of roots.

Healthy forests also use large quantities of water. Research in the mid-South shows that about two-thirds of annual rainfall is either evaporated from vegetation surfaces (interception) or transpired through leaf tissues (Lawson 1967; Scoles et al. undated; Ursic 1985). By rapidly depleting soil moisture, forests increase retention storage within the profile, thereby reducing the likelihood of soil saturation and overland flow during precipitation events.

Managed forests are most vulnerable to erosion and sedimentation during harvesting and regeneration activities and in the construction and maintenance of forest roads. Important factors affecting the severity of erosion and sedimentation are (1) increased exposure of soil to falling or flowing water, (2) increased water available for runoff due to reduced evapotranspiration, (3) compaction of soil or interruption of macropore flow, and (4) energy of falling or flowing water (e.g., canopy drip heights, slope gradients, rainfall amounts and intensities).

If harvesting and regeneration activities significantly disturb the forest floor and expose and compact the soil, erosion and sedimentation rates may increase. Furthermore, a reduction in evapotranspiration caused by harvesting increases the amount of water available to detach and transport sediment into streams. Removal of the plant canopy and disturbance of the forest floor also subject exposed mineral soil to the direct energy of falling raindrops or overland flow.

The actual outcome of harvesting and regeneration operations depends upon the extent to which forest managers can reduce forest floor disturbance and soil compaction or implement measures to mitigate any adverse impacts. "Best management practices" (BMPs) are strategies adopted to reduce the environmental effects of management activities. The Federal Water Pollution Control Amendments enacted by Congress in 1972 required that states adopt BMPs to control, to the extent feasible, all nonpoint sources of water pollution, including silviculture. Limited research done prior to 1972 indicated that generalizations about silvicultural effects on soil losses and water quality are limited by complex, dynamic interrelations among factors controlling erosion. Spatial and temporal variations in soil particles, climatic regimes, site factors, and specific forest practices limit the extrapolation of research results from one region to another. Efforts to develop and test prediction models have been hampered by a lack of comparable data from controlled field experiments over a broad geographic range. Research conducted in the mid-South during the past two decades has provided a wealth of information on this complex issue. The studies described here involved small watersheds where specific forest practices could be implemented and evaluated under carefully controlled conditions relatively free of the confounding effects of extraneous variables.

Sediment from Undisturbed Forests

Generally sediment losses from undisturbed forests are minimal. However, in the Gulf Coastal Plain where streambeds and banks are comprised principally of soil materials or previously deposited sediments, forest streams may run muddy with heavy sediment loads during or after a large storm event. Most, if not all, of this sediment may originate in the stream channels (Beasley 1979; Ursic 1977; Ursic and Douglass 1979). This is in contrast to the mountains where streambeds and banks are usually protected by rock cover. Sediment losses from small undisturbed forested watersheds throughout the mid-South range from 20 to 30 kilograms per hectare (kg/ha) in the mountains to 30–400 kg/ha in the Coastal Plain (table 1).

Table 1. Mean annual water yields (streamflow) and sediment losses from undisturbed watersheds in the mid-South

Physiographic Province	Location	Forest Type	Water Yield (cm)	Sediment Loss (kg/ha)	Discharged Weighted Sediment Loss (mg/l)	Reference
Gulf Coastal Plain	Arkansas Flatwoods	Mature pine	12.3	33	27	Beasley and Granillo 1988
	Mississippi Uplands	40-yr old pine	16.5	183	111	Schreiber and Duffy 1982
		Mature pine	48.3	403	83	Ursic 1977
		Mature pine	2.9	365	1,259	Beasley 1979
		Depleted hardwoods	45.2	196	43	Ursic 1982
		Depleted hardwoods	12.2	224	183	Ursic 1970
	Texas Uplands	Mature pine	2.7	97	360	Blackburn et al. 1986
Athens Plateau	Arkansas	Mature pine-hardwoods	18.4	67	36	Beasley et al. 1986
Ouachita Mountains	Arkansas	Mature pine	32.0	32	10	Miller et al. 1988a, 1988b
	Oklahoma	Mature pine-hardwoods	19.2	18	10	Miller 1984
Ozark Mountains	Arkansas	Upland hardwoods	5.8	22	38	Rogerson 1976

This corresponds to stream discharge-weighted losses of 10–40 mg/l (or 0.001–0.004 tons per acre-inch of streamflow) in the mountains to 30–1,300 mg/l (or 0.003–0.147 tons per acre-inch) in the Coastal Plain (table 1). Extreme variability in the Coastal Plain can be attributed to stream channel slope gradients and morphology—including degradation and aggradation related to previous land use (Ursic 1986).

Silvicultural Impacts: Water Yields

Trees extract large quantities of water from the soil and transpire it through their foliage. Individual trees may use from two to three hundred liters per day. When forests are harvested, some excess water normally shows up either as overland flow (if the soil is compacted or saturated) or as streamflow at some point downslope.

Increases in water yields from harvesting small watersheds in the mid-South were generally significant yet variable. Increases ranged from over 40 centimeters in Mississippi and the Athens Plateau of Arkansas, to 10–20 cm in the Arkansas flatwoods and mountains and the Texas Coastal Plain (table 2). Only one study reported a reduction in water yield from harvesting and site preparation (Miller 1984). The study, located in the Ouachita Mountains of southeastern Oklahoma, involved clearcutting followed by tree crushing and ripping (contour subsoiling) prior to replanting. The ripping treatment created detention storage and apparently interrupted the normal flow of subsurface water through macrochannels.

Silvicultural Impacts: Sediment Losses

Harvesting alone, under some circumstances, may increase sediment production by exposing and compacting soil and increasing the amount of water available for runoff. However, research has shown that even with clearcutting, significant soil disturbance seldom occurs on more than 10 percent of the harvest area (Campbell et al. 1973; Dickerson 1968). Most sediment losses from silvicultural activities are associated with mechanical site preparation during the regeneration process. First-year sediment losses from mechanical site preparation after clearcutting ranged from less than 300 kg/ha for the Arkansas flatwoods and Ouachita Mountains of Arkansas and Oklahoma, to about 3,000 kg/ha in the Texas Coastal Plain and over 12,000 kg/ha on steep, highly erodible slopes in northern Mississippi (table 2). It is important to note that the Mississippi study was not a nor-

mal silvicultural operation. It was designed to investigate a "worst-case scenario" where erosion-control pine plantations on previously eroded land were clearcut and regenerated. Furthermore, the study did not involve BMPs, which could have protected the stream channels from extensive scouring that accounted for much of the sediment. All of the studies showed a substantial reduction in sediment losses by the second or third posttreatment year due to rapid regrowth of vegetation (Beasley and Granillo 1985).

Mean slope gradient and groundcover following site preparation accounted for much of the variation in sediment losses among study locations. Slopes were steepest on the Ouachita Mountains and Texas watersheds, however, an extensive cover of rock fragments on Ouachita Mountain slopes and streambeds protect soils against the erosive forces of water; consequently, sediment losses were low. On the other hand, the moderately steep slopes of the Texas Coastal Plain watersheds had a high percentage of exposed soil; therefore, sediment losses were relatively high. Even though exposed soil was high on the Arkansas Coastal Plain watersheds, slopes were flat, hence sediment losses were low.

Some site preparation methods proved to have less impact on water quality than others. At the Arkansas Athens Plateau site, chemical site preparation resulted in significantly less sediment production than mechanical site preparation (Beasley et al. 1986). At the Texas Coastal Plain site, roller chopping produced less sediment than shearing and windrowing (Blackburn et al. 1986).

Studies in the Arkansas flatwoods (Beasley and Granillo 1988) and Ouachita Mountains (Miller et al. 1988b) showed that the first selection harvest in an uneven-aged management system resulted in less sediment than clearcutting and mechanical site preparation. However, uneven-aged management requires harvests on a regular cycle of five to seven years. The cumulative impact of reopening roads and skid trails for repeated harvests may negate any presumed advantage with respect to water quality (Scoles et al. undated).

Water Quality Effects of Fertilization and Pesticide Use

Fertilization

Forest fertilization in the South has gained in popularity during the last thirty years. During 1998, 0.486 million hectares of pine plantations were fertilized, and it is esti-

Table 2. Mean annual water yields and sediment losses resulting from harvesting and regeneration activities in the mid-South

Location	Treatment	Yrs. after Tmt.	Water Yield (cm)	Sediment Loss (kg/ha)	Discharged Weighted Sediment Loss (mg/l)	Reference
Gulf Coast Plain						
Arkansas	clearcut/shear/windrow/	1	13.2	264	208	Beasley and Granillo 1988
Flatwoods	burn/replant	2	44.7	63	14	
		3	32.8	83	24	
	1st Selection thin to	1	5.1	13	28	
	achieve uneven-age	2	33.8	26	7	
	distribution	3	14.5	15	9	
	Controls—no disturbance	1	1.0	4	22	
		2	31.0	19	6	
		3	17.5	46	24	
Mississippi	clearcut/shear/windrow/	1	45.1	12,800	2,838	Beasley 1979
Uplands	burn/cover crop/replant	2	28.0	2,220	794	
	clearcut/roller chop/	1	50.8	12,540	2,471	
	burn/replant	2	34.5	2,310	670	
	clearcut/shear/windrow/	1	50.7	14,250	2,808	
	burn/bed on contour/replant	2	23.6	5,540	2,346	
	Controls—no disturbance	1	2.9	620	2,127	
		2	2.8	110	393	
Texas Uplands	clearcut/shear/windrow/	1	14.6	2,937	2,119	Blackburn et al. 1986
	burn/replant	2	5.0	80	167	
		3	6.2	35	54	
		4	6.1	165	331	
	clearcut/roller chop/	1	8.3	25	30	
	burn/replant	2	3.4	6	15	
		3	4.4	5	12	
		4	3.5	16	47	
	Controls—no disturbance	1	2.6	33	126	
		2	1.2	5	42	
		3	2.1	5	23	
		4	1.4	28	203	
Athens Plateau						
SW Arkansas	clearcut/shear/windrow/	1	32.5	535	165	Beasley et al. 1986
	burn/replant	2	60.8	1,005	165	
		3	50.0	308	62	
	clearcut/chemical site	1	15.6	251	161	
	prep/burn/replant	2	39.6	205	52	
		3	25.9	90	35	
	Controls—no disturbance	1	15.9	71	45	
		2	22.0	147	67	
		3	26.3	46	17	

(*continued*)

Table 2. *Continued*

Location	Treatment	Yrs. after Tmt.	Water Yield (cm)	Sediment Loss (kg/ha)	Discharged Weighted Sediment Loss (mg/l)	Reference
Ouachita Mountains						
Arkansas	clearcut/roller chop/	1	31.5	237	75	Miller et al. 1988a, 1988b
	burn/replant	2	27.4	90	33	
		3	75.7	177	23	
	1st Selection thin to	1	31.5	36	11	
	achieve uneven-age	2	25.6	36	14	
	distribution	3	71.3	84	12	
	Controls—no disturbance	1	21.4	12	6	
		2	18.2	15	8	
		3	56.4	68	12	
SW Oklahoma	clearcut/tree crush/	1	22.5	282	125	Miller 1984
	burn/rip (contour	2	11.1	35	32	
	subsoiling)/replant	3	13.6	15	11	
		4	22.1	43	19	
	Controls—no disturbance	1	31.9	36	11	
		2	6.2	8	13	
		3	14.7	5	3	
		4	23.8	24	10	

mated that the annual rate of forest fertilization in the southeastern United States is now greater than the sum of all forest fertilization in the rest of the world (NCSFNC 1999). Most forest fertilization is part of "intensive" management of high-yielding pine plantations, rather than "extensive" management of natural stands of pines or hardwoods. Unlike agricultural systems, which may be fertilized annually, forest fertilization usually occurs once or twice in a typical fifteen- to thirty-five-year southern pine rotation, although recent recommendations call for more frequent applications. Currently, prescriptions for loblolly pine (*Pinus taeda* L.) advocate fertilization at plantation establishment with 45–56 kg/ha of phosphorus (P), followed by a second fertilization near midrotation with 168–224 kg/ha of nitrogen (N) alone or in combination with 28–56 kg/ha of P. Fertilization of forest stands with other nutrient elements is uncommon, although there has been increasing interest recently in using potassium (K) and boron (B). Alternatively, forest tree nursery fertilization frequently involves a broader range of nutrient elements, including micronutrients. However, we confine much of our discussion to N and P due to availability of data.

Nitrogen

Nitrogen is usually applied to forests as urea $((NH_2)_2CO$, 46 percent N), ammonium nitrate (AN; NH_4NO_3; 33.5 percent N), or diammonium phosphate (DAP; $(NH_4)HPO_4$; 18 percent N)(Allen 1987). Plants acquire N in the inorganic form, supplied directly by AN and DAP, but urea must undergo conversion to ammonium (NH_4^+) before plant uptake. The transformations of these fertilizers to nitrate (NO_3^-) and NH_4^+ that occur after fertilization are of most importance to water quality.

High concentrations of NO_3^- in streamwater are of concern because of possible health risks; for example, methemoglobinemia (blue-baby) syndrome in infants can be caused by excessive NO_3^- in drinking water. The maximum concentration of NO_3^--N for safe drinking water has been set at 10 mg-N/L (US EPA 1986). Nitrite (NO_2^-) is also potentially toxic but is very transient and easily oxidized to NO_3^-. The average concentration of NO_3^--N in major North American river systems is less than 1 mg-N/L (GEMS 1997). Because NO_3^- is an anion and is very soluble in water, it is highly mobile in soils (Havlin et al. 1999).

Ammonium is not toxic, although the nonprotonated form, ammonia (NH_3), is. The equilibrium between NH_3 and NH_4^+ depends somewhat on temperature and strongly on solution pH, with the percentage of NH_3 decreasing markedly as pH declines. The percentages of NH_3 are 0.1, 1.0, 10.0, and 50 at pH 6.0, 7.0, 8.0, and 9.0, respectively (Schmidt 1982). Since the pH of forested streams in the southern United States is normally in the range of 4.0 to 6.5 (NCASI 1999), much of the NH_3–NH_4^+ pool in these streams will be in the nontoxic NH_4^+ form. The EPA's most recent criteria for NH_3 are for total NH_3 ($NH_3 + NH_4^+$), the toxicity of which does not appear to vary with temperature (U.S. EPA 1998). The maximum acute concentrations of NH_3 expressed as mg/L of NH_3-N when salmonids are absent are 48.8, 36.1, 19.9, 8.40, 3.20, and 1.32 for pH 6.5, 7.0, 7.5, 8.0, 8.5, and 9.0, respectively. Concentrations for waters containing salmonids are 0.67 times those mentioned. For chronic exposures, concentrations are 3.48, 3.08, 2.28, 1.27, 0.57, and 0.25 for pH 6.5, 7.0, 7.5, 8.0, 8.5, and 9.0, respectively.

There are no water quality standards for organic-N or urea-N, but acute toxicity studies have shown that several thousand mg-N/L as urea are required for any toxic effects, which is orders of magnitude greater than concentrations measured in forested streams.

Phosphorus

Phosphorus fertilization in southern forestry mainly involves fertilization near the time of plantation establishment on poorly drained P-deficient soils of the lower Coastal Plain. Trees usually absorb phosphorous (P) in the phosphate form $H_2PO_4^-$. The "superphosphates" are the principal phosphorus fertilizers used in forestry when only phosphorus is required. Most commonly, concentrated superphosphate (about 19% phosphorus) and normal superphosphate (about 9% phosphorus) are used. DAP (about 20% phosphorus) is used when both nitrogen and phosphorus are desired. Ground rock phosphate is used sparingly in forestry and usually only on very acidic soils, particularly during mechanical site preparation when the fertilizer can be incorporated into the soil.

Phosphate is not toxic, although elemental phosphorus is. The major concern over phosphates in aquatic communities is excessive eutrophication. This nutrient enrichment leads to algal blooms, and subsequent bacterial decomposition of the algae can deplete aquatic oxygen. The U.S. Environmental Protection Agency (1986) has suggested guidelines for total phosphorus to prevent eutrophication: it should not exceed 50 µg/L in streams entering lakes or reservoirs, 25 µg/L in lakes or reservoirs, and 100 µg/L in other flowing waters not directly discharging to lakes or impounds.

Research on Fertilization Impacts on Surface and Subsurface Water Quality

Tables 3 and 4 contain a summary of studies done in the Southeast on surface and subsurface water response, respectively, to forest fertilization. As already noted, data are lacking for Texas sites.

Campbell (1989) showed that maximum concentrations of various N species and phosphate-P in streamwater after fertilization never approached the maximum values for safe drinking water (table 3). Water samples were taken from water draining the fertilized plantation for thirty days before and after fertilization. Concentrations of all ions returned to pretreatment levels within three weeks following fertilization.

Herrmann and White (1996) fertilized a six-year-old loblolly pine plantation and left a companion stand unfertilized as a control on the Coastal Plain of North Carolina (table 3). The fertilizer was applied aerially without avoidance of a drainage ditch system. Maximum nutrient concentrations in the drainage water were observed within one week following fertilization and returned to control levels after thirty weeks. Nutrient concentrations were well below those considered unsafe for drinking water. Herrmann and White (1996) estimated that direct application of fertilizer into streams accounted for 70–80 percent of the nutrient export from fertilization.

Fromm and Herrmann (1996) fertilized the stand that served as a control for Herrmann and White (1996) using ground-based equipment and the previously fertilized stand as a control. Maximum concentrations of N and P in streamwater from the fertilized watershed were lower than those from the control, likely because of the ground application and avoidance of the streams.

Research has also been conducted on the effects of forest fertilization on groundwater chemistry. Wheeler et al. (1989) measured leaching of NO_3^--N through a moderately well drained, slowly permeable soil under a young loblolly pine plantation and an uneven-aged, mixed shortleaf (*Pinus echinata*)/loblolly pine stand in the upper Coastal Plain of Arkansas (table 4). The plantation was fertilized at ages three and four with 70 kg N/ha. The uneven-aged stand received 230 kg N/ha annually for two years. Soil solution NO_3^--N concentration under the fer-

Location, Stand Type	Treatment (kg/ha)	Application Method	Period or Treatment	Chemical Concentration (mg/L)								Reference
				Nitrate-N		Ammonium-N		Organic N		Phosphate-P		
				max	annual average	max	annual average	max	annual average	max	annual average	
Coastal plain, North Carolina, loblolly pine	170 N, 28 P as urea and DAP	ground, streams avoided	pre-fert		0.6		0.1		0.9		0.04	Campbell 1989
			post-fert	1.2		3.8		9.3		0.18		
Coastal plain, North Carolina, loblolly pine	210 N, 40 P as urea and DAP	aerial, streams not avoided	control	0.31	0.02	0.81	0.12	1.22	0.68	0.052	0.015	Herrmann and White 1996
			post-fert	0.14	0.03	3.63	0.51	14	1.59	1.11	0.170	
Coastal plain, North Carolina, loblolly pine	145 N, 24 P as DAP	ground, streams avoided	control	0.7	0.8	0.11	0.04	1.1	0.7	0.18	0.07	Fromm and Herrmann 1996
			post-fert	1.0	0.14	0.12	0.04	1.1	0.8	0.07	0.03	
Piedmont, North Carolina, loblolly pine	110 N as AN, 13 P, 40 K, 12 S	ground, streams avoided	pre-fert		0.1		0.1					Sanderford 1975
			post-fert	0.1		0.2						
Coastal plain, Florida, slash pine	40 N, 50 P	ground, streams avoided	pre-fert		<0.1		<0.1		0.9			Fisher 1981
			post-fert	0.1		0.4		2.7				
Florida, slash pine, 1.5 yr old	225 N, 90 P, 45 Ca	ground applied over 4 yr, stream buffer	control			1.1	0.2			0.23	<0.1	Riekirk 1989
			fertilized			1.5	0.2			0.7	<0.1	

tilized plantation increased from 0.5 mg/L to a maximum of less than 6 mg/L immediately after fertilization both years and declined to less than 3 mg/L in the year following the second fertilization. There were no detectable differences in NO_3^--N between urea and AN fertilization. Fertilizing the uneven-aged stand led to more persistent and greater concentrations of NO_3^--N in soil solution. As in the even-aged stand, there was an initial peak that was related to the fertilizer being flushed through the system before it could be incorporated.

Grant (1991) found that N+P fertilization of a fifteen-year-old Georgia loblolly pine stand gave the highest NH_4^+-N concentrations in soil water, with peak concentrations of 0.9 mg/L (table 4). Maximum concentrations of NO_3^--N never exceeded 0.6 mg/L after all fertilizations tested, compared to 0.1 mg/L for the control. Segal et al. (1987) measured N concentrations in water wells following fertilization of a young slash pine (*Pinus elliottii*) stand on a poorly drained sand with subsurface soil hori-

zons that impeded vertical water movement. They found that average concentrations of NH_4^+-N and NO_3^--N remained below 3 mg/L and 7 mg/L, respectively.

A review of the aforementioned studies and others (NCASI 1999) revealed that concentration of NO_3^--N in soil solutions is generally less than 3 mg/L for nonfertilized soils but frequently peaks beyond 10 mg/L after fertilization. Many of the reviewed studies showed that concentrations remained above 10 mg/L for at least a year after fertilization, but authors of the review concluded that the highest values were likely not representative of operational fertilization practices. For instance, some of the highest values were seen after repeated annual fertilization, weekly fertigation, or heavy applications of nitrogen-rich sludge. The reviewers also concluded that high soil solution concentrations usually do not translate into high streamwater concentrations due to nitrogen removal and dilution. None of the reviewed studies revealed high NH_4^+ concentrations (NCASI 1999).

| Location, Stand Type | Treatment (kg/ha) | Application Method | Period | Chemical Concentration (mg/L) | | | | Reference |
| | | | | Nitrate-N | | Ammonium-N | | |
				max	ann. ave.	max	ann. ave.	
Arkansas, 3–4 yr loblolly pine	140 N as urea and AN	applied over 2 years, water sampled at 90–360 cm	2 yrs	<6				Wheeler et al. 1989
Arkansas, uneven-aged shortleaf/ loblolly pine	230 N as urea and AN	applied over 2 years, water sampled at 90–360 cm	2 yrs	25–30				Wheeler et al. 1989
Florida, slash pine plantation	34 N, 13 P, 28 K + micro-nutrients	single application, sampled at 80 cm			<7		<3	Segal et al. 1987
Georgia, 15-yr loblolly pine	control 225 N 225 N, 55 P 225 N, 44 P, 110 K	single application, sampled at 90–150 cm	1 yr. post fert.	<0.1 0.1 0.1 0.55			0.9	Grant 1991

Source: Table adapted from Binkley et al. 1999. NCASI Tech. Bull. No. 782. Reprinted by permission of NCASI.

To summarize the effects of forest fertilization on water quality, research has shown that changes in nutrient concentrations in water depend very much upon whether the fertilizer is allowed to enter water bodies or watercourses basically unaltered. Also, the largest changes in streamwater chemistry have been measured following fertilization with AN and with high rates or repeated doses of fertilizers. Nutrient concentrations in streamwater draining fertilized forests remain well below maximum concentrations permitted by drinking water standards. Maintaining untreated buffers along streams is a recommended practice. Nitrate concentration peaks above the recommended levels considered safe for drinking water have been measured in soil solution, but these usually do not translate into similar streamwater concentrations. Peak concentrations are usually transitory, particularly in streamwater.

Pesticides

In this chapter, the term *pesticide* refers to any chemical used to kill or control an organism that is detrimental to human activities, including herbicides, insecticides, fungicides, nematicides, acaricides, and rodenticides.

Herbicides are by far the most common pesticide in southern forestry today, so most of this review concerns this class of pesticide. Herbicides are used primarily to reduce or eliminate undesirable vegetation in order to channel more site resources to the crop species. Forestry use of insecticides and fungicides is most frequent in nurseries and seed orchards, where management is most intense and economic impacts of pests can be greatest. Although modern pesticides have been a boon to forest management, only twenty of the current 890 active ingredients of pesticides registered in the United States comprise more than 95 percent of all pesticides used in forestry (Michael 2000). Furthermore, although forests occupy 32 percent of all land in the United States, they receive only 1 percent of all pesticides used, and less than 1 percent of all forest land is treated annually (Michael 2000). Southern forest management is fairly intense relative to the remainder of the United States. In the twelve southern states, herbicide use increased 53 percent from 1996 to 1998, and a total of 256,345 ha were treated with herbicides in 1998, most through aerial application (Dubois et al. 1999).

Most modern pesticides are organic chemicals that are used at low rates and have good to excellent selectivity for the pest to be controlled. Organic pesticides can act more specifically than inorganic pesticides (Banks et al. 1992). Pesticides are usually applied in liquid form but can also be applied in dry form, usually as granules. Most concerns about environmental impacts of pesticides are related to off-site movement into aquatic systems, both during and after application. This movement is controlled by natural processes that can be summarized in two general categories: transfer processes and degradation processes, both of which can affect pesticides during and after application (Banks et al. 1992). Transfer processes change the location or availability of a pesticide to the target organism without changing the chemical structure or properties of the pesticide. Degradation processes change the chemical structure and alter or reduce the potency of the pesticide to the target organism. Transfer processes include physical drift, volatilization, adsorption, leaching, surface erosion, and plant or animal uptake. Degradation processes include photochemical, microbial, and chemical degradation and plant or animal metabolism (Banks et al. 1992). Major forestry pesticide characteristics are listed in table 5.

Herbicides

Fewer than a dozen herbicides account for the majority of silvicultural usage, both in terms of frequency and total applied amounts (Neary et al. 1993). These are 2,4-DP, dicamba, fosamine, picloram, sulfometuron methyl, tebuthiuron, 2,4-D, triclopyr, hexazinone, glyphosate, and imazapyr, the last five of which are the most common. Those used in seed orchards are usually from this same list, whereas nursery herbicides include the former list plus atrazine, bifenox, DCPA, diphenamid, napropamide, oxyflourofen, sethoxydim, and simazine (Neary et al. 1993).

Hexazinone is a selective triazine herbicide that is low in both toxicity and risk to aquatic and terrestrial organisms since toxicity thresholds are not commonly exceeded. Hexazinone residue and fate are better documented than those of any other southern forestry herbicide, likely due to its widespread usage and the fact that it is soil active. Miller and Brace (1980) reported concentrations as high as 2,400 µg/L from accidental di-

Table 5. Major forestry pesticide physical, chemical, environmental, and toxicological properties

Pesticide	Half-Life[a] (d)	Photo-Degradation	Microbial Degradation	Hydrolysis	Volatilization	LD50[b] (mg/kg)	LC50[c] (mg/L)
Herbicides							
2,4-D	28	minor	yes	yes	yes	375	168.0
Dicamba	25	no	yes	no	no	757	135.0
Fosamine	10	no	yes	no	no	24,400	278.0
Glyphosate	60	minor	yes	no	low	4,320	120.0
Hexazinone	30	yes	yes	no	low	1,690	370.0
Imazapyr	30	yes	yes	no	no	5,000	100.0
Picloram	60	yes	yes	yes	no	8,200	21.0
Sulfometuron	10	no	yes	yes	no	5,000	12.0
Triclopyr	45	rapid	yes	no	low	630	148.0
Insecticides							
Azinphosmethyl	30	yes	yes	yes	no	12	0.2
Carbofuran	60	no	yes	yes	no	8	0.2
Fenvalerate	35	yes	yes	yes	no	451	>0.1
Lindane	90	yes	yes	no	yes	88	>0.1
Malathion	20	yes	yes	yes	no	2,800	0.1

Source: Table adapted from Neary et al. 1993.

a. Average half-life in days.

b. LD50, technical grade for rats, based upon formulation

c. LC50 for bluegill sunfish, 96 hours.

rect application of hexazinone pellets to streamwater. However, concentrations fell within twenty-four hours to 110 μg/L and after ten days were down to less than 10 μg/L. Hexazinone was applied aerially to 20 percent of another watershed without direct application to the stream and was never detected in streamwater during a seven-month sampling period following application (Neary 1983).

Ground application of hexazinone has produced similar results to aerial applications concerning the greater impacts from direct application to watercourses. Hexazinone pellets were broadcast on four ephemeral, first-order watersheds in the upper Piedmont of Georgia (Neary et al. 1983). Streamflow occurred only after storms, and runoff from twenty-six storms was collected for one year following application. Residues peaked in the first storm (442 μg/L) and declined steadily thereafter. Loss of hexazinone from the treated sites averaged only 0.53 percent, with two storms accounting for nearly 60 percent of the off-site transport. In contrast, hexazinone was applied to an Arkansas watershed as a liquid spot application without treating the ephemeral stream channels (Bouchard et al. 1985). Even though application rates were higher than in the Georgia study, hexazinone residues were never detected in storm runoff. Base flow from the Arkansas watershed carried low concentrations of hexazinone (less than 14 μg/L) for over a year, and the total amount of herbicide transported out of the watershed was 2 to 3 percent of that applied.

Michael et al. (1998) aerially applied hexazinone as a pellet and as a liquid to watersheds in the Alabama Piedmont at a rate of 6.72 kg/ha, three times the rate prescribed for the study site. An untreated watershed served as a control. Hexazinone half-life in days for the pelleted form was 26–59 for plants, 55 for litter, 68 for bare soil, and 74 for soil under litter. For the liquid form, hexazinone half-life was 19–36 days for plants, 56 for litter, 77 for bare soils, and 275 for soil under litter. Maximum stream concentrations (422 μg/L for the pellets and 473 μg/L for the liquid) were observed during application and resulted from direct overspray. Hexazinone stream concentrations peaked several times during stormflow in the first thirty days and were diluted by three to five times 1.6 km downstream. Exposure of macroinvertebrates to hexazinone did not alter benthic community structure. Taxa richness did not differ significantly between treatments and control.

Sulfometuron methyl is a herbicide normally used for herbaceous weed control in newly established pine plantations. It was applied as water-dispersible granules and pellets to small watersheds in Florida with a five-meter streamside buffer strip (Neary and Michael 1989). Concentrations of residues detected in streamflow were low (less than 7 μg/L), did not persist beyond one week, and did not penetrate to groundwater that was less than one meter deep.

Triclopyr is a forestry herbicide favored for control of woody plants during site preparation as well as directed spray applications in existing young pine plantations. It was applied to small Florida watersheds in both the amine and ester formulations by a ground sprayer. Monitoring of both streamflow and groundwater (less than 1 m deep) for five months following application did not show any detectable residues of triclopyr (Bush et al. 1988).

Picloram is usually used in site preparation as a spray, or can be injected through tree bark, or can be sprayed directly on a freshly cut stump to prevent subsequent sprouting. An aerial application of picloram in the upper Coastal Plain of Alabama resulted in a streamflow concentration of 50 μg/L during the treatment and a peak stormflow concentration of 241 μg/L fourteen days later (Michael et al. 1989). Picloram concentrations were greater than 10 μg/L for the first hundred days after treatment and then less than 2 μg/L after 140 days through nearly one year. Streamflow concentrations were well below toxic levels for animals but were in the toxic range (greater than 10 μg/L) for sensitive plants.

Michael and Neary (1993) summarized several studies that monitored the environmental fate of forestry herbicides in the southern United States (table 6). Herbicide residues in surface water from injection-treated sites ranged from not detectable to 21 μg/L, for soil spot-applied from six to 442 μg/L, for broadcast by ground equipment from 1 to 10 μg/L, and for broadcast aerially from not detected to 2,400 μg/L. The very high residues from spot treatment on one site resulted from placing pellets directly in ephemeral drains. Michael and Neary (1993) concluded that herbicide contamination of surface water was very variable and depended upon method and rate of application, product formulation, and site-specific characteristics. Highest concentrations occurred in streams in ephemeral peaks during the first three storms following application. Streamside management zones (SMZs) greatly reduced the amount of herbicide entering streams. Soil persistence was highly variable and dependent upon many site characteristics, whereas plant residues dissipated rapidly with half-lives less than forty days.

Table 6. Maximum observed herbicide residues in streamflow from research sites in the southern U.S.

Herbicide	Location	Application Form[a]	Application Method[b]	Application Rate[c]	Surface Water[d]
Hexazinone	Arkansas	L	spot	2.0	14
Hexazinone	Alabama	L	spot	2.3	8
Hexazinone	Alabama	L	spot	2.9	24
Hexazinone	Alabama	L	spot	2.9	37
Hexazinone	Alabama	L	spot	2.9	23
Hexazinone	Georgia	L	spot	1.6	6
Hexazinone	Georgia	L	spot	1.6	9
Hexazinone	Florida	L	BCG	1.7	1.3
Hexazinone	Alabama	P	BCA	0.8	2,400
Hexazinone	Georgia	P	spot	1.7	442
Hexazinone	Tennessee	P	BCA	1.7	ND
Imazapyr	Alabama	L	BCA	2.2	680
Imazapyr	Alabama	L	BCA	2.2	130
Picloram	Georgia	L	inj	0.3	ND
Picloram	Georgia	L	inj	0.3	ND
Picloram	Georgia	L	inj	0.3	6
Picloram	Kentucky	L	inj	1.3	21
Picloram	Kentucky	L	inj	0.3	10
Picloram	Tennessee	L	inj	0.6	4
Picloram	Alabama	P	BCA	5.6	241
Picloram	North Carolina	P	BCG	5.0	10
Sulfometuron methyl	Mississippi	P	BCA	0.4	23
Sulfometuron methyl	Mississippi	DG	BCA	0.4	44
Sulfometuron methyl	Florida	P	BCG	0.4	5
Sulfometuron methyl	Florida	DG	BCG	0.4	7

Source: Table adapted from Michael and Neary 1993.

a. Liquid (L), dispersible granules mixed in water (DG), pellet/granule (P).

b. Stem injection (inj), soil spot application (spot), broadcast aerially (BCA), broadcast by ground (BCG).

c. Active ingredient applied in kg/ha.

d. Expressed as µg/L; ND is not detected.

Insecticides

As previously noted, most forestry insecticide use is confined to nurseries and seed orchards. However, widespread applications infrequently occur for such insect outbreaks as gypsy moth (*Lymantria dispar* L.) and southern pine beetle (*Dendroctonus frontalis* Zimmermann). Recently, insecticides such as tebufenozide are being recommended for Nantucket pine tip moth (*Rhyacionia frustrana* Comstock). The most common nursery and seed orchard insecticides include carbaryl, chlorpyrifos, diazinon, dimethoate, and fenvalerate. Acephate, diflubenzuron, dimilin, lindane, and trichlorofon are used in the control of large insect outbreaks. Additional insecticides used in seed orchards for control of cone and seed insects include azinphosmethyl, carbofuran, malathion, and permethrin (Neary et al. 1993). Of the total amount of insecticides used in American agriculture, it is estimated that only 0.01 percent are used in southern pine nurseries (South 1994).

Bush et al. (1986) reported very high concentrations in surface runoff after a ground application of 19.0 kg/ha of carbofuran in the Georgia Piedmont. This was a very high application rate for a forestry pesticide. Although concentrations reached as high as 7,820 µg/L in the year following application, carbofuran residues did not persist from year to year and were variable between years for the next three years.

Summary

Research shows that if silvicultural manipulations are carefully conducted, water quality impacts are relatively minor and of short duration. Even intensive even-aged management involving clearcutting and mechanical site preparation resulted in sediment losses that are low relative to those derived from other activities, such as construction and row-crop agriculture. Established forests protect and rebuild the soil resource and yield high quality water. It is only during the harvest and regeneration stage that soils are disturbed and exposed. Harvest cycles in the South range from ten to fifty years, depending upon management objectives. In contrast, row-crop soils are cultivated and exposed to the erosive power of falling and flowing water every year.

In recent years, mechanical site preparation activities have become much less intensive, often involving ripping (contour subsoiling) and clearing only the strips where seedlings are to be planted. The ripping treatment breaks up impervious soil layers, creates detention storage, and promotes infiltration of surface water. Furthermore, SMZs are now being left even on ephemeral streams— that is, those that flow only during a storm event. These strips of trees and brush left along drainages often trap sediment before it reaches the stream. These BMPs can further reduce the water quality impacts of silviculture.

In general, forestry use of pesticides poses a low pollution risk to groundwater due to its dispersed nature, low frequency of application, and low rates (Neary et al. 1993). In fact, Neary and Michael (1996) concluded that vegetation control from mechanical means can increase annual erosion by nearly 7 percent, whereas chemical control of competing vegetation did not increase natural erosion rates. The greatest potential hazard to groundwater comes from handling concentrates—(transport of formulations; storage; spilling during mixing; and loading, disposal, and rinsing of containers)—not from operational application of dilute mixtures (Neary et al. 1993). Furthermore, most forestry use of pesticides is confined to small-scale watersheds containing ephemeral or intermittent streams. Surface water sources used for drinking water are larger reservoirs or lakes wherein any pesticides added through forest management would be diluted to extremely low concentrations or subject to breakdown from the aforementioned degradation processes. Also, these water sources are not usually considered to be drinking water without treatment before consumption.

Forestry pesticides have not been identified in surface or groundwater at sufficiently high concentrations to impair drinking water quality. Avoiding direct application to water will generally preclude water contamination. Following accepted BMPs will enable the safe use of forestry pesticides. For instance, applicators should:

- Follow the manufacturer's label and all federal and state laws and regulations.
- Plan the operation to avoid the pesticide being applied off target or moving off target.
- An SMZ should be established and managed to protect water quality.
- Buffer areas should be established around all sensitive areas.
- All equipment used for transport and application must be properly maintained and adjusted to prevent leakage and spills.

References

Allen, H. L. "Forest Fertilizers: Nutrient Amendment, Stand Productivity and Environmental Impact." *Journal of Forestry* 85, no. 2 (1987): 37–46.

Banks, P. A., Schroeder, J., and J. B. Weber. *Fate of Pesticides in the Environment.* Las Cruces, N.M.: Marathon-Agricultural and Environmental Consulting, 1992.

Beasley, R. S. "Intensive Site Preparation and Sediment Losses on Steep Watersheds in the Gulf Coastal Plain." *Soil Sci. Soc. of Am. J.* 43 (1979): 412–17.

Beasley, R. S., and A. B. Granillo. "Soil Protection by Natural Vegetation on Clearcut Forest Land in Arkansas." *J. Soil and Water Conserv.* 40 (1985): 379–82.

———. "Sediment and Water Yields from Managed Forests on Flat Coastal Plain Sites." *Water Resour. Bul.* 24 (1988): 361–66.

Beasley, R. S., A. B. Granillo, and V. Zillmer. "Sediment Losses from Forest Management: Mechanical vs. Chemical Site Preparation after Clearcutting." *J. Environ. Qual.* 15 (1986): 413–16.

Blackburn, W. H., J. C. Wood, and M. G. DeHaven. "Stormflow and Sediment Losses from Site-Prepared Forestland in East Texas." *Water Resour. Res.* 22 (1986): 776–84.

Bouchard, D. C, J. L. Lavy, and E. R. Lawson. "Mobility and Persistence of Hexazinone in a Forested Watershed." *Journal of Environmental Quality* 14 (1985): 229–33.

Bush, P. B., D. G. Neary, and J. W. Taylor. "Effect of Triclopyramine and Ester Formulations on Groundwater and Surface Runoff Water Quality in the Coastal Plain." *Proc. Southern Weed Science Society* 39 (1988): 262–70.

Bush, P. B., D. G. Neary, J. W. Taylor, and W. L. Nutter. "Effects of Pesticide Use in a Pine Seed Orchard on Pesticide Levels in Fish." *Water Resources Bulletin* 22 (1986): 817–27.

Campbell, P. G. "Water Quality Mid-year Report." Weyerhaeuser Research and Development Report, New Bern Forestry Research Station, New Bern, N.C., 1989.

Campbell, P. G., J. R. Willis, and J. T. May. "Soil Disturbance by Logging with Rubber-tired Skidders." *Jour. Soil and Water Conserv.* 8 (1973): 218–20.

Dickerson, B. P. "Logging Disturbance on Erosive Sites in North Mississippi." Research Note SO-72. USDA Forest Service, Southern For. Exp. Sta., New Orleans, La. 1968.

Dubois, M. R., K. McNabb, and T. J. Straka. "Costs and Cost Trends for Forestry Practices in the South." *Forest Landowner* 58 (1999): 3–8.

Fisher, R. F. "Impact of Intensive Silviculture on Soil and Water Quality in a Coastal Lowland." In *Tropical Agricultural Hydrology*, ed. R. Lal and E. W. Russell, 299–309. New York: John Wiley and Sons, 1981.

Fromm, J. H., and R. B. Herrmann. "Jones 5 Fertilizer Runoff Monitoring—1992." Weyerhaeuser Research and Development Report, Proj. No. 050-9010, Southern Environmental Field Station, New Bern, N.C. 1996.

Global Environment Monitoring Programme (GEMS). "Atlas of Global Freshwater Resources." United Nations Environment Program, 1997. URL http://www.cciw.ca/gems/atlasgwq/ as of May 8, 2000.

Grant, M. J. Potassium Nutrition of Midrotation Loblolly Pine (*Pinus taeda* L.) Plantations on the Georgia Coastal Plain. M.S. thesis, Department of Forestry, North Carolina State University, Raleigh, 1991.

Havlin, J. L., J. D. Beaton, S. L. Tisdale, and W. L. Nelson. *Soil Fertility and Fertilizers; An Introduction to Nutrient Management,* 6th ed. Upper Saddle River, N.J.: Prentice Hall, 1999.

Herrmann, R. B., and W. M. White. "Jones 5 Fertilizer Runoff Monitoring—1983." Weyerhaeuser Research and Development Report, Proj. No. 050-9010, Southern Environmental Field Station, New Bern, N.C. 1996.

Lawson, E. R. "Throughfall and Stemflow in a Pine-hardwood Stand in the Ouachita Mountains of Arkansas." *Water Resour. Res.* 3 (1967): 731–35.

Michael, Jerry L. "Pesticides Used in Forestry and Their Impacts on Water Quality." In *Proceedings of the 53rd Annual Meeting, Southern Weed Science Society,* January 24–27, 2000, Tulsa, Okla. Champaign, Ill.: Southern Weed Science Society, 2000.

Michael, J. L., and D. G. Neary. "Herbicide Dissipation Studies in Southern Forest Ecosystems." *Environmental Toxicology and Chemistry* 12 (1993): 405–10.

Michael, J. L., D. G. Neary, and M. J. M. Wells. "Picloram Movement in Soil Solution and Streamflow from a Coastal Plain Forest." *Journal of Environmental Quality* 18 (1989): 89–95.

Michael, J. L., E. C. Webber, D. R. Bayne, J. B. Fischer, H. L. Gibbs, and W. C. Seesock. "Hexazinone Dissipation in Forest Ecosystems and Impacts on Aquatic Communities. *Can. J. For. Res.* 29 (1998): 1170–81.

Miller, E. L. "Sediment Yield and Storm Flow Response to Clearcut Harvest and Site Preparation in the Ouachita Mountains." *Water Resour. Res.* 20 (1984): 471–75.

Miller, E. L., R. S. Beasley, and E. R. Lawson. "Forest Harvest and Site Preparation Effects on Stormflow and Peakflow of Ephemeral Streams in the Ouachita Mountains." *J. of Env. Quality.* 17 (1988a): 212–18.

———. "Forest Harvest and Site Preparation Effects on Erosion and Sedimentation in the Ouachita Mountains." *J. of Env. Quality.* 17 (1988b): 219–25.

Miller, J. H., and A. C. Brace. "Streamwater Contamination after Aerial Application of Pelletized Herbicide." Research Note SO-255. USDA Forest Service, Southern For. Exp. Sta., New Orleans, La. 1980.

National Council of the Paper Industry for Air and Stream Improvement (NCASI). *Water Quality Effects of Forest Fertilization.* Technical Bulletin No. 782. Research Triangle Park, N.C.: NCASI, 1999.

North Carolina State Forest Nutrition Cooperative (NCSFNC). 28th Annual Report. College of Forest Resources, North Carolina State University, Raleigh, 1999.

Neary, D. G. "Monitoring Herbicide Residues in Springflow after an Operational Application of Hexazinone." *Southern Journal of Applied Forestry* 7 (1983): 217–23.

Neary, D. G., P. B. Bush, and J. E. Douglass. "Off-site Movement of Hexazinone in Stormflow and Baseflow from Forest Watersheds." *Weed Science* 31 (1983): 543–51.

Neary, D. G., P. B. Bush, and J. L. Michael. "Fate, Dissipation and Environmental Effects of Pesticides in Southern Forests: A Review of a Decade of Research Progress." *Environmental Toxicology and Chemistry* 12 (1993): 411–28.

Neary, D. G., and J. L. Michael. "Effect of Sulfometuron Methyl on Groundwater and Stream Quality in Coastal Plain Forest Watersheds." *Water Resources Bulletin* 25 (1989): 617–23.

———. "Herbicides: Protecting Longterm Sustainability and Water Quality in Forest Ecosystems." *New Zealand Journal of Forestry Science* 26, no. 1–2 (1996): 241–64.

Riekirk, H. "Forest Fertilizer and Runoff Water Quality." *Soil and Crop Science Society of Florida Proceedings* 48 (1989): 99–102.

Rogerson, T. L. "Hydrologic Characteristics of Mixed Hardwood Catchments in the Ozark Plateau." Pp. 327–33 in *Proc. First Central Hardwood Forest Conf.,* ed. J. S. Fralish, G. T. Weaver, and R. C. Schlesinger. Carbondale: Southern Illinois University, 1976.

Sanderford, S. G. *Forest Fertilization and Water Quality in the North Carolina Piedmont.* Technical Report no. 53. Raleigh: School of Forest Resources, North Carolina State University, 1975.

Schmidt, E. L. "Nitrification in Soil." In *Nitrogen in Agricultural Soils,* ed. F. J. Stevenson. Agronomy Monograph no. 22. Madison, Wis.: American Society of Agronomy, 1982.

Schreiber, J. D., and P. D. Duffy. "Sediment and Nutrient Transport from Pine Watersheds of the United States Southern Coastal Plain." In *Hydrologic Research Basins and Their Use in Water Resources Planning,* Proc., Int. Sym., Bern, Switzerland, September 21–23, 1982. Bern: Sonderh, Landeshrydrologie, 1982.

Scoles, S., S. Anderson, D. Turton, and E. Miller. *Forestry and Water Quality: A Review of Watershed Research in the Ouachita Mountains.* Circular E-932, Water Quality Series, Okla. Coop. Ext. Serv., Div. Agri. Sci. and Nat. Resour., Okla. State University. Undated.

Segal, D. S., D. G. Neary, G. R. Best, and J. L. Michael. "Effect of Ditching, Fertilization, and Herbicide Application on Ground Water Levels and Ground Water Quality in a Flatwood Spodosol." *Soil and Crop Science Society of Florida Proceedings.* 46 (1987): 107–12.

South, D. B. "Managing Pesticides and Nitrogen in Southern Pine Nurseries and Some Ways to Reduce the Potential for Groundwater Contamination." Auburn University School of Forestry Departmental Series no. 14, Auburn, Ala. 1994.

Ursic, S. J. "Hydrologic Effects of Prescribed Burning and Deadening Upland Hardwoods in Northern Mississippi." Research Note SO-542. USDA, Forest Service, Southern For. Exp. Sta., New Orleans, La. 1970.

———. "Water Quality Impacts of Harvesting and Regeneration Practices." In *Proc. "208" Symp.: Non-Point Sources of Pollution from Forested Land,* October 19–20, 1977. Carbondale: Southern Illinois University, 1977.

———. "Hydrologic Changes after Replacing Hardwoods with Southern Pine." In *Hydrological Res. Basins and their Use in Water Res. Planning: Proc., Int. Sym.,* Bern, Switzerland, Sept. 21–23, 1982. Bern: Sonderh, Landeshydrologie, 1982.

———. "Water Management, an Integral Element of Forest Management Planning." In *Proc., Southern Forest Symposium.* Atlanta, Ga. 1985.

———. "Sediment and Forestry Practices in the South." In *Proc. Fourth Federal Interagency Sedimentation Conf.,* Las Vegas, Nev. Vol. 1, sec. 2. 1986.

Ursic, S. J., and J. E. Douglass. "Effects of Forestry Practices on Water Resources." In *W. Kelly Mosley Envir. Forum,* Auburn, Ala. 1979.

U.S. Environmental Protection Agency (EPA). *Quality Criteria for Water.* EPA-440/5-86-001. Washington, D.C.: Office of Water Regulations and Standards, 1986.

———. 1998 Update of Ambient Water Quality Criteria for Ammonia. 1998. URL http://www.epa.gov/OST/standards/amonia.html as of May 10, 2000.

Wheeler, L., T. T. Ku, and R. J. Colvin. "The Effects of Silvicultural Practices on Soil Water Chemistry of Southern Pine Forests." In *Proceedings of the Fifth Biennial Southern Silvicultural Research Conference,* Memphis, Tenn., November 1–3, 1988. USDA Forest Service General Technical Rep. SO-74, 1989.

CHAPTER 19

Long-Term Trends in the Water Quality of Barton Springs, Austin, Texas

Martha A. Turner and David A. Johns

Environmental Resource Management Division

Watershed Protection Department, City of Austin

Abstract

Barton Springs, the major discharge point for the Barton Springs segment of the Edwards aquifer, is not only the primary habitat for the endangered Barton Springs salamander (Eurycea sosorum), *but it also supplies a portion of Austin's drinking water, provides winter and drought baseflow to the Colorado River downstream, and is an important recreational resource. Significant changes in Barton Springs' water quality have not been previously identified. However, with the passage of time, increased data collection efforts, and improved data separation methodology, several significant time trends have been documented. These trends in water quality are potentially related to watershed urbanization over the period of record (1975–99). Increasing specific conductance, sulfate, turbidity, and total organic carbon trends were noted to be significant. A decreasing trend in dissolved oxygen concentrations was also significant in Barton Springs. Significant trends were not noted in other parameters that are commonly considered pollutants, such as nutrients and total suspended solids. Constraints associated with using this type of data analysis for future predictions are discussed.*

The Edwards aquifer is one of the most prolific aquifers in the state, providing large volumes of high quality water to well users, feeding the state's largest springs, and supplying important baseflow to numerous river systems. The Edwards aquifer in the Balcones fault zone extends in a belt from Kenny County in southwest Texas to Bell County in north-central Texas. The Barton Springs segment of the Edwards aquifer extends from a groundwater divide near Kyle northward approximately twenty miles to the Colorado River in Austin. It is the single most important groundwater resource in the Austin area.

The fourth largest spring in Texas (Brune 1981), Barton Springs is the largest discharge point in the Barton Springs segment of the aquifer. Barton Springs has an average discharge of 50 cubic feet per second (cfs) with a maximum discharge of 166 cfs occurring in May, 1941, and a minimum discharge of 9.6 cfs occurring in March, 1956 (USGS 1995). Barton Springs is also known as Main or Parthenia Spring and has a series of associated spring outlets: Old Mill (also known as Sunken Gardens, Walsh, or Zenobia Spring), Eliza (Concession or Elks Pit), Upper Barton Springs, and Cold Springs (Deep Eddy). They discharge into Town Lake upstream of the Green Water Treatment Plant and therefore contribute to the drinking water supplies of the City of Austin (COA). The pool built around Barton Springs is a major attraction for the City and a revenue source for the Parks and Recreation Department. The Barton Springs salamander (*Eurycea sosorum*) inhabits four springs (Barton, Old Mill, Eliza, and Upper Barton Springs), and in April, 1997, the U.S. Fish and Wildlife Service (USFWS) listed the species as endangered.

The Barton Springs Edwards Aquifer (BSEA) consists

of the Georgetown Formation and Edwards Group (Rose 1972; Senger and Kreitler 1984; Slagle et al. 1986; Small et al. 1996). Several members within the Edwards are recognized at the surface and in the subsurface (Rose 1972; Small et al. 1996). The Barton Springs Zone (BSZ), the area contributing water to Barton Springs, can be divided into two geographic components: the recharge zone, defined as the surface outcrop of the Georgetown and Edwards limestones where water directly enters the aquifer, and the contributing zone, the area up gradient (upstream) of the recharge zone, generally underlain by the Glen Rose Formation where most of the water recharging the aquifer originates (Santos, Loomis and Associates 1995). The recharge zone for the BSEA covers an area of approximately ninety square miles The contributing zone for the BSEA comprises the watersheds of Barton, Slaughter, Williamson, Bear, Little Bear, and Onion creeks, covering an area of approximately 264 square miles

The Edwards aquifer is a karst aquifer. Porosity in the Edwards includes matrix porosity, generally intergranular voids of primary or secondary origin responsible for diffuse flow, and conduit porosity, secondary macroscopic voids associated with bedding surfaces, fault and fracture planes, and fossil molds responsible for conduit flow. These voids occur in the epikarst, or unsaturated zone, and the phreatic, or saturated zone. Dissolution by recharging waters has progressively enlarged openings in the limestone and dolomite host rock, creating an integrated network of conduits allowing rapid recharge from surface water and rapid groundwater movement to discharge points. Recharge waters enter the aquifer through point features such as caves, or solution-enlarged fractures, or as diffuse recharge through upland soils and bedrock surfaces.

Most water enters the aquifer through point recharge features in the creek beds of the six main creeks crossing the recharge zone. The difference in flow loss in different creek segments is probably most dependent on the number and size of point recharge features in the creek channel, which are related to particular geologic strata outcrops. A water balance study by the Center for Research in Water Resources has estimated that over 75 percent of the water discharging from the springs is provided by Onion Creek (46 percent) and Barton Creek (31 percent; Barrett and Charbeneau 1996). Previous researchers have documented the close relationship between rainfall and rapid response in discharge from the springs (Slade et al. 1986). Spring discharge can increase 20 to 30 cfs within twenty-four hours following heavy rains and 65 cfs within days

following very heavy rains. For example, Barton Springs discharge increased from 65 cfs to 130 cfs in four days following twelve inches of rain over five days in December of 1991 (USGS 1992).

Numerous investigators have studied the BSEA. Papers by Adkins (1933), Rodda and colleagues (1966), Fisher and Rodda (1969), and Rose (1972) provide the framework for Edwards stratigraphy. Mapping by Rodda and co-workers (1970) and Garner and Young (1976) are the most commonly used geologic maps of the Austin area. More detailed mapping of the recharge zone is presented by Small and colleagues (1996). Detailed hydrogeologic and water chemistry studies by the U.S. Geological Survey, Bureau of Economic Geology, and Texas Water Development Board have provided the basis for understanding recharge and chemical composition of the aquifer (Andrews et al. 1984; Slade et al. 1986; Senger and Kreitler 1984; Baker et al. 1986). A recent study by the Barton Springs/Edwards Aquifer Conservation District (Hauwert and Vickers 1994) documented several specific occurrences of water quality degradation within the aquifer and defined a probable major flow path in the vicinity of Sunset Valley leading toward Barton Springs. A City of Austin report (COA 1997) summarized spring chemistry, possible impacts due to urbanization, and rain impacts to the springs. Recent tracing studies in the aquifer have provided new information on contributing areas to specific springs, groundwater flow routes, and travel times from recharge features to discharge points (Hauwert et al. 1998). Many University of Texas graduate theses have focused on the Edwards.

Geochemically, Barton Springs water is a calcium bicarbonate–type water. Data show that Barton Springs is consistently in a relatively narrow field on Piper diagrams, trending slightly toward enrichment in sodium, chloride, and sulfate during low flow conditions (Senger and Kreitler 1984; Slade et al. 1986; COA 1997). During high flow conditions, particularly when the aquifer is receiving large volumes of recharge, Barton Springs concentrations are close to those of surface water. This is indicative of the rapid nature of groundwater migration in the Edwards when water has less contact time with host rocks and may reflect the large volume of recharge to the aquifer from creeks relatively close to the springs.

The chemical quality of Barton Springs has been the subject of considerable scrutiny as environmental and land development interests debate the effects or potential effects of urbanization on water quality of the springs. These examinations have focused primarily on whether the quality of water in Barton Springs has changed through the years. Unfortunately, historical chemical data for Barton Springs are sparse and not adequate to evaluate long-term time trends over the entire development history of the Barton Springs Zone. Time trend studies based on more recent chemical data from the U.S. Geological Survey (USGS), from the late 1970s through the early 1990s, have been inconclusive as to whether there have been increases in concentrations of many constituents commonly associated with nonpoint-source pollution, particularly nutrients and metals. Barrett and Charbeneau (1996) concluded that nitrate in Barton Springs has remained essentially unchanged from 1979 to 1995.

Several factors complicate time trend analysis, including natural variation in chemical concentration, rapid migration of storm waters in the aquifer, timing of sample collection in relation to storms, and the relationship of spring discharge volume to constituent concentrations (i.e., some decrease as flow increases). Senger and Kreitler (1984) documented the inverse relationship of discharge to sodium, chloride, and sulfate concentrations. Their evidence indicated that during periods of low discharge, water from the "bad-water" line crept into the main body of the aquifer; mixed with fresher aquifer water, increasing constituent concentrations; and discharged from Barton Springs. Andrews and colleagues (1984) and Slade and colleagues (1986) documented the relationship between bacteria and rainfall and illustrated the relationship between high discharge volumes and low specific conductance. Andrews also noted the inverse relationship between recharge volume and nitrate-nitrogen. Slade (1986) and Slade and co-workers (1986) documented the correlation between heavy rainfall and high turbidity in Barton Springs.

Austin's staff analysis of data collected since these early 1980s reports generally confirms the relationships previously discussed. Analysis of data collected by the USGS from 1978 to 1993 indicates that turbidity and bacteria are higher in spring samples following storms (defined in data sets as samples with bacteria concentrations greater than 100 colonies/100 mL) and specific conductance and magnesium were lower following storms. A number of chemical constituents are inversely related to spring discharge (i.e., they decrease as flow increases). These include total dissolved solids, specific conductance, nitrate-nitrogen, total nitrogen, magnesium, sodium, chloride, sulfate, and fluoride. Dissolved oxygen is directly related to discharge, with high concentrations during periods of

high spring discharge. T-tests of chemical constituents based on high flow versus low flow, with low flow being defined as spring discharge of less than 50 cfs, indicate a number of constituent relationships with flow conditions. Alkalinity, total dissolved solids, nitrate-nitrogen, hardness, magnesium, sodium, chloride, sulfate, and fluoride were all in lower concentrations during high discharge conditions. Dissolved oxygen and total suspended solids and fecal coliform bacteria were all higher during high discharge conditions.

Significant changes in Barton Springs water quality have not been previously identified. However, with the passage of time, increased data collection efforts and improved data separation methodology, several significant time trends have been documented.

Methodology

Data collected at Barton Springs by the U.S. Geological Survey, Austin Travis County Health Department, and City of Austin were used. This is a comprehensive data set in both period of record, 1975–99, and number of parameters.

Data reflecting two abnormal conditions, Barton Springs pool maintenance drawdown and a sewer line failure, were removed from the data set before analysis was begun. Data from these events are not representative and could obscure trends in parameter levels caused by long-term watershed impacts rather than localized short-term influences.

The remaining data were then separated into three flow categories: baseflow without recharge, baseflow with recharge, and stormflow. This separation was performed because the factors affecting water quality in the springs differ with the flow condition. During recharge, the water quality at the springs partially reflects the current water quality in the creeks, whether it is baseflow or stormflow (COA 1997). Under baseflow without recharge, the spring discharge would primarily reflect the long-term changes in aquifer water quality.

Discharge quality was used to separate stormwater from baseflow. Because neither rainfall in the large contributing area nor flow in the recharging creeks, nor Barton Springs flow rate, is a conclusive measure of the influence of stormflow conditions on the springs, water quality was used as a separation indicator. If fecal coliform counts were greater than 100 mg/L or total suspended solids were greater than 10 mg/L, then the data were labeled as indicative of storm conditions.

Daily flow in Barton Creek at Loop 360, inside the recharge zone, was examined to determine if recharge was occurring. If the flow was greater than zero then it was assumed that the data could be categorized as recharge. At times recharge may have been occurring in other watersheds when there was no flow in Barton Creek at Loop 360. However, from examination of concurrent gauge records in the recharge zone, this separation based on a single gauge is accurate in the vast majority of cases.

This partitioning of the data into flow categories is imperfect but conservative. That is, data placed in the wrong flow category will likely increase the variability in that category and obscure any actual trends occurring under that flow condition.

Analysis

Multiple linear regression analysis was used to determine whether parameter levels were changing over time. Dependent variables included each water quality parameter for three flow classes: baseflow with recharge, baseflow without recharge, and stormflow. The independent variables were spring discharge and time. A relationship between spring discharge levels and parameter levels for some parameters has been previously demonstrated at Barton Springs (Senger and Kreitler 1984; COA 1997). Hence, spring discharge was entered first in the regression model, followed by time. It could thus be determined whether time accounted for a significant amount of variation in the parameter levels in addition to the variance already accounted for by spring discharge. Relationships between water quality constituents and time, which are significant at the $P < 0.05$ or the $P < 0.10$ level were identified.

If a significant time trend was found for a parameter in the regression analysis, then the magnitude of the change in the constituent concentrations over time was calculated. For parameters with a significant relationship with spring discharge, the slope of the regression equation was used to normalize the concentrations to those that would have been expected at an average discharge of 50 cfs. The equation used to normalize the data was:

Normalized concentration = original concentration
+ (regression coefficient for discharge)
* (50 cfs—spring discharge).

Median concentrations were calculated for each five-year period from 1975 to 1999 using the original data if the relationship with spring discharge was not significant or the normalized data if it was significant. Medians were used, rather than means, to reduce the impact of outliers and of values that are in the wrong flow category due to uncertainties in the data separation process.

The earliest sampling dates are in either the 1975–79 or the 1980–84 period, depending on parameter. The increase or decrease in a parameter was determined by difference in the period medians from the earliest and most recent five-year period. The percent change in the parameter concentrations was determined from the size of the change in the concentrations divided by the median concentration level during the earliest period.

Results

Parameters with significant changes over time included specific conductance, dissolved oxygen, organic carbon, sulfate, and turbidity. Regression r-squares, model and coefficient probabilities, coefficient estimates and standard errors are shown in table 1. Those numbers indicating regression coefficients for time that were significant at the 0.10 level but not at the 0.05 alpha level are noted in table 1. The regression model, including both discharge and time variables, was significant at the 0.05 level in all cases.

Significant relationships to spring discharge for parameters with significant changes over time are also listed in table 1. In general, dissolved oxygen increases with increasing discharge, whereas specific conductance, sulfate, and turbidity decrease with increasing discharge. Organic carbon is not significantly related to spring discharge under any flow condition.

The size, percentage, and direction of the change in these five parameters with significant time trends are summarized in table 2. The paragraphs below describe the significant changes identified for each individual parameters by this analysis.

Figure 1 shows the measured dissolved oxygen concentrations during baseflow, both with and without recharge, with matching discharge levels. A decrease over time at both high discharge levels (mid-1980s, early 1990s, and late 1990s) and low ones (late 1970s, around 1990, and mid-1990s) is apparent. The need for separating the variation due to discharge from the variation due to time is evident from this plot. During baseflow, when recharge was not occurring, dissolved oxygen levels have decreased significantly over time. Figure 2 shows these dissolved oxygen concentrations normalized to a discharge of 50 cfs. The median normalized dissolved oxygen concentration has

Table 1. Regression r-squares, model and coefficient probabilities, coefficient estimates, and standard errors

| Parameter/Flow Condition | Model | | Regression Coefficients | | | | | |
| | | | Discharge | | | Time | | |
	PR>F	R-Square	PR>|t|	Estimate	Standard Error	PR>|t|	Estimate	Standard Error
Dissolved Oxygen								
Baseflow without recharge	<0.0001	0.59	<0.0001	0.03	0.004	0.0016	−0.00015	0.00004
Total Organic Carbon								
Stormflow	0.0404	0.1	0.7538	0.01	0.03	0.0116	0.0009	0.0003
Specific Conductance								
Baseflow without recharge	<0.0001	0.34	<0.0001	−1.19	0.14	0.0663[a]	0.0037	0.002
Baseflow with recharge	0.0002	0.18	0.0304	−0.45	0.21	<0.0001	0.0106	0.0024
Stormflow	<0.0001	0.29	<0.0001	−0.98	0.14	0.0257	0.0051	0.0023
Sulfate								
Baseflow with recharge	0.0062	0.36	0.0163	−0.15	0.06	0.0016	0.0023	0.0006
Turbidity								
Stormflow	<0.0001	0.19	0.0001	−0.12	0.03	0.064[a]	0.001	0.0005

a. Significant at the 0.1 level but not at the 0.05 level.

Table 2. Change in constituent levels over two to twenty-five years

| Parameter | Flow Condition | Normalized Period Medians | | | |
		1975–79 or 1980–84[a] Median	1995–99 Median	Change over Approx. 20 Years	Percent Change
Dissolved Oxygen (mg/L)	Baseflow without recharge	6.8	5.7	−1.1	−16%
Organic Carbon (mg/L)	Stormflow	1.5	3.4	1.9	127%
Specific Conductance (μS/cm)	Baseflow without recharge	655	677	22[b]	3%
	Baseflow with recharge	590[a]	646	56	9%
	Stormflow	624	642	18	3%
Sulfate (mg/L)	Baseflow with recharge	28.3[a]	38.8	10.5	37%
Turbidity (NTU)	Storm flow	5.3	7	1.7[b]	32%[b]

a. Actually 1980, 1983, and 1984, since 1981 and 1982 were removed from the analysis due to a sewer line break.

b. Significant at the 0.1 level but not at the 0.05 level.

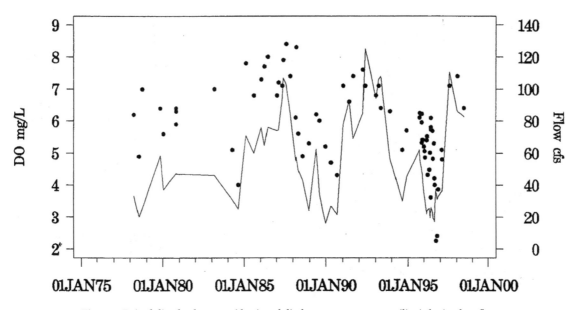

Figure 1. Paired dissolved oxygen (dots) and discharge measurements (line) during baseflow.

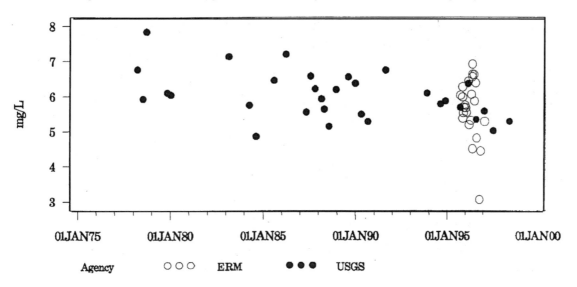

Agency   ○ ○ ○   ERM   ● ● ●   USGS

Figure 2. Normalized dissolved oxygen during baseflow without recharge.

decreased approximately 1.1 mg/L over the last twenty-five years, from 6.8 to 5.7 mg/L, a decrease of 16 percent.

During nonrecharge and low spring discharge levels, the measured dissolved oxygen concentration sometimes drops below 4 mg/L. Independent time series measurements levels by the City of Austin of dissolved oxygen in Barton Springs have been below 4 mg/L approximately 11 percent of the time during an approximately four-year period of recent record. These data were not included in the regression and magnitude of change analyses since the water quality separation variables were not concurrently measured. Since the range of dissolved oxygen levels tol-

erated by the endangered Barton Springs salamander (*Eurycea sosorum*) is unknown, any decreases in dissolved oxygen are of concern.

Organic carbon has increased during stormflow only. This increase is shown in figure 3. The outliers, which were not plotted, were 18.2 mg/L in 1990 and 42 mg/L in 1998. The size of the increase in median concentration over the last twenty-five years is 1.9 mg/L, from 1.5 to 3.4 mg/L. This is an increase of 127 percent. Perhaps increased deposition of degradable organic carbon in the aquifer during stormflow may lead to decreases in dissolved oxygen during baseflow when there is no recharge occurring.

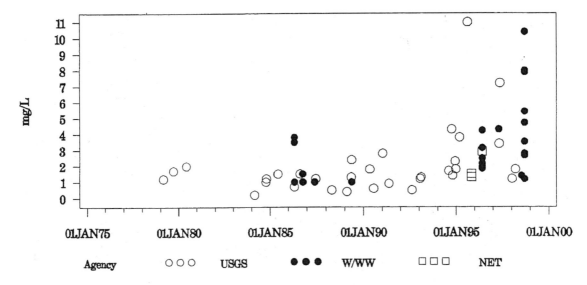

Figure 3. Total organic carbon during stormflow.

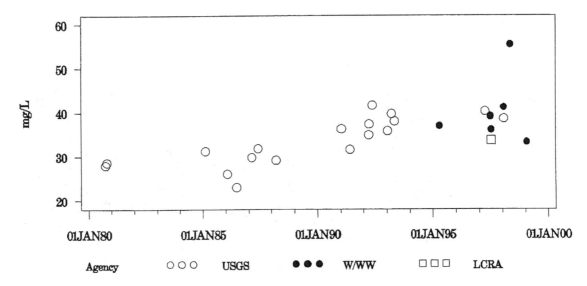

Figure 4. Normalized sulfate during baseflow with recharge.

However, the cause and effect relationship between organic carbon and dissolved oxygen trends cannot be determined with concurrent sampling alone.

Specific conductance has increased during all flow conditions over the past twenty to twenty-five years. The largest change is observed during baseflow with recharge and is estimated to be a 9 percent change. Stormflow changes are estimated to be 3 percent, and during baseflow without recharge, the change is also 3 percent. These concentrations are not plotted because changes of 3 and 9 percent are not visually apparent. The median normalized concentration during baseflow without recharge increased from 655 to 677 µS/cm. For comparison, these

concentrations both lie between the mean baseflow concentrations of 566 µS/cm for much smaller rural springs and 867 µS/cm for much smaller springs in newer urban settings in the Jollyville Plateau (COA 1999). However, the increase noted in Barton Springs may be an indicator of future change in Barton Springs to more of an urban spring chemical signature.

Sulfate has increased during baseflow when recharge is occurring. Median normalized sulfate concentrations have increased approximately 10.5 mg/L, from 28.3 to 38.8 mg/L. This is an increase of 37 percent over a twenty-year period. The normalized concentrations are shown in figure 4. Sulfate levels have been found to be fairly consistent

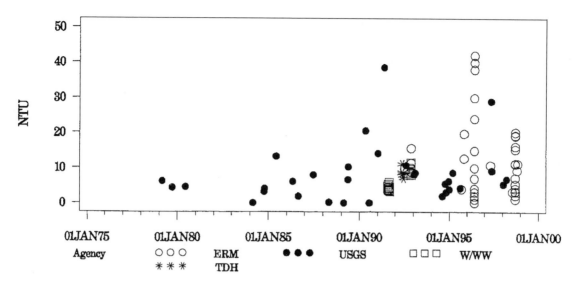

Figure 5. Normalized turbidity during stormflow.

Table 3. Percent of turbidity concentrations in selected ranges for three time periods

Period NTU	Baseflow without Recharge		Baseflow with Recharge		Stormflow	
	0–2 NTU	>2 NTU	0–2 NTU	>2 NTU	0–12 NTU	>12
1975–89	100%		82%	18%	100%	
1990–94	97%	3%	85%	15%	95%	5%
1995–99	75%	23%	28%	72%	67%	33%

NTU = nephelometric turbidity unit.

indicators of urbanization in much smaller springs in the Jollyville Plateau region of the Austin area and the contributing zone of Barton Creek (Johns 1994; Johns and Pope 1998; COA 1999). In the Jollyville Plateau area, mean concentrations in rural springs ranged from 12 to 26 mg/L, whereas mean concentrations in newer urban springs ranged from 43 to 59 mg/L (COA 1999). The current median concentrations in Barton Springs lie between these two groups. Again, this increase may be an early indicator of the effects of watershed urbanization that are not reflected in more commonly considered nonpoint-source pollutants.

Turbidity has increased significantly over time during stormflow. Turbidity is significantly inversely proportional to spring discharge. The average increase in normalized stormwater turbidity is 1.7 NTU, from 5.3 to 7 NTU. This is an increase of about 32 percent over the past twenty years. Normalized stormwater turbidity concentrations are shown in figure 5. It should be noted that the comprehensive sampling of several recent storms, in an

effort to measure turbidity over the entire stormflow hydrograph, affects the significance of the regression. Only single grab samples were obtained for most other storm events. Replacement of storm event data with the median concentration causes the regression to be nonsignificant (P < 0.15); however, the regression is still significant (P < 0.06) when the event data is replaced with the maximum single grab taken over the storm event.

Changes in turbidity during baseflow are not significant due to the variability of the data and the large number of very low concentrations, but there is some indication that change is occurring. Table 3 shows the percentage of turbidity measurements that fell within various ranges for three periods. Prior to 1990, under baseflow conditions, 82 percent of the turbidity levels during recharge were less than 2 NTU, and all stormflow turbidities were less than 12 NTU. In the past five years, 72 percent of the baseflow turbidity levels during recharge conditions were between 2 and 12 NTU, and 33 percent of stormflow turbidities were between 12 and 50 NTU. Although short-term turbidity increases are expected during storm conditions as a watershed is urbanized, baseflow increases in turbidity may also be an early indicator of such watershed changes.

Future Conditions

While trends in Barton Springs water quality have been demonstrated statistically, the projection of these changes into the future is problematic. The regression model r-square is not high in most cases. Many factors that affect the water quality of Barton Springs, such as antecedent weather conditions, spill events, and construction loads, are not included in the model. These factors can not be adequately characterized over the entire period from 1975 to 1999 and thus could not be included in the model. Hence, the regression model should not be used to predict water quality concentrations for any particular date in the future. The prediction of average water quality at Barton Springs also poses difficulties. The regression model is linear. Water quality changes in response to environmental stresses may be linear over a certain range of stress levels and then change abruptly once a threshold is reached. Thus predictions of average conditions made by extrapolating the rate of change during the past twenty years will likely be inaccurate. Future rates of change will depend on the rates of change in environmental stressors and possible threshold conditions. Insofar as we can prevent increases in environmental stresses in the contributing and recharge zone of Barton Springs, increased degradation of the water quality at the springs may be prevented.

Additional parameters of interest may be increasing, but the increase is not yet large enough or the sample size is too small to demonstrate a statistically significant trend at this time. Continued monitoring and periodic updates of these analyses may identify trends in these parameters, especially where there are indications of change not yet supported by statistics. Examples include turbidity under baseflow conditions as discussed; turbidity following storms, where anecdotal evidence suggests lower levels in the past; and nitrate-nitrogen where recent low flow concentrations are greater than under similar conditions in the past.

Conclusions

The analysis of long-term water quality records from Barton Springs indicates statistically significant changes in water quality, which could be related to watershed ur-

banization. Increasing conductivity, sulfate, turbidity, and total organic carbon trends were noted to be significant. A decreasing trend in dissolved oxygen concentration was also found to be significant. Significance and presence of trends is variable depending on flow conditions (i.e., baseflow vs. stormflow, recharge vs. nonrecharge).

Increases in conductivity and sulfates during baseflow conditions may be an early indication of ongoing long-term changes in spring chemistry. We have observed that these two parameters are typically elevated in springs in small urbanized watersheds as compared to similar springs in undeveloped watersheds. The data are not yet sufficient to determine if the trends are accelerating over time.

Increases in turbidity and organic carbon during stormflow conditions and the decreasing trend in dissolved oxygen during baseflow conditions may be a result of increased transport of organic matter into the aquifer and subsequent decay. Although these changes do not represent an immediate threat to aquatic life, they should be monitored closely as they may precede increases in other parameters of concern (nutrients, total suspended solids, pesticides/herbicides).

The noted changes took place over a twenty-five-year period and do not indicate imminent impairment of uses, or impacts to aquatic life, or warrant drastic modification in the City's current initiatives to protect the springs. The trends also do not support any relaxation in protective measures currently in place.

If noted trends continue and accelerate, increases in turbidity and decreases in dissolved oxygen may be the first concerns in relation to impacts on the Barton Springs salamander. If, as in smaller springs, watershed urbanization results in higher concentrations of more conventional pollutants such as nutrients and suspended solids, degradation of habitat due to siltation and more frequent and severe algae blooms may be of concern.

Significant trends were not noted in other parameters that are commonly considered pollutants, such as nutrients and total suspended solids. Continued monitoring and periodic updates of these analyses are warranted to detect any changes in pollutants that would be of more immediate concern to maintaining water quality for drinking water supplies and maintenance of high quality habitat for aquatic life.

References

Adkins, W. S. "The Mesozoic Systems in Texas." In *The Geology of Texas*, vol. 1: *Stratigraphy*. Edited by E. H. Sellards, W. S.

Adkins, and F. B. Plummer, 239–517. Bulletin 3232. University of Texas, Austin, 1933.

Andrews, F. L., T. L. Schertz, R. M. Slade, Jr., and Jack Rawson. *Effects of Storm-Water Runoff on Water Quality of the Edwards Aquifer near Austin, Texas.* U.S. Geological Survey Water-Resources Investigations Report 84-4124, 1984.

Baker, E. T., Jr., R. M. Slade, Jr., M. E. Dorsey, L. M. Ruiz, and G. L. Duffin. *Geohydrology of the Edwards Aquifer in the Austin Area, Texas.* Texas Department of Water Resources Report 293, 1986.

Barrett, M. E., and R. J. Charbeneau. *A Parsimonious Model for Simulation of Flow and Transport in a Karst Aquifer.* Technical Report 269. Center for Research in Water Resources, University of Texas, Austin, 1996.

Brune, Gunnar. *Springs of Texas.* Fort Worth: Branch-Smith, 1981.

City of Austin (COA). *The Barton Creek Report.* COA, Drainage Utility Department (DUD), Environmental Resource Management (ERM). Water Quality Report Series COA-ERM/1997, 1997.

———. *Jollyville Plateau Water Quality and Salamander Assessment,* COA, WPD, ERM. Water Quality Report Series COA-ERM/1999-01, 1999.

Fisher, W. L., and P. U. Rodda. "Edwards Formation (Lower Cretaceous)," in *Texas: Dolomitization in a Carbonate Platform System.* Bureau of Economic Geology Geologic Circular 69-1. University of Texas, Austin, 1969.

Garner, L. E., and K. P. Young. *Environmental Geology of the Austin Area: An Aid to Urban Planning.* Report of Investigations 86. Austin: Bureau of Economic Geology, 1976.

German, E. R. *Analysis of Nonpoint-Source Ground-Water Contamination in Relation to Land Use: Assessment of Nonpoint-Source Contamination in Central Florida.* Prepared in cooperation with the Florida Department of Environmental Protection. U.S. Geological Survey Water-Supply Paper 2381-F, 1996.

Hauwert, N. M., D. A. Johns, and T. J. Aley. *Preliminary Report on Groundwater Tracing Studies within the Barton and Williamson Creek Watersheds, Barton Springs/Edwards Aquifer.* Barton Springs/Edwards Aquifer Conservation District and City of Austin/Watershed Protection Department, 1998.

Hauwert, N. M., and S. Vickers. *Barton Springs/Edwards Aquifer Hydrogeology and Ground Water Quality.* Barton Springs/Edwards Aquifer Conservation District Report to the Texas Water Development Board, 1994.

Johns, D. A. "Ground Water Quality in the Bull Creek Basin, Austin, Texas." In *Edwards Aquifer: Water Aquifer and Land Development in the Austin Area, Texas.* Edited by D. A. Johns and C. M. Woodruff, Jr. Geological Society Guidebook 15. Austin, 1994.

Johns, D. A., and S. R. Pope. "Urban Impacts on the Chemistry of Shallow Groundwater: Barton Creek Watershed, Austin, Texas." *Gulf Coast Association of Geological Societies Transactions* 48 (1998): 129–38.

Rodda, P. U., W. L. Fisher, W. R. Payne, and D. A. Scofield. *Limestone and Dolomite Resources, Lower Cretaceous Rocks, Texas.* Report of Investigations 56. Austin: Bureau of Economic Geology, 1966.

Rodda, P. U., L. E. Garner, and G. L. Dawe. *Austin West, Travis County, Texas.* Geologic Quadrangle Map 38. Austin: Bureau of Economic Geology, 1970.

Rose, P. R. Edwards Group. *Surface and Subsurface, Central Texas.* Report of Investigations 74. Austin: Bureau of Economic Geology, 1972.

Santos, Loomis and Associates. *Barton Springs Contributing Zone Retrofit Master Plan,* vol. 2, *Assessment of Water Quality.* Prepared for the City of Austin Environmental and Conservation Services Department, 1995.

SAS Institute. *SAS/STAT® User's Guide.* Version 6, 4th ed., vol. 2. Cary, N.C.: SAS Institute, 1989.

Senger, R. K., and C. W. Kreitler. *Hydrogeology of the Edwards Aquifer, Austin Area, Central Texas.* Report of Investigations 141. Austin: Bureau of Economic Geology, 1984.

Slade, R. M., Jr., M. E. Dorsey, and S. L. Stewart. *Hydrology and Water Quality of the Edwards Aquifer Associated with Barton Springs in the Austin Area, Texas.* U.S. Geological Survey Water-Resources Investigations Report 86-4036, 1986.

Slagle, D. L., A. F. Ardis, and R. M. Slade, Jr. *Recharge Zone of the Edwards Aquifer Hydrologically Associated with Barton Springs in the Austin Area, Texas.* U.S. Geological Survey Water-Resource Investigations Report 86-4062, 1986.

Small, Ted A., John A. Hanson, and Nico M. Hauwert. *Geologic Framework and Hydrogeologic Characteristics of the Edwards Aquifer Outcrop (Barton Springs Segment), Northeastern Hays and Southwestern Travis Counties, Texas.* U.S. Geological Survey Water-Resources Investigations 96-4306, 1996.

U.S. Geological Survey (USGS). *Water Resources Data: Texas, Water Year 1992.* U.S. Geological Survey Water-Data Report TX 92-3, 1993.

U.S. Geological Survey (USGS). *Water Resources Data: Texas, Water Year 1995.* U.S. Geological Survey Water-Data Report TX 95-3, 1996.

U.S. Geological Survey (USGS). *Water Resources Data: Texas, Water Year 1998.* U.S. Geological Survey Water-Data Report TX 98-3, 1999.

CHAPTER 20

Educating the Public about Water Resources Research at Texas Universities

Ric Jensen

Assistant Research Scientist

Texas Water Resources Institute

Texas A&M University

Abstract

This chapter describes the use of content analysis of New Waves, *the research-based newsletter of the Texas Water Resources Institute (TWRI), as well as an analysis of research projects funded by the institute. The goal is to ascertain whether TWRI research and public information programs during the 1990s accurately reflect a multi-university focus, as is the goal of the National Water Resources Research Institute (NIWR). TWRI seeks to be a resource for all the universities in Texas, not just Texas A&M. Results show that roughly 60 percent of the research projects allocated by TWRI were awarded to Texas A&M University (TAMU). Roughly 83 percent of projects funded by TWRI were given to scientists affiliated with the TAMU system. In contrast, the articles presented in* New Waves *represent a much broader portrayal of research by various universities. Although Texas A&M University research was cited most often (roughly 20 percent), substantial coverage was also given to the University of Texas at Austin (11 percent), Texas Tech University (6 percent), the Texas Agricultural Experiment Station (6 percent), Texas A&M–Corpus Christi, the University of Houston, and Southwest Texas State University (4 percent*

each). The reason the institute's research program largely focuses on Texas A&M may be explained by the fact that, in addition to administering a competitive program funded by NIWR, TWRI also supports research activities within the TAMU System Agriculture Program. Perhaps a more accurate reflection of TWRI research funding would be to look solely at research projects specifically awarded through NIWR funds. On the other hand, New Waves *was created with the intent of featuring news about research projects throughout Texas and has largely accomplished this purpose. Perhaps a better way of evaluating the content of* New Waves *might be to conduct another content analysis that would omit TWRI research projects from the articles that are examined. In other words, part of the reason the newsletter may seem to emphasize Texas A&M research so much is that we presented many research projects funded by the institute, several of which were funded at TAMU. In sum, I think the case can be made that TWRI does a fairly good job at funding research projects at multiple universities throughout Texas, especially when compared to the vast majority of water resources research centers in Texas, which serve only to support a specific university. Additionally,* New Waves *works to present research-based in-*

formation from several universities, in stark contrast to the publications of other water resources centers, which promote or disseminate only research news from the host college.

The intent in this chapter is to describe briefly the role of the Texas Water Resources Institute (TWRI) in fostering collaboration between many universities, both in research and in public information.

A content analysis of individual articles from issues of the TWRI *New Waves* newsletter was performed for the period 1990 through 2000. Efforts were made to group articles in terms of the number of instances in which TWRI involved different universities as well as by the types of issues discussed. In addition, education efforts of the institute are presented, as is its work in reaching out to initiate collaborative projects. Finally, personal insights of the author are provided about the means that may be most promising in communicating water resources information in the future.

A premise of this analysis is that the *New Waves* newsletter is to some extent representative of the work of TWRI and, in a broad sense, of the extent to which various Texas universities are involved in water resources research. However, it would be logical to extend this work to gather additional information on broad water resources issues investigated by other groups as well as more quantifiable institutional data on activities in this field performed by universities throughout Texas.

The Unique Role of the Institute

To understand the work of the institute, a brief overview of the history, scope, and role of its program is needed. TWRI is part of a national group of water resources research institutes, which were established by the U.S. Congress in the 1960s. One institute is designated as the representative for its state; TWRI represents Texas. For the most part, institutes are located at land grant universities.

Throughout the history of this program, the mission of the institutes has been clearly designated. Some of the fundamental principles that institutes work to achieve include administering a small competitive grants program open to all the universities in its state, strengthening the capacity and enthusiasm of universities to become involved in water resources research, and supporting graduate students so that future water resources professionals can be trained. In addition, many institutes (including TWRI) have made it a priority to communicate the research and extension efforts of all the universities in each state to the public.

Therefore, even though there are many water resources centers located at universities throughout Texas (table 1),

Table 1. Selected environmental and water resources centers at Texas universities

University	Resource Center
Lamar University	Gulf Coast Hazardous Substance Research Center
Sam Houston State	Texas Regional Institute for Environmental Studies
Texas State University–San Marcos	Edwards Aquifer Research and Data Center
Tarleton State University	Texas Institute for Applied Environmental Research
Texas A&M International University	Center for Earth and Environmental Studies
Texas A&M University	Sea Grant Program
TAMU–Commerce	Water Resources Center
TAMU–Galveston	Galveston Bay National Estuary Program
TAMU–Kingsville	Wellhausen Water Resources Center
Texas Christian University	Center for Remote Sensing
Texas Tech	Water Resources Center
University of Houston–Clear Lake	Environmental Institute of Houston
University of North Texas	Institute for Applied Sciences
University of Texas–Austin	Center for Research in Water Resources
University of Texas–El Paso	Center for Environmental Resources Management
University of Texas–San Antonio	Center for Water Research
University of Texas–Pan American	Center for Coastal Studies
West Texas A&M University	Dryland Agriculture Institute

for the most part these units serve a different role than TWRI in that they typically serve only the host institution and do not fund research, service, and information activities at different universities. The only exceptions may be the National Estuary Programs supported by the U.S. Environmental Protection Agency, focused on Galveston Bay and Corpus Christi Bay (these programs sponsored studies over a limited period) and the Gulf Coast Hazardous Substance Research Center at Lamar University, which supports the work of a consortium of universities dealing with hazardous waste issues.

TWRI is unusual in other ways. Because the institute is an operating unit of the Texas Agricultural Experiment Station and the Texas A&M University System Agriculture Program, TWRI has often been active in issues related to agriculture, natural resources, wildlife and fisheries science, and other rural concerns. As a result, the institute has often funded small research and education efforts within the Texas A&M University System and the Texas A&M University Agriculture Program. Recently, TWRI has become active in spurring ad hoc efforts to assemble teams of scientists from different disciplines, typically involving numerous academic departments and units from the Texas A&M University System.

How This Analysis Was Conducted

An informal content analysis of articles presented from 1990 to 2000 in the TWRI quarterly newsletter *New Waves* was conducted. The newsletter is written and edited by the author of this chapter. Its purpose is to explain the work of TWRI to the public in easily understood terms. In addition, the newsletter provides summaries of research and service efforts at universities throughout Texas, even if they are not related to TWRI. In particular, a thought-ful effort is made to craft the newsletter so that it presents a broad-based and representative view of work at the many colleges in Texas, not just Texas A&M or the Texas A&M University System.

Roughly a thousand individual articles were published in *New Waves* during this period. It should be noted, though, that only articles specifically mentioning the work of a particular university were classified for this assessment. To perform the content analysis, subject categories intended to represent the major concerns about water resources issues were arbitrarily selected by the author. The appropriateness of these classifications can be debated. As each article was examined, it was assigned to subject categories.

Most articles were assigned to multiple subject categories. Thus the number of articles segregated overrepresents the actual number of projects sponsored by TWRI as well as the number of articles that have been published in *New Waves*. However, it is thought that this analysis will accurately convey the relative proportion of spotlighting of various universities and the subjects that have been discussed most often.

Activities by TWRI during This Period

A listing of various universities involved in TWRI projects is shown in table 2, and the topics of these projects are shown in table 3. A total of 112 articles discussed projects funded by TWRI.

Obviously, the vast majority of the research supported by TWRI was at Texas A&M University (69 articles, or 61 percent) and within the universities of the Texas A&M University System (94 articles, or 83 percent). This includes more than one article about TWRI projects associated with the Texas Agricultural Extension Service (10 ar-

Table 2. TWRI projects, grouped by university

University	No. Projects	University	No. Projects
North Texas	1	Texas Christian University	2
Sam Houston State	1	Tarleton State	2
Texas State University	3	Texas Tech	1
Texas A&M University	69	University of Houston	1
TAMU–Commerce	1	University of North Texas	1
TAMU–Galveston	1	University of Texas	7
TAMU–Kingsville	2	University of Texas–Dallas	1
Texas Agricultural Experiment Service	9	University of Texas–San Antonio	1
Texas Agricultural Extension Service	10		

Table 3. TWRI Projects, grouped by subject

Subjects	No. of Projects	Subjects	No. of Projects
Agriculture and irrigation	19	On-site wastewater systems	3
Aquaculture	3	Policy issues	29
Aquatic biology	9	Pollution	17
Coastal issues	3	Recreation	1
Computer modeling	23	Rivers & lakes	20
Conservation and reuse	8	Rural issues	2
Dams	8	Salinity	3
Drought	2	Texas–Mexico issues	2
Economics	13	Wastewater	3
Education	12	Water quality	12
Erosion and sediments	4	Water use	3
GIS & remote sensing	9	Water and wastewater management	23
Groundwater	14	Water and wastewater treatment	4
Human health and drinking water	3	Wetlands	3
Hydrology and runoff	11	World wide web	9
Industries and hazardous waste	4		

ticles), Texas Agricultural Experiment Station (9), Texas A&M University–Kingsville (2), and Tarleton State University (2). Still, it should be pointed out that projects were also funded at seven universities that are not part of the Texas A&M family, including seven projects at the University of Texas at Austin (6.2 percent) and two studies at Texas State University (2.7 percent).

Since TWRI was given increased control over which universities would be selected for funding two years ago, three of four projects awarded were to colleges not part of the Texas A&M University System. The point is that one may make the case that TWRI does work to support research at different universities throughout Texas, even though it has to be taken into account that one of the primary missions of the institute is to facilitate and strengthen work at Texas A&M.

Another way of examining the work of the institute is via the subject categories, which approximate the types of work TWRI has funded. In all, thirty-one topics containing 279 articles were identified. A rough analysis shows that the types of research and service work supported by TWRI most often focused the following themes (in order): policy issues and water rights (29 articles, or 10.2 percent), water and wastewater management (23 articles, 8.8 percent), computer modeling (23 articles, 8.8 percent), studies of reservoirs, lakes, and rivers (20 articles, 7 percent), agriculture and irrigation (19 articles, 6.5 percent), and pollution (17 articles, or 6 percent). In general, this

demonstrates that the institute has embraced the use of high tech methods, such as computer modeling, to investigate water issues. Additionally, the protection and maintenance of water quality continues to be a major thrust.

Articles Published in the *New Waves*

During the 1990s *New Waves* presented 1,042 articles giving news about water resources activities from forty-seven universities in Texas (table 4). In fact, it may be difficult to find a Texas university working with water resources research or service that was not featured in the newsletter. Consistently, TWRI has worked to incorporate the work of as many universities as possible in *New Waves*.

Breaking down the articles according to the university or unit featured (for example, the Texas Agricultural Extension Service) shows that the institutions most often highlighted include the state's flagship colleges—Texas A&M (296 articles, or 19.7 percent) and the University of Texas at Austin (119 articles, 11.4 percent). The high number of instances in which Texas A&M was included is explained in large part by the fact that the newsletter works to feature the work of TWRI. Much of the work of the institute involves collaboration between TWRI and many TAMU departments.

Other universities and academic units that were often mentioned include Texas Tech University (69 articles, or

Table 4. *New Waves* articles, grouped by university

University	No. of Articles	University	No. of Articles
Abilene Christian	2	TAMU–Kingsville	34
Angelo State	1	TAMU Sea Grant	3
Baylor	29	Texas Agricultural Experiment Station	62
Central Texas College	1	Texas Agricultural Extension Service	31
Concordia Lutheran	1	Texas Engineering Extension Service	3
Hardin-Simmons	1	Texas Transportation Institute	4
Incarnate Word	1	Texas Christian University	17
Lamar	23	Texas Southern University	4
Midwestern State	1	Texas Tech	69
North Texas State	38	Texas Women's University	1
Prairie View A&M	6	University of Houston	42
Rice University	38	University of Houston–Clear Lake	10
St. Mary's University	1	University of Texas	119
Sam Houston State	4	University of Texas–Arlington	17
Southern Methodist	10	University of Texas–Brownsville	5
Stephen F. Austin	14	University of Texas–Dallas	7
Texas State University–San Marcos	41	University of Texas Marine Sciences	13
Sul Ross State	1	University of Texas Medical Schools	12
Tarleton State	29	University of Texas–El Paso	17
Texas A&M University	206	University of Texas–Pan American	15
Texas A&M International	7	University of Texas–Permian Basin	1
TAMU–Commerce	11	University of Texas–San Antonio	14
TAMU–Corpus Christi	43	West Texas A&M	12
TAMU–Galveston	20		

6.6 percent), the Texas Agricultural Experiment Station (62, 5.9 percent), Texas A&M University–Corpus Christi (43, 4.1 percent), the University of Houston (42, 4 percent), Texas State University (41, 3.9 per cent), the University of North Texas and Rice University (38 articles each, 3.6 percent), Texas Agricultural Extension Service (31, 2.9 percent), Baylor University (29, 2.7 percent), Tarleton State University (29, 2.9 percent), Lamar University (23, 2.2 percent), and Texas A&M University–Galveston (20, 1.9 percent). Additionally, a number of universities were spotlighted more than ten times (roughly 1 percent of all the articles), including Stephen F. Austin State, Southern Methodist, and Texas Christian University, the University of Houston–Clear Lake, the University of Texas at Arlington, El Paso, and San Antonio, University of Texas–Pan American, UT Marine Sciences Institute, and West Texas A&M University.

What sorts of insights does this information provide? In most cases, the universities that were most often written about in *New Waves* share at least one of the follow-ing features. First, they are typically larger institutions that invest in research (such as Texas A&M University and the University of Texas at Austin). Second, these universities are often correlated with the presence of a water resources or environmental center at their campus (for example, Texas A&M University–Corpus Christi housed the Coastal Bend National Estuary Program) or have developed a core of expertise in one or more areas associated with water resources. For instance, Stephen F. Austin State University does a lot of work with the biology of inland streams, while Rice University has worked extensively with groundwater pollution and remediation. Finally, some universities have been frequently covered as a result of their excellent public affairs functions, which are the most ambitious at informing us (and other trade magazines and newsletters) of research at their schools. Texas A&M–Kingsville comes to mind in this regard.

A brief analysis by subject (see table 5) yields a total of 2,795 presentations in *New Waves* in a slightly different set

Table 5. *New Waves* articles, listed by topic

Article Topics	No. of Articles	Article Topics	No. of Articles
Agriculture and irrigation	158	Lakes and rivers	201
Aquaculture	29	Landscapes	19
Aquatic biology	170	Navigation and transportation	34
Coastal issues, bays, and estuaries	118	On-site wastewater systems	12
Climate and climate change	48	Policy issues and water rights	154
Computer modeling	124	Pollution	209
Conservation and reuse	73	Range lands and forests	20
Dams	18	Recreation	19
Drought	22	Rural issues	20
Economics	65	Salinity	35
Education	27	Subsidence	3
Energy	10	Texas–Mexico issues	51
Erosion and sediments	29	Wastewater	19
Flooding	28	Water and wastewater management	169
GIS and remote sensing	89	Water quality	108
Groundwater	145	Water and wastewater treatment	119
History and archaeology	52	Water use	73
Human health and drinking water	60	Wetlands	28
Hydrology and runoff	117	World wide web	29
Industrial and hazardous wastes	91		

of subjects than the breakdown in table 2, more specifically reflecting the large number of stories published in the newsletter. Results of this analysis suggest that the emphasis of the greatest number of articles was on pollution (209 articles, or 7.5 percent), followed by studies of lakes and rivers (201, 7.2 percent), work in aquatic biology (170, 6.1 percent), water and wastewater management (169, 6.1 percent), agriculture and irrigation (158, 5.6 percent), policy issues and water rights (154, 5.5 percent), and groundwater (145, 5.2 percent). Other subjects featured somewhat regularly (at least 60 times, or roughly 2 percent) are coastal issues including bays and estuaries, the development and use of computer models, economics, water conservation, recycling and reuse, human health and drinking water, industrial and hazardous wastes, the use of remote sensing and geographic information systems, efforts to study water quality, water and wastewater treatment, and water use.

One could perhaps make the case that the articles are somewhat representative of Texas' major water resources issues. They certainly seem to a large extent to mirror many of the concerns of water managers and planners in the state, although more detailed analysis would be useful.

Comparing TWRI Efforts with Articles Published in *New Waves*

Comparing TWRI work with articles in *New Waves* does show some potentially interesting trends. For example, the greatest number of TWRI projects were awarded to (in order) Texas A&M University, the Texas Agricultural Extension Service, Texas Agricultural Experiment Station, and University of Texas at Austin. The universities most often mentioned in *New Waves* were much the same, although in a different ranking (Texas A&M University followed by the University of Texas at Austin, Texas Tech University, the Texas Agricultural Experiment Station, Texas A&M University–Corpus Christi, and the University of Houston).

In a similar vein, the subjects of TWRI projects are somewhat similar to topics presented in the newsletter. A rough analysis shows that the topics of research and service work supported by TWRI most often focused on the themes of water and wastewater management, computer modeling, studies of reservoirs, lakes and rivers, agriculture and irrigation, pollution, and groundwater. Results of this analysis suggest that the emphasis of the largest number of *New Waves* articles was on pollution, followed by studies of lakes and rivers, work in aquatic biology, water and wastewater management, agriculture and irrigation, policy issues and water rights, and groundwater (145 articles or 5.2 percent). Major discrepancies were in the subjects of aquatic biology (which featured prominently in *New Waves* but not in TWRI projects) and computer modeling (which was often a feature of TWRI projects but was not among the topics most often featured in *New Waves*).

Other Educational Activities of TWRI

The *New Waves* newsletter is just one of the many educational efforts of TWRI. The technology transfer and information dissemination efforts of the institute also include the hosting of major conferences, publishing technical reports, additional newsletter series, and, more recently, use of the World Wide Web (WWW) and Internet list servers.

During the 1990s, the institute has sponsored and cosponsored many major conferences in which research-based information is presented to scientists, policy makers, and the public. Topics of TWRI conferences have centered on such issues as state water planning efforts, water quality in rivers, lakes, and groundwater systems, pollution prevention, the influence of agricultural activities on water quality, water conservation, the development and use of computer models to better manage water systems, and Texas-Mexico border issues. Whenever possible, TWRI publishes proceedings from these conferences.

Over the years, the institute has sponsored many newsletters discussing regional and national water resources issues as well as efforts at Texas universities. Currently, TWRI produces three other quarterly newsletter series: *Texas Water Resources* is a six-page newsletter that focuses on a single topic and provides an in-depth look at a specific water resources concern; *Texas On-Site Insights* informs readers of new developments in on-site wastewater treatment systems and how to manage these units; and *Texas Water Savers* discusses trends in water conservation reuse and recycling. It is noteworthy that the *Texas On-Site Insights* and *Texas Water Savers* are largely supported by external funds.

Since 1996, TWRI has been active in WWW sites and Internet list servers. For example, the main Web site of the Institute is "Texas WaterNet" (http://twri.tamu.edu). This site contains the full text and photos of articles published in TWRI newsletters, a directory of water resources experts at Texas universities, abstracts of technical reports, descriptions of projects funded by the institute, links to many other web sites, and many other features. The site is equipped with powerful search features which enable users to combine search terms and seek information from specific portions of home pages. In addition, TWRI has also developed WWW sites to support its work in on-site wastewater treatment, water conservation, and environmental and natural resources issues.

At the same time, TWRI has also been moderating and hosting Internet list servers related to specific water-related topics. These efforts send e-mail messages to individual subscribers' addresses. After messages have been distributed, they are archived onto the TWRI World Wide Web sites. The e-mail list servers are quite useful in rapidly communicating timely information, and they allow people both to ask questions and to comment on issues to a larger group. In essence, the e-mail list servers create a type of "virtual community" in which people can participate in live discussions across broad distances. The list servers sponsored by TWRI include "WaterTalk" (which includes a wide range of water resources issues), "SepticTalk" (focusing on on-site wastewater treatment), and "TX-Water-Ed" (emphasizing water conservation). So far, roughly five hundred individuals are signed up to receive messages from these list servers.

At times, the institute has supported other purely educational efforts. These include an evaluation of the extent to which public school teachers were using the Internet in the mid-1990s for classroom science teaching, developing a CD-ROM for public school use to teach about environmental science and natural resources issues, and incorporating water-based themes into a children's museum.

In many instances, these educational efforts (along with related work in technology transfer) have resulted in the application and implementation of work being done by scientists at Texas universities.

Trends for Future TWRI Communication to the Public

Traditionally, TWRI has conducted its public information program through the use of traditional methods— printing newsletters and reports and mailing them to consumers. About five years ago, the institute changed its direction slightly. For the present it is continuing to produce printed newsletters and reports but, at the same time, is posting these materials onto the WWW and circulating them via e-mail.

In the future, we are considering abandoning the

printed publications and going to a purely Internet- and WWW-based strategy. This would mean that users would have to have access to the Internet so as to download information and would have to pick up the cost of printing it themselves. The advantage would be that TWRI would free up funding by abandoning printed publications and would be adopting and using the latest and most efficient technologies.

A critical issue that must be considered, however, is the extent to which the institute may risk abandoning traditional customers by switching over to the Internet-only mode. Many people who currently rely on TWRI communications for information live in rural areas and may not be ready or willing to lose printed information in favor of e-mail or the web. Therefore, we may find less of a need for, and less use of, our educational efforts if we abandon printed publications.

Summary and Conclusion

Throughout the 1990s, the Texas Water Resources Institute has served a unique role in providing resources to support university efforts in water research across Texas. This is evidenced by the number of universities funded by the Institute and the broad spectrum of research topics the insti-

tute has sponsored. In much the same way, the education program of TWRI is also, at its core, multidisciplinary and multi-university. The institute intentionally strives to present a wide array of information about many universities and subjects. The *New Waves* newsletter, in particular, can be used to illustrate the inclusive nature of the institute's programs. A content analysis shows that this series has successfully showcased the work of many universities in Texas as well as discussing diverse water issues.

At the same time, it must be recognized that TWRI, like many other institutions, constantly needs to reassess the nature of present efforts, both in terms of the types of materials being developed and as regards how they are being delivered. At some point, the institute needs to evaluate seriously if it should switch over totally to Internet-based products, abandon printed works, and consider emerging technologies.

Related Works

Jensen, R. "Increasing Awareness about On-Site Wastewater Issues in Texas: Work of the Texas Water Resources Institute in Newsletters, World Wide Web Sites, and Internet List Servers." In *Proceedings of the 2000 Conference of the Texas On-Site Wastewater Treatment Research Council*, Waco.

CHAPTER 21

Reuse as a Viable Option in Water Resource Development

A Discussion of the Legal Framework Governing Reuse Projects

Edmond R. McCarthy, Jr.

Partner

Jackson, Sjoberg, McCarthy and Wilson, L.L.P.

Michael A. Gershon

Senior Associate

Lloyd, Gosselink, Blevins, Rochelle, Baldwin and Townsend, P.C.

Abstract

Development of reuse water projects certainly depends upon technical requirements and economic practicalities of the end user. In many parts of the state facing scarce resources, reuse is fiscally practical, and communities have begun to look at reuse projects more seriously. Aside from the economic analyses and specific technical requirements of the end user—whether an industrial cooling facility or golf course—the Texas Legislature has tailored the statutory framework governing reuse water projects, and the Texas Commission on Evnironmental Quality (TCEQ), formerly the Texas Natural Resource Conservation Commission (TNRCC), has adopted regulations implementing these statutes.

This chapter examines the parameters of the pertinent statutory provisions governing these projects and the TCEQ's implementing regulations. The chapter focuses on some of the more significant legal hurdles to consummating a reuse project, including water quality requirements, the necessity of a "bed-and-banks" permit for indirect reuse, instream flow restrictions, and consideration of conflicting claims to the water as a property right.

An irreplaceable necessity for all living things, water is probably our most precious resource. Unlike many other natural resources, water is a "renewable resource." The supply, however, is finite.

Through the natural "water cycle," water resources on average are replenished through precipitation in roughly the same quantity each year.[1] That average, however, includes periods of prolonged drought and of heavy rainfall. Demand, resulting from increased population, and to support industrial and related applications, is quickly outstripping the renewable capability of the resource.[2] Accordingly, the extremes in the average must be anticipated and planned for by water managers. The available rainfall must be captured and conserved for use during the periods of drought.[3] Building additional reservoirs to capture and store the rainfall when it occurs, however, does not increase this finite renewable resource. Instead, such reservoirs provide the traditional water supply strategy of storage to make the finite resource available for extended periods during the droughts that are also part of the hydrologic cycle.

As the population of Texas continues to mushroom, water managers must develop and implement strategies to increase, enhance, and whenever possible, renew and/or extend the "usability" of Texas' limited surface and groundwater resources.[4] Reuse of the available water resources, along with other nontraditional strategies, must be implemented to meet both existing and growing water demands.[5]

Overview of Reuse Development

During his tenure as chairman of the former Texas Water Commission, the late Buck Wynne jokingly used to introduce his presentations at environmental law seminars around the state with the following quote: "The good news is we will all soon be drinking treated wastewater. The bad news is there will not be enough to go around."[6]

Historically, the reuse of water in Texas focused primarily on commercial or industrial operations, and agricultural applications. Reuse of water for municipal and domestic purposes has not only been minimal, but in many instances it was avoided. On the municipal side, the development of "reuse water" as a municipal potable water supply strategy has been hampered by both the available technology and its cost. It has also been avoided because of the historical, philosophical, and political resistance of both municipal suppliers and end users to acknowledging that the use of treated effluent for potable purposes was both viable and inevitable.[7]

Ironically, the traditional methodology for the disposal of municipal wastewater—that is, discharges from wastewater treatment plant outfalls into state water courses—has resulted in the municipal reuse in discharges in the sense of potable reuse by individuals downstream of treated wastewater. Albeit inadvertent or unintentional, we have been recycling reuse water for years.

Similarly, large industrial users have discharged wastewater (both treated and untreated) back into water courses for years. Tailwater from agricultural applications has also contributed to downstream flows and, consequently, been reused. Accordingly, to a large extent, we have been practicing an unorganized form of water reuse throughout our history.

Until recently, such unorganized reuse caused us to focus primarily on the development of standards for wastewater discharges to improve the quality of the effluent returned to state water courses. This emphasis on treatment quality was for the protection of health and human safety as well as for the environmental needs of the water courses themselves and the habitats they support. Exploiting the recycled water (at least "treated wastewater") for its water supply potential, however, was not regularly considered because of what naively had been considered to be abundant supplies of fresh water.

The consequence of recycling water that has once been used beneficially is to put it to beneficial use at points downstream, by other municipalities that draw water from the river for their municipal supplies as well as by agricultural and industrial users. It also provides for inflows for bays and estuaries and other environmental instream uses, including water for aquatic and riparian habitats and recreation.

In response to our recent water crisis resulting from drought conditions and growing population and resultant demand for additional supplies, water policy "gurus" have focused on the organized reuse of treated wastewater in the development of water supply strategies for the future. As one might expect, industrial and agricultural use of such wastewater flows has developed more quickly than use for potable water supplies for domestic and municipal needs. In part, the nonpotable applications have developed more quickly because of the economic incentives to reduce production costs.[8] At the municipal level, however, use of treated wastewater for *nonpotable* purposes has been evolving over the last twenty years.[9]

Wastewater reuse, or the use of so-called reclaimed water and greywater, has several potential benefits. The reclaimed water can be used to meet nonpotable demands, including industrial applications and irrigation use for parks, golf courses, and other landscaping needs.[10] Developing new strategies for use of reclaimed water provides a substitute for potable purposes and frees up and/or extends the availability of other water supplies for potable uses. Use of reclaimed water without returning it to water courses, so-called direct reuse, has been lauded by environmentalists as more protective of our environment. Reclaimed water can be made available for groundwater recharge as well as aquifer storage and recovery projects, with the recharged reclaimed water becoming available for both potable and nonpotable water purposes.[11] The use of reclaimed water, rather than disposal in on-site septic systems, not only creates additional water supplies but provides greater protection to native groundwater quality.[12]

Throughout the years, water planning officials have recognized that the freedom Texans once enjoyed to live almost anywhere in the state has been curtailed by a combination of the demand for water caused by an increase in population growth in the state and the natural climatogical characteristics of Texas, which become aggravated during recurring drought conditions.[13] As the population of Texas exploded in the midst of recurring drought conditions and dwindling water supplies, and given the absence of any new water storage reservoirs coming online and the high costs and long lead time to build new reservoirs, municipal water purveyors began to rethink how reusing their own reclaimed water might be a viable option.[14] In response, the legislature took steps to regulate the use of state water courses to transport and capture reclaimed water as a source of potable municipal water supplies.[15] The TCEQ provides guidelines for the use of reclaimed water in its chapter 210 rules.[16]

Additionally, the creation of the regional water planning process, as a result of modifications to the state water planning process in Senate Bill 1, pushed the development of water strategies down to the local level. Regional planning groups from around the state, appointed by the Texas Water Development Board, are charged with assessing available water strategies and preparing a recommendation for inclusion in the state plan. According to a study by the Texas Water Resources Institute (TWRI) at Texas A&M University, the critical elements of regional planning studies of potential water development strategies include the following five elements:

(1) Improved conservation;
(2) Reuse;
(3) Reallocation of existing supplies;
(4) Demand reduction; and
(5) Drought management strategies.[17]

These five critical elements were broken down in the study into twenty water demand management and supply strategy options.[18]

TWRI conducted a survey of the sixteen statewide regional planning groups in which the groups were asked to participate in a "preference-feasibility analysis" of the twenty options. The groups were asked to rank each of the options on a five-point scale of preference ranging from "do not prefer" to "strongly prefer." Similarly, regarding feasibility, the groups were asked to rank each of the options from "not feasible" to "very feasible." In connection with their ranking of the feasibility of a particular option, the groups were required to answer a questionnaire that had them consider any combination of economic, environmental, legal, political, or technical factors that limited the feasibility of the strategy option. The results of the study were tabulated and graphed by TWRI.[19] The data results speak loud and clear. On a statewide basis, reuse is one of the most preferred and feasible water strategy options available to regional planners.[20]

This conclusion regarding reuse, in varying degrees, includes the reuse of treated wastewater, requiring residential reuse of greywater, and requiring industrial reuse systems. While not touting the report as conclusive, it certainly supports the notion that reuse of our limited water resources is a water strategy to be favorably considered at the local, regional, and statewide levels.

Direct versus Indirect Reuse

The development of an organized approach to the implementation of water reuse has also sparked a debate over the virtues and vices of direct reuse versus indirect reuse. In addition to varying requirements associated with reuse of water based upon the quality of its treatment, legal questions exist depending upon whether the so-called reclaimed water originated as privately owned groundwater or state-owned surface water. Depending upon the source of the water, the authorization requirements also vary based on whether the reclaimed water is to be directly or indirectly reused.

Direct reuse contemplates that water having been beneficially used for its intended purpose is then recirculated in a closed system for a secondary beneficial use. In an industrial or commercial context, a closed system contemplates water being piped between points of use, treatment, and reuse. In an agricultural context a "closed" system may contemplate the use of tailwater retention ponds coupled with open irrigation ditches and canals to move water between points of use and reuse within the closed irrigation system. Alternatively, a municipal or domestic system might transport the beneficially used water in a closed collection system to a wastewater treatment plant, where it is treated to the required quality level and then transported directly from the wastewater treatment plant, again in a closed system, to the point of end use.

In the first scenario, water used in industrial applications is sometimes recirculated in a closed system and reused after only minimal or no treatment. Water quality requirements do not mandate any significant treatment, including removal of solids or other chemical treatment, prior to recirculation in a closed system for some industrial applications.

In the scenario concerning municipal or domestic reuse, wastewater is treated in a wastewater facility permitted by TCEQ and then piped directly from the wastewater treatment plant to locations for reuse, such as in irrigation for parks, golf courses, or playing fields, and/or is pumped to industrial users.[21] In most instances, the reuse water is treated but not to potable standards. However, research and technological developments present growing opportunities for piping water directly from a wastewater treatment plant to a water treatment plant which will then continue to treat the reclaimed water to a potable level.

Indirect reuse, on the other hand, involves the transportation of water that has been beneficially used to a point of reuse without the use of a closed system. Examples of indirect reuse include agricultural applications. Tailwaters from crop irrigation are often captured and then transported in open canals or down water courses for diversion and additional agricultural purposes a second, third, or fourth time. Additionally, as is contemplated in subsections 11.042(b)–(c) of the Texas Water Code, municipal and domestic wastewater collected and treated at a wastewater discharge plant would be discharged through a wastewater outfall to a water course and would then flow downstream to a point of intended use. It is this latter form of indirect reuse that creates the most excitement—for both water purveyors and environmentalists.

Water purveyors are looking for the opportunity to capture the reclaimed water and transport it downstream for additional use at the lowest possible cost. Using the "bed-and-banks" of a state water course to transport reclaimed water downstream has almost no capital costs associated with it in the sense of having to build and construct pipelines, pumping stations, or storage facilities. The largest cost of this type of transport involves accounting for "carriage losses" and the possible reductions in the amount of flow that can be diverted based upon special conditions imposed by the TCEQ in a bed-and-banks authorization.[22] Direct reuse in a closed system, on the other hand, requires the capital investment in pipelines, booster pumps, and storage facilities as well as easements and rights-of-way for construction of such facilities.

Environmentalists assert that direct reuse is better for the environment. Indirect reuse, they argue, results in the water course being used to "polish" the wastewater or provide additional incremental levels of treatment once the water is discharged into the stream. The argument is flawed, however. The discharge can only occur legally if done pursuant to a wastewater discharge permit issued by TCEQ pursuant to chapter 26 of the Texas Water Code, with all of its water quality protections. The argument also ignores the potentially more invasive impacts on the environment caused by the construction of pipelines and other facilities required to accomplish direct reuse. Additionally, the capital investment significantly increases the cost of the project. All of these costs are ultimately transferred to the system customers through rates. The higher cost components associated with direct reuse may cause a project to be economically infeasible in many instances.

Wastewater Permitting Considerations and Use of Reclaimed Water

As part of the wastewater discharge permit process, reuse can and should be addressed. In other words, if you expect to recycle some of your wastewater, either by direct or indirect reuse, it should be incorporated into your wastewater permit or amendment application. Issues to be addressed in that permitting process, as appropriate, include the volume of discharge to be reused; location and type of reuse (this may impact the level of treatment required); identification of any party or parties who will or may reuse the water; whether reuse will be direct or indirect; and whether any contract exists for the reuse.

By addressing these issues in an anticipatory fashion during the permitting process, delay and additional cost of further permitting at a future date can be avoided. A corollary to addressing anticipated reuse in the wastewater permitting processes is to request reuse authorization in the water rights permitting process.

General requirements for the use of reclaimed water, as well as the related issues of treatment quality criteria and design and operational requirements for the beneficial use of reclaimed water, are addressed in the TCEQ regulations at chapter 210.[23] Authorization to use reclaimed water does not provide a substitute for a discharge permit issued under chapter 305 if a discharge into the waters of the state is contemplated.[24]

Chapter 210 requires that a producer of "reclaimed water" use it in accordance with the terms and conditions of its wastewater permit. If the producer is not the intended user, then the applicable notice and authorization requirements under chapter 210 are triggered.[25] Chapter 210 does not apply to reuse authorized by a permit issued pursuant to chapter 305 of the TCEQ rules governing "consolidated permits" or on-site wastewater treatment systems authorized by chapter 285.[26]

Prior to providing reclaimed water to a third party, the producer must provide written notice to the TCEQ Executive Director *and* receive written approval.[27] The notice requirements are enumerated in section 210.4. If the "provider" of the reclaimed water is not the "producer," the notice must include a copy of an agreement with the producer authorizing the transfer and identifying the origin.[28] If the producer intends to use the reclaimed waters within the boundaries of a wastewater facility permitted by the commission, no notice is required. However, the producer must otherwise comply with the Chapter 210 requirements. If there are any "major changes" in the use of the reclaimed water after the required notice and approval have been completed, a new notice must be filed and approval obtained. Major changes include such things as the location of use, the type of use, and the addition of new producers.[29] Prior to using reclaimed water within the Edwards aquifer recharge zone, the project must be approved pursuant to chapter 213 as well as chapter 210 of the rules.[30]

The producer, provider, and user of the reclaimed water all have specific minimum responsibilities specified in chapter 210. To ensure its beneficial use, reclaimed water can only be supplied on a "demand basis." The user has the right to refuse delivery at any time. As a result, any plan for using reclaimed water should have an adequate storage component. Notwithstanding the demand condition, the user must comply with a proper agreement between the parties related to the reclaimed water—for example, take or pay provisions and providing adequate storage.[31]

Treated wastewater eligible for use as "reclaimed water" is categorized in chapter 210 as Type I and Type II reclaimed water. Type I reclaimed water can be used for residential irrigation; irrigation of public parks, golf courses, school yards, and athletic fields; fire protection (hydrants and building sprinkler systems); irrigation of food crops, including contact with the edible part of the crop, unless the crop will undergo a pasteurization process; pasture irrigation for "milking animals"; maintaining water levels in ponds, reservoirs, etc.; and toilet flushing.[32]

Type II reclaimed water use is more restrictive, requiring that public access and the likelihood of human exposure be limited. Type II water can be used for irrigation of "remote" sites; irrigation of sites bordered by walls or fences and where access is controlled by the site owner or operator; irrigation of public access areas if public access is restricted during the irrigation, such as on a golf course at night or in cemeteries; irrigation of crops *if* reclaimed water is not likely to have direct contact with the edible part of the crop; irrigation of animal feed crops—other than pastures for milking animals; water impoundments where direct human contact is unlikely; soil compaction or dust control at construction sites; cooling tower make-up water; and irrigation and other nonpotable uses at a wastewater facility.[33]

Delivering Reuse Water Down the Banks and Beds of State Water Courses

Section 11.042 of the Texas Water Code, entitled "Delivering Water Down Banks and Beds," contains the statutory authority for the TCEQ to issue what are commonly known as bed-and-banks permits. Prior to 1997, the statute only contemplated state regulation of the use of the bed and banks of state water courses to convey water out of storage in a reservoir to a downstream place of use or diversion by an appropriator for a beneficial use authorized under chapter 11 of the Texas Water Code.[34] Section 11.042 was silent with regard to the use of the bed-and-banks of a state water course to convey treated wastewater pursuant to a commission-issued permit, prior to the passage of Senate Bill 1 in 1997.[35]

In Senate Bill 1, however, the Legislature enacted specific authority for the TCEQ to issue bed-and-banks permits from and after September 1, 1997, for waters other than those being released from storage.[36] Pursuant to the amended section 11.042, TCEQ purportedly obtained authority to regulate persons wishing to reuse water that originated as either state water or as privately owned groundwater *if* the water is to be discharged into a state water course for conveyance downstream for diversion and reuse. The amended statute expressly requires a permit be obtained prior to the diversion and reuse of any such return flows.[37]

In addition to accounting for the traditional carriage losses associated with bed-and-banks permits, the statute purports to authorize TCEQ to impose special conditions on the bed-and-banks reuse project *if* it determines the same are necessary to protect an existing water right that was granted based on the use or availability of the historic return flows of the privately owned groundwater that previously had not been part of a reuse project.[38] Such special conditions can also be imposed upon reuse bed-and-banks permits to help maintain instream uses, including aquatic and riparian aquarium habitats and recreational uses and freshwater inflows to bays and estuaries.[39] Additionally, the amended statute requires that in the event the amount of the discharge of groundwater-based effluent increases in the future, if the discharging party wishes to divert and reuse any future increases in the volume of reclaimed water discharged, authorization must be obtained to reuse the increases before the increase occurs.[40]

The legislature also made clear that persons wishing to use, convey, and subsequently divert *state* water returned to a water course must obtain TCEQ's prior approval in the form of a bed-and-banks authorization. This new subsection (c) applies to discharges of treated wastewater that originates as "state water" diverted pursuant to a permit. It is also broad enough to apply to use of raw water—regardless of whether its origin is surface or groundwater—transported by artificial means from its source to a river for subsequent transport downstream to the point of diversion and use.[41]

The legislature prescribed that the authorization to use the bed-and-banks of the state water course pursuant to subsection 11.042(c) could also be made subject to special conditions to address the "impact of the discharge, conveyance and diversion" on existing permits, certified filings, or certificates of adjudication, instream uses, and freshwater inflows to bays and estuaries."[42] Additionally, to address concerns about water quality impacts arising from such bed-and-banks reuse projects, the Legislature mandated that water discharged into a water course not cause any degradation of water quality to a degree that the stream segment classification for the affected water course would be lowered.[43]

Applying for a Bed-and-Banks Authorization

The TCEQ has not had many opportunities to explore or implement the provisions of section 11.042 as amended by Senate Bill 1. In fact, the TCEQ has yet to develop an application form for obtaining bed-and-banks permits. Instead, persons wishing to obtain authorization to use the bed-and-banks of a state water course to transport water, regardless of its source, must use either the TCEQ's form for an original water right pursuant to section 11.121 or an application to amend an existing water right pursuant to

section 11.122 of the Texas Water Code. These forms are used because they contain the general information necessary for TCEQ staff evaluation, such as the proposed use, the location of the affected stream segment, the source of the water, the point(s) of diversion, and the identification of intervening and downstream water rights. The TCEQ's forms must, however, be customized to address the particulars of the proposed reuse project and the bed-and-banks authorization, including whether it involves reuse or merely transport.

Based upon the 1997 amendments to section 11.042(b)–(c) in Senate Bill 1, TCEQ has adopted new rules regarding additional information required for proposals to convey groundwater-based effluent in the bed and banks of a state water course and to convey water (other than water from storage and a reservoir or groundwater-based effluent) in the bed and banks of a state water course.[44] Section 295.112 of the TCEQ regulations contains a list of additional application requirements peculiar to a person who either has discharged, or intends to discharge, groundwater-based effluent into a state water course and then divert and use the discharged water.[45] The rule also provides that the method and calculation of the carriage losses is subject to review and approval by TCEQ Executive Director. In other words, the applicant faces a moving target.

Section 295.113, which was developed to address subsection 11.042(c), requires similar information to that described in section 295.112. However, because the water involved is surface water, additional requirements exist. These include a certified copy of the underlying water right. If the reuse water proposed to be conveyed results in an interwatershed or interbasin transfer, then the authorization process for the bed and banks permit will be combined with the authorization for the interbasin transfer. Section 295.113 also allows for an application under its provisions to be combined with an application for a wastewater discharge permit in a consolidated permit proceeding. As with section 295.112, section 295.113 expressly provides that the method and calculation of carriage losses are subject to review and approval by TCEQ Executive Director.

Conclusion

In many areas of Texas facing a scarcity of water resources, water planning officials search for economically viable options to maximize and firm up existing supplies. Reuse projects have the potential to meet each of these objectives. As a water supply source, reuse water presents one of the most predictable renewable sources available. The Texas Legislature has responded to this need for creative solutions by structuring a framework for developing reuse projects, and TCEQ has enacted regulations to allow for implementing these projects. Although water reuse is a relatively new and uncharted course for many Texas communities, this water development strategy offers a viable solution for those willing to take the leadership in implementing such a project. If we are to meet the challenge of developing sufficient reliable water supplies for the future, all forms of reuse must be incorporated as essential elements of all water strategies in Texas. More important, such strategies must be implemented.

The following whimsical poem by Verne N. Rockcastle tells the tale of our water cycle from a perspective that is uniquely appropriate for the consideration of water reuse.

Recycled

The glass of water you're about to drink
Deserves a second thought, I think
For Avogadro, oceans and those you follow
Are all involved in every swallow,
The molecules of water in a single glass
In number, at least five times, outclass
The glasses of water in stream and sea,
Or wherever else that water can be.
The water in you is between and betwixt.
And having traversed is thoroughly mixed.
So someone quenching a future thirst
Could easily drink what you drank first!
The water you are about to taste
No doubt represents a bit of waste
From prehistoric beast and bird—
A notion you may find absurd.
The fountain spraying in the park
Could well spout bits of Joan of Arc,
Or Adam, Eve, and all their kin;
You'd be surprised where your drink has been!
Just think! The water you cannot retain
Will some day hence return as rain.
Or be held as the purest dew.
Though long ago it passed through you![46]

Only time will tell whether reuse will become a viable tool for water development strategists or simply another source of business for lawyers. Let us hope the strategists win!

Notes

1. Postel, "Water and World Population Growth," *Journal of the American Water Works Association*, April, 2000, 131–33.

2. Hoffman, "Texas Water Reuse Update," 25th Water Conference for Texas, Texas Water Resource Institute, December 1–2, 1998, Austin (available online at http://twri.tamu.edu/www.twriconf/w4tx98); Postel, "Water and World Population Growth."

3. Hoffman, "Texas Water Reuse."

4. Kaiser, Lesikar, Shafer, and Gerston, "Water Management Strategies and Ranking the Options," Texas Water Resource Institute, Texas A&M University System (available online at http://tx-water-ed.tamu.edu/strategies www.tx-water-ed.tamu.edu/strategies.html http://tx-water-ed.tamu.edu/strategies); see also Hoffman, "Texas Water Reuse"; Postel, "Water and World Population Growth."

5. "Scientists worldwide see that already-used water is a key to preventing a water-supply crisis." Golberg, "Reuse Water to Prevent a Water Crisis," Academy of Natural Sciences, February, 1994 (available online at www.acnatsci.org/erd/ea/reuse_water.html).

6. Source unknown.

7. Hoffman, "Texas Water Reuse."

8. According to Texas Water Development Board data, as of 1997, Texas was reusing 159.1443 MGD of municipal wastewater. Of that amount, 57.8829 MGD was consumed by industrial applications, 67.6273 MGD was utilized by agriculture in irrigation applications, and 33.4842 MGD was consumed in "other" unspecified uses—many of which appear to include landscape, golf course, ball field, and parkland irrigation. TWDB, "Municipal Wastewater Reuse in Texas 1997" (available on line at www.twdb.state.tx.us/assistance/conservation/reuse_1997.htm).

9. "San Patricio Squeezes Reuse from New Cogen Plant," Texas WaterNet, Texas Water Resource Institute, Texas A&M University System (available online at http://twri.tamu.edu.twripubs/WtrSavrs/v5n4/article-08); www.twri.tamu.edu/./twripubs/WtrSavrs/v5n4/article-08.html); Hoffman, "Texas Water Reuse"; Kaiser et al. "Water Management Strategies."

10. 30 TAC Ch. 210.

11. This practice is utilized by the City of El Paso, Texas. See Roebuck, "City of El Paso Water Conservation and Reuse of Wastewater Program," 1997 Water Conservation Conference Presentations (available online at www.cagesun.nmsu.edu/AGRICULTURE/wcc/epconser/index.html); cf. "Florida Water Plan Nears Approval: State Seeking EPA's Permission to Store Tainted Liquid in Ground," *Houston Chronicle*, April 13, 2001, p. 4A. To "head off dividing water shortages," Florida proposes injection of up to 1.7 billion gallons per day of "untreated, partly contaminated" water into the ground.

12. 30 TAC Ch. 285; Chubb, "Greywater: An Untapped

Source of Texas Water," February 17, 2000 (available online at www.twri.tamu.edu/./septictalk/archive/2000-Feb/Feb-17.3 .html); "Strategic Management Implications of Water Reclamation and Reuse on Water Resources," NC AWWA/WEA Reclaimed Water Conference, April 10, 1996, prepared by the North Carolina Division of Water Resources (available online at www.p2pays.org/ref/01/00035.htm#aquifer); "Review of Reuse of Reclaimed Water," Report no. 96-61, Office of Program Policy Analysis in Government Accountability, Florida Legislature, March 3, 1997; "Water Reuse Summary for Fiscal 1996–97," Los Angeles County Sanitation District (http://www .lacsd.org/webreuse/refy9697.htm); "San Patricio Squeezes Reuse"; Hoffman, "Texas Water Reuse"; Kaiser et al. "Water Management Strategies"; Payne, *Groundwater Recharge and Well: A Guide to Aquifer Storage Recovery* (CCRC Press Inc., 1995), 250–51; Rochelle, "Return Flows: Permitting and Planning Implications," 25th Water Conference for Texas, Texas Water Resource Institute, December 1–2, 1998, Austin (available online at http://twri.tamu.edu/www.twriconf/w4tx98).

13. *Technical Papers on Selected Aspects of the Preliminary Texas Water Plan*, Texas Water Development Board, Report 31 (September, 1996); "Introduction," in *The Texas Water Plan*, Texas Water Development Board (November, 1968); McNeely and Lacewell, *Water Resource Uses and Issues in Texas* (College Station: Texas Agricultural Experiment Station, Texas A&M University, August, 1978), p. 7; *A Plan for Meeting the 1980 Water Requirements of Texas*, Texas Board of Water Engineers (May, 1961), pp. 3–6; Texas Water Development Board, *Water for Texas: A Comprehensive Plan for the Future*, 2 vols., Document GP-4-1 (Austin: TWDB, November, 1984).

14. Oliver, "Water Reuse and Watershed Management: Tarrant Regional Water District's Reuse Project," Texas Water Law Conference, May 8, 1998, Dallas (CLE International), p. 21; Hoffman, "Texas Water Reuse"; Kaiser et al., "Water Management Strategies"; *Water for Texas Today and Tomorrow*, Texas Water Development Board, Document no. GP-6-1 (December, 1992), pp. ix, 24–25.

15. Act of June 19, 1997, 75th Leg., Ch. 1010 §2.06, 1997 Tex. Gen. Laws 3620 (amending §11.042 by adding Sub-Sections (b)–(d); Gooch, "Surface Water Rights Permitting Issues: Regulatory Considerations in Getting and Amending Permits," Texas Water Law Conference, May 4–5, 2000, Houston (CLE International).

16. 30 TAC ch. 210; see Tex Water Code §26.0311(b), directing TCEQ to adopt rules for use of "greywater"; see generally Gooch, "Surface Water Rights Permitting Issues."

17. Kaiser et al. "Water Management Strategies."

18. Ibid.

19. Ibid.; Chenault, "Wide-Ranging Opinion Revealed in Texas Water Survey," Texas Water Resource Institute, Texas A&M University System, March 10, 2000 (available online at http://www.agnews.tamu.edu/stories/AGEN/Mar1000a.htm; and http://tx-water-ed.tamu.edu/strategies).

20. Kaiser et al. "Water Management Strategies"; Chenault, "Wide-Ranging Opinion."

21. 30 TAC Ch. 210 (Use of Reclaimed Water); Ch. 305 (Consolidated Permits).

22. Texas Water Code §11.042.

23. 30 TAC §210.2.

24. Ibid., §210.5; 30 TAC Ch. 305.

25. 30 TAC §210.1.

26. Ibid; 30 TAC Ch. 305, Ch. 285.

27. 30 TAC §210.4.

28. 30 TAC §210.4(b).

29. 30 TAC §210.4(c), §210.4(e).

30. 30 TAC §210.4(d).

31. 30 TAC §210.6, §210.7.

32. 30 TAC §210.32, §210.32(1).

33. 30 TAC §210.32(2)

34. 11.042(a), Texas Water Code; see generally Gooch, "Surface Water Rights Permitting Issues."

35. Rochelle, "Return Flows"; Act of June 19, 1997, 75th Leg., Ch. 1010, 1997 Tex. Gen Laws 3610.

36. Act of June 19, 1997, Ch. 1010, §2.06.

37. Texas Water Code §11.042(b); see generally Gooch, "Surface Water Rights Permitting Issues."

38. Texas Water Code §11.042(b). Carriage losses include reductions in the volume of streamflow resulting from evaporation and bank seepage. A person wishing to use a water course to convey a volume of water downstream must account for and *not* divert the amount of water included in the calculated carriage losses.

39. Texas Water Code §11.042(b).

40. Ibid.; Rochelle, "Return Flows."

41. Texas Water Code §11.042(b).

42. Ibid; also Hoffman, "Texas Water Reuse."

43. Texas Water Code §11.042(c).

44. 30 TAC §295.112, §295.113.

45. 30 TAC §295.112(b).

46. Water Magazine.Com, December 27, 2000 (available online at www.watermagazine.com/reuse.htm).

PART V

International
Issues
in the
Rio Grande
Valley

This section contains case studies of what is perhaps the most water-stressed region of Texas: the Lower Rio Grande Valley. This area, including El Paso, faces severe shortages within the next twenty-five years as groundwater becomes depleted and surface water is scarce. On the Mexican side of the river, the situation is much worse due to cultural differences, a restrictive treaty, and impoverished communities. International agreements and interstate laws hamper the region's efforts to improve its water resources.

Robert Schmidt offers an overview of the El Paso–Juarez situation in terms of current water supplies. This region, the largest border community in the world, is located in possibly the driest ecological niche in Texas. The bolsons from which the two communities draw the majority of their water resources are drained to depletion.

This forces area managers to search for surface water sources. They are considering future options such as desalination and recycled wastewater.

Richard A. Marston and William J. Lloyd discuss the spatial disconformities that exist between supply and demand and across jurisdictions in El Paso, Juarez, and New Mexico. They suggest that federal intervention will be needed to govern the water allotments for everyone in this border region.

Ranjan S. Muttiah and colleagues look at the area's water in terms of salinity. High salt content damages water-processing equipment and kills crops as well as posing a serious health threat. He discusses modeling the salinity of the Rio Grande by incorporating flow-salinity relationships into the Soil and Water Assessment Tool (SWAT) hydrology model.

Finally, Mitchell L. Mathis looks at the whole binational border region in terms of economics, living conditions, agriculture, ecology, and population. In order for this region to survive, the whole area must adopt better water management and waste disposal strategies. For this to occur, the two countries will have to develop more international institutional cooperation.

CHAPTER 22

Water Resources of Far West Texas

El Paso–Ciudad Juarez

Robert H. Schmidt

Department of Geological Sciences

University of Texas at El Paso

Abstract

Most of the settlements in the region depend upon well water, but historically the Rio Grande has been the main focus of the region's water. The important population center has approximately two million inhabitants, making this the world's largest adjoining border community. At present, diversions from the Rio Grande provide 44 percent of the total water supply, and accounting for the remainder of El Paso's water supply are wells in the Hueco Bolson (37 percent) and the Mesilla Bolson (19 percent). Ciudad Juarez is completely dependent upon the Hueco Bolson for its domestic water. The groundwater supply for El Paso is expected to last about twenty-five years, and Ciudad Juarez's five years. Water rights, pipelines from surface reservoirs, desalination and blending of locally available brackish water, obtaining groundwater from distant water ranches, and the blending of treated wastewater are all possibilities for the future, but cooperation for a much needed regional approach is definitely lacking. Political, legal, and economic turmoil is unfortunately the future.

Far West Texas is an area dominated by the Chihuahuan Desert, Basin and Range topography, and the Rio Grande Valley. In this area, the western appendage of Texas is bounded by the Rio Grande (known in Mexico as the Rio Bravo del Norte), which forms the international border in the south and west, and in the north by the 32nd parallel, which is the New Mexico state line. This isolated, arid region has been almost wholly dependent upon the great river throughout most of its history, but during the last hundred years, well water has increased in use to the point that it represents more than 90 percent of the water consumption in El Paso and Ciudad Juarez. As we move into the new millennium, surface water will again be the most important source of water for El Paso. Just across the border, Ciudad Juarez is still 100 percent dependent upon groundwater, and it will be for the foreseeable future (fig. 1).

Although most of the settlements and people in the region currently depend upon well water, historically the Rio Grande/Rio Bravo has been the main focus of the region's water. By far the most important population center is the El Paso–Ciudad Juarez metroplex. The combined population of approximately two million habitants makes this the world's largest adjoining border community. As a result of the dominance or primacy that this urban area enjoys, it is the major focus of this study. Although Ciudad Juarez (population 1.3 million) is not within the boundaries of Texas, it cannot be ignored when discussing water and water resources of the region because of the city's historical significance and sheer size.

At present, the El Paso Water Utility (EPWU) produces

Surface Water: Rio Grande/Rio Bravo

In the El Paso–Ciudad Juarez region and surrounding area, there are no perennial rivers or important sources of surface water other than the Rio Grande. It is the fifth longest river in North America and the continent's twentieth largest river in volume, occupying a watershed that is equal in size to 11 percent of the continental United States, and it is the only significant surface drainage feature for the region. However, it is not in the same category as the world's major rivers. Its unimpressive waterflow prompted Will Rogers to remark that "the Rio Grande is the only river I ever saw that needed irrigation." The Rio Grande/Rio Bravo has its headwaters in the San Juan Mountains of southwestern Colorado, flows through New Mexico and Texas, and empties into the Gulf of Mexico. Its total length is approximately 3,135 kilometers (www.epa.gov/rivers/98rivers/fsriogra.html). Slightly more than 2,000 km of its length forms the international border between Texas and the Mexican states of Chihuahua, Coahuila, Nuevo Leon, and Tamaulipas. The total drainage area of the Rio Grande basin is 868,945 km^2 (IBWC 1996), but it contains large areas, especially along its southwestern boundaries, that yield little to no runoff to the river. The productive or contributing area of the watershed is approximately 456,700 km^2 or just 53 percent of the total. The total storage capacity of reservoirs in the basin is nearly 14.5 billion m^3. In combined total capacity, the reservoirs in the United States and Mexico are nearly equal (7.7 billion m^3 in the United States; 7.0 billion m^3 in Mexico). An additional 7.4 billion m^3 of reservoir capacity is provided by the international Amistad and Falcón impoundments. Prior to the construction of the international Falcón Dam in 1938, the annual flow of the Rio Grande to the Gulf of Mexico below Brownsville averaged 3.2 billion m^3 for the years 1934–52. Since that period, the annual flow has averaged 974 million m^3 (IBWC 1996).

For nearly all practical purposes, especially from a hydrologic perspective, the Rio Grande/Rio Bravo operates as two rivers. Because of heavy demands upstream, there is little to no waterflow for about 225 kilometers downstream from the El Paso–Juarez valley to its confluence at Ojinaga-Presidio just west of the Big Bend National Park, Texas. Here Mexico's Rio Conchos, which is the largest tributary to the Rio Grande/Rio Bravo in the entire basin, contributes between 23 and 27 percent of all the water that flows in the total river system (computation by Schmidt based upon IBWC data).

Water from the upper portion of the Rio Grande has

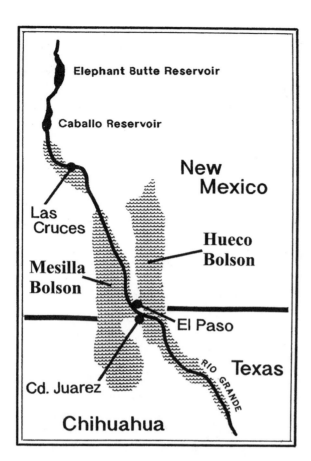

Figure 1. Major water features (boundaries of bolsons, fresh and brackish water, based upon several unpublished maps by the EPWU, and Reinert, pers. comm., 2001).

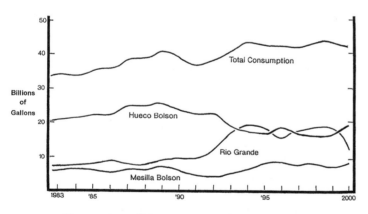

Figure 2. Annual EPWU sources and consumption. Annual total, raw water data (ground + diversions) from Sperka (2001).

approximately 43 billion gallons of raw water annually (Sperka 2001). Diversions from the Rio Grande provide 44 percent of the total, and accounting for the remainder are wells in the Hueco Bolson (37 percent) and the Mesilla Bolson (19 percent; fig. 2).

been a focus of conflict since the late nineteenth century. Rapid increases in irrigation set state against state and country against country, eventually leading to the construction of Elephant Butte Dam 220 km upstream from El Paso. This structure, which has a capacity of 2.55 billion m³, together with diversion dams and canal systems, was completed in 1916. Although the somewhat unexpected compaction and shrinkage of clay initially increased the reservoir capacity, about 25 percent of the volume has been lost to siltation. Eventually, when the capacity of Elephant Butte has diminished substantially, the dam can be raised three to four meters. In order to provide more storage capacity and help regulate discharge, Caballo Dam was completed in 1938 (capacity 409 million m³). In addition to water storage for downstream uses, the dams, levees, rectification, and channelization provide protection against flooding. Hydroelectric power is generated at Elephant Butte Dam. Originally conceived for flood control and additional storage, Caballo Dam was finally built as a multipurpose feature that permitted near year-round power generation at Elephant Butte Dam (Resch 1965). Even after completion of this second dam, conflicts continued. Most recently, the nearly continuous conflicts have become acute, especially those related to El Paso's ever increasing need for domestic water coupled with the impending depletion of its aquifers. Appropriately, Albert Utton (1999) points out that the Rio Grande/Rio Bravo has served as a laboratory during the twentieth century, producing "a variety of methods for apportioning the use of international/interstate rivers as well as dealing with drought in an international/interstate drainage basin." Although the laboratory has aged, from all appearances and for better or worse, it appears that the grand, brave river will be on the cutting edge for more experimentation.

Groundwater

El Paso's groundwater is obtained from about a hundred producing wells in the Hueco and Mesilla bolsons. The majority of the wells are in the Hueco Bolson and reach a bottom from about 180 to 365 m (Sperka, pers. comm., 2000). The Mesilla-Canutillo wells are shallower, the production zone mainly above 160 m. Generally, the groundwater reserves are located in unconsolidated clastic sediments found in the broad intermontane structural basins. It was not until the 1970s that the reality of relying on a rapidly diminishing water source began to set in. A rapid population explosion on both sides of the border coupled

with the realization of a substantially diminished ground water supply and increased pumping costs as a result of soaring petroleum prices all contributed to greater utilization of and reliance on the Rio Grande/Rio Bravo.

Water Use

El Paso uses a little over 40 billion gallons of water each year. This equates to 165 gallons per person per day with the rest being utilized for industrial uses, parks, etc. As the city's population continues rapidly increasing, the per capita daily consumption has dropped from approximately 200 gallons to 165 gallons during the last decade, a decrease of 18 percent. In order to meet the consumption demands of nearly 160,000 metered customers, the EPWU oversees approximately 2,000 miles of pipeline, 150 workable wells, and more than 50 reservoirs with a total storage capacity of 150 million gallons.

El Paso's climate extremes and water use closely mirror one another. Peak water use generally occurs very near the summer solstice and minimum water use occurs around the winter solstice, with Christmas day often being the lowest (Rittmann 1996). This has created one of EPWU's biggest ongoing problems. Along with a rapidly diminishing water supply, the EPWU must face significant seasonal differences in water use. Although the seasonal consumption variation has improved dramatically during the last couple of decades, summer water requirements are still more than twice that of winter (approximately 185 million gallons per day vs. 70 mgd). In 1984, the difference increased 3.7 times (167 mgd vs. 45 mgd; Rittmann 1984, 1996). Although general awareness of water conservation has been important overall, the main reason behind the narrowing of seasonal water consumption variation is the substantial decrease in water used on lawns during the hot, dry summer months. About 40 percent of all the city's potable water is used for outdoor irrigation. Approximately 70 percent of the seasonal increase is attributed to lawn care. The other 30 percent is utilized by evaporative cooling, a category of consumption that may never see much of a reduction. El Paso's very dry air, summer temperatures, 1,220-meter altitude, and average maximum extreme temperature of 40°C, coupled with income levels among the lowest in the United States, make evaporative cooling the overwhelming choice. Desert landscaping or xeriscaping, regulation of days and hours when watering can take place, and improvements to keep water on the property and out of the streets account for most of the more efficient use of water. In addi-

Table 1. Users of the Hueco Bolson Aquifer, 1999

User	acre-feet*	percent
Cuidad. Juarez	121,593	63.5
City of El Paso	51,127	26.7
Industrial and public supply	13,000	6.8
Ft. Bliss Military Reservation	4,713	2.4
Chaparral, N.M., private wells	1,075	0.6
Total	191,508	100.0

*One acre-foot equals 325,850 gallons.

tion to general water savings, the more even requirements across the seasons result in lowering the cost of infrastructure for the water supply capacity (e.g., reservoirs, pumping, piping).

Long, heavy demands on the Hueco Bolson have left El Paso with a domestic water supply from the aquifer of only twenty to twenty-five years. Small quantities of precipitation, high evaporation rates, and modest injection of reclaimed-recycled water contribute little to the recharge of the Hueco Bolson. All of the various water users in El Paso account for only 36 percent of the water pumped from Hueco Bolson (table 1). The other 64 percent is consumed by the city of Juarez. Ciudad Juarez obtains 100 percent of its water from the Hueco Bolson's aquifer. This has most experts predicting that there will be potable water for only about another five years. The projection is based upon a study by the U.S. Geological Survey (USGS) and represents the difference between user demand (about 120,000 acre-feet per year) and pumping-storage capacity (an estimated 600,000 acre-feet of recoverable fresh water).

The amount of recoverable fresh water remaining in the Hueco Bolson is calculated by the USGS at 7.5 million acre-feet. Just a little over half of this reserve is in the Texas portion of the bolson, 40 percent in New Mexico, and just 8 percent remains in adjoining Chihuahua. Heavy demands on the Mexico side of the border began about twenty-five years ago. This coincided with the beginning of the Border Industrialization Program, popularly referred to as the *maquiladora* industry, and its eventual evolution to the present North American Free Trade Agreement. Very rapid population growth, nearly quadrupling during this period, accompanied these developments.

The Mesilla Bolson, on El Paso's west side, supplies approximately 15 percent of the city's needs. The rapidly growing city of Las Cruces, forty-five miles upstream from El Paso, obtains 100 percent of its domestic water from this aquifer. Although the aquifer contains an estimated 60 million acre-feet, most of it lies in the adjacent southern Doña Ana county of New Mexico. Most of the recharge, which is approximately equal to withdrawals, is believed to be derived from seepage provided by the Rio Grande.

Ciudad Juarez

This large border city depends entirely upon well water from the southern portion of the Hueco Bolson for its domestic supply. With a large and very rapidly expanding population, the future looks bleak. Ciudad Juarez continues to grow at over 4 percent annually in spite of an extremely limited water supply, and it is rapidly depleting its only current source of water. Water resources and the future supply have been a neglected topic until very recently, and even today progress appears to be tenuous. Total per capita consumption of about 100 gallons each day is about two-thirds that of El Paso, and recent stepped-up enforcement has improved the proportion of water users paying their bills, increasing in one year from 58 to nearly 70 percent (Ramirez-Cadena 1999). An additional and deep-seated problem facing the Juarez water and sanitation authority, according to Humberto Uranga, spokesman for the Junta Municipal de Agua y Saneamiento, is that "people will need to reconsider (water) as a benefit they have to conserve and for which they have to pay" (Ramirez-Cadena 1999). "It's a cultural idea of government obligation. These people think that the water comes free with the little piece of land they own" (Stack 1999). Mexican law does not permit disconnecting households from their water supply for nonpayment. There is also a real need to replace the existing system of pipelines, which has developed numerous leaks, and to provide new additions. It is estimated that these improvements would cost approximately $800 million. But the real challenge for the future is having water at all. With the dwindling water supply from the Hueco Bolson, government officials are moving quickly to investigate the possibilities of utilizing water from the Mesilla Bolson to the west, tapping into the Conejos-Medanos aquifer about sixty kilometers to the south, and eventually utilizing surface water from the Rio Grande. But there are numerous obstacles aside from a notable lack of effective planning and financial support. About two dozen exploratory wells have been drilled into these aquifers, but sheer distance from the city, the presence of the Sierra de Juarez, and the estimated costs of $40 million all hinder their development (Simonson 2000). The desire to convert Mexico's surface water allotment into suitable quality for human consumption would require substantial planning and funding for a nonexistent treatment plant. In addition, the 1906 treaty that allocated 60,000 acre-feet of Rio Grande water to Mexico earmarked it specifically for agricultural use. Redirection of water use would add an unknown but sizable number of Juarez area farmers, and those who depend upon their products and business, to the list of casualties.

Water Rights

Two sets of water rights—ground and surface—govern the El Paso–Ciudad Juarez water supply. Groundwater use is subject to the Texas law of capture and it is basically unregulated (Fahy 1995). Because of a substantial drop in the water table (greater than 30 m), intrusion of brackish water, and early retirement of wells, this has been the preferred method to meet the local demands of residential and municipal users as well as a large military presence and industries such as oil refineries and copper smelters. As a result of unregulated water withdrawal, the El Paso Water Resources Management Plan projects that groundwater from the Hueco Bolson, which historically has been by far the most significant source, will be depleted within twenty-five years. Hence the naturally renewable (if properly managed) surface water of the Rio Grande will be relied upon as the primary source for the public water supply. This is made even more appealing by the fact that present 95 percent of the Rio Grande's average annual flow is utilized for irrigation agriculture. It is probably inevitable that urban demands will eventually succeed in acquiring a major share of the river's water. But the political, legal, and economic obstacles are many, and the time frame will no doubt leave much to be desired.

Surface water is governed by Texas statutes that have evolved over the last 150 years. The current adjudication system based upon prior use began with the law of Spanish sovereignty, passing through English common and riparian laws (Fahy 1996). This doctrine of prior appropriation—"first in time is the first in right"—applicable in many western states with large areas of arid and semiarid climates, was also adopted by New Mexico in 1907 (Utton 1999). At present, approximately seventy thousand acres in the El Paso area are subject to Texas surface water rights. This allows each parcel of land to receive an equal allotment based upon the river's annual runoff. Property owners in these areas, as designated by the Rio Grande

Project, are responsible for paying taxes to the local irrigation district whether they use or do not use the river's raw water. This situation allows the EPWU to provide one-time cash compensation to lease the surface water rights from property owners who no longer need the untreated irrigation water. The EPWU is then responsible for paying the taxes and providing for the cleaning of the affected canals under the agreement. The leases, which are in affect for seventy-five years and are filed with the county clerk's office, are carried with the property to successive owners. After seventy-five years, the surface water rights revert back to the original signer. For many decades, this has been an ongoing process for increasing El Paso's water supply.

Reclaiming and Recycling

Average daily water consumption in El Paso is approximately 110 million gallons. About 40 percent of this is lost to outdoor uses. Therefore, more than half of all the city's water is returned as effluent. As observed by Guild (1990), this "is the only water resource that will increase with population." This water, after primary treatment, has historically been returned to the river, where it is utilized for irrigation. However, in the overall water scheme, the City of El Paso does not receive exchange credit for this water. As a result, the Public Service Board decided in 1978 to build a plant that could extensively treat and disinfect 10 million gallons a day of wastewater to produce water that meets government standards for drinking water. The plant was completed in 1984. Because government regulations forbid reclaimed sewage to be used directly in a potable water supply, the treated water is injected into the aquifer in the Hueco Bolson. After years of moving through the aquifer, it eventually finds its way into the city's water supply.

Reusing sewage water is not uncommon. St. Petersburg, Florida turned to wastewater in 1979. Other communities such as Tucson, Arizona, and Irvine, California, soon followed (Kolenc 1990). The reclaiming, recycling process is increasing rapidly across the United States as water supplies are being depleted. Although most of the sewage continues to go to irrigation agriculture, reused water is being applied more and more to golf courses, parks, school grounds, and for industrial processes as well as finding its way into domestic use. More recently in El Paso, the recycling and distributing of wastewater has expanded to four primary treatment plants. In an ongoing process, additional water reclamation projects are being phased into the system. El Paso Electric Company. is the city's largest reclaimed water customer, utilizing 2.5 to 3.5 million gallons of reclaimed water daily. The electrical generation plant began using recycled water about fifteen years ago (Simonson 1999). A common concern about using treated sewage is that it contains increased salt levels. On the plus side, the recycled water contains nitrates that fertilize the grass and other plants at golf courses and parks.

Recently Rittmann (2001) introduced two new ideas that involve the blending of Rio Grande water with similar amounts of treated wastewater and the blending of well water from the Mesilla Bolson with return-flow river water during the winter months. This would eliminate pumping the Hueco Bolson aquifer and provide artificial recharge of the freshwater zone. Purportedly Rittmann's concept would be far less expensive than desalination because El Paso water plants have the capability of treating raw sewage, and this method would not require much in the way of major changes to plant processes—and would not have the environmental consequences and cost of disposing of the salts and minerals associated with desalination.

Desalination and Blending Locally Available Brackish Water

Most people associate desalting water with expensive projects and oceans. In far West Texas there are some real possibilities for utilizing desalination methods for large quantities of brackish water in the Hueco Bolson. The USGS has estimated that approximately four million acre-feet of slightly saline water remain in the bolson's aquifer. This quantity of groundwater is just slightly less than the amount of fresh water that has been pumped from the freshwater aquifer since pumping began. The state's first desalting plant was constructed in 1967 at Dell City, a small agricultural community about 110 km east of El Paso. Since the requirements regarding salt content in Texas domestic water changed from not more than 500 to not more than 1,000 parts per million in the mid-1970s, brackish water has been mixed with water having lower salt content to achieve state standards and extend the life of the aquifer.

In 2001, the EPWU and the military base of Fort Bliss obtained a joint grant for more than $50 million to build what will be the largest inland desalination plant in the United States. Upon completion, the plant would provide about one-fifth of El Paso's present consumption. But the operational cost of desalination is not low. The process requires large quantities of electricity and imposes the additional expense of disposing of the extracted salts and minerals. Treating brackish water would produce an estimated seven tons of salt daily. The disposal of the large quantities of salts and minerals remains one of the most important drawbacks of desalination. One possible albeit small and partial solution that has been proposed and is under investigation at University of Texas–El Paso is the use of solar ponds to generate electricity. These ponds utilize salt, which serves as an insulator that traps heat at the bottom of the ponds. Thus, solar ponds could supply power to a desalination plant while providing utilization for some of the salts and minerals.

In the El Paso area, three small desalination plants are operating. These include the El Paso Electric Company, Phelps-Dodge copper smelter, and a small subdivision on the eastern edge of the county. At the Haciendas del Norte Estates, approximately 220 customers are supplied with treated water through reverse osmosis.

Recently Horizon City, just east of El Paso, announced plans to build a reverse osmosis water treatment plant (Ramirez-Cadena 2000). Horizon City is a rapidly growing community of approximately thirty-five hundred spread over ninety-one square miles. The plant, which will cost an estimated $6.3 million, will be leased back to the water authority. There is a buyout clause in the contract that will allow the authority to buy the processing plant. Home dwellers have expressed concerns that (1) it is built for developers, (2) water rates will increase, and (3) the 160-acre pond will not be safe and clean.

Ranches, Ranches, and More Ranches

Far West Texas has to be noted for having a greater variety of ranchers than any other place in the nation. In more or less historical order, the area has been associated with cattle ranching, followed by petroleum and hunting ranches, radioactive waste ranches, and most recently "water ranches." In 1992 and 1994, the El Paso Water Utility purchased two water ranches in order to obtain the water rights to the underlying aquifers. These ranches are located more than 190 km east of El Paso. The Wildhorse Ranch near Van Horn and the Antelope Valley Ranch near Valentine overlie groundwater basins that can be used to ensure future water supplies. Although substantially more expensive than treating surface water, these potential but distant subsurface sources are currently viewed as emergency supplies to be used only if adequate domestic water cannot be acquired nearby.

Recently, El Paso's Public Service Board (PSB) agreed to let a private land developer conduct a major study of new water resources for the city (Crowder 2000). Hunt Building Corporation, the largest private owner of undeveloped land in El Paso, will spend an estimated $1 million to identify optional water sources and methods of obtaining, treating, and delivering water to customers. The study and another complementary engineering study will greatly expedite the process, save the PSB substantial expenditures that it cannot presently afford, and do so without cost to users or taxpayers. These studies will be available to the public. The major focus of the studies involves the feasibility of piping water from ranches near Valentine and Van Horn. A large aquifer underlying the Dell City area will also be considered, but this alternative would require the construction of an expensive desalination plant. This area enjoys substantial recharge from the surrounding mountains, including Texas' highest, the Guadalupe Mountains. The Dell City aquifer may receive annual recharge of as much as 100,000 acre-feet. In return for Hunt Corporation's involvement, the company would no doubt benefit from a competitive edge for future construction and other related projects. Apparently in anticipation, the Hunt Corporation has been purchasing property in the area.

Water Quality

With dwindling water supplies and a rapidly growing population, and hence demand, the border city of El Paso is being forced to wean itself from groundwater sources and rely entirely on river water. Given that the Rio Grande is generally perceived as a badly polluted river, there is considerable concern about the quality of drinking water. There is no doubt that this river—one of the globe's longest, with low water volume and serving as an international boundary between Mexico and the United States for more than half its length—is easily polluted and readily conjures up thoughts of a virtual cesspool. In 1993, the environmental group American Rivers listed the Rio Grande and its largest tributary, the Rio Conchos, as the most polluted in North America. The Rio Grande has also been referred to as the continent's most endangered river.

At present, El Paso Water Utilities customers derive their water from three sources. Although some receive water from only one source, most customers consume water from two sources—groundwater and the Rio Grande—depending upon their location and the time of year. Although the area's high quality groundwater needs only to be chlorinated prior to delivery, the surface water taken from the Rio Grande requires substantially more intensive and expensive mechanical treatment. Too often forgotten is that petroleum costs and hence energy rates have been at relatively low levels. The surge in petroleum costs in the 1970s saw pumping costs soar, and the processing of surface water became less costly than expense of groundwater. Costs of operation spent on electrical power for pumping increased from about 10 percent in the early 1970s to nearly 50 percent in the mid 1980s. Not only did energy costs increase, but deeper wells required higher lifts. This situation had an unforeseen benefit in that it served as a wakeup call to begin utilizing river water in serious quantities. Even today, El Paso utilizes groundwater for 100 percent of its drinking water from around the first of October through mid-February, leaving the surface water treatment plants idle and hence underutilizing expensive facilities.

The main culprit in all the intermingling of fact and fiction concerning the river's pollution in the El Paso area is the inflow of raw sewage from Ciudad Juarez. This *agua negra* (black water) results from the lack of sewage treatment for a city of 1.3 million people, and the 20 million gallons of raw sewage that they produce each day. By comparison, El Paso, a city with slightly less than half the population of Ciudad Juarez, treats between 60 and 70 million gallons of sewage daily. Two main canals carry the agua negra through the city, and it eventually enters the Rio Grande more than 130 km downstream near Fort Hancock. At this point, the flow of the Rio Grande is almost nonexistent and it is far below the diversions for the water treatment plants of El Paso. But the situation with the agua negra is not a pleasant prospect. There are serious concerns that this raw sewage, which already finds its way into the Rio Grande and associated canals, can be used to irrigate cropland. This possibility can be exacerbated during times of drought. The very real temptation to pump raw sewage to irrigate crops during these times could contaminate the resulting food products. The most probable results would be the spread of diseases such as shigella, salmonella, and cholera. This serious health hazard would affect both sides of the border, because the contaminated food could easily be brought across the border. One hopes this situation will soon be alleviated. Two wastewater treatment plants are planned, with one nearing completion. The Border Environment Cooperation Commission and the Juarez Junta Municipal de Agua y Saneamiento are the agencies responsible for the $31.1 million projects.

Another not uncommon dilemma in Juarez is the lack of water service to the outlying *colonia* areas. An investigative inquiry by Stack and Ramirez-Cadena (1999) indicated that 7 percent of users or fourteen thousand families in Juarez do not have access to city water. These people rely upon private tank trucks for their domestic water supplies. This circumstance has led to an unfortunate situation of unlimited and unknown consequences concerning the use of water barrels that were never intended for that purpose. Reports occasionally surface that colonia residents who do not have water hookups purchase metal barrels to store drinking water that they purchase from water-truck vendors. According to one news report, a Juarez merchant who regularly imports scrap metal from El Paso sells the drums to colonia residents. In one case it was found that at least ten of the barrels had previously been used to store toxic chemicals such as PCBs and malathion. If any remnants of the contaminants remained in these drums, they could pose a definite risk to human health (Ramirez-Cadena 1999).

From all documentable indicators, it appears that El Paso is exemplary in its water treatment. The longest ongoing problem of using Rio Grande water is silt. Silt has a particle size much smaller than sand but larger than clay. Although there is no definitive study for documentation, the Rio Grande is generally perceived as having the highest silt charge of any river in the United States. Apparently in an attempt to rectify this situation, many of the smaller tributaries to the Rio Grande have retention dams, the main function of which is retaining silt, with water retention a matter of lesser importance. The earliest water treatment in the El Paso area dates back to at least the 1800s. At that time, the local inhabitants used mashed prickly pear pads to help clean the river water. The pads were mixed with water in barrels to settle silt particles and help neutralize the river's sometimes musty taste and odor. Musty tastes and odors are occasionally present today. They are caused by harmless microscopic algae that proliferate rapidly, particularly in reservoirs during the hot summer months.

Because Rio Grande water travels more than eight hundred kilometers from its source and is detained in several reservoirs before it reaches El Paso, the possibility of contamination is substantial. This, coupled with El Paso's long association with the Rio Grande and its unique border health situation, has resulted in treatment plants that are exemplary in design and operation. El Paso has been a documented pioneer in water treatment. The water utilities began filtering drinking water in 1943, forty-seven years before it was federally mandated. Recently, El Paso has been a progressive leader in ozonation and particularly chlorine dioxide processing. As a result, the water is treated to achieve levels that far exceed the requirements established by the U.S. Environmental Protection Agency. El Paso water treatment plants are ranked nationally in the top 3 percent of surface water plants for their treatment design and water quality. In addition, the Texas Natural Resource Conservation Commission has classified El Paso as a "superior source of public water."

El Paso and Ciudad Juarez have what is considered hard water. The presence of two main elements, calcium and magnesium, cause the moderately hard water (75–150 mg/L) classification that typifies most of El Paso. The Canutillo-Mesilla wells, which supply El Paso's northwest side, are the lowest in mg/L, and the Lower Valley wells the highest (Rittmann n.d.). If the pH is too high, carbon dioxide is added to reduce the water to a pH of about eight. This level minimizes scaling in pipes and household appliances and provides a noncorrosive water. As previously noted, water standards in Texas changed in the mid-1970s regarding parts per million of minerals allowable for domestic water. The change from 500 to 1,000 ppm meant that more brackish water is mixed with water having a lower salt content, thus achieving state standards.

A not uncommon complaint pertains to the relatively warm water coming out of taps, especially during the summer months. There are three sources for this warmth. The first is a low-volume, shallow river flowing through a southerly desert, with the contribution of tailwaters that drain back into the river from dozens of fields using flood irrigation. The second is mild geothermal heating associated with the Canutillo-Mesilla wells. These wells produce water that is above 36°C as it comes out of the wellhead. During the summer months in particular, water is in such heavy demand that it does not have the time to cool much while being held in city reservoirs. This situation has been somewhat alleviated by some impressive waterflow management. Human-induced urban microclimatic aspects are the third reason for the relatively warm water that comes out of taps. Because Paseños enjoy mild winters and a general absence of permafrost, and because of occasional plumbing shortcuts that have occurred over time, water lines are typically located near the surface (the city code requires a total depth of twelve inches). The result is warmer water during the summer. In some situations, a combination of shallow water pipes near or in direct contact with low albedo surfaces, such as black asphalt parking lots and city streets, results in water temperatures that may be relatively high even after the water has passed through a refrigerated water cooler.

Fluoride

A question commonly asked is if flouride is added to El Paso's water. Some people view flouride in drinking water as a negative. Others welcome it, because it is known to retard the formation of cavities in teeth. Bottled water does not usually contain flouride, and therefore many dentists do not recommend it for children. Flouride occurs naturally in El Paso's water supply, the quantity apparently varying from source to source and seasonally. The concentration is usually about 0.9 to 1.0 ppm. The American Dental Association recommends 1 ppm with a maximum level of 4 ppm (El Paso Water Utilities 1998). Healthwise, the naturally occurring minimum level is accepted as adequate given El Paso's relatively warm climate. The prevailing conceptual theory is that warm climate inhabitants drink a greater volume of water than do those in colder areas.

Lithium

Over time, the most widely publicized topic concerning El Paso's water has been the natural occurrence of lithium. Although the amount of lithium is small, it is high compared to that in other cities in Texas and in the United States. Apparently the soils and rocks around the greater El Paso area contain high levels of lithium, which is eroded and leached from natural deposits into the river and to a much lesser extent into the wells that supply the city.

Lithium has been well documented as generally effective in the treatment of and as a prevention for manic depression and for depression without manic episodes. What attracts state, national, and worldwide interest is that for decades El Paso has had substantially lower rates of violent crimes and suicides, both for cities of similar size and in rates per hundred thousand inhabitants. As an example, El Paso's murder rate is only about half the national average. In 2002, El Paso was ranked the second safest large city (> 500,000 inhabitants) in the nation. The city has ranked third-safest since 1997. This has led some scientists and others of less rigorous backgrounds to theorize that the city's community water supply, which contains higher amounts of lithium, is a major contributor to the lack of violence. There is no doubt that El Paso is a friendly and laid-back city. This has led to humorous accusations of El Paso being "a hotbed of apathy."

Detractors of the general domestic tranquility–lithium comparison point out that in order to get the same amount of lithium as is present in one standard capsule, a person would have to drink six hundred gallons of city water. Also, until very recently, domestic water consumed in El Paso was largely derived from deep wells, and only 10 to 15 percent derived from the Rio Grande, which has much higher concentrations of lithium. But the low violent crime rates do not seem to correlate well with social factors, which are commonly cited without documentation. The city has one of the nation's worst records for indicators such as family and per capita incomes, unemployment, and educational attainment—and then there is the general perception of border cities being wild, unruly places. Apparently Paseños do not read the textbooks. In contrast, Ciudad Juarez has one of the highest violent crime rates in Mexico, and perhaps the world. One could speculate that part of the reason is that Juarez relies totally upon well water, which is substantially lower in lithium. But it should be noted that the negative statistics for Ciudad Juarez are a relatively recent phenomenon, beginning in the mid-1980s; that this border city has a large floating population consisting of recent migrants and highly mobile residents; and that many if not most of the violent crimes are related to drug trafficking and drug cartel control.

Another reasonable and somewhat persuasive factor that needs to be considered is that of long-term use. This is a compelling factor when coupled with the forgotten aspects of this matrix—that the El Paso area has a mild to hot, arid climate and a large labor force with minimal job skills, where outdoor working and living conditions are much more common than in most places. These factors certainly promote heavier consumption of water than the norm. Drinking substantial quantities of water that contain higher than normal amounts of lithium for decades, including during the formative years, is certainly a realistic possibility for the low violent crime and suicide rates. Obviously rigorous statistical research with a spatial–water source perspective is needed to produce something more than ongoing speculations.

In the early 1970s, researchers from the University of Texas Medical Branch in Galveston found that lithium in

Table 2. Geographical distribution of lithium content for El Paso

Sample	Lithium ppb*
Canutillo Station	18
Treatment plant effluent	168
Mesa Wells area (composite)	30
Airport area (composite)	58
Lower Valley (area composite)	64
Nevins Station	30
Filtered canal water	160
Cielo Visto Booster Station	65

*One part per billion (ppb) is one drop in 10,000 gallons—about the size of an average above ground swimming pool.

El Paso's water ranged from a low of 18 parts per billion (or mg/L) from the Canutillo wells to over 160 ppb at the river treatment plants, which are the main source of water for the city's central area and south side (table 2). The high levels recorded at the treatment plants were representative of using Rio Grande water from March to October. River water causes the metallic salts found in the soil to go into solution, which increases the lithium content. To date no one has tested for and studied lithium levels in Juarez.

The Future

Basically, all sources agree that the region's population will continue to grow. Presently El Paso, Ciudad Juarez, and Las Cruces are amongst the fastest growing urban areas in North America. Estimates project doubling of population within thirty-five years. El Paso's high fertility rate is the city's main source of growth. Immigration, both legal and illegal, and changing government policies, including amnesty, have played and may continue to play an important role in population numbers (table 3).

The tremendous population expansion experienced in Ciudad Juarez during the last several decades has been driven by an exploding maquiladora industry and its predecessors. These export-assembly plants are presently concentrated in Mexico's northern border states and account for 46 percent of the nation's exports, employing nearly 1.2 million workers (Dimeglio 1999). Although Ciudad Juarez has the largest number of maquila workers, its future growth will probably be constrained by its inability to provide infrastructure.

The much smaller city of Las Cruces, New Mexico, has experienced a very rapid but much shorter period of pop-

Table 3. Population and water requirements in El Paso County

Year	Population	Average Use (gal./person/day)	Annual Req. (million gal.)
1920	77,560	80	2,265
1930	102,421	81	3,028
1940	96,810	95	3,357
1950	130,003	134	6,358
1960	276,687	165	16,660
1970	322,261	195	22,551
1980	(443,080)	(200)	32,345
1990	(520,822)	200	38,207
2000	728,000	164	43,500
2025	1,050,000	160	61,320

Note: Small differences exist between daily consumption and annual requirements resulting from total billed water and total water in the distribution system and in the rounding of acre-feet used in earlier record keeping.

Sources: Sperka 2000; and an unpublished report entitled "Water Requirements and Available Resources of El Paso, Texas," n.d. (1970+), 11 pp.; and 2025 population projection from Department of Planning and Development, City of El Paso.

ulation growth than the substantially larger metropolitan areas just downstream. Its recent population explosion and the impact of this on water resources are unclear. Las Cruces obtains its water from the Mesilla Bolson with supplements from a second aquifer in the Jornada Bolson. At present, the city has no claims to Rio Grande surface water. However, Las Cruces does own farmland in the valley and has considered the possibility of constructing a plant to treat river water within the next twenty years.

Aside from the ongoing improvements in conservation, reclaiming, recycling, blending, and desalination, as previously discussed, additional proposed solutions to secure El Paso's future water needs include increasing the quantity of surface water available from the Rio Grande by negotiation with upstream farmers in the Elephant Butte Irrigation District. Of the Elephant Butte water, just a little over half goes to New Mexico users, with the remainder going to Texas. A federal lawsuit is under way to determine the ownership of Rio Grande water below the Elephant Butte reservoir. The ongoing battle over water rights is complicated and costly and has far-reaching and long-term implications. A second proposed solution involves encouraging and educating farmers to use water more efficiently. This includes various means for reducing evapotranspiration, such as drip irrigation, and switching to crops that require less water. Chiles, pecans, onions, alfalfa, and cotton—the valley's major crops—have high water requirements, especially given present farming methods. The situation is further complicated because growers commonly supplement their surface water allotment with well water. But the Rio Grande is the major source of recharge for the shallow aquifer system, and the water not lost through crop production and evapotranspiration flows back into the river. Thus, surface and groundwater are inextricably linked. Also, under current law, water from the Elephant Butte reservoir in New Mexico is only to be used for agriculture (Ford and Canup 1999). Farmers retain their water rights only as long as they put the water to beneficial use. Therefore, if a farmer practices conservation, the unused portion of his right is not recognized as a beneficial use. However, there is no doubt that water conservation technology and the incentive to use it are vital to the area's agriculture and urban future.

A further solution to securing El Paso's water needs is to construct a conveyance to transport water directly from Caballo Dam to the El Paso area. There are several options or scenarios to accomplish this goal of providing surface water year-round while improving water quality before treatment. A means long under consideration involves building a concrete-lined ditch alongside the existing river channel. Aside from the hazard this would represent and the political and legal considerations of obtaining right-of-way, there would still be substantial losses to evaporation, the potential for being polluted, and the costs of bridging an open canal. Recent assessments conclude that a pipeline extending from a location near Caballo Dam to the El Paso area appears to be another possibility. The problems noted for an open channel would be minimized or nonexistent if a pipeline were used.

Another issue to be resolved is the quality of water received in El Paso. In a 1991 court settlement, El Paso is to receive 376,858 acre-feet of water annually. Approximately 44 percent of that water is supposed to be low in dissolved solids, less than 350 ppm. According to an investigative report, El Paso is receiving water with dissolved solids of at least 1,200 ppm (Scharrer 1999).

At present, it appears that a very large water treatment plant will be constructed in El Paso's upper valley to process river water. In addition, an existing treatment plant's capacity would be increased substantially. A sixty-inch, thirty-mile-long pipeline would take water from the river treatment plant over the north end of the Franklin Mountains at Anthony Gap to the rapidly expanding area of northeast El Paso. The life of the river through El Paso would be seriously impacted—a fact that has not gone unnoticed by environmentalists. They hope the regional water situation will offer an opportunity for a much needed ecological restoration. Unfortunately, proposed alternatives to the foregoing plans and proposals, such as placing the processing plant below El Paso, while highly desirable, do not seem to be realistic economically. In addition, it should be noted that aside from centuries of planned and unplanned alterations, including nearly a hundred miles of rectified river channel below Caballo Dam, the Rio Grande is, unfortunately, substantially altered from anything resembling a natural environment. This portion of the Rio Grande represents one of the most managed and modified river channels anywhere.

Other considerations that could impact the river's future surface water supply and management are activities involving the middle Rio Grande above Elephant Butte reservoir. Not only is the silvery minnow, a species near extinction, found in this area, but Albuquerque, New Mexico's largest urban area, has taken an interest in this section of the Rio Grande as a source of domestic water. Albuquerque has formulated a water strategy that has recently turned attention to the use of surface waters in place of pumping groundwater (www.abq.gov/). Albuquerque now obtains 100 percent of its water from aquifers. It also has one of the highest rates of per capita water consumption in the Southwest at 204 gallons per day. The city now wants to use San Juan–Chama river water (48,200 acre-feet annually), which is a sizable amount of the Rio Grande's flow (Belin 2000). In addition, Albuquerque is proposing to use some of its daily sixty million gallons of sewage effluent for irrigation and nonpotable purposes rather than returning it to the river. These activities of course would have substantial negative impacts on the ecological well-being of what is left of the Rio Grande. There are also plans by the Bureau of Reclamation and the U.S. Army Corps of Engineers to expand and reactivate the sixty-mile-long Low Flow Convergence Channel adjacent to the Rio Grande above Elephant Butte reservoir. This canal is designed to transport water more efficiently during dry periods. Environmental groups are not standing idly by; nine major organizations have formed the Alliance for Rio Grande Heritage.

All the ongoing projects and proposed solutions to provide for future needs center on increased use of Rio Grande surface water and cooperative regional approaches to assure a high quality sustainable water supply.

At present, various conflicts including a federal court gag order, supersensitive negotiations, and potential litigation make it difficult if not impossible to predict exactly when, where, and how tomorrow's water needs will meet the demands of the world's largest border community.

References

Bath, C. Richard. "Transboundary Resource Management Models: Applicability to the El Paso–Ciudad Juarez Region for Groundwater Managment." *Transboundary Resources Report* 10, no. 1 (1996): 1–3.

Belin, Letty. "Collaboration and Court Action on the Rio Grande." *Rio Grande Sierran* (Sierra Club newsletter), March–April, 2000, 1, 6.

Chavez, Octavio E. "Mexican Perspective." *Transboundary Resources Report* 12, no. 1 (1999): 5–8.

Cliett, Tom. "Groundwater Occurrence of the El Paso Area and Its Related Geology." In *Guidebook of the Border Region*, ed. D. A. Cordova, S. A. Wengerd, and J. Shommaker, 207–14. (New Mexico Geological Society, 1969).

Crowder, David. "PSB Agrees to Free Study of New Water Resources." *El Paso Times*, May 6, 2000, 1, 2A.

Day, J. C. "The Hueco Bolson on the Rio Grande River." *International Aquifer Management* 18, no. 1. (January, 1978): 163–80.

Dimeglio, Steve. "Tax Deal Could Make or Break Maquiladoras." *Denver Post*, December 5, 1999, 6L.

El Paso Water Utilities. Drinking Water Report. Information note. 1998.

Fahy, Michael P. "Impact of Prevailing Water Laws on the Development of Potable Water for El Paso, Texas." Abstract, Assoc. Eng. Geol. and Groundwater Res. Assoc. Annual Meeting, 1995, 46. M. Fahy is a water rights engineer with the Public Service Board, El Paso.

———. "History of Water Rights." *Kern Place Newsletter* 16, no. 3 (May, 1996): 3.

Ford, D'Lyn, and Terry Canup. "The Giving River." *New Mexico Resources* (Spring 1999): 2–7.

Guild, Kirke. Cited in Vic Kolenc, "Special Report: Before the Well Runs Dry," *El Paso Herald-Post*, October 24, 1990, 4A.

Hernández, John W. "An Analysis of the Drought of 1996 in the Middle Rio Grande Valley of New Mexico." *Transboundary Resources Report* 12, no. 1 (1999): 3–5.

———. "Interrelationship of Ground and Surface Water Quality in the El Paso–Juarez and Mesilla Valleys." *Natural Resources Journal* 18, no. 1 (January, 1978): 1–9.

House, John W. *Frontier on the Rio Grande.* Oxford: Clarendon Press, 1982.

Ingram, Helen. "Lesson Learned and Recommendations for Coping with Future Scarcity." *Transboundary Resources Report* 12, no. 1 (1999): 9–11.

International Boundary and Water Commission, United States and Mexico (IBWC). *Binational Study Regarding the Presence of Toxic Substances in the Rio Grande/Rio Bravo and its Tributaries along the Boundary Portion between the United States and Mexico.* Final Report, September, 1994.

———. *Flow of the Rio Grande and Related Data.* Water Bull. no. 66. U.S. Dept. of State, 1996.

JMAS. *Diagnostico de los Indices de Vulnerabilidad a la Contaminacion del Sistema Acuifero de la Zona Urbana de Cd. Juarez, Chih.* Juanta Municipal de Agua y Saneamiento, Departamento de Geohidrologia. Reporte Tecnico No. DS GEO-08/97.

Kolenc, Vic. "Special Report: Before the Well Runs Dry—A Toast to El Paso's Future Drawn from Recycled Sewage." *El Paso Herald-Post*, October 24, 1990, 1, 4A.

Lloyd, W. J. "Growth of the Municipal Water System in Ciudad Juarez, Mexico." *Natural Resources Journal* 22 (1982): 943–55.

Lloyd, W. J., and Richard A. Marston. "Municipal and Industrial Water Supply in Ciudad Juarez, Mexico." *Water Resources Bull.* 21, no. 5 (October, 1985): 841–49.

Lloyd, W. J., and Robert H. Schmidt, Jr. "Land Use in the Basin and Range Topographic Province of Trans-Pecos, Texas." In *New Mexico Geological Society Guidebook*, 31st Field Conference, Trans-Pecos Region, 1980, 305–10.

Marston, R. A., and W. J. Lloyd. "River Budget for the Rio Grande, El Paso-Juarez Valley." *J. of Arid Environments* 8 (1985): 109–19.

Ramirez, Renee, "River Water for Lawns: Can the Bargain Last?" *El Paso Inc.* 1, no. 41 (June 23, 1996): 1.

Ramirez-Cadena, Cindy. "Juarez Water Has Murky Mixed Future." *El Paso Times*, August 22, 1999, 16.

———. "Horizon City Builds Treatment Plant." *El Paso Times*, March 2, 2000, 1, 2.

Reinert, Scott. Associate hydrogeologist, El Paso Water Utilities. Pers. comm., 2001.

Resch, W. F. General Descriptive Statement: The Rio Grande Project, New Mexico–Texas. Unpubl. report, 1965.

Rincon V., Carlos A. "Disponibilidad de aguas superficiales y su demanda futuro a lo largo de la franja fronteriza desde Ciudad Juarez." *Natural Resources Journal* 22 (October, 1982): 847–53.

———. "disponibilidad de Aguas Superficiales y Su Demanda Futuro a lo Lago de la Franja Fronteriza Desde Ciudad Juarez." *Natural Resources Journal* 22 (October, 1982): 939–41.

Rittmann, Douglas. "El Paso Has Options in Its Search for Adequate Fresh Water Sources." *El Paso Times*, June 2, 2001, 11A.

———. El Paso Water Story. Unpubl. N.d.

———. Water Systems Division manager, El Paso Water Utilities (now an environmental consultant). Pers. comm., several dates.

Scharrer, Gary. "Officials Get Ready to Dive into Litigation over Water Deal." *El Paso Times,* February 28, 1999, 3B.

Shupe, Steven J., and John Folk-Williams. *The Upper Rio Grande: A Guide to Decision Making.* Western Network, 1988.

Simonson, Sharon. "Treated Waste Water Gains Popularity." *El Paso Times,* August 22, 1999, 6, 21.

———. "Juarez Could Run Dry in 5 Years." *El Paso Times,* February 27, 2000, 1, 21.

Sperka, Roger. Annual Water Production Report for the Year of 2000. Interoffice memorandum, 2001.

———. Hydrogeologist, El Paso Water Utilities. Pers. comm., 2000.

Stack, Megan. "Water Is Most Pressing Problem for Many Families in Juarez." *El Paso Times,* August 22, 1999, 12.

Utton, Albert E. "Water and the Arid Southwest: An International Region under Stress." *Transboundary Resources Report* 8, no. 2 (1994): 5–6.

———. "Coping with Drought: The Case of the Rio Grande/ Rio Bravo." *Transboundary Resources Report* 12, no. 1 (1999): 9–11.

Van Metre, P. C., B. J. Mahler, and Edward Callander. *Water-Quality Trends in the Rio Grande/Rio Bravo Basin Using Sediment Cores from Reservoirs.* U.S. Geological Survey, U.S. Dept. of Interior. Washington, D.C.: U.S. Government Printing Office, 1997.

Washington Valdez, Diana. "Getting Water Clean Will Cost, Study Finds." *El Paso Times,* March 9, 2000, 1, 2.

———. "Juarez Hunts New Sources of Water as Crisis Looms." *El Paso Times,* February 14, 2001, 1, 2.

CHAPTER 23

Geographical Hydrology
of the El Paso–Ciudad Juarez Border Region

Richard A. Marston

School of Geology

Oklahoma State University

William J. Lloyd

Department of Geography

California State University

Abstract

The purpose of this chapter is to describe and explain the spatial disconformities that exist in water supply, water demand, and jurisdiction over water resources for the El Paso–Ciudad Juarez border region. Population growth and increasing per capita consumption of water have led to increasing demands for water, especially for municipal and industrial uses. Adequate supplies to meet this demand exist in the Hueco and Mesilla bolsons, but supplies are not shared between the portions of New Mexico, El Paso, and Juarez that comprise the border region. As a consequence, groundwater is being mined and groundwater quality is being degraded. Supplies of fresh water will soon be depleted in Ciudad Juarez and the City of El Paso. Federal intervention will be required to renegotiate interstate and international agreements that govern water allocation in the border region. Other alternatives, such as desalination and importation, are too expensive.

Water resources in the El Paso–Ciudad Juarez border region are shared between three states (Chihuahua, Texas, New Mexico) and two countries (Mexico, United States). With approximately two million inhabitants, the El Paso–Ciudad Juarez urban region comprises the largest adjoining border community in the world. The rapidly growing population in an area of sparse rainfall creates some significant challenges for water management. Water is scarce for physical reasons but also because of legal, political, and economic factors. Many earlier studies, principally those by state and federal water management agencies, have ignored the hydrologic interdependencies between El Paso and Juarez, resulting in incomplete understanding of the impending water crisis. The regional disconformities are the basis of predictions we present on water availability through the twenty-first century within the El Paso–Juarez border region. We begin by describing the water demand and use in the region. This is followed by an outline of the available water supplied by the Rio Grande and alluvial-filled grabens known as bolsons. We conclude with a discussion of water management concerns and predictions on the degree to which water demand can be met by available supplies in the future. The political units in this study are the City and County of El Paso in Texas, Doña Ana County in New Mexico (in which Las Cruces is the largest city), and Ciudad Juarez and the Juarez Valley in Chihuahua, Mexico. This chapter comprises an updated and abbreviated version of previously unpublished consultants' reports by the authors that provided an exhaustive review on the status of border region water resources (Lloyd and Marston 1984; Marston 1981, 1985, 1986a, 1986b, 1986c; Marston and Lloyd 1984; Marston, Lloyd, and Dupuy 1985; Marston, Lloyd, and Peeples 1983; Marston, Peeples, and Raksaskulwong 1985).

Water Demand and Use

The estimated populations of El Paso County and Ciudad Juarez in the year 2000 are 730,000 and 1.3 million, respectively (table 1). The population of Ciudad Juarez has grown from 500,000 in 1970, largely due to the creation of more than 70,000 new assembly plant jobs under Mexico's Border Industrialization Program. The per capita municipal and industrial (M&I) use of water in El Paso has been reduced from a peak of 757 liters per day (lpd) between 1980 and 1990 to a current 620 lpd. This has been achieved largely through voluntary water conservation measures, including xeriscaping of residential and commercial property. Over the same period, per capita M&I water use in Ciudad Juarez increased 40 percent to 378 lpd. This increase reflects efforts of the Junta Municipal de Aguas y Saneamiento, the agency responsible for providing water service in Ciudad Juarez, to (1) increase the percentage of homes that have inside plumbing; (2) increase the level of commercial and industrial demand; (3) improve the efficiency of the water distribution system; and (4) expand the production and distribution system (Lloyd 1982). The M&I demand in Juarez was greatly underestimated in early models developed by the Texas Department of Water Resources. The M&I demand for water accounts for about one-fourth of the total water use in both El Paso and Juarez. However, M&I activities account for 60 percent of the income and employment.

Irrigation agriculture comprises 75 percent of the total demand for water in the border region. This water is used to grow cotton, alfalfa, chiles, and pecans. Urban water needs compete directly with agricultural demands. The City of El Paso purchases water rights from farmers for conversion to M&I uses. Agriculture accounts for 75 percent of the total water demand but provides only about 5 percent of the income and employment. The public debate over this issue hinges on the much greater financial return for M&I uses compared to agricultural uses.

Water Supply

Water supplies are derived from the Rio Grande, shallow groundwater in alluvium of the Rio Grande Valley, and deep groundwater reserves in two large bolsons (fig. 1; White 1983). The Rio Grande is fully appropriated under the current set of complex international and interstate agreements (Day 1975). An average of 72,000 cubic meters per year are provided to the City of El Paso and about 74,000 cubic meters per year are diverted to the Juarez Valley. The allotment for Mexico is restricted for agricultural uses. In the El Paso–Juarez border region, approximately 95 percent of river water is used for agriculture.

The Hueco Bolson is a north-south-trending tectonic trough with basin fill deposits up to 2,700 meters thick, extending from southern New Mexico through westernmost Texas into Chihuahua, Mexico. Groundwater reserves are deep, with important vertical and horizontal patterns to water quality. The largest portion of fresh water is on the west side of the Hueco Bolson within the upper 430 meters of fluvial sands and gravels of the Camp Rice Formation. Total dissolved solids increase to the east and south. The total estimated storage of fresh water is 27.1 billion cubic meters, with 37 percent in New Mexico, 45 percent in Texas, and 18 percent in Mexico. Withdrawals from the Hueco Bolson in Ciudad Juarez and the

Table 1. Water demand along the El Paso–Juarez border

	City & County of El Paso, Tex.	Cd. Juarez & Juarez Valley	Regional Total
Est. 2000 population	730,000	1,300,000	2,030,000
Per capita M&I use (liters/day)	620	378	998
Total M&I use (MCM/year)	165	179	344
Agricultural use (million cu^3/year)	412	230	642

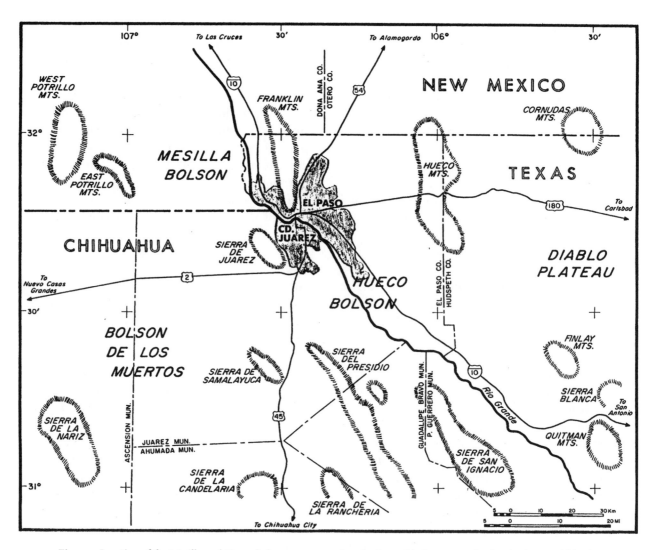

Figure 1. Location of the Mesilla and Hueco bolsons among major physiographic features and urbanized area within the El Paso–Juarez border region.

Juarez Valley exceed those in El Paso County. Since the 1920s, the rate of pumping has exceeded the rate of recharge; currently, the former exceeds the latter by a factor of twenty-five. Very little is withdrawn in the New Mexico portion of the Hueco Bolson. The annual precipitation in the border region is only 210 millimeters, and most of this is evaporated. Insignificant recharge occurs at the margin of bolsons from the mountain runoff of arroyos. Additional recharge occurs in the Texas portion of the Hueco Bolson from seepage out of the Rio Grande and from injection wells used to store treated effluent from the sewage treatment plant in northeast El Paso.

The total estimated storage in the Mesilla Bolson is 42.9 billion cubic meters, but 97.7 percent of this is stored in New Mexico and the remainder in Texas. The portion of the Mesilla Bolson in the Rio Grande Valley has been developed for agricultural use, although urban growth in this direction has led to increasing withdrawals for M&I use. Exploration has failed to find measurable fresh water stored in the Mexican extension of the Mesilla Bolson, known as the Bolson de los Muertos, where fluvial sands and gravels are replaced by lacustrine clays. This portion is largely undeveloped.

Water Management Concerns

Groundwater Mining

Measurements of groundwater elevations in the Hueco Bolson early in the twentieth century demonstrated that groundwater was moving in a gentle hydraulic gradient toward the Rio Grande Valley from both sides of the border. Once this groundwater reached the Rio Grande Valley, it turned southeast and moved down the valley. The development of major urban well fields in east El Paso has created major cones of depression, diverting the deep bolson water away from rural communities. In Ciudad Juarez, water is supplied from individual wells to the immediate neighborhoods; wells are not linked together in an integrated water distribution system. Thus, the Junta Municipal de Aguas y Saneamiento does not have the ability to spread out the groundwater demand on the aquifer, nor is it able to move water from one part of the city to another. Hence, the drawdown on the aquifer has been greatest in the central business district of Ciudad Juarez, where population density and per capita consumption are highest (Lloyd 1982). El Paso and Juarez place demands on the same deep Hueco Bolson water. Cones of depression have intersected across the border, causing up to thirty-five meters of drawdown in the last fifty years. The gradient of the piezometric surface has been altered, causing 4,000 cubic meters per day to flow from Texas into Mexico and, where the groundwater is flowing northward, 750 cubic meters per day from Mexico into Texas. The net flow into Mexico amounts to 1 percent of the M&I demand in El Paso. Groundwater mining is encouraged by the rule of capture that dominates Texas groundwater law; land owners can pump as much groundwater as possible from beneath the land they own, irrespective of impacts on adjacent landowners, unless it can be proven that pumping is undertaken with malicious intent against adjacent landowners. The malicious action clause has not yet been successfully employed in the Texas courts.

In 1965, the U.S. Geological Survey (USGS), El Paso Water Utilities, and Texas Water Development Board compiled an electrical analogue model of the Hueco Bolson in order to predict effects of water demand on the aquifer. This model was made obsolete by the realignment and cement lining of the Rio Grande through the El Paso–Ciudad Juarez urban area. In 1976, the USGS developed a two-dimensional digital model of the aquifer (Meyer 1976), but this greatly underestimated the demand in the City and County of El Paso. The Texas Department of Water Resources updated the USGS model in 1979, with new projections as a result (Knowles and Alvarez 1979). However, this model vastly underestimated the demand for water in Juarez and did not account for the distribution of drawdown and directions of urban growth in Juarez.

Lee Wilson and Associates (1981) projected water demand in the border region for the hundred-year period 1980–2079. Their model assumed that agricultural use would remain steady. M&I use in El Paso and Juarez would increase 2 percent per year from 1980 to 2019, slowing to 1.2 percent from 2020 to 2079. Their model further assumed that M&I would increase only 1 percent per year in Doña Ana County, New Mexico, consistent with estimates used in more recent modeling efforts. We have applied these assumptions of water demand to our estimates of water supply derived from published sources and our own finite difference models (Lloyd and Marston 1985). If freshwater supplies are fully shared, water should be sufficient beyond 2079 in El Paso County, Doña Ana County, and in Ciudad Juarez and the Juarez Valley. Without full sharing of freshwater, however, political boundaries will place a constraint on optimal spacing of wells in El Paso and Juarez (Day 1978). As a result, Doña Ana County will enjoy sufficient fresh water far beyond the year 2079, but El Paso County will exhaust fresh water by the year 2060. Seventy-one percent of the freshwater storage will be depleted in the Juarez Valley between 1972 and 2010, and fresh water will be exhausted by the year 2020. Further shifts can be expected in the rates and directions of groundwater flow, with even more diversion toward major cones of depression in urban well fields.

This scenario is particularly bleak for M&I users in El Paso and Ciudad Juarez. El Paso Water Utilities has considered a number of alternatives to extend the supply. We have already mentioned the water saved through conservation and wastewater recycling. Emphasis is currently being given to proposals for increasing supplies of water from the Rio Grande. This would be accomplished by constructing lined (and perhaps covered) canals that would divert the Texas allocation of Rio Grande water from as far upstream as Caballo Dam in New Mexico. The prospect of renegotiating the Rio Grande Compact has also been considered, but little incentive exists for either Colorado or New Mexico to consider this alternative. Colorado's allocation is fully appropriated, and New Mexico wishes to reserve its portion of Rio Grande water to promote future development of the Mesilla Valley, to reserve the water for irrigated agriculture, or to sell at a higher price to El Paso. Litigation was brought by El Paso in the 1970s against the State of New Mexico claiming infringement of interstate commerce through New Mexico's refusal to sell groundwater to El Paso from the Mesilla and Hueco bolsons. El Paso submitted sixty well permit applications in the New Mexico portion of the Hueco Bolson and 266 well permit applications in the New Mexico portion of the Mesilla Bolson. New Mexico's position has been upheld, so state officials can afford to wait and, should they wish, sell water to El Paso at a later date. No incentive exists for Texas to renegotiate the 1944 treaty with Mexico that governs allocation of Rio Grande water (Day 1975).

Projected effects of increasing water demand in the Mesilla Bolson have been modeled for the Rio Grande alluvium in one layer and, in a second layer, the upper 300 meters of the Santa Fe Group, which contains deeper, fresh bolson water. A third dimension was added to the model to simulate downward leakage of groundwater from the alluvial groundwater to the deeper bolson aquifer. Modeling was constrained by the lack of data on hydraulic head and aquifer coefficients (transmissivity, storativity). When the withdrawals from El Paso's 266 proposed wells were included, drawdown of up to 30 meters was predicted in one simulation and up to 122 meters in a second simulation, with differences between the two simulations attributed to the aquifer coefficients that were applied. Either simulation would trigger a change in direction of groundwater flow away from the Mesilla Valley, but seepage out of the Rio Grande would not be significantly increased. This is because the river is hydraulically disconnected from groundwater in the alluvium in the Mesilla Valley of New Mexico.

Seepage from the Rio Grande

The present-day El Paso–Juarez Valley is entrenched 60–80 meters into the Hueco Bolson. The Rio Grande exchanges water with the alluvium, which is up to 60 meters thick over the Hueco Bolson deposits. The unconfined groundwater in the Rio Grande alluvium lies only 3–5 meters below the surface and may be hydraulically connected to the river in places. The Rio Grande alluvium contains dissolved solids in concentrations that fluctuate according to the amount of fresh water that enters the alluvium from the river.

We examined the changing importance of seepage in the Rio Grande since 1889 for the reach between gauges at El Paso and Fort Quitman, 133 km downstream (Marston and Lloyd 1985). The proportion of streamflow between El Paso and Fort Quitman that was lost to seepage and evaporation was reduced dramatically by river management. Channel rectification was completed in 1938 to stabilize the border between Texas and Mexico along this reach. The rectification program, conducted by the Bu-

reau of Reclamation under the authority of the International Boundary and Water Commission, also served to decrease river losses in the following five ways:

(1) The length of the channel between El Paso and Fort Quitman was reduced 45 percent, from 240 to 133 km.
(2) Overbank ponding areas were eliminated by reducing the floodplain width between new artificial levees.
(3) The wetted perimeter of the channel was reduced so that a lower portion of the flow was in contact with the bed and banks of the channel where seepage could occur.
(4) The channel bed elevation was lowered, allowing greater opportunity for the river to intercept shallow subsurface flow and irrigation return flow and to receive arroyo runoff.
(5) Transpiration losses were reduced through control of streamside phreatophytes (salt cedar) on the U.S. side of the floodplain.

The seven-kilometer-long Chamizal segment of the Rio Grande through urbanized El Paso and Ciudad Juarez was paved with concrete in 1968. The net effect of the channel rectification program and Chamizal Project was to reduce the amount of water supplied to the Rio Grande alluvium. In the El Paso urban area, problems of subsidence have been reported as the water table was lowered and clays were dewatered. Farther down valley, the water table has not been lowered, but the dilution of total dissolved solids (TDS) in the alluvial groundwater has been reduced, and TDS levels are on the increase. TDS increases progressively as one moves down valley, from about 1,000 mg/l in alluvial groundwater near El Paso to 3,700 mg/l near Fort Quitman. A minimum annual runoff of 360 million cubic meters is needed at El Paso to provide sufficient water for leaching of salts from farm soils and to dilute river water for later application. This threshold runoff value has been attained in only two out of every five years since 1950. To augment river flow further, it will be necessary to undertake the following: (1) store more water in reservoirs of northern New Mexico to avoid the high evapotranspiration loss downstream; (2) add a cement lining to irrigation canals and to the Rio Grande channel; and (3) level irrigation fields, coordinate irrigation schedules, and improve phreatophyte control in the irrigation canals and on the Mexican side of the floodplain.

Increased TDS in Surface Water and Groundwater

Unconfined groundwater in the Rio Grande alluvium is hydraulically connected to leaky confined groundwater in the Hueco Bolson deposits that lie beneath the Rio Grande alluvium. Prior to heavy development of the deeper Hueco Bolson aquifer, the piezometric surface for the bolson aquifer was at a higher elevation than the water table for the Rio Grande alluvial groundwater. This meant that seepage through the discontinuous clays separating the two was in the upward direction. The fresh bolson water was diluting the alluvial groundwater charged with dissolved solids from centuries of irrigation agriculture. Excess pumping from the Hueco Bolson aquifer has lowered the piezometric surface to an elevation below the constant water table elevation. As a consequence, the direction of seepage has been reversed; the low quality alluvial groundwater leaks downward into the bolson aquifer. The alluvial aquifer is becoming more brackish, as is the deeper bolson aquifer. We suggest that one mechanism responsible for this increase in TDS is upconing. A well that penetrates the freshwater zone pulls water horizontally and vertically toward the screened sections. The interface between fresh water and salt water cones up toward the bottom of the well. If a critical pumping rate is exceeded, the freshwater-saltwater interface will reach the screened section of the well. Our modeling suggests that the 1,000 mg/l isochlor in the Hueco Bolson underlying Ciudad Juarez moved upward more than 200 meters just between 1972 and 1979 (Lloyd and Marston 1985). Some have also suggested that brackish groundwater is moving through El Paso del Norte from the Mesilla Valley into the El Paso–Juarez Valley (Phillip Goodell, pers. comm., 1999). Some combination of aquifer leakage, upconing, and lateral migration of brackish groundwater is causing an annual increase of 10 mg/l in wells of El Paso and 30 mg/l in twelve wells of Ciudad Juarez for which data are available.

Conclusions

We have pointed out that water supplies in the El Paso–Juarez border region are not located where the demand is greatest. Moreover, water supplies are divided among different political jurisdictions, each with its own economic, legal, and political mandates to protect and develop its water for the best interests of its citizens, regardless of impacts on neighbors. Sufficient supplies of water exist in the Mesilla Bolson, Hueco Bolson, and Rio Grande to supply all the needs in the twenty-first century of Doña Ana County, the City and County of El Paso, Ciudad Juarez, and the Juarez Valley. However, these supplies must be shared or Ciudad Juarez and El Paso County will run out of fresh water, perhaps as soon as the years 2020 and 2060, respectively. Under present water law, New Mexico is not compelled to share groundwater from its portion of the Hueco and Mesilla bolsons with El Paso, nor is New Mexico obligated to share its allotment of Rio Grande water with El Paso. Moreover, international treaties between the United States and Mexico allow little flexibility to reallocate groundwater or Rio Grande water. Conjunctive management of the Rio Grande and groundwater is not possible under the current water laws of Texas. For legal and political reasons, as much as for physical reasons, the El Paso–Ciudad Juarez border region finds itself in a crisis regarding future water demand and supply. Groundwater mining and the related increase in dissolved solids will render much of the current supply unusable in the next few decades. Intervention by the highest levels of federal government would provide the level of attention needed to address the crisis; parochial state government and antiquated laws will not serve the best interests of all citizens living in this large and growing border community.

References

Day, J. C. "Urban Water Management of an International River: The Case of El Paso-Cd. Juarez." *Natural Resources Journal* 15 (1975): 453–70.

———. "International Aquifer Management: The Hueco Bolson on the Rio Grande River." *Natural Resources Journal* 18 (1978): 163–80.

Knowles, T. R., and H. J. Alvarez. *Simulated Effects of Groundwater Pumping in Portions of the Hueco Bolson in Texas and New Mexico during the Period of 1973 through 2029.* Texas Department of Water Resources Report LP-104, 1979.

Lee Wilson and Associates. "Water Supply Alternatives for El Paso." Consultant's report prepared for the El Paso Water Utilities and Public Service Board, El Paso, 1981.

Lloyd, W. J. "Growth of the Municipal Water System in Ciudad Juarez, Mexico." *Natural Resources Journal* 22 (1982): 943–55.

Lloyd, W. J., and R. A. Marston. "Municipal and Industrial Water Supply in Ciudad Juarez, Mexico: Current Status and Future Prospects." Consultant's report prepared for Ford Motor Company, Dearborn, Mich., 1984.

———. "Municipal and Industrial Water Supply in Ciudad Juarez, Mexico." *Water Resources Bulletin* 21 (1985): 841–49.

Marston, R. A. "Compliance by Steere Tank Lines with Texas

New Industrial Solid Waste Management Rules." Consultant's report prepared for Danny R. Anderson, Consultants, El Paso, 1981.

———. "Geology Report: Application for Texas Department of Water Resources Part B Permit, Border Steel Mills Hazardous Waste Facilities." Consultant's report prepared for Danny R. Anderson, Consultants, El Paso, 1985

———. "Bibliography of Water Resources in the El Paso Border Region." Consultant's report prepared for Lee Wilson and Associates, Santa Fe, N.M., 1986a.

———. "Environmental Planning Maps for the City and County of El Paso." Consultant's report prepared for El Paso Department of Planning, Research and Development, El Paso, 1986b.

———. "Well Logs for El Paso County, Texas." Consultant's report prepared for Charles B. Reynolds, Consultants, Albuquerque, N.M., 1986c.

Marston, R. A., and W. J. Lloyd. "Potential Groundwater Supply in the Vicinity of Horizon Lake, El Paso County, Texas." Consultant's report prepared for Horizon Communities Improvement Association, El Paso, 1984.

———. "River Budget for the Rio Grande, El Paso–Juarez Valley." *Journal of Arid Environments* 8 (1985): 109–19.

Marston, R. A., W. J. Lloyd, and J. R. Dupuy. "Water Resources of the Hueco Bolson, Tularosa Basin, Mesilla Bolson, Lower Rio Grande, and TransPecos Region of Texas." Annotated bibliography and selected abstracts. Consultant's report prepared for Lee Wilson and Associates, Santa Fe, N.M., 1985.

Marston, R. A., W. J. Lloyd, and W. J. Peeples. "Water Resource Development Options for Southeast El Paso County." Consultant's report prepared for Horizon Communities Improvement Association, El Paso, 1983.

Marston, R. A., W. J. Peeples, and M. Raksaskulwong. "Electrical Surveys for Groundwater in the Vicinity of the Mountain Shadow Lakes Project, El Paso County, Texas." Consultant's report prepared for Horizon Communities Improvement Association, El Paso, 1985.

Meyer, W. R. *Digital Model for Simulating Effects of Groundwater Pumping in the Hueco Bolson, El Paso Area, Texas, New Mexico and Mexico.* U.S. Geological Survey Water Resources Investigation 58-75, 1976.

White, D. E. *Summary of Hydrologic Information in the El Paso, Texas, Area, with Emphasis on Ground-water Studies, 1903–1980.* U.S. Geological Survey Open-File Report 83-775, 1983.

CHAPTER 24

Instream Salinity Modeling
of Mid–Rio Grande and Wichita Basins

R. S. Muttiah, S. Miyamoto, M. Borah, and C. H. Walker

Texas Agricultural Experiment Station, Temple (Muttiah, Walker)

Texas Agricultural Experiment Station, El Paso (Miyamoto, Borah)

Abstract

The salinity of Rio Grande at Lake Amistad and Wichita at inflow into the Red River were modeled by incorporating flow-salinity relationships into the Soil and Water Assessment Tool (SWAT) hydrology model. The flow-salinity relationships for streams were analyzed by irrigated and nonirrigated seasons. Major processes involved were evaporative-concentration and dilutive mixing in flowing water. Stream bank influences were modeled through stream soil-water routing and riparian leaf area index. Model results against measured values showed reasonable agreement for Lake Amistad but poor comparisons for Wichita. Wichita results were poor because of the role played by salt dissolution from geologic formations, an irrigation canal, and damping of salinity peaks by Lake Kemp.

Salinity is a serious problem for utilities supplying potable water and in agricultural irrigation. Increased salinity in streams can damage water processing equipment through sedimentation and rusting and can also lead to public health concerns. Crop and orchard growers relying on irrigation are concerned about reduced yields due to salt toxicity on plants. In South Texas, the Amistad reservoir has seen a rise in salinity from about 500 parts per million (ppm) in 1968, when it was completed, to present concentrations near 1,000 ppm (Miyamoto et al. 1995). The Wichita basin on the border with Oklahoma also has elevated salinity levels that range above 1,000 ppm at the outlet into the Red River.

This chapter presents preliminary results of modeling salinity in large river basins using the routing component of the Soil and Water Assessment Tool (SWAT) model. Modeling of instream salinity offers water policy makers the option of rapidly checking impact of riparian management and reservoir release on downstream salinity. The SWAT model was developed by the Agricultural Research Service of the U.S. Department of Agriculture as lead agency, in collaboration with the Texas Agricultural Experiment Station in Temple, Texas. The SWAT hydrology and nonpoint-source model, which runs on a daily time step, has landscape and stream water routing components. The salinity routines discussed in this chapter were incorporated into the stream routing portion of the model. The SWAT model was applied by hydrologic cataloging units (HCUs) in two river basins in Texas: in the middle Rio Grande (fig. 1) and the Wichita basin (fig. 2). The HCU data sets used for the model runs were obtained from earlier work on the hydrologic unit modeling of the United States (HUMUS; Arnold et al. 1999). The 1:250,000 scale data sets consisted of daily climate on precipitation, maximum and minimum temperature, land use and land cover data from the U.S. Geological Survey (USGS) Land Use Data map, State Soil Geographic (STATSGO) soils, elevation and slopes from 3 arc second digital elevation models, and baseflow day periods. The HUMUS model runs were made from 1960 to 1989.

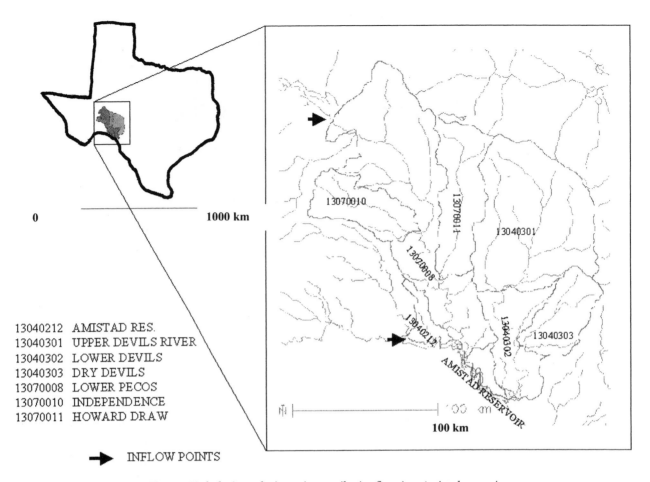

13040212 AMISTAD RES.
13040301 UPPER DEVILS RIVER
13040302 LOWER DEVILS
13040303 DRY DEVILS
13070008 LOWER PECOS
13070010 INDEPENDENCE
13070011 HOWARD DRAW

➡ INFLOW POINTS

Figure 1. Hydrologic cataloging units contributing flows into Amistad reservoir.

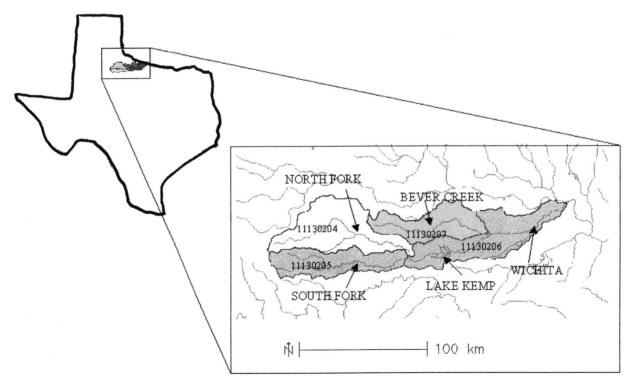

Figure 2. Wichita basin streams and hydrologic cataloging units.

Method

The flow charts in figures 3 and 4 depict the logic of the routing component in SWAT and the salinity routines. Stream water routing in sloping streams was accomplished by use of the storage coefficient method, which assumes a triangular-shaped lead crest (Williams 1969). The storage coefficient specifies outflow fraction as function of inflow and stored volume. Final volume of water flowing out of streams is based on a daily water mass balance accounting for evaporation, transmission losses, and water abstraction for consumptive use. Concentration of salt flowing out of streams is estimated from (monthly) mass balance involving (1) irrigation return flows; (2) flushing of salts concentrated on stream banks through soil-water evaporation and plant transpiration—salt flushing occurs during flooding events; (3) salt dissolution in geologic formations (assumed constant); and (4) instream mixing and concentration of salts by evaporation.

The primary driver of instream salinity modeling in SWAT was the monthly relationship between flow and salinity derived by plotting flow (Q) in units of millions of cubic meters against salinity (C) in units of milligrams per liter. In the stream segments where irrigation was important, flow-salinity relationships were derived for irrigated and nonirrigated seasons. The outflow salinity concentration was assumed to follow an exponential relationship for evaporative processes and a linear relationship for simple mixing processes. The following relationships were assumed:

(1) for evaporative processes:
$$C = C_{RO}e^{[a_R(1 - Q/Q_{RO})]}, \text{ when } Q < Q_{RO},$$

(2) for dilutive mixing processes:
$$C = [C_{RO} + C_I(Q/Q_{RO})]/(Q/Q_{RO})$$

Where C_{RO} and Q_{RO}, respectively, are the salt concentration and monthly flow prior to evaporation on the flow-salinity plot, a_R is an empirical coefficient estimated by $a_R = (\ln C)/C_{RO}$ when Q is zero, and C_I is inflow concentration.

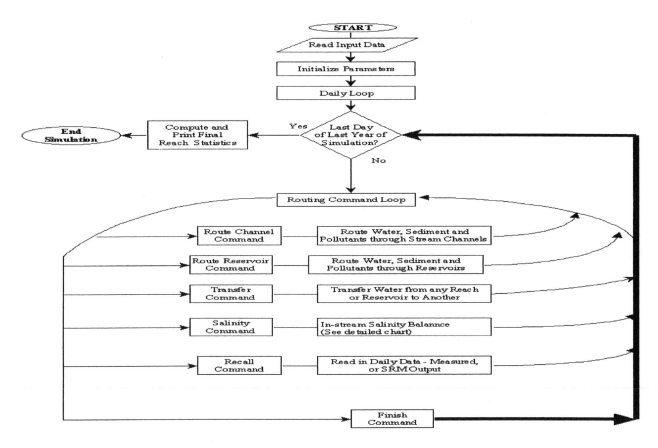

ROTO ROUTING COMPONENT

Figure 3. In stream routing component of the SWAT model.

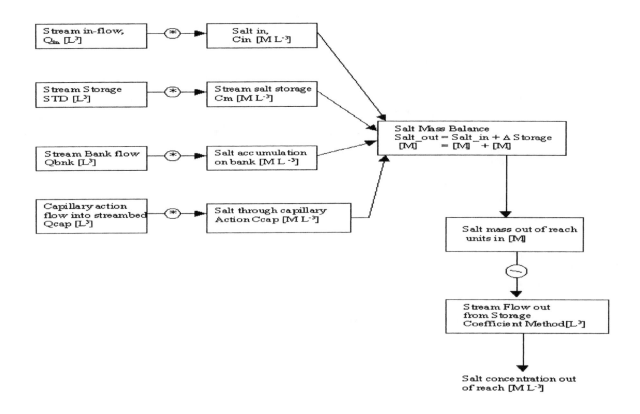

SALINITY MASS BALANCE COMPONENT (See text for discussion)

Figure 4. Instream salt balance model.

Figure 5 shows the flow and salinity relationship for the middle Rio Grande at Fort Quitman. Data for the months of October through February were taken as representative of the nonirrigated season and from March through September as irrigated season. The C_{RO} and Q_{RO} were determined by fitting equation (1) to values that passed through the most points above C_{RO} and Q_{RO}. Equation (2) denotes those points where there is leveling off of salinity to a constant. Similarly, figure 6 shows the salinity and flow relationship for the Wichita river at Charlie. Note that equation (1) is shown in the figure as equation 5, and equation (2) in the figure is shown as equation 7.

The stream bank was simulated using a two-layer soil. The water movement was simulated using the SWAT soil-water subroutines, which accumulate moisture in soil layers between wilting point and field capacity. Salts also accumulate on foliage of salt-tolerant vegetation through a tranpiration-driven process. The amount of salt accumulated on the soil surface through soil-water evaporation and riparian vegetation transpiration was assumed as

$$(3) \quad C_{sf} = [e_s + a_2(LAI)^{(e_s)c}]$$

where the soil-water evaporation of salts is $e_s = a_1(SW)^b$, and LAI is the leaf area index of riparian vegetation. Due to lack of empirical data, the constants a_1, a_2, b, and c were assumed as $a_1 = a_2 = 1$, b = 2, and c = 1.5. We expect to generate refined estimates from research on concentrative processes on stream banks over the next few years. The accumulation of salts on foliage was assumed to follow a similar nonlinear relationship, with SW replaced by the leaf area index of foliage (the model uses a phenological plant growth model).

Monthly stream inflows for the middle Rio Grande were input at HCU 13040212 in the main stem of the Rio Grande, and HCU 13070008 for inflows into the Pecos. Since inflows were used for modeling the river basin, the SWAT predicted flows at outlet into Amistad can be expected to follow measured flows. The initial salinity concentrations in all stream segments were set at 500 mg/l, a value near the average salinity measured in the

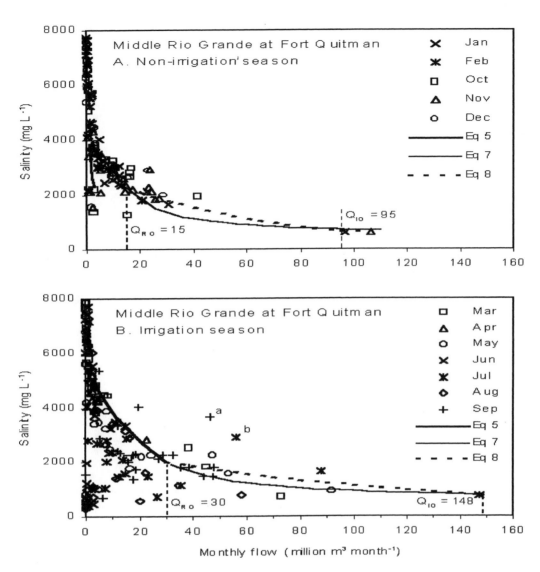

Figure 5. Flow-salinity relationship for the Middle Rio Grande at Fort Quitman.

Amistad International Reservoir in the early 1960s. The average baseflow salinity for the Pecos basin was estimated at 2,000 mg/L from flow-salinity plots, and the rest of mid–Rio Grande baseflow salinity was estimated at 250 mg/L.

The Wichita was modeled without use of measured inflows into the river system. The SWAT predicted outflows were therefore validated against measured flows at the outlet of the Wichita basin at the Charlie gauge. The initial value of stream salinity was set at 1,000 mg/l based on salinity measurements at Charlie. The average baseflow concentration of 10,000 mg/l in the north and south forks of the Wichita was estimated from the flows in those subbasins, mostly springs. The Wichita Irrigation District

canal is the major source of salinity in return flows (estimated at 3,000 ppm).

The salinity data for streams bordering Mexico were obtained from the International Boundary and Water Commission (IBWC). Salinity for the Wichita (chloride concentration) was estimated from regression of conductivity, which was measured on a daily basis against chloride, which was irregularly sampled (see Walker 2000 for details).

Results and Discussion

Figure 7 shows the SWAT predicted flow and the USGS measured flows at the Charlie gauge at the Wichita outlet.

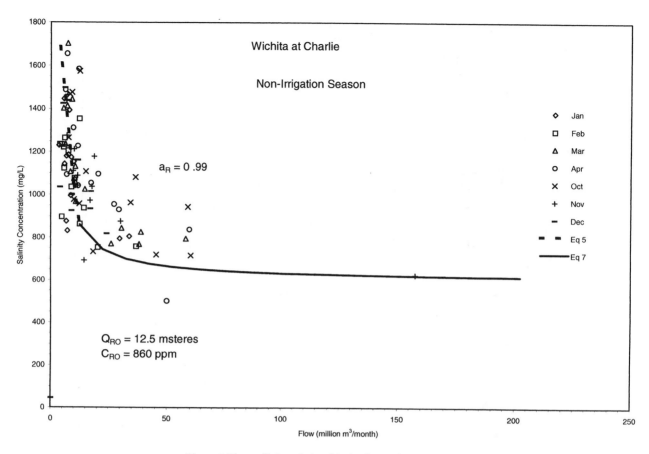

Figure 6. Flow-salinity relationship for the Wichita at Charlie.

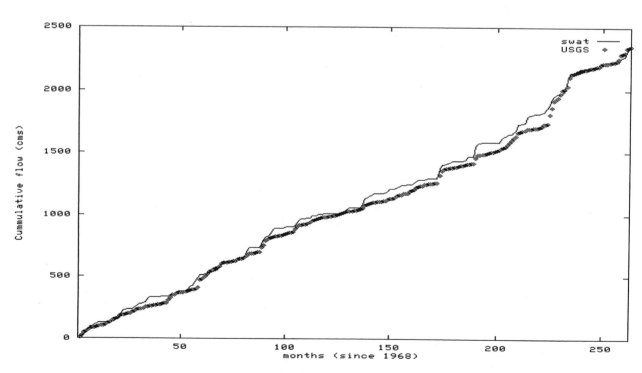

Figure 7. The SWAT predicted and measured flows at Charlie, Wichita basin.

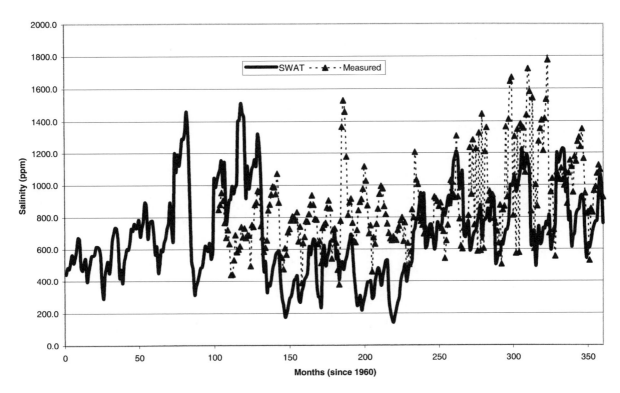

Figure 8. Predicted and observed salinity at inflow into Amistad reservoir.

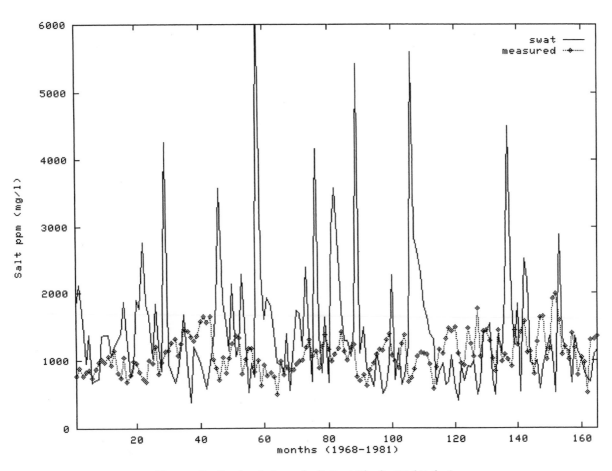

Figure 9. Predicted and observed salinity at Charlie, Wichita basin.

Calibration was performed by decreasing curve numbers for antecedent moisture II (default) conditions by 24, and setting the groundwater (deep root) extraction coefficient to 0.2. No adjustments were made to the STATSGO soil parameters. Since inflows were used, and no USGS gauge was located at points into Amistad reservoir, no calibration/validation was performed for the Amistad runs.

Figure 8 shows the modeled and IBWC observed salinity at Amistad (water quality station at outflow of reservoir). While the model is able to predict the tendency toward higher salinity levels, and even approaches the final salinity levels about 1989, there is significant underprediction for several years. Interestingly, the model results suggest that due to upstream flow releases, the seasonal nature of salinity increases and decreases have abated compared to the pre-dam periods, while absolute salinity concentration in Amistad has risen. Another contributing factor toward the low side of prediction capabilities of SWAT is that Rio Conchos (salinity range 500–1,500 ppm) from Mexico was not modeled. The model predictions show limitation of the routing component without an adequate lake mixing model for salinity.

Figure 9 shows the modeled and observed salinity for the Wichita basin. The model significantly overpredicts the peaks but has ability to capture the general salinity trend. It is likely that the peaks in the Wichita are damped by the presence of Lake Kemp, which has been observed to decrease salinity of inflows at outflow by several orders of magnitude.

Conclusions

While the SWAT-salt model has the ability to predict the general trend in observed salinity at two of the tested watersheds, absence of a lake mixing model for salinity limits predictive capability. Further work is required for determining the empirical coefficients governing salt flushing along stream banks.

References

Arnold, J. G., R. Srinivasan, R. S. Muttiah, and P. M. Allen. "Continental Scale Simulation of the Hydrologic Balance." *J. AWRA* 35, no. 5 (1999): 1037–51.

Miyamoto, S., L. B. Fenn, and D. Swietlik. "Flow, Salts, and Trace Elements in the Rio Grande: A Review." TR-169, Texas Water Resources Institute. College Station, Texas, 1995.

Williams, J. R. "Flood Routing with Variable Travel Time or Variable Storage Coefficients." *Trans. ASAE* 12, no. 1 (1969): 100–103.

CHAPTER 25

Water in the Lower Rio Grande Border Region

A Binational Perspective

Mitchell L. Mathis

Mitchell Center for Sustainable Development

Houston Advanced Research Center

Abstract

This chapter considers various water issues in the drought-prone Lower Rio Grande/Río Bravo basin on the Texas-Mexico border.[1] While the emphasis is on the Texas portion of the region, the binational context is also discussed. The focus is on six key factors—population growth, water supply, water use, water quality, ecology, and the institutional context of water management—as well as future scenarios of water scarcity, including a scenario of increased water use upstream in the Mexican Rio Conchos watershed. One of the chapter's underlying themes is that most water problems in the Lower Rio Grande/Río Bravo basin are complex and have a binational element, hence their solution will likely require innovative interdisciplinary approaches and a binational management response. The chapter concludes that despite a wide range of opportunities to use existing water supplies more efficiently, greater institutional cooperation—within and between Texas and Mexico—is required to improve regionwide water management and move the region toward a more sustainable future.

Over the course of the last century, Rio Grande water has supported the development of intensive agriculture as well as rapid population growth in the lower part of the binational river basin, despite frequent droughts and chronic water scarcity. As the region enters a new century, a booming urban population—the twin cities of Brownsville and Matamoros, McAllen and Reynosa, and Laredo and Nuevo Laredo are in the region—and growing industrial and agricultural sectors are creating unprecedented demands on scarce surface water resources. Since 1994, a severe and prolonged drought has exacerbated water shortages in the region, testing the limited water supply and existing institutions for water management on each side of the river as never before. In terms of both availability and quality, water is a central and possibly limiting factor for future development in the region.

To examine the vital linkages between water and development in the lower part of the Rio Grande/Río Bravo basin, the Houston Advanced Research Center (HARC), in collaboration with the Instituto Tecnológico y de Estudios Superiores de Monterrey (ITESM), undertook a major four-year interdisciplinary research effort (Schmandt et al. 2000). The HARC-ITESM assessment approached the binational region, and the watershed within which it is located, as a complex interconnected system. To carry out the assessment, a multidisciplinary group of researchers from Mexico and the United States was organized into six teams: (1) water supply and demand, (2) water quality, (3) population, (4) socioeconomics, (5) ecology, and (6) water management.[2] As in many watersheds, knowledge and information about the Lower Rio Grande/Bravo basin is fragmented, disjointed, incomplete, and sometimes inaccurate. The main objective of the assessment was to integrate and analyze existing information and data across disciplinary and geopolitical boundaries in order to establish a more complete understanding of current and future conditions regarding water and development of the binational region. This chapter reviews some of the key findings of the HARC-ITESM assessment and provides additional analysis of the complex water challenges of the Texas portion of the Lower Rio Grande/Río Bravo basin.

The Rio Grande/Río Bravo Basin

The Rio Grande is the fifth largest river in North America. It runs north-south from its source in the Rocky Mountains of southern Colorado to El Paso, Texas. From there it turns southeast and for over twelve hundred miles serves as the border between Mexico and Texas. Due to intensive human development and water use in Colorado,

New Mexico, and West Texas, the river runs dry south of El Paso during much of the year. As a result, the Lower Rio Grande/Río Bravo, from Fort Quitman, Texas, to the Gulf of Mexico, has effectively become a separate watershed. Below Fort Quitman, two tributaries—the Río Conchos from Mexico and the Pecos River from the United States—are the main sources of inflow into the main stem of the river.[3]

For the Lower Rio Grande/Río Bravo, as for any river that derives its flow from deep-convection precipitation, the flows are what are known as "flashy," or a series of sharp rises followed by recessions of stage. As a result of the region's semiarid climate, major rainfall events are widely spaced in time. Most of the rainfall is absorbed by the watershed due to the dry, desiccated nature of the terrain. Consequently, these spikes of precipitation typically do not create appreciable increases in streamflow in the main stem of the Lower Rio Grande. Only for very large rainfall events, or a closely timed series of several smaller occurrences, does a storm hydrograph appear in the river. Thus, the long-term river hydrograph (see fig. 1) of the Lower Rio Grande is characterized by long periods of low

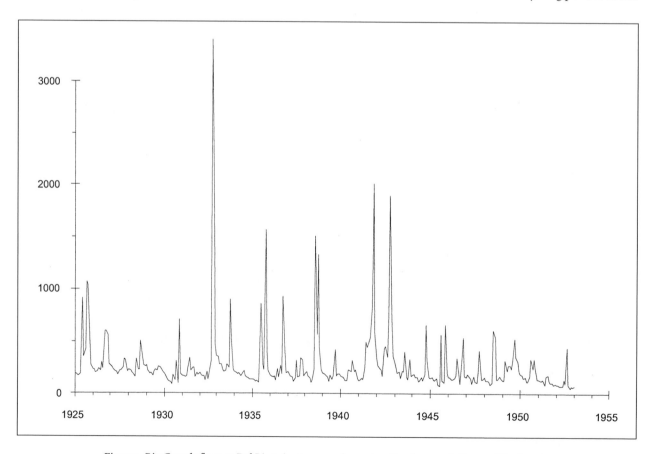

Figure 1. Rio Grande flows at Del Rio prior to reservoir construction (1925–53). Source: Ward 1998a.

Table 1. Binational allocation of Rio Grande water below Fort Quitman, Treaty of 1944

Mexico	United States
All waters in San Juan and Alamo rivers	All waters in Pecos and Devil's rivers (plus waters from several minor tributaries and springs
2/3 of flow reaching the Rio Grande from Conchos, Las Vacas, Salado, San Diego, San Rodrigo, and Escondido rivers	1/3 of flow reaching the Rio Grande from Conchos, Las Vacas, Salado, San Diego, San Rodrigo, and Escondido rivers, but not less than 350,000 acre-feet/year averaged over 5-year cycles (ending whenever the U.S. storage capacity is filled)
1/2 of flow in Rio Grande main channel below lowest international storage dam	1/2 of flow in Rio Grande main channel below lowest international storage dam
1/2 of all other flows not specifically allotted	1/2 of all other flows not specifically allotted

flow punctuated by very high flow events on an interval of several years (Ward 1998a).

The Treaty of 1944 (U.S. Department of State 1946) is at the center of Texas-Mexico water issues concerning the lower Rio Grande watershed downstream of Fort Quitman. Among other things, the treaty formally establishes between Texas and Mexico the current division of the flows to the Rio Grande from the tributaries below Fort Quitman, which are summarized in table 1. The treaty also authorized the construction and binational operation of Falcón and Amistad international reservoirs under the auspices of the International Boundary and Water Commission (IBWC). Falcón reservoir was completed in 1953 and Amistad reservoir was completed in 1969.

The Falcón and Amistad reservoirs, which are operated as a tandem system, dominate the hydrology of the Lower Rio Grande/Río Bravo basin. The reservoir system allows for the capture and storage of the runoff on the watershed from the large, infrequent meteorological events, thus performing the dual functions of protection against floods as well as provision of a more reliable water supply for users downstream.[4] The water supplied by the Falcón-Amistad system supports intensive agriculture in the lower part of the basin, growth of the region's municipalities and industries, and a wide variety of flora and fauna that comprise the region's unique mix of highly diverse ecosystems.

The Binational Lower Rio Grande/Río Bravo Border Region

The Lower Rio Grande/Río Bravo Border Region (LRGB) receives the vast majority of its water as runoff from the larger watershed that extends far upstream. As defined in Schmandt and colleagues (2000), the LRGB includes six Texas counties—Cameron, Hidalgo, Starr, Webb, Willacy, and Zapata—and ten *municipios* in the state of Tamaulipas—Matamoros, Valle Hermoso, Río Bravo, Reynosa, Gustavo Díaz Ordaz, Camargo, Miguel Alemán, Mier, Guerrero, and Nuevo Laredo. The Texas portion of the LRGB is called the Texas Lower Rio Grande Valley (TV), in keeping with local terminology (fig. 2), while the Mexico portion is known as the Tamaulipas Border Region (TBR).[5]

Figure 2. Map of the Texas Lower Rio Grande Valley. Source: Schmandt et al. 2000.

The LRGB represents a rich mix of cultures, traditional lifestyles, and rural and urban communities. The region is characterized by rapid population growth and urban development; intensive irrigation, occasional floods, and frequent droughts; significant and increasing industrial *maquiladora* production, a highly integrated binational economy in terms of goods, services, investment, and labor; high incidence of poverty; and significant ecological degradation. Following are some of the key findings of the HARC-ITESM assessment regarding water in the LRGB.

Population

As shown in figure 3, the LRGB has experienced rapid population growth since the 1950s, a trend that will continue over the next several decades. From 1950 to 1995 population rose from around 680,000 to more than 2.1 million—an increase of more than 200 percent. Over this period, the population in the Texas Valley (TV) grew from approximately 381,000 to nearly one million, more than 150 percent, while the Tamaulipas Border Region absorbed a 300 percent increase in population, which rose from approximately 299,000 in 1950 to almost 1.2 million in 1995. Much of the increase is the result of in-migration from the interior of Mexico.

Over the next thirty years the total population of the LRGB is expected to more than double to an estimated 4.9 million in 2030, with 2.3 million people living on the Texas side of the river and 2.6 million in the Tamaulipas

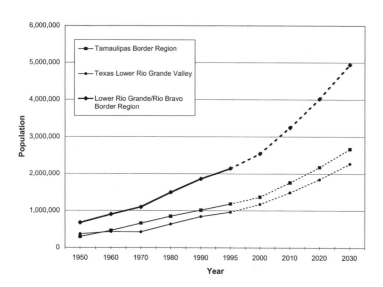

Figure 3. Historical and projected population growth in the Lower Rio Grande Border Region. Source: Adapted from Schmandt et al. 2000.

Border Region. Since the completion of Falcón Reservoir in 1953, the population of the LRGB will have increased by a whopping 600 percent by the year 2030, placing increasing pressure on the region's scarce water resources.[6] This rapid growth in population will be concentrated almost entirely in the region's urban areas and will exact tremendous demands on existing water treatment, delivery, and sewerage infrastructure.

Water Supply

The Falcón-Amistad reservoir system is the source of nearly all—more than 90 percent—of the LRGB's water.[7] The two reservoirs have a total combined storage capacity of 11,382 million cubic meters (Mm^3), 6,475 Mm^3 at Amistad and 4,907 Mm^3 at Falcón. Approximately 73 percent of this total capacity—4,100 Mm^3 at Amistad and 3,200 Mm^3 at Falcón—is allocated to conservation storage, the remaining 27 percent to flood control (Ward 1998a, Lower Rio Grande Valley Development Council 1999). Of the conservation storage in the two reservoirs, the United States is allocated 56.2 percent at Amistad and 58.6 percent at Falcón, with Mexico receiving the remainder.[8] These allocations of conservation storage are treated much like separate bank accounts, and wide differences in the percentage of water remaining in the two countries' conservation pools are common. As of this writing, the ownership of the reservoir contents stands at 33 percent of total conservation capacity allocated to the United States and 8 percent is Mexico's portion of total conservation capacity (IBWC 2000).

The infrequent high flow rainfall events that occur on the watershed play a major role in filling the reservoirs, which otherwise are in a general state of drawdown (Ward 1998a).[9] This pattern—a sharp rise in storage content in response to a major storm event, followed by a prolonged period of drawdown—is clearly seen in figure 4, which depicts the contents of the two reservoirs measured daily from January, 1990 to June, 2000. The most recent year in which the annual average of the combined contents of both reservoirs surpassed 100 percent of storage capacity was 1992.[10] The annual average of reservoir contents fell to about 84 percent of capacity in the subsequent year and dropped to 60 percent in 1994. Since 1995 to the time of this writing, the annual average of the combined reservoir contents has hovered around 30 percent of their total reservoir capacity; however, on several occasions, the contents dropped below 25 percent. During this period, the contents of Falcón fell to as low as 8 percent of its

Combined Reservoir Contents

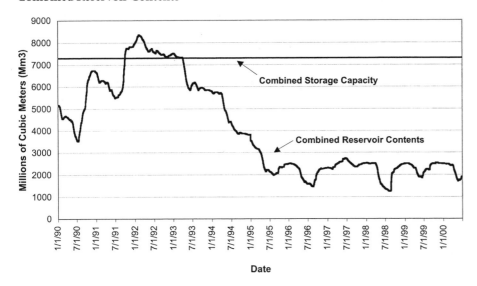

Amistad Reservoir Contents

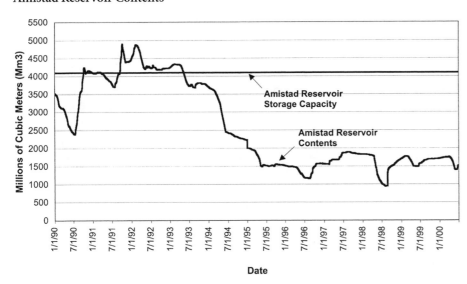

Falcon Reservoir Contents

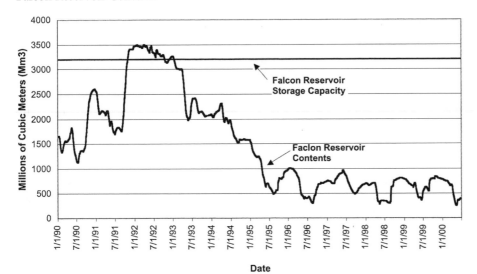

Figure 4. Contents of Amistad and Falcón reservoirs, 1990–2000.

conservation capacity, while Amistad's contents dropped to as low as 16 percent of capacity.

Reservoir operation is a complex process driven by the hydrological state of the reservoirs, demands from downstream users, judgment weighing the risk of flood versus drought, and the political contexts within the two countries. Generally, Falcón is drawn down first. This is hydrologically prudent since it maximizes the available storage downstream and thus enables rainfall events to be captured whether they occur on the Amistad or Falcón watershed. As noted earlier, reservoir releases occur for one of two purposes, either flood pool evacuation or to satisfy delivery requests from downstream users.

The central focus of water in the HARC-ITESM assessment required extensive hydrological analysis of the region. Ward (1998a, b, 1999a, b) and Navar (1998, 1999) developed models to analyze reservoir operation, diversion for agricultural, municipal and industrial uses, and the distribution of instream flow in the Lower Rio Grande/Río Bravo watershed. These models allow simulation of reservoir operation and river flow under a range of past, current, and postulated future conditions.

Using the hydrological record from 1945 to 1960 and population projections, Ward (1998b) simulated current operation of the Falcón-Amistad reservoir system under conditions that include the region's worst drought of the twentieth century (1950–54) as well as several floods. The current reservoir system did not exist during this period and has never been subjected to such extreme drought conditions, except under the current drought. In the absence of complete data from the current drought, Ward's (1998b) drought-of-record analysis uses the historical record to analyze the simulated performance of the reservoir system under extreme drought conditions. This analysis serves as a meaningful benchmark against which data from the current drought can be compared once they have been thoroughly analyzed.

Ward's (1998b) analysis of water supply also included simulations under four future scenarios of water scarcity:

(1) *Population Growth between Falcón and Amistad*: This scenario adjusts the analysis of the 1945–60 hydrology to account for increased water use between Falcón and Amistad reservoirs due to projected population growth to the year 2030.[11]

(2) *Full Conchos Development*: Despite present shortfall of flow from the Río Conchos watershed, the average inflow into the Río Grande/

Bravo from the Río Conchos (and other minor tributaries in Mexico) has historically been much greater than the amount required by treaty.[12] This scenario is based on the possibility that in the future Mexico will utilize all Conchos water except the treaty amount.

(3) *Superdrought*: Removal from the 1945–60 hydrological data of a single, isolated anomalous weather event (Tropical Storm Alice) that occurred during drought of record creates a more likely representation of the "worst possible drought."

(4) *Worst Case:* Population growth between Falcón and Amistad, full Conchos development, and superdrought scenarios are combined.

Because water supply available in the Falcón-Amistad system varies greatly over time, Ward (1998a, b, 1999a, b) utilized firm yield—a key concept in reservoir planning—as a quantitative indicator of water supply that allows comparison across the complex and variable conditions of the water supply scenarios described. Firm yield is defined as the maximum constant flow that the reservoir system can deliver without failure, even in the depths of the drought of record. In the case of the Falcón-Amistad reservoir system, it should be emphasized that firm yield serves only as an indicator and that the system has never been operated under a firm yield approach. According to Ward's (1998a) calculations, the firm yield of the tandem Falcón-Amistad reservoir system under the 1945–60 hydrology is 2774.4 Mm^3 per year (231.2 Mm^3/month). Texas' share, based on the allocation of the conservation pools for the two reservoirs, is approximately 1,500 Mm^3/yr. This is corroborated by the 1,472 Mm^3/yr (1,194,000 acre-ft/yr) firm yield calculated in the Lower Rio Grande Development Council's (1999) "Integrated Water Resource Plan" based on IBWC data from the longer period 1945–96.

In the HARC-ITESM assessment, Ward (1998b) used the firm yield for the 1945–60 drought-of-record scenario as a benchmark against which the firm yield calculated under the four future scenarios of water supply described could be compared. Of these scenarios, the one with the single greatest impact on the firm yield of Falcón-Amistad is that of future development and increased water use on the Río Conchos watershed in Mexico. Under this scenario, the firm yield of the reservoir system was 23 percent less than the benchmark firm yield under the 1945–60 hydrology. The effect of deleting Tropical Storm

Table 2. Falcón-Amistad firm yield under various hydrological scenarios, in million m³/month

Population Growth	1945–60 Hydrology	Full Conchos Development	Superdrought	Worst Case*
1990	229.6	176.7	201.7	157.5
	(0%)	(−23%)	(−12%)	(−31%)
2010	229.6	175.9	199.6	157.5
	(0%)	(−23%)	(−13%)	(−31%)
2030	229.6	175.9	198.8	157.5
	(0%)	(−23%)	(−13%)	(−31%)

Conchos Development + Superdrought

Source: Ward 1993a.

Alice from the hydrological record results in about a 10 percent decrease in the firm yield of the combined system. Between the two reservoirs, the effect of population growth on water supply was minimal, reducing the firm yield under the 1945–60 hydrology by less than 1 percent. The "worst-case" scenario, combining the three future scenarios, showed a reduction of the firm yield by around 30 percent for a value of 1,890 Mm³/yr (157.5 Mm³/month), of which Texas' share would be approximately 1,100 Mm³/yr. These reductions in water supply are summarized in table 2.

Water Use

As long as water is available in the Falcón-Amistad conservation pools of Mexico and Texas, the IBWC will release water as requested by the appropriate entities from the two countries.[13] Agricultural, industrial, and municipal users comprise the bulk of the demand for waters from the international reservoir system, with agricultural use making up the vast majority of this demand. The river channel serves as the conduit for delivery of these released flows to their ultimate users. Mexico diverts its share of the water mainly at a single point, the Anzaldúas Canal. In Texas, water is diverted in smaller quantities at a number of points along the river. The volumes of water diverted vary greatly from month to month, season to season, and year to year.

As water is diverted from the river channel to various users in both Mexico and the United States, the remaining flow in the channel is concomitantly reduced. The river flows at Brownsville or Matamoros are typically reduced to 20 percent or less of the flow measured immediately below Falcón Reservoir and dropped to zero during the drought of record. Inflows of Rio Grande water into the Gulf of Mexico have ceased entirely during the current drought. Yet the instream flow of the Lower Rio Grande/Río Bravo is necessary to achieve dilution of wasteloads discharged to the river channel, to extrude salinity intruding up the channel from the Gulf of Mexico, and to maintain various ecosystems in and along the river as well as in the estuary and inshore bays of the Gulf. Thus, in addition to agricultural as well as municipal and industrial uses, instream uses of water must be included as a third broad category of water use.[14]

Using IBWC data from 1972 to 1990, Ward (1999a) calculated average total diversions, from Mexico and Texas combined, at approximately 2,532 Mm³/yr (211 Mm³/month).[15] Navar (1999) examined IBWC records from 1980 to 1993 and found that the total average monthly diversions for Mexico and Texas were nearly equal—approximately 115 Mm³/month (1,380 Mm³/yr) for Mexico and 113 Mm³/month (1,356 Mm³/yr) for the TV. Data from the Texas Water Development Board (TWDB) show total 1990 water use for the TV to be 1,724 Mm³/yr, with estimates for 2000 at over 1,800 Mm³/yr. TWDB projects that in the year 2030, water use in the TV will likely be more than 1,900 Mm³/yr.

As in most other parts of Texas, agriculture is by far the largest user of water in the LRGB, historically comprising between 75 to 85 percent of total water use.[16] This compares with irrigation's share of about two-thirds of total water use in Texas overall. More important, while groundwater is the source of approximately 70 percent of the water used for irrigation purposes statewide, in the TV nearly 99 percent of irrigation water comes from the Rio Grande/Río Bravo. Data from TWDB show that water used for irrigation in the TV varies widely from year to year but has remained more or less constant over the past decade (1984–95), averaging around 1,300 Mm³/yr. Looking to the future, TWDB projects a slight decline (6.5 percent) over the next three decades, falling from 1,559 Mm³ in 2000 to 1,395 in 2030. Such reductions are consistent with the existing trend of slowly declining acreage of irrigated land that began in the mid-1970s.[17]

At present, the combined municipal and industrial (M&I) uses in the TV amount to around 300 Mm³/yr. Driven by projections of population growth for the TV, municipal and industrial use of water is estimated almost to double, reaching more than 500 Mm³/month by 2030 (Schmandt et al. 2000). In terms of Texas' portion of the 1945–60 firm yield for the Falcón-Amistad reservoir system as described, M&I will require around 30 percent of the water supply. This share rises to 44 percent if firm yield under the worst-case scenario is used (Ward 1998b).

To compare water supply with water use, Ward (1999a) developed an index called "irrigation shortfall"—based on recent uncurtailed agricultural use and municipal and industrial demand on both sides of the river—as a measure of water scarcity.[18] Given the existing priority of municipal and industrial uses over agricultural irrigation in both Texas and Mexico, this index assumes that the former are satisfied first, and the latter receives the remainder. At current levels of municipal and industrial water use and using Ward's methodology, the irrigation shortfall measure for the TV is approximately 16 percent below the estimated uncurtailed irrigation demand. This suggests that under drought conditions, the Falcón-Amistad reservoir system cannot supply enough water to meet the current municipal and industrial uses, nor can it meet the uncurtailed demands of agricultural irrigation. The periodic shortages of irrigation water during the drought of the past several years reinforce this finding.

The irrigation shortfall index was also calculated under each of the future scenarios described.[19] The effects of population growth in the TV to the year 2030, and the corresponding increases in municipal and industrial water demands, increase the irrigation shortfall indicator to about 25 percent of potential irrigation demand. Under the worst-case water availability scenario, the shortfall would increase to more than 50 percent of potential irrigation demand. The irrigation shortfall indexes calculated under the various scenarios are summarized in table 3.

Certainly part of the region's future water shortfall could be met by declining water use in agriculture due to the continued conversion of land from agricultural to urban uses. Nonetheless, Ward's (1999a) analysis suggests that as pressure on the LRGB's water resources increases, due to urban population growth and increased water use on the Río Conchos watershed upstream in Mexico, agri-

Table 3. Irrigation shortfall index under various scenarios

2030 Scenarios	Shortfall (Million m³/yr)	Shortfall*
1945–60 Hydrology	241.8	16%
Population Growth	369.0	25%
Full Conchos Development	717.0	48%
Superdrought	568.2	38%
Worst Case	836.4	55%

*In terms of estimated potential irrigation demand (1,500 Million m³/yr).

Source: Adapted from Ward 1999a.

culture will almost certainly face future reductions in the supply of water available for crop irrigation.

Water Quality

As urban population growth and economic development continue, both in the LRGB and in the watersheds above the Falcón and Amistad reservoirs, the *quality* of the region's water is taking on ever greater importance. Historically, wastewater from the Mexico border communities has been discharged directly into the Rio Grande/Río Bravo with minimal or no treatment. Toxic discharges have been documented downstream from population centers in the lower basin and are most prevalent near the maquiladora industrial parks (IBWC 1994; TNRCC 1994). In response to these threats, concerted efforts from Mexico as well as the binational arena and the United States are now being directed at increasing wastewater treatment capacity in the Mexico portion of the LRGB. Nonetheless, water quality will continue to be a major concern for the region as more water is used for municipal and industrial purposes, which generally require higher quality than does agriculture.

To assess the existing water quality of the Lower Rio Grande/Río Bravo for the HARC-ITESM project, Vogel-Martinez and colleagues (1998) compiled existing historical data from a number of Mexican and U.S. sources and found that although the Lower Rio Grande/Río Bravo generally exhibits adequate water quality trends relative to current standards, there is cause for some specific concerns. At times, high levels of total dissolved solids (TDS) exist in the study area, but this could be due to natural brines associated with flows from the Pecos River rather than to identifiable point- or nonpoint-source loads within the lower basin. High concentrations of constituents such as chlorides and sulfates that make up TDS are also found, especially under low flow conditions, and have occasionally rendered the river water unsuitable for agricultural irrigation and other uses.

Vogel-Martinez and colleagues (1998) found ample evidence that untreated point and/or nonpoint wastewater discharges are causing elevated levels of fecal coliform concentrations in the Lower Rio Grande/Río Bravo's waters. Levels of total suspended solids (TSS) are high throughout the Lower Rio Grande. There is some evidence that organic loads to the Lower Rio Grande/Río Bravo system raise dissolved oxygen (BOD_5) levels slightly but not enough to cause deleterious impacts to dissolved oxygen resources under the flow conditions at which measurements were made. The limitation of the data did not permit identification of specific sources of toxic substances, but those toxic effects that were found were most noticeable downstream from the largest cities along the river.[20]

Dramatic impacts on water quality were found to be related to low flow conditions that coincide with a substantial rise in the concentration of dissolved solids. Armstrong (1999) analyzed the response of dissolved oxygen under the future water availability scenarios described previously.[21] He found that under the low flow conditions emerging under these scenarios, and as waste loads to the river increase, the dissolved oxygen concentrations fall farther and farther below the normal standard of five mg/L.[22] Under these conditions, the dissolved oxygen concentrations are such that further treatment of wastewaters would be needed to meet Texas' dissolved oxygen standards.[23] This was true under all of the scenarios and serves to underscore the important, but often overlooked, relationship between quantity of stream flow and water quality. Problems with other constituents are also likely under decreasing flow conditions. Armstrong (1999) concludes that the combination of low flow and high mineral content in the Lower Rio Grande/Río Bravo is likely to be exacerbated in years ahead with continued diminished flows due to uses of water upstream as well as increases in wastewater discharges. This, in turn, could reduce the amount of water of sufficient quality to supply agriculture, domestic, municipal, and ecosystem demands.

Ecosystem

The LRGB lies in one of the most biodiverse regions in North America, a unique confluence of flora and fauna found in the deserts to the west, coastal areas to the east, the temperate zone to the north, and tropical and subtropical regions to the south.[24] Population and economic growth as well as irrigated agriculture and reservoir construction have had a significant impact on the region's ecology.[25] The region's ecosystem is thus under tremendous pressure and is an important but often neglected user of the Rio Grande/Río Bravo water.

For the HARC-ITESM assessment, Edwards and Contreras (1997) use fish communities as an indicator of the ecological health of the river.[26] They examine historical data on the river's fish populations and find that major alterations to the riparian ecosystem have occurred steadily over the course of the last century. The river from Falcón to Brownsville-Matamoros has lost many of its freshwater species, while exotic or estuarine and even marine species are found in increasing numbers. This trend is particularly pronounced near the mouth of the river. These faunal changes appear to be correlated with decreasing streamflows, the proliferation of exotic species, and increases in chemical pollution.

Building on the data in Edwards and Contreras (1997), Contreras and co-workers (1999) develop an index of biological integrity (IBI), and a broader index of bio-ecological integrity (IBEI), for evaluating the condition of the riverine ecosystem of the Lower Rio Grande/Río Bravo.[27] Their IBI consists of a number of metrics (see, e.g., Karr and Chu 1997) regarding the fish populations in the river, such as number of species, number of individuals within each species, classification by river habitat, feeding habits, and whether the species is native or introduced. The broader IBEI incorporates the metrics used in the IBI as well as measures of the quality of the riverine habitat, including various chemical measures of water quality (pH, dissolved oxygen, dissolved and suspended solids, and a number of chemical pollutants) and other indicators of pollution (turbidity, odor, scum, and evidence of fish mortality). In contrast to the conclusions of the water quality analysis, the resulting ratings of the condition of riverine ecosystem under both the IBI and IBEI are poor for nearly all locations in the region. Contreras and colleagues (1999) list habitat destruction, decreased streamflow, rising ambient water temperature, turbidity and siltation, salinization and pollution, and invasive species as contributing factors.

Edwards and Contreras (1997) and Contreras and colleagues (1999) conclude that streamflow and other habitat requirements for a healthy river ecosystem downstream from Falcón are not met today and will probably decline further as human demands for water increase into the future.

Water Management

As elsewhere along the Texas-Mexico border, water management in the Lower Rio Grande/Río Bravo is complex, involving international, federal, state, and local institutions. At the international level, in accordance with the Treaty of 1944, the Mexican and U.S. sections of the IBWC work cooperatively to carry out responsibilities that include undertaking and managing binational water infrastructure projects, such as the Falcón and Amistad reservoir system, and monitoring each nation's water accounts, as described briefly earlier. The two sections of the IBWC are part of the state departments of their respective countries. While the Treaty of 1944 establishes a quantitative allocation of river water between Mexico and Texas, no such agreement exists to deal with the binational aspects of water quality, minimum instream flow for ecosystem maintenance, and other environmental issues. Despite the regular occurrences of drought, no formal binational mechanism for drought management exists.

At the state level, jurisdiction over Texas' water resources falls under two agencies: the Texas Water Development Board and the Texas Natural Resource Conservation Commission (TNRCC). The TWDB is responsible for statewide water planning while the TNRCC, as part of its regulatory responsibility over the state's environmental quality and natural resources, regulates the state's water resources. The Rio Grande watermaster is an office within the TNRCC designated with the specific responsibility of managing Texas' share of Rio Grande water, requesting delivery of water to irrigation districts and cities according to the unique system of water rights that exists for this stretch of the river.[28]

At least one regional water planning entity is found in the TV, the Rio Grande Regional Water Planning Group (Rio Grande RWPG). This was established when the 75th Texas Legislature passed Senate Bill 1 in 1997 in response to the growing awareness of the state's vulnerability to drought and to the limits of existing water supplies. The stakeholder-based planning group is charged with assessing the adequacy of current water supplies, forecasting water demands for the region, and developing strategies to ensure adequate water supply for the region over the next fifty years. The Rio Grande RWPG is one of sixteen such regional planning groups established by SB 1 to coordinate long-term water planning at the regional level.[29]

The Rio Grande RWPG recently completed its regional water plan, which was submitted to the TWDB in January, 2001. This plan, along with the regional water plans from the other SB 1 regional planning groups, will be included in a new state water plan. Regional water plans will subsequently be updated every five years.

Local institutions in the TV include nearly thirty irrigation and water improvement districts as well a number of city water utilities. These entities hold water rights to the U.S. portion of the Rio Grande water in the form of permits issued by the TNRCC. They request deliveries of water from the Rio Grande watermaster, who works with the IBWC to coordinate releases from the Falcón-Amistad reservoir system. These local entities then divert the water to which they are entitled from the Rio Grande and distribute it to their end users. In some cases, irrigation or water improvement districts deliver water to city water utilities in addition to their member agricultural producers.

Finally, in addition to these planning and management entities, the Lower Rio Grande Valley is one of the few places in the United States with a functioning market for water rights.[30] In this market, existing water rights can be either sold or leased in a voluntary transaction between a willing buyer and seller. Most major transactions occur as a transfer of water from agricultural water right holders to cities. This market provides a degree of flexibility regarding the reallocation of water between agricultural, municipal, and industrial interests.

While it is unlikely that techniques such as cloud seeding and desalination will become feasible on a large scale in the near future, there is much that can currently be done to make better use of the existing water supplied by the river. The reuse of highly treated municipal wastewater for nonpotable uses, such as turf and landscape irrigation and certain industrial uses, represents an increasingly popular option.[31] Wastewater reuse recently ranked highest among a wide range of potential water management strategies in the Rio Grande RWPG, considering both feasibility and preference (see Kaiser et al. 2000), and represents a significant new source of future municipal water in the group's regional plan.

A second possibility involves changing the way the Falcón-Amistad reservoir system is operated. Two basic changes to reservoir operation exist that could increase the available water supply from the Falcón-Amistad reservoir system: increase the storage capacity or curtail releases during droughts. Though these changes in reservoir operation could increase somewhat the water supply available to the Lower Rio Grande/Río Bravo basin, reservoir simulation by Ward (1999b) suggests that neither of these strategies, nor a combination of the two, could entirely eliminate the estimated shortfall in supply.

Ultimately, the issue of water scarcity must be dealt with by making efficient use of the existing water supplied by the Rio Grande. Currently, large amounts of water are lost in the process of delivering it to municipal and agricultural users. Significant amounts of water are also lost through inefficient irrigation practices at the farm level. These inefficiencies are cause for concern but also represent tremendous opportunity. Schmandt and colleagues (2000) find that a relatively modest 9–17 percent reduction in the water used by agriculture could supply the estimated increases in municipal and industrial demand to the year 2030. Various technologies for more efficient water delivery and irrigation are currently available that can achieve this reduction while allowing agriculture to continue to produce.[32] Municipal conservation efforts—adopting measures mainly at the household level that allow cities to do more with less water—also represent a potentially significant opportunity, though it is relatively small compared with the water savings possible in agriculture.

Irrigators can be highly adaptive to reductions in water availability and can compensate by changing crop selection and implementing more efficient irrigation technology. Schmandt and co-workers (1998) describe the efforts of one irrigation district in the TV that has reduced water use by 40 percent by voluntarily undertaking improvements to its water delivery infrastructure, without economic loss. The same district fared better than many of its neighboring districts in the face of diminished water supplies during the current drought.

To simulate the impacts of a permanent reduction in water availability on the agricultural sector in the TV, Hazelton (1999) used an empirical U.S. agricultural sector model (ASM).[33] In this simulation three scenarios are analyzed: (1) no change in water available for irrigation; (2) a permanent 20 percent reduction in water available for irrigation; and (3) a permanent 40 percent reduction in water available for irrigation. This analysis provided important insight into the way in which farmers might respond to changes in water availability. The simulation indicated that under an assumed 20 percent exogenous and permanent reduction in water availability, farmers would respond primarily by changing cropping patterns, reducing by 20 percent or more the acreage devoted to irrigation, and increasing dryland production. Under a 40 percent reduction of water for irrigation, farmers are likely to retain the cropping pattern under the 20 percent reduc-

tion scenario and also introduce more efficient irrigation technology. Thus, even though twice as much water is being withheld, the impact on the economy in this simulation is slightly *less* than under the 20 percent reduction scenario due to improved efficiency of water use.[34]

Hazelton (1999) notes that the magnitude of the loss of farm proprietor's net income in this modeling exercise is surprisingly low, amounting to only $8.7 million under the 20 percent reduction scenario and to $5.4 million under the 40 percent reduction scenario. The resulting loss in personal income under the 20 percent reduction scenario is about $29 million, falling to $27 million under the 40 percent reduction scenario. This compares with total personal income in the region of $10.6 billion and is well within the range of recent variations in farm income due to drought and market conditions. Farm employment drops by about 16 percent, but Hazelton (1999) points out that only about 3.1 percent of the total earnings in the region come from farm income and agricultural services.

Future Challenges

While the demographic, social, political, economic, and institutional landscapes in the Texas Lower Rio Grande Valley will all change over the next thirty years, drought will continue to be an inevitable part of the regional geography. Ironically, however, perhaps the most important impacts to the future water supply of the LRGB will be consequences of human activities. Because of the increased pressure placed on the region's limited water resource by the growing population and regional economy, and the institutional context within which water management is currently carried out, there exists an array of potential conflicts in the basin: between agriculture and industry, between economic development and preservation of environmental quality, between rural and urban areas, between upstream and downstream users and between Texas and Mexico.[35]

Thus, one of the basic challenges in the Lower Rio Grande/Río Bravo basin is to balance multiple demands by municipal, industrial, agricultural, and ecological users of the region's limited water resources. Improving the efficiency with which water is delivered and used will play a large role in meeting this challenge. Cooperative "win-win" opportunities between cities and agricultural producers exist. For example, agricultural water rights can be transferred to municipalities through the Lower Rio Grande water market. Cities can offer to pay for improvements to agricultural irrigation infrastructure in exchange for the water saved. However, the balancing of competing water demands must also take into account that as more and more river water is used for municipal and industrial uses, the quality of the water will play a more important role. This highlights the often-overlooked relationship between the quantity and quality of water in the river. Finally, the water needs of the ecosystem—which provides a number of crucial services in the region including the basis for a growing ecotourism industry—must also be accounted for.

The TV does not exist in isolation but as part of a complex interconnection of social, economic, ecological, and hydrological systems that extend throughout the larger binational watershed. Water supply in the LRGB is heavily dependent on activities upstream, primarily in the Río Conchos watershed in Mexico. The *quality* of Rio Grande water upon which the Texas Lower Rio Grande Valley depends is also strongly linked to activities in Mexico. This underscores the strong interdependencies surrounding water that inextricably bind together both the Texan-Mexican and upstream-downstream portions of the watershed. Recognizing that the web of interdependencies between the TV and Mexico fundamentally includes water, a second challenge regarding water resources is to incorporate a broader, binational perspective into local or regional water planning and policy efforts.

Whether the Lower Rio Grande/Río Bravo basin moves toward a more sustainable future concerning its water resources is largely a question of management. Potentially, the river can supply enough water, of acceptable quality, to support the domestic water needs of 4.9 million people projected to be living in the Lower Rio Grande/Río Bravo Border Region in 2030. To make this possible, agricultural use of water will have to be modestly reduced. Market mechanisms and mutually beneficial arrangements between cities and irrigation districts can bring about more efficient water use, making the rural-urban reallocation one of cooperation rather than conflict. However, without changes in water management to reflect minimum ecological water needs, not enough water will be left instream to maintain riverine and riparian ecosystems. As new wastewater treatment capacity continues to come on line, mostly in Mexico, water quality in the river may improve, although these improvements could be offset by increased concentration of pollutants due to decreased streamflow caused by increased water use. The complex array of local, state, regional, federal, and international institutions involved in water management presents a formidable challenge. Yet greater institutional cooperation—both within

the Texas Lower Rio Grande Valley and with Mexican counterparts across the river—will be fundamental to improving regionwide water management and maneuvering the Lower Rio Grande/Río Bravo basin toward a more sustainable future.

Notes

1. This chapter draws extensively on results from the project "Water and Sustainable Development in the Binational Lower Rio Grande/Río Bravo Basin" (Schmandt et al. 2000), conducted jointly by the Houston Advanced Research Center (HARC) and the Instituto Tecnológico y de Estudios Superiores de Monterrey (ITESM). The project was funded by a grant awarded to HARC in 1995 from the EPA/NSF STAR Partnership for Environmental Research Program, Water and Watersheds Program, EPA Grant no. R 824799-01-0. The project involved close collaboration among a team of researchers, and this chapter draws heavily upon their work. I would thus like to acknowledge Neal Armstrong, Salvador Contreras-Balderas, Robert Edwards, Jared Hazleton, José de Jesus Navar-Chaidez, Liliana Chapa-Alemán, and Enrique Vogel-Martinez, whose work is cited throughout. I am especially grateful to Jurgen Schmandt and Ismael Aguilar-Barajas for their leadership and invaluable contributions, and to George Ward, whose expertise and input regarding the hydrological analysis was invaluable to the project and contributed greatly to this chapter. Of course, all errors and omissions remain my responsibility alone.

2. See Mathis (1999) for details regarding the interdisciplinary methodology developed for the project.

3. Secondary tributaries include the Devil's River on the U.S. side and the San Juan and Salado rivers on the Mexico side.

4. Electricity is produced at both dams but as an ancillary function.

5. Although the Monterrey Metropolitan Area, located in the upper reaches of the San Juan River subbasin of the Lower Rio Grande/Río Bravo watershed, is not definitionally part of the LRGB and does not use water from the Rio Grande/Río Bravo, the two areas are highly interconnected in terms of hydrology, geography, economy, culture, and migration. Thus Schmandt et al. (2000) also include the Monterrey Metropolitan Area in their study.

6. If the Monterrey Metropolitan Area is included in the analysis, the population of the basin will grow from 5.1 to 11.1 million.

7. Groundwater is generally of poor quality, with high levels of salinity, nitrates, and sediments, and is currently not widely used.

8. The allocations between the United States and Mexico of Falcón and Amistad reservoirs' conservation storage was determined binationally through the IBWC as part of the agreements between the two countries to build the reservoirs.

9. For example, shortly after the completion of Falcón Reservoir in 1953, the largest flood on that reach of the river occurred. The entire flood was captured in the new reservoir, filling it to more than 90 percent of its conservation capacity less than a year after its completion. By early 1957, the reservoir contents had dwindled to 6 percent of conservation capacity (Ward 1998a).

10. Because Falcón and Amistad are operated as a single system, the state of their water supply is best represented by considering the combined total storage contents and capacities of the two reservoirs.

11. Note that most of this population growth occurs in the twin cities of Laredo and Nuevo Laredo.

12. The Treaty of 1944 specifies that the combined flow from Mexico of the Conchos, Las Vacas, Salado, San Diego, San Rodrigo, and Escondido rivers shall not be less than 350,000 acre-feet per year (432 Mm³/year or 36 Mm³/month), averaged over five-year cycles. The average of the total of these flows for the period 1924–90 is approximately 163 Mm³/month, nearly five times the required treaty amount, while the average for the Conchos alone, at 81 Mm³/month, is more than double this amount (Ward 1998b).

13. Navar (1999) calculated that the combined U.S. and Mexico diversions account for approximately 88 percent of the reservoir releases measured below Falcón, with the remainder attributed to excess flows from the reservoir system during large rainfall events.

14. The Texas Water Development Board also collects data on water used for livestock, mining, and electrical production, but these uses involve minor amounts in the TV.

15. In the history of the Falcón-Amistad system, 1972 is a crucial year: it was the first time both reservoirs simultaneously achieved 100 percent of storage capacity, and it is assumed that the tandem operation of the reservoir system effectively began at that time.

16. Irrigation use varies greatly from year to year, depending not only on hydroclimatology and season but on crop selection, economic conditions, and the availability of water in the international reservoirs (and the ability of the farmers and water managers to forecast all of these at least a growing season in advance). Precisely determining the amount of these diversions allocated between agricultural and M&I use is complicated by the fact that in some cases, water diverted to agricultural users, such as irrigation districts, is used to supply municipal demands as well. Measuring the allocation between agricultural and M&I use is further confounded in the portion of the study dealing with Mexico. In contrast to agriculture in the Texas Lower Rio Grande Valley, which derives virtually all of its irrigation water from the Rio Grande, agriculture in the TBR uses water from the Rio Grande as well as from other tributaries, such as the Río Alamo and Río San Juan. Moreover, a portion of the water from the single Mexican agricultural diversion from the Rio Grande/Río Bravo at the Anzaldúas Drain is allocated to municipal and industrial use.

17. Navar (1999) and Hazelton (1999) find a gradual decrease in irrigated acreage in both the Mexican and Texas portions of the LRGB over the past two decades. The decline in irrigated acreage is due to a number of factors, including more acreage being set aside for compliance with federal farm programs in Texas, poor economic conditions in the agricultural sector during the past decade, a decline in the number and size of farms, conversion of farmland to municipal uses, and technological advancements in crop production.

18. To derive a rough estimate of uncurtailed irrigation demand, Ward (1999a) averages the five highest annual irrigation demands from 1980 to 1993 (just before the current drought). Based on these calculations, the uncurtailed irrigation demand for the TV is estimated at around 1,500 Mm³/yr. He estimates the upper limit of uncurtailed combined irrigation demand for *both* sides of the river to be approximately 3,000 Mm³/year.

19. In this exercise, constant-flow firm yield releases from the reservoir system are designated for delivery to meet downstream demands. As discussed earlier, firm yield operation is a hypothetical construct, since firm yield is in actuality not a consideration in the operation of the Falcón-Amistad system. Instead, reservoir operation is a complex process involving hydrological, socioeconomic, and political factors.

20. Concentrations of toxic substances appear lower than might have been expected based on the suspected loadings of toxic substances to the Lower Rio Grande/Río Bravo system, but data are patchy.

21. QUAL-TX, a water quality model developed for Texas by the Texas Natural Resource Conservation Commission (TNRCC), was used to model water quality, particularly dissolved oxygen, in the Lower Rio Grande/Río Bravo under a set of hydrological conditions defined by the water availability scenarios and for three time periods: 1990, 2010, and 2030. An input file developed by the TNRCC for the Rio Grande/Río Bravo was modified to represent the diversions in the watershed better. In addition, the input file was augmented with loading data from Mexico so that waste loads from *both* sides of the river were represented. River flow and diversion flows used were low flows, which would exacerbate the impacts of oxygen-demanding materials into the river. Summertime temperature conditions were also used to stress the dissolved oxygen system further.

22. Specifically, two dissolved oxygen sag curves were noted in the river, the first below the Reynosa wastewater input and the second below the Brownsville Southside Plant input.

23. This assumes that water quality standards would not be relaxed because of flows decreased below the 7Q2 level.

24. The existing natural plant communities support a wide variety of native wildlife that uses these habitats for feeding, nesting, and for protection. Nearly seven hundred species of wildlife have been documented from the study area (Jahrsdoefer and Leslie 1988); of these, more than eighty-six vertebrate species are either already listed by governmental organizations

as Endangered or Threatened or are considered target species that may require immediate protection (Malstrom and Jordan 1994).

25. The original grasslands and brush of the region have been largely cleared. In its natural state the Lower Rio Grande/Río Bravo river channel is bounded by a dense riparian flood forest thicket, but less than 5 percent of the original ecosystem remains along the binational stream corridor. Palm groves and wetlands are also threatened. Agricultural production has generated environmental impacts that include decreased water quality and eutrophication, salinization, soil modification, and the destruction of habitat (Mikesell 1992; Jahrsdoerfer and Leslie 1988).

26. See, for example, Karr (1981).

27. Contreras et al. (1999) extend the methodology of Karr (1981) and Lyons et al. (1994) for evaluating the condition of river ecosystems using multiple criteria.

28. The office of watermaster is not common in the state. Only one other watermaster's office exists, the South Texas watermaster's office, which has jurisdiction over a number of rivers in South Texas.

29. The Rio Grande Regional Water Planning Group includes Maverick, Webb, Zapata, Jim Hogg, Starr, Hidalgo, Willacy, and Cameron counties. Prior to the creation of the SB 1 planning group, the Valley Water Policy and Management Council worked on water issues in a smaller region that included only Starr, Hidalgo, Willacy, and Cameron counties.

30. See Chang and Griffin (1990) and Hurlbut (2000) for details regarding the Lower Rio Grande Valley water market.

31. For an overview of wastewater reuse on the Texas-Mexico border, see Mathis (2001).

32. The Rio Grande RWPG estimates that the cost of such improvements would average $150 per acre-foot of water saved for delivery infrastructure and $225 per acre-foot of water saved due to on-farm measures.

33. Note that this exercise does not consider *short-term* water reductions, such as those that occur during drought.

34. It should be noted that the results of the modeling exercise are based on the unrealistic assumption of the existence of a market price for water that perfectly reflects its full economic value.

35. During the current drought, political conflict over water supply has escalated between Texas and Mexico (e.g., McGraw 2000) and between municipal and rural interests in the Mexican states of Tamaulipas and Nuevo Leon (see Aguilar 1999).

References

Aguilar-Barajas, I. "Interregional Transfer of Water in Northeastern Mexico: The Dispute over El Cuchillo." *Natural Resources Journal* 39, no. 1 (1999): 65–98.

Armstrong, N. "Water Quality Modeling in the Lower Rio Grande/Río Bravo." HARC/CGS Working Paper Series, Water and Sustainable Development in the Binational Lower Rio Grande/Río Bravo Basin, Houston Advanced Research Center, The Woodlands, 1999.

Chang, C., and R. Griffin. "Water Marketing as a Reallocative Institution in Texas." *Water Resources Research* 1 (1990): 879–90.

Contreras-Balderas, S., R. Edwards, M. Lozano-Vilano, and M. Garcia-Ramírez. "Integrated Environmental Assessment of the Binational Lower Rio Grande/Río Bravo Basin." HARC/CGS Working Paper Series, Water and Sustainable Development in the Binational Lower Rio Grande/Río Bravo Basin, Houston Advanced Research Center, The Woodlands, 1999.

Edwards, R., and S. Contreras-Balderas. "Ecological Conditions in the Lower Rio Grande/Río Bravo Basin." HARC/CGS Working Paper Series, Water and Sustainable Development in the Binational Lower Rio Grande/Río Bravo Basin, Houston Advanced Research Center, The Woodlands, 1997.

Hazelton, J. "Socio-Economic Profile and Trends in the Texas Lower Rio Grande/Río Bravo Basin." HARC/CGS Working Paper Series, Water and Sustainable Development in the Binational Lower Rio Grande/Río Bravo Basin, Houston Advanced Research Center, The Woodlands, 1999.

Hurlbut, D. "The Texas Lower Rio Grande Water Market." Ph.D. dissertation, Lyndon B. Johnson School of Public Affairs, University of Texas at Austin, 2000.

International Boundary and Water Commission (IBWC). *Binational Study Regarding the Presence of Toxic Substances in the Rio Grande/Río Bravo and its Tributaries along the Boundary Portion between the United States and Mexico.* El Paso: IBWC, 1994.

———. "Updated Rio Grande National Ownership of Waters Stored at the International Amistad and Falcon Dams." Accessed Oct. 20, 2000, at http://www.ibwc.state.gov/wad/storage.htm.

Jahrsdoerfer, S. E., and D. M. Leslie, Jr. *Tamaulipan Brushland of the Lower Rio Grande Valley of South Texas: Description, Human Impacts, and Management Options.* Biological Report 88, no. 36. Washington, D.C.: U.S. Fish and Wildlife Service, 1988.

Kaiser, R. A., B. J. Lesikar, C. S. Shafer, and J. R. Gerston. "Water Management Strategies: Ranking the Options." Discussion paper. Texas A&M University System, 2000.

Karr, J. R. "Assessment of Biotic Integrity Using Fish Communities." *Fisheries* 6, no. 6 (1981): 21–27.

Karr, J. R., and E. W. Chu. *Biological Monitoring and Assessment: Using Multimetric Indexes Effectively.* EPA 235-R97-001. University of Washington, Seattle, 1997.

Lower Rio Grande Valley Development Council (LRGVDC). "Description of Water Supply Requirements." In *Integrated Water Resources Plan: Final Report.* McAllen, Tex.: LRGVDC, 1999.

Lyons, J., S. Navarro-Pérez, P. A. Cochran, A. Santana, and

M. Guzmán-Arroyo. "Index of Biotic Integrity Based on Fish Assemblages for the Conservation of Streams and Rivers in West-Central México." *Conservation Biology* 9, no. 3 (1994): 569–84.

Malstrom, H. L., and W. R. Jordan, eds. *Environmental Issues of the U.S.-Mexico Border Region: A Workshop Summary.* Technical Report 166. College Station: Texas Water Resources Institute, Texas A&M University, 1994.

Mathis, M. "Using New Approaches to Environmental Decision-Making: An Application of Integrated Assessment Methods to Water Resource Issues in the Binational Lower Rio Grande Basin." *Policy Studies Review* 16, no. 3–4 (1999): 138–67.

———. "Reuse of Wastewater on the Texas-Mexico Border." Mitchell Center for Sustainable Development Discussion Paper, Houston Advanced Research Center, The Woodlands, 2001.

McGraw, D. "A Boiling Tex-Mex Water War." *U.S. News and World Report,* May 1, 2000, 24.

Mikesell, R. F. *Economic Development and the Environment: A Comparison of Sustainable Development with Conventional Development Economics.* New York: Mansell Publishing, 1992.

Navar, J. "Surface Water Supply and Demand in the Lower Río Bravo/Rio Grande Watershed." HARC/CGS Working Paper Series, Water and Sustainable Development in the Binational Lower Rio Grande/Río Bravo Basin, Houston Advanced Research Center, The Woodlands, 1999.

———. "Water Supply and Demand Scenarios in the Río San Juan Watershed." HARC/CGS Working Paper Series, Water and Sustainable Development in the Binational Lower Rio Grande/Río Bravo Basin, Houston Advanced Research Center, The Woodlands, 1998.

Schmandt, J., C. Stolp, and G. Ward. *Scarce Water: Doing More with Less in the Lower Rio Grande.* U.S.-Mexican Policy Report no. 8. Austin: Lyndon B. Johnson School of Public Affairs, 1998.

Schmandt, J., I. Aguilar-Barajas, M. Mathis, N. Armstrong, L. Chapa-Alemán, S. Contreras-Balderas, R. Edwards, J. Hazleton, J. Navar-Chaidez, E. Vogel-Martinez, and G. Ward. "Water and Sustainable Development in the Binational Lower Rio Grande/Río Bravo Basin." Final Report to EPA/NSF Water and Watersheds Grant Program, Grant no. R 824799-01-0, Houston Advanced Research Center, Center for Global Studies, The Woodlands, 2000.

TNRCC (Texas Natural Resource Conservation Commission). "Regional Assessment of Water Quality in the Rio Grande Basin: Including the Pecos River, the Devils River, the Arroyo Colorado and the Lower Laguna Madre." TNRCC, Watershed Management Division, Austin, Texas, 1994.

U.S. Department of State. "Utilization of Waters of the Colorado and Tijuana Rivers and of the Rio Grande." *Treaty Series 994, Treaty between the United States of America and Mexico,* Government Printing Office, Washington, D.C., 1946.

Vogel-Martinez, E., L. Chapa-Alemán, and N. Armstrong. "Water Quality in the Lower Rio Grande/Río Bravo." HARC/CGS Working Paper Series, Water and Sustainable Development in the Binational Lower Rio Grande/Río Bravo Basin, Houston Advanced Research Center, The Woodlands, 1998.

Ward, G. "Hydrological Analysis of the International Reservoir Operation on the Lower Rio Grande/Río Bravo." HARC/CGS Working Paper Series, Water and Sustainable Development in the Binational Lower Rio Grande/Río Bravo Basin, Houston Advanced Research Center, The Woodlands, 1998a.

———. "Hydrological Scenarios in the Lower Rio Grande/Río Bravo Basin." HARC/CGS Working Paper Series, Water and Sustainable Development in the Binational Lower Rio Grande/Río Bravo Basin, Houston Advanced Research Center, The Woodlands, 1998b.

———. "Water Demands and Flows in the Lower Rio Grande/Río Bravo Basin." HARC/CGS Working Paper Series, Water and Sustainable Development in the Binational Lower Rio Grande/Río Bravo Basin, Houston Advanced Research Center, The Woodlands, 1999a.

———. "Water Supply Strategies for the Lower Rio Grande/Río Bravo Basin." HARC/CGS Working Paper Series, Water and Sustainable Development in the Binational Lower Rio Grande/Río Bravo Basin, Houston Advanced Research Center, The Woodlands, 1999b.

ISBN 1-58544-326-3

9 781585 443260

90000